Reviews of the Unabridged Version

"The great merit of Köstenberger's and Patterson's volume is its three-dimension account of biblical interpretation. The authors rightly focus on the history, literature, and theology of the Bible—what they call the hermeneutical triad. Call it hermeneutics in real 3-D. A three-stranded hermeneutical cord may not be easily broken, but it's easy to grasp by following this introductory textbook. Another merit is the authors' reminder that biblical interpretation is not only about method but about virtue: a heart-felt humility before the divine text is as important as any heady procedure."

—Kevin J. Vanhoozer,
Research Professor of Systematic Theology, Trinity Evangelical Divinity School

"This book on biblical interpretation combines training in exegesis with a basic knowledge of hermeneutics. It urges careful consideration of historical, literary, and theological issues. Thus, historically, it includes helpful chronological charts, and much on cultural history. Its literary focus includes canon, genre, and language. Its theological dimension includes application. Genre is crucial: thus narrative, poetry, and wisdom are distinguished in the Old Testament; and parable, epistles, and apocalyptic, in the New. Why responsible interpretation requires toil and labor receives careful explanation. This book contains plenty of common sense, sanity, and love of Scripture. I commend it especially to students, teachers, and even pastors, as helping all of us to use the Bible responsibly and fruitfully."

—Anthony C. Thiselton,
Professor Emeritus of Christian Theology, University of Nottingham

"There are certain topics of must-reading for serious Bible students—hermeneutics is at the top. There are certain books of must-reading for a topic—Andreas Köstenberger's work on hermeneutics is one of them. It is clear, concise, and yet deep, and manages to cover most of the needed areas. Thus it becomes an invaluable guide for the student working through the labyrinth of issues that make up the task of biblical interpretation. It will enable the reader to bridge the gap from understanding biblical portions in their original cultural context and from showing their relevance to a modern audience. I recommend it very highly."

—Grant Osborne,
Professor of New Testament, Trinity Evangelical Divinity School

"In this triad dance of history, literature, and theology, as they move across the floor of biblical interpretation, Köstenberger and Patterson excel at sorting through and clearly presenting massive amounts of material across a wide spectrum of cognate disciplines. Written in a down-to-earth style, the book is as accessible as it is broad, as practical as it is informed on contemporary discussions of these difficult matters. From the particulars of Greek grammar and discourse analysis to helpful introductions on canon, biblical theology, and appropriate application, here one again and again finds a welcome orientation to the bread-and-butter concepts, sound practices, and tools needed for handling the biblical text responsibly and the spiritual posture for approaching it reverently. I am impressed and looking forward to putting this book in the hands of my students, who will find here a rich, expansive resource from which to draw guidance for years to come."

—George H. Guthrie,
Benjamin W. Perry Professor of Bible, Union University

"This book distills a wealth of wisdom from two seasoned scholars whose expertise spans both Testaments. Chapters are up to date without succumbing to the trendy. There is attention to both the theory and practice of interpreting Scripture, obligatory given the title. But the novel element of this volume is at least twofold. (1) It unabashedly privileges Scripture as recording a *history* that produced *literature* which conveys *theology* of eternal redemptive importance. (2) It strikes a balance between these three elements in a readable and engrossing style. No book on this subject can do everything. But this one is without peer as a classroom resource supporting the triadic reading it calls for at a level that is neither brutally rudimentary nor unrealistically advanced. It will enhance the teaching of this subject and draw students into the excitement of navigating hermeneutical frontiers."

— Robert W. Yarbrough,
Professor of New Testament, Covenant Theological Seminary

FOR THE LOVE OF GOD'S WORD

An Introduction to Biblical Interpretation

Andreas J. Köstenberger
and Richard D. Patterson

For the Love of God's Word: An Introduction to Biblical Interpretation

This is an abridgment and revision of *Invitation to Biblical Interpretation: Exploring the Hermeneutical Triad of History, Literature, and Theology,* © 2011 by Andreas J. Köstenberger and Richard D. Patterson.

Published by Kregel Publications, a division of Kregel, Inc., 2450 Oak Industrial Dr. NE, Grand Rapids, MI 49505-6020.

ISBN 978-0-8254-4336-7

Printed in the United States of America

19 / 5 4 3 2

To all who love God's Word:

"Oh, how I love your law!
I meditate on it all day long."
—Psalm 119:97

CONTENTS

PREFACE

Writing a hermeneutics text is not an easy task. Having taught courses on biblical interpretation on the college, graduate, and doctoral levels for many years, we can attest to the fact that hermeneutics is one of the hardest subjects to teach—but also one of the most important. The present volume is dedicated to all serious students of Scripture who love God's Word and want to mine it for its precious spiritual truths and life-changing practical insights.

The book you're holding in your hands (or reading on your screen) is an abridgment of *Invitation to Biblical Interpretation*. We're grateful to those who suggested preparing this essential digest of the larger book for high school, home school, and college students and anyone who is interested in a solid course of instruction on studying and applying God's Word. Special thanks are due Nathan Ridlehoover, who used a draft of this book in class and made numerous helpful suggestions for connecting with readers and keeping jargon at bay.

In *For the Love of God's Word*, we have retained all the essential core knowledge from *Invitation to Biblical Interpretation*. We cut or thinned out advanced material (e.g., history of interpretation, original languages, and discourse analysis). Also cut were sample exegesis sections and material on preaching from the different genres of Scripture. The material at the end of chapters was trimmed (especially bibliographies). The chapter on figurative language was cut, but some core information moved to the chapter on poetry and wisdom literature.

We gratefully acknowledge the loving support of our wives, Margaret and Ann, during the process of writing the original volume and preparing this abridgment. They have faithfully stood by our side for many years. Thank you so much!

I (Andreas) would also like to express my gratitude to my esteemed colleague and friend, Dick Patterson, for embarking with me on the adventure of writing this text. I could not have asked for a better collaborator, equally conversant with and committed to exploring the historical, literary, and theological dimensions of Scripture. It has been a great privilege to work with you, Dick, and your seasoned scholarship sets a wonderful example for others to emulate.

I would also like to acknowledge the debt of gratitude I owe to those who, by instruction and example, taught me how to interpret the Bible: my first hermeneutics teacher, Robertson McQuilkin; my Greek exegesis instructor, William Larkin; my advanced hermeneutics teacher, Grant Osborne; and my doctoral mentor, D. A. Carson. While I have charted my own course, standing on the shoulders of these spiritual giants has enabled me to see farther than I would otherwise have been able to see. Especially Grant Osborne's *Hermeneutical Spiral* and D. A. Carson's *Exegetical Fallacies* have made a lasting impact on me, and in many ways this volume represents a tribute to the formative influence of these men.

I (Dick) would like to express my gratitude to my distinguished and well-respected colleague and friend, Andreas Köstenberger, for his vision, direction, and dedication to the completion of this text. I have profited from my interaction with the fruits of his dedicated scholarship and have enjoyed collaborating with him in our mutual concern for the "hermeneutical triad." It has been my privilege to be asked to serve with you, Andreas. Your wide-ranging expertise and commitment to Christ have set a high standard for all of us to follow.

I would also acknowledge the contributions to my training by the excellent graduate faculty at UCLA in my early days, such as Giorgio Buccellati, and my dear mentor and professor of Greek and theology, Marchant King, all of whom not only provided vital information, but also shared both their love of the subject matter and their lives with me. I also acknowledge the contributions of so many colleagues in the Evangelical Theological Society, whose commitment to Christ and his Word have served as motivating examples to me to make God's Word my guidebook for life (Ps. 119:111).

Finally, we would like to express our gratitude to Liz Mburu, Corin Mihaila, Alan Bandy, and Scott Kellum for writing serious first drafts of the original chapters on the Gospels and parables, the Epistles, apocalyptic, and application, and to Michael Travers for providing some material on figures of speech.

To God alone be the glory!

A PERSONAL NOTE TO TEACHERS, STUDENTS, AND READERS

This book is teaching a simple method for interpreting the Bible, the *hermeneutical triad* of history, literature, and theology. In essence, we propose that for any passage of Scripture, you'll want to study the *historical setting*, *literary context*, and *theological message*. The first element of the hermeneutical triad is *history*. Studying the historical setting provides a proper grounding, since all Scripture is rooted in real-life history. God revealed himself in history, and the genres and language in which God chose to reveal himself reflect the historical context.

Second comes *literature*. Studying the literary context is the focus of Bible study, since Scripture is a piece of writing, a text that has three major components: (1) canon; (2) genre; and (3) language. In studying the literary dimension of Scripture, we locate a passage's place in the canon, determine its genre, and interpret it in keeping with its genre characteristics, doing justice to the language used (which normally will involve outlining the passage to determine its flow of thought and performing relevant word studies).

Third is the climax of biblical interpretation: *theology*. While the biblical message is grounded in history and conveyed through literature, exploring the theology of a given passage of Scripture is the ultimate goal in interpretation, since, as mentioned, Scripture is first and foremost God's revelation or self-disclosure to us.

Throughout the book, we use the hermeneutical triad as a compass on our interpretive journey through the canonical landscape. Thanks for joining us on this exciting journey of life-giving discovery and adventure. May God richly bless you as you serve him and study his Word.

Your fellow servants,
Andreas Köstenberger and Dick Patterson

CHAPTER 1 OBJECTIVES

1. To convince the reader of the need for, and the rewards of, skilled interpretation.
2. To persuade the reader of the cost of failed biblical interpretation.
3. To set forth the essential characteristics of the biblical interpreter.
4. To preview the purpose and plan of this book.
5. To introduce the student to the hermeneutical triad of interpreting Scripture.

CHAPTER 1 OUTLINE

A. Introduction

B. Need for Skilled Biblical Interpretation

C. Cost of Failed Biblical Interpretation

D. Characteristics Required of the Biblical Interpreter

E. Purpose and Plan of This Book

F. Developing Interpretive Virtues

G. Guidelines for Biblical Interpretation: Overall Method

H. Key Words

I. Assignments

J. Key Resources

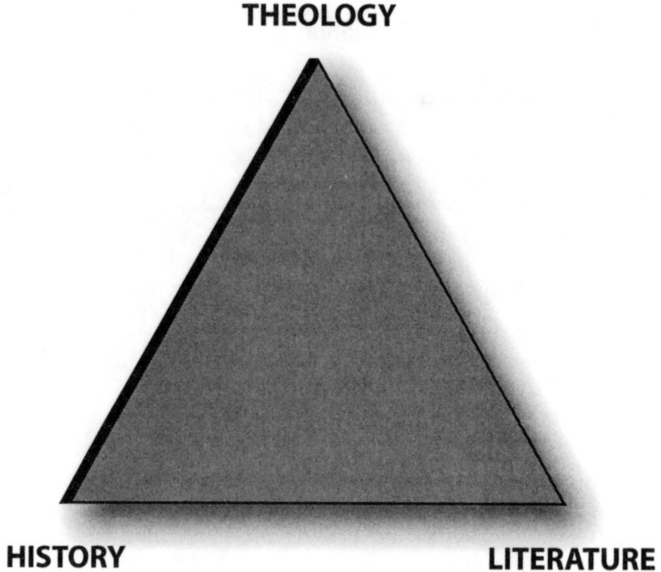
THEOLOGY
HISTORY
LITERATURE

Chapter 1

INTRODUCING THE HERMENEUTICAL TRIAD: HISTORY, LITERATURE, AND THEOLOGY

INTRODUCTION

COME ON IN, AND STAY for a while! Make yourself at home, and acquire vital skills in understanding the most important book ever written—the Holy Scriptures. The volume you are holding in your hands invites you to embark on the quest of sound biblical interpretation or as it is also called, "hermeneutics." As in Jesus's parable of the wedding feast, the invitation goes out to all who care to listen. And as in Jesus's parable, the terms are not set by those invited but by the one who issues the invitation and by the book to be interpreted.

In our quest to understand the Bible, *author*, *text*, and *reader* each have an important part to play. Every document has an author, and the resulting text is shaped by his or her intention. It is this authorial intention the interpreter must aim to recover. The text is not "just there," left to be interpreted any way a given reader chooses. When my friend talks to me, I dare not give her words my own preferred meaning. The rules of proper communication demand that I seek to understand the meaning *she* intended to convey.

It follows that the text of Scripture, likewise, is not neutral, that is, malleable to a great variety of interpretations that lay equal claim to represent valid readings of a given passage. Nor is the text autonomous, that is, a law unto itself, as if it existed apart from the author who willed and wrote it into being. It is an authorially shaped and designed product that requires careful and respectful interpretation.

There is therefore an important *ethical* dimension in interpretation. We should engage in interpretation responsibly, displaying respect for the text and its author. There is no excuse for interpretive arrogance that elevates the reader above text and author. The "golden rule" of interpretation requires that we extend the same courtesy to any text or author that we would want others to extend to our statements and writings (Matt. 7:12). This calls for respect not only for the intentions of the human authors of Scripture but ultimately for God who chose to reveal himself through the Bible by his Holy Spirit.

This volume is based on such respect both for the ultimate author of Scripture and for its human authors. We are committed to taking the text of Scripture seriously and to practicing discerning listening and perception. We aim to take into account the relevant historical setting of a given passage and to pay close attention to the words, sentences, and discourses of a particular book. We purpose to give careful consideration to the theology of the Bible itself and to interpret the parts in light of the canonical whole. Last but not least, we seek to operate within the proper framework of the respective genres of Scripture.

Why would we want to take the time and exert the effort to learn to interpret Scripture correctly? First of all, we will want to do so because we are seekers of *truth* and because we realize that truth sets free while error enslaves. Many cults have arisen because of their flawed interpretation of Scripture. There is an even more powerful motivation, however: embarking on the quest for accurate biblical interpretation out of our *love* for God, his Word, and his people. If you and I truly love God, we will want to get to know him better, and this involves serious study of his Word.

As seekers of truth and as lovers of God and others, then, we set out to discover revealed truth and to acquire biblical wisdom as one sets out to mine gold and precious stones. Our conviction that God's Word is the most precious commodity there is fuels a desire to extract even the last ounce of meaning from the biblical text no matter how much effort or learning it takes to recover it. In our quest for revealed divine truth, we will be prepared to pay whatever price it takes to hear God speak to us in and through his Word and to proclaim his life-giving message authentically and accurately to others.

NEED FOR SKILLED BIBLICAL INTERPRETATION

"Do your best," Paul wrote in his final missive to his foremost disciple, "to present yourself to God as one approved, a workman who does not need to be ashamed and who correctly handles the word of truth" (2 Tim. 2:15). In a day when people are confronted with a flood of information and are struggling to keep up and set priorities, Paul's words bring into sharp focus what ought to be our primary object of study: Scripture, "the word of truth." Like Peter, we ought to say, "Lord, to whom shall we go? You have the words of eternal life" (John 6:68). We ought to be driven by a hunger and thirst for righteousness (Matt. 5:6); we ought to be longing for the life-transforming, "living and active" word of God (Heb. 4:12).

In keeping with Paul's exhortation, we need to work hard at interpreting Scripture. We must "do our best" as "a worker." Biblical interpretation is hard work. The one who wants to master the handling of God's Word must be like the apprentice of a master craftsperson. Over time, and through practice, that apprentice will learn to skillfully use many tools. Likewise, the biblical interpreter must know what interpretive tools to use and how to use them. This is what it means to "correctly handle" the word of truth.

While the analogy holds well between the realm of craftsmanship and biblical interpretation, the argument is clearly from the lesser to the greater. If it is important for craftspeople to wield their tools skillfully, how much more important must it be for those who are called to handle God's "word of truth" with utmost care and expertise? No sloppy or shoddy work will do. Everything must be done in proper sequence, appropriate proportion, and with the purpose of producing an end product that pleases the one who commissioned the work. Background information, word meanings, the context of a given passage, and many other factors must be judiciously assessed if a valid interpretation is to be attained.

Also, no worker labors without regard for the approval of the one who assigned a particular task. Once again, the argument is from the lesser to the greater: for in the case of biblical interpretation, the one to whom we have to give an account is none other than God himself. It is *his* approval we are seeking, for if God approves, no one else's approval, or disapproval, ultimately matters. Our love for God and our conviction that God's Word is so precious that we ought to spare no effort to comprehend it as precisely as possible will be powerful motivators as we embark on our interpretive journey. In so doing, we will long to hear God's words of approval, "Well done, good and faithful servant. Enter the joy of your master."

COST OF FAILED BIBLICAL INTERPRETATION

Not only are there great rewards for faithful biblical interpretation, there is also a considerable cost if we fail in this effort. This cost, too, is mentioned in 2 Timothy 2:15. It is shrinking back in shame at God's judgment by the one who is unwilling to acquire the skills needed to interpret Scripture accurately. The equivalent of improper biblical interpretation is shoddy workmanship, due either to a lack of skill or carelessness. In the area of hermeneutics, this translates into fallacies arising from neglect of the context, prooftexting (reading one's preferred meaning *into* the text rather than deriving it by careful study *from* the text), improper use of background information, and other similar shortcomings.

Scripture is full of examples of those who failed in the task of biblical interpretation and were severely chastised, because their failure did not merely bring ruin on these individuals themselves but also on those they taught and influenced. A case in point are the false teachers Hymenaeus and Philetus, who erroneously taught that the final resurrection had already taken place (2 Tim. 2:17–18). Biblical interpretation is not an individualistic enterprise. Rather, it takes place in the community of believers, and the failure or success of the interpretative task affects not merely the interpreter but other believers as well.

Biblical interpreters are charged with a sacred task: handling Scripture with accuracy. They are entrusted with a sacred object, God's Word of truth, and their faithfulness or lack thereof will result in God's approval or in personal shame. God's Word commands our very best because, in the ultimate analysis, it is not a human word, but the Word of God. This means that our interpretive enterprise must rest on a robust doctrine of biblical revelation and a high view of Scripture—as Jesus taught, Scripture is "the word of God" and thus "cannot be broken" (John 10:35). Though conveyed through human means, using human language and thought forms, Scripture is ultimately the product of divine inspiration and therefore completely trustworthy.

CHARACTERISTICS REQUIRED OF THE BIBLICAL INTERPRETER

Rather than adopting a critical stance toward Scripture, we should rather submit to it as our final authority in all areas of life. An essential quality required of the biblical interpreter is therefore *humility*. As sinners saved by grace, we must humbly submit to Scripture rather than arrogantly asserting our right to critique Scripture in light of our modern or postmodern presuppositions and preferences. Instead of accepting only the teachings we find acceptable in keeping with contemporary sensibilities, we should be prepared to conform our presuppositions and preferences to the teachings of Scripture and to act accordingly. We must come to Scripture willing to obey what it says.

Part of this humility is acknowledging our finiteness and need for instruction and correction. As Paul wrote in his final letter to Timothy, "All Scripture is God-breathed and is useful for teaching, rebuking, correcting and training in righteousness, so that the man of God may be thoroughly equipped for every good work" (2 Tim. 3:16–17). Proper instruction and, if necessary, correction are therefore a function of Scripture itself, though God may choose to administer these through those who rightly interpret the Bible and teach it to others (cf. 2 Tim. 2:2).

Note also that biblical interpretation is not an end in itself but interpretive competence equips the interpreter for "every good work" (2 Tim. 3:17; cf. Eph. 2:10). Rather than being exclusively, or even primarily, a scholarly pursuit, interpretation is required of every believer. While it is true that God has given to the church certain individuals who are to serve as teachers and pastors (Eph. 4:11), he expects *every* believer to progress toward spiritual maturity (Col. 1:28–29). For this reason, we all should assume responsibility for our spiritual growth and make every effort to grow in our ability to handle God's Word accurately and with increasing skill (2 Pet. 3:17–18).

Another quality that is essential for the biblical interpreter is to *listen carefully* to the Word and to study it *perceptively*. In a time when listening is largely a lost art and many are approaching Scripture primarily for the purpose of validating their own predetermined conclusions, this is a much-needed reminder. In James's words, and in keeping with Old Testament wisdom, interpreters should be "quick to listen" and "slow to speak" (Jas. 1:19). As the ancient preacher pointed out, "Guard your steps when you go to the house of God. Go near to listen rather than to offer the sacrifice of fools . . . Do not be quick with your mouth, do not be hasty in your heart to utter anything before God. God is in heaven and you are on earth, so let your words be few" (Eccl. 5:1–2). Deplorably, the opposite is far more common: people are often quick to air their opinions but slow to hear the actual Word of God. Listening to Scripture requires discipline, self-restraint, wisdom, and love for God.

One final set of desirable (in fact, essential) attributes for biblical interpreters: they should be *regenerate* (that is, have experienced spiritual rebirth) and be *Spirit-filled and led*. The role of the Spirit in biblical interpretation warrants extended treatment, but for a start read Paul's concise treatment in 1 Corinthians 2:10b–16:

> The Spirit searches all things, even the deep things of God. For who among men knows the thoughts of a man except the man's spirit within him? In the same way no one knows the thoughts of God except the Spirit of God. . . . The man without the Spirit does not accept the things that come from the Spirit of God, for they are foolishness to him, and he cannot understand them, because they are spiritually discerned. The spiritual man makes judgments about all things, but he himself is not subject to any man's judgment . . .

While Paul wrote these words in order to address a specific issue in the Corinthian church, his remarks are also highly relevant for all of us who embark on our interpretive journey. If we do not have the Spirit—or if we have the Spirit but do not listen to him and depend on him for spiritual insight from God's Word—our interpretations will invariably fall short. Only the interpreter who depends on the Holy Spirit in his interpretive quest will likely be successful in discerning God's special, Spirit-appraised revelation.

While a given interpreter may indeed be devoid of faith and the Holy Spirit and still understand some of the words in Scripture, he will lack the spiritual framework, motivation, and understanding to grasp a given passage in its whole-Bible context. What is more, he will not be able to carry out what Scripture asks of him, because it is only regeneration and the Holy Spirit that enable him to do so. For this reason, anyone who has a sincere desire to understand the Bible will want to make sure that he or she is the kind of person who can receive God's words of truth.

PURPOSE AND PLAN OF THIS BOOK

Foundational to the plan of this book is the conviction that those who want to succeed in the task of biblical interpretation need to proceed within a proper interpretive framework, that is, the hermeneutical triad, which consists of the three elements interpreters must address in studying any given biblical passage: a book's *historical setting*, its *literary dimension*, and its *theological message*.

Since Christianity is a historical religion, and all texts are historically and culturally embedded, it is important that we ground our interpretation of Scripture in a careful study of the relevant historical setting. Since Scripture is a text of literature, the bulk of interpretive work entails coming to grips with the various literary and linguistic aspects of the biblical material. Finally, since Scripture is not merely a work of literature but inspired and authoritative revelation from God, the goal and end of interpretation is theology. Using the hermeneutical triad as a compass will ensure that Bible students stay on track in their interpretive journey.

As an interpreter sets out to explore a particular biblical text, he will first research its historical setting. After grounding his study in the real-life historical and cultural context of the biblical world, he will orient himself to the canonical landscape. This will place a given passage in its proper salvation-historical context. Next, he will consider the literary genre of a passage. He should imagine the different genres found in Scripture as topographical features such as valleys, mountain ranges, or plains, each of which exhibit characteristic features and call for appropriate navigational strategies. The historical and literary investigation will be followed by theological study. Finally, the interpreter will take a close look at the specific linguistic features of a text—the literary context and word meanings.

The hermeneutical triad, then, will serve as an overall method for studying any passage of Scripture. As a result, the interpretive apprentice will be well on the way to becoming a skilled worker who does not need to be ashamed, having developed the necessary skills for handling God's Word. The interpretation of Scripture, in turn, is not the end in itself but only a means to an end: the application of biblical truth to life. Using proper interpretive tools and resources and finding a path from text to sermon for each biblical genre are important. Thus sound interpretation becomes the solid foundation for the application and proclamation of biblical truth to life.

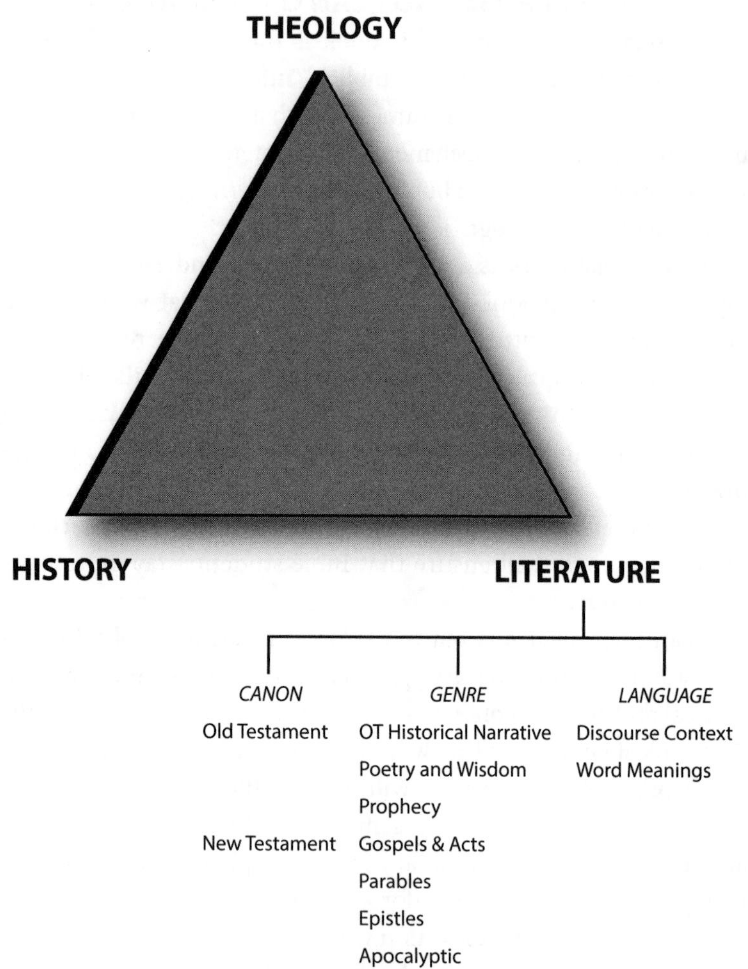

1.1. The Hermeneutical Triad in Detail

DEVELOPING INTERPRETIVE VIRTUES

As we have seen, following the proper method is vital for interpretation. But interpretation is more than simply adhering to a given method. What matters is not merely the final product (an accurate interpretation of a given passage) or even the procedure used to arrive at a given interpretation (one's method), but the person of the interpreter himself. Interpretation therefore also involves cultivating a set of interpretive virtues or competencies such as the following:

1. historical-cultural awareness;
2. canonical consciousness;
3. sensitivity to genre;
4. literary and linguistic competence;
5. a firm and growing grasp of biblical theology;
6. an ability to apply and proclaim passages from every biblical genre to life; and
7. wisdom for continuing the interpretive task.

Acquiring and polishing these skills will be well worth the effort. Doing so will bring glory to God and great blessing to the interpreter and through him or her to God's people. As you are growing in these virtues and competencies, and as you are following a proper method, you are more likely to arrive at the proper interpretation of a given passage.

God spoke the universe into being by his Word (Gen. 1:3, 6, 9, etc.). In OT times, God spoke to the Israelites "at many times and in various ways" through the prophets (Heb. 1:2), but "in these last days he has spoken to us by a son" (Heb. 1:3)—Jesus, the preexistent, incarnate Word (1:1, 14). The OT "prophets, though human, spoke from God as they were carried along by the Holy Spirit" (2 Pet. 1:21), and by extension, the NT authors did the same (cf. Eph. 2:20) in producing the "God-breathed" holy Scriptures (2 Tim. 3:16).

Our role as interpreters, in response, is not merely to be *recipients* of that Word but to be fitting *participants* in this penultimate stage of the drama of redemption as history moves inexorably toward the final consummation of God's plan of salvation. Toward that end, we must not only determine what Scripture is saying (meaning) but also what it means to us today (significance) and what convictions, affections, and actions it calls for on our part. So, let's get started on our journey!

As interpreters, we need to not only know the Scripture's meaning but also its significance!

GUIDELINES FOR BIBLICAL INTERPRETATION: OVERALL METHOD

1. Determine the historical setting of the passage and identify relevant cultural background issues.
2. Locate your passage in the larger canonical context of Scripture.
3. Determine your passage's literary genre and use appropriate interpretive principles for interpreting each genre, including those for figurative language.
4. Identify the major theological theme(s) in the passage and determine the passage's contribution to your understanding of the character and plan of God in dealing with his people.
5. Determine the structure of the entire book you are studying and discern how your passage fits within the overall structure.
6. Conduct a comprehensive word study of any significant term in your passage.
7. Apply the passage to your own life and communicate your insights to others.

KEY WORDS

Dual authorship, Hermeneutics, Inerrancy, Infallible, Inspiration, Prooftexting, Sufficiency of Scripture.

ASSIGNMENTS

1. Give examples from Scripture and from your own personal experience that illustrate the benefits of proper biblical interpretation and/or the cost of failed biblical interpretation.

8. Discuss the importance of each of the three major aspects of the hermeneutical triad—history, literature, and theology—and show how neglect of any one of these aspects results in imbalanced interpretation.

KEY RESOURCES

Grudem, Wayne A., gen. ed. *The ESV Study Bible*. Wheaton: Crossway, 2008.

Plummer, Robert L. *40 Questions about Understanding the Bible*. Grand Rapids: Kregel, 2009.

PART 1

HISTORY

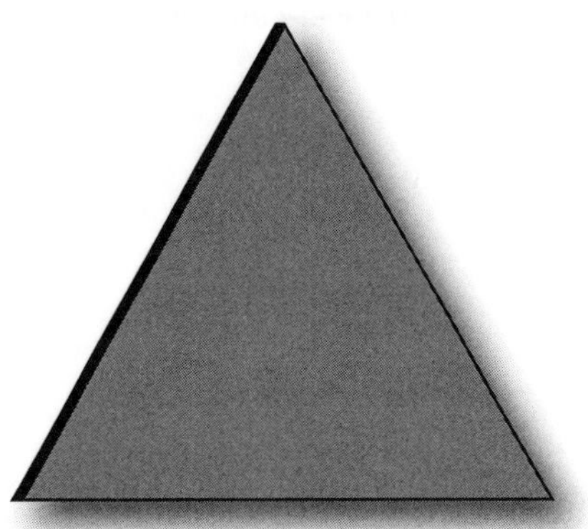

CHAPTER 2 OBJECTIVES

1. To underscore the crucial importance of understanding the historical-cultural background of a given biblical passage.

2. To demonstrate the trustworthiness of the biblical record.

3. To stress the need for determining the author's purpose regarding the specific details he has chosen to record.

4. To provide a set of interpretive guidelines for applying the principles embedded in the historical-cultural data of the Bible to a given contemporary situation.

CHAPTER 2 OUTLINE

A. History and Biblical Interpretation

B. Chronology

C. Archaeology

D. Conclusion

E. Guidelines for Interpreting Historical-Cultural Background

F. Key Words

G. Assignments

H. Key Resources

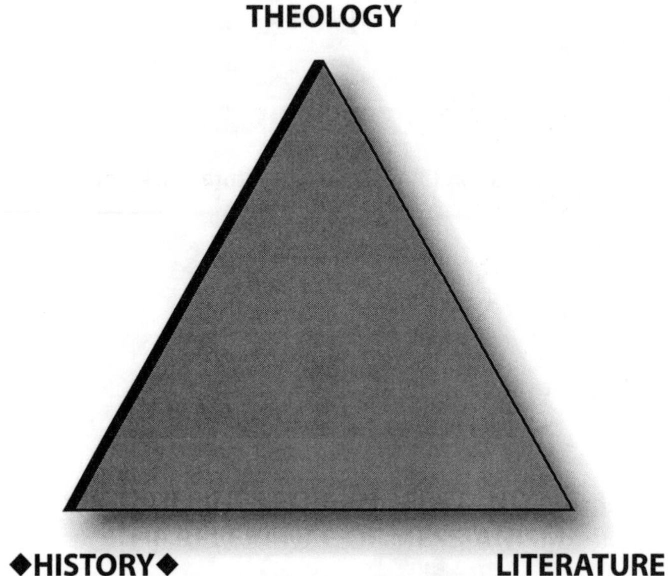
THEOLOGY
◆HISTORY◆
LITERATURE

Chapter 2

SETTING THE STAGE: HISTORICAL-CULTURAL BACKGROUND

HISTORY AND BIBLICAL INTERPRETATION

In order for the interpretation of Scripture to be properly grounded, it is vital to explore the historical setting of a scriptural passage, including any cultural background features. An informed knowledge of the historical and cultural background is imperative also for applying the message of Scripture. J. Scott Duvall and J. Daniel Hays (2005: 100) put the issue well:

> Since we live in a very different context, we must recapture God's original intended meaning as reflected in the text and framed by the ancient historical-cultural context. Once we understand the meaning of the text in its original context, we can apply it to our lives in ways that will be just as relevant.

Emphasizing the importance of historical information, of course, does not mean that every available piece of background data will necessarily be germane for the interpretation of a given biblical passage. The relevance of a particular piece of information must be carefully weighed and assessed. Certainly, background information should never override what is stated explicitly in the text. Conversely, understanding the background of a given passage is often vital for proper interpretation and application.

For our present purposes, the most important hermeneutical question relates to the relationship between history and literature, the first and second element in the hermeneutical triad. Literature, in the ancient Greek and Hebrew languages, immediately reinforces the notion of texts, different from our own, with unique historical and cultural development. These texts not only require translation into an understandable language (English) but also the study of historical-cultural aspects embedded within them since both the biblical languages and other parts of biblical culture and history are inextricably intertwined.

It is commonly acknowledged that it is vital to study Scripture in its proper context, and that context, in turn, properly conceived, consists of both historical and literary facets; so there is no need to justify the necessity of responsible historical research as part of the interpretive process. The necessity of historical research also underlies major reference works such as study Bibles, Old and New Testament introductions, commentaries, and other standard reference works.

In this regard, it is important not to unduly divide the historical and literary dimensions of Scripture but to keep them in proper balance. The very fact that the triad consists of history, literature, *and* theology shows the need for historical research to be balanced by a proper focus on the text (literature) and sufficient attention given to theology (God's self-revelation in the sacred, historically embedded text). On the other hand, interpreters should avoid methods that are unduly critical of the Bible's historicity and eschew the reductionism that comes with reading Scripture merely as literature while keeping history at bay.

CHRONOLOGY

Reading the Bible reveals the great distance in time between the events recorded in Scripture and today; in its pages are not only events of long ago but also customs that are quite foreign. In order to grasp their significance, an understanding of the people, events, and customs of the Bible in their proper historical milieu is necessary. In this chapter, then, we will provide surveys of biblical chronology, archaeology, and historical-cultural background research, beginning with a general historical framework for biblical interpretation.

OLD TESTAMENT PERIOD

Primeval Period

Primeval history covers the period between Genesis 1–11, encompassing the time span between Creation to the birth of Abram. Despite the fact that we cannot determine with any degree of finality dates for primeval history, Genesis 1–11 is a crucial part of biblical history, reflecting not mere textual realities but historical realities that have served to shape the present world. The world in which we live is the one that God created as good, that was corrupted by the Fall, in which God established his covenant with Noah, and in which God made his promise to Abraham. If these are not historical realities, then the Christian faith is merely one among many mythological understandings of the world. True faith is rooted in a text that reveals not merely literary but also *historical* reality.

Historical realities are communicated through texts, and by their very nature, texts are selective in what they record. For this reason, there can never be a full account of every minute historical detail. Rather, the biblical authors recorded the most significant historical events for understanding who God is, what he is doing in the world, and what he calls humanity to do in response. In this way, the biblical text provides the interpretive framework for understanding human history. What is more, the biblical story line focuses particularly on *salvation history*, that is, the record of God's mission in carrying out his plan of redemption for sinful humanity in and through the Messiah. This section on chronology seeks to understand that history as given by the biblical text.

The creation narrative of Genesis 1–2 is part of the larger purpose of the five books of Moses (the Pentateuch) as a whole. This purpose is to demonstrate to Israel that their covenant God, Yahweh, is also the Creator of the entire universe. In this context, locating the creation of the world at an exact point of time in the past is secondary to understanding the creation narrative in the context in which it was originally written. In these early stages of Israel's history, the people were constituted as a nation by Yahweh, the Creator, who had established his covenant with Noah, Abraham, and Moses.

This creation, according to the scriptural witness, is followed by the fall of humanity into sin. Though God created all things as "good," Adam's sin brings death to all creation; yet God at once begins to make provision for overcoming death and restoring all things by speaking of the promised seed, a child from Eve who will end sin's rule (Gen. 3:15). Despite God's promise to end sin's reign by crushing the head of the serpent, the primeval period demonstrates that humanity spiraled downward until "[t]he LORD saw how great man's wickedness on the earth had become, and that every inclination of the thoughts of his heart was only evil all the time" (Gen. 6:5).

In the midst of this world of sin, God keeps a remnant of people who are faithful to him. In the flood narrative, all flesh is destroyed, except for Noah's family (Genesis 6–9); thus, the promise of the seed endures. Following the flood, the Noahic covenant confirms that God will sustain the natural cycle in order to set a firm stage for the redemption of all things by the promised seed (Genesis 9). The story of the tower of Babel serves to show the need for the redemption of all nations (Genesis 10–11). The answer for creation's plight and the nations' deliverance will come through God's covenant with Abraham.

Patriarchal Period

Most of the patriarchal period is set in the archaeological era known as the Middle Bronze Period (c. 2000–1600 B.C.). In the biblical literature, the patriarchal period begins in Genesis 12 with God's calling of and covenant with Abram and carries through the lives of Abraham, Isaac, Jacob, and Joseph until the end of Genesis (2092–1877/6 B.C.). Much of the biblical literature, including the material covering the patriarchal period, is written to demonstrate God's faithfulness to the promises he made to Abra(ha)m in Genesis 12, 15, and 17.

The Hebrew people, and therefore God's covenant promises and the deliverance of all that God had created, face a great challenge through the people's bondage in Egypt (1876–1447 B.C.). The book of Exodus opens up with the Hebrews growing so numerous that the Egyptian pharaoh decrees the slaughter of all the newborn male children, and thus the promise of the seed is threatened. Yet "God heard their groaning, and God remembered his covenant with Abraham, with Isaac, and with Jacob" (Exod. 2:24).

From the Exodus to the United Monarchy

God remembers the covenant through the exodus of the Hebrew people from Egypt, arguably the most important event for the constitution of the nation of Israel (1447/6 B.C.). Through the exodus and the Mosaic covenant established at Sinai, God calls Israel into being as a nation set apart for him. God then continues to be faithful to his covenant promises by taking the people across the Jordan to settle the land that he promised Israel's forefathers (1407/6 B.C.).

The period of the judges ensues as God continually raises up leaders to bring Israel back to faithfulness to the covenant (1367–1064 B.C.).

The united monarchy then begins with the anointing of Saul as king (1044 B.C.) and consists of the reigns of Saul, David, and Solomon. With regard to biblical literature, this era is significant because the Psalms and wisdom literature flourished during this time period as David and Solomon became the archetypal psalmist and embodiment of wisdom, respectively.

The period of the united monarchy also proved to be significant with respect to the covenant promises of God. God made a covenant with David, saying,

> When your days are over and you rest with your fathers, I will raise up your offspring to succeed you, who will come from your own body, and I will establish his kingdom. He is the one who will build a house for my Name, and I will establish the throne of his kingdom forever (2 Sam. 7:12–13).

This covenant with David continued God's faithfulness to his prior covenants, specifying that the promised seed, God's Messiah, would come in and through the line of David (see Matt. 1:1–17). Later, Solomon builds the temple as the place where God has chosen to make his name dwell (957 B.C.). After Solomon's death, the nation is divided into the northern and the southern kingdoms, called Israel and Judah, respectively.

Divided Monarchy

The era of the divided monarchy encompasses the period from the death of Solomon until the collapse of the northern and southern kingdoms in 722 B.C. and 586 B.C, respectively. This is a lively time in the history of the ancient Near East, which sees the ascendancy of the Neo-Assyrian Empire (745–612 B.C.), the rise of the Neo-Babylonian (or Chaldean) Empire (626–539 B.C.), and a brief resurgence of Egypt (664–525 B.C.). Israel's location in the midst of these competing powers provides frequent pressure upon the twin kingdoms. That pressure will lead to Israel and Judah's breaking of the covenant and her spiritual apostasy and worship of other gods. Breaking the covenant, in turn, means that Israel and Judah incur the curse of the Mosaic covenant—exile from the promised land (586–516 B.C.).

Exile and Return

The northern kingdom (Israel) is exiled by the Assyrians in 722 B.C., and the southern kingdom (Judah) follows suit when it falls into Babylonian captivity. If the exodus serves as the paradigmatic event of redemption, the exile represents the paradigmatic event of judgment. Though it is Israel's—not God's—unfaithfulness that ushers in divine judgment, now that the Jews have gone into exile they question God's faithfulness to his covenant. God promised that Israel would be in the land permanently, that his name would dwell in the temple indefinitely, that David would have a son on the throne forever, and that all nations would be blessed through Israel. Yet, other nations took Israel captive in judgment and destroyed the temple. Nevertheless, in spite of Israel's failure to fulfill her side of the covenant arrangement, God would prove faithful.

In due course, God calls the Persian ruler, Cyrus, to defeat the Babylonians who captured Israel (Isa. 44:24–45:7), and he issues a decree to bring God's people back to the Promised Land (538 B.C.). Subsequently, the people begin to rebuild the temple in 536 B.C. Under the ministries of Ezra and Nehemiah, the temple is completed in 516 B.C. God proves faithful, and the people are restored from exile. Though the temple is rebuilt, however, it is not as glorious as Solomon's temple, nor does the glory of God descend to take up his presence there again. God's fulfillment of his promises awaits a future time.

2.1. BIBLE CHRONOLOGY: 2167–430 B.C.		
DATE	**EVENT/PERSON**	**SCRIPTURE**
2167–1992	Abraham	Genesis 11:26–25:11
2092–1877/76	Patriarchal Age	Genesis 12–50
1876–1447	Bondage in Egypt	Exodus 1–12:30
1447/6	The Exodus	Exodus 12:31–15:21
1407/6	Entrance into Canaan under Joshua	Joshua
1367–1064	Period of the Judges	Judges
1064–1044	Samuel	1 Samuel 7:2
1044–1004	Saul	1 Samuel 10; cf. Acts 13:21
1011–971	David	2 Samuel 5:5
971–931	Solomon	1 Kings 11:42
931	Division of the Kingdom	1 Kings 12:19
722	Assyrian Exile	2 Kings 17:6
605	First deportation to Babylon	Daniel 1
598	Second deportation to Babylon	2 Kings 24; 2 Chronicles 36
586	Third deportation to Babylon	Jeremiah 38–45
538	Decree of Cyrus allowing return	Ezra 1–4
520	Work on temple renewed under Darius	Haggai; Ezra 5–6
483–74	Xerxes and Esther; Purim	Esther
458	Return of Ezra to Jerusalem	Ezra 7–10
444	Artaxerxes allows Nehemiah to return	Nehemiah
430	End of Old Testament prophetic period	Malachi

The Writing Prophets

The Lord's writing prophets ministered during the eras of the divided monarchy, and the exile and return. Though their messages were primarily directed toward God's people, they also at times interacted with the surrounding nations (see chapters 5 and 7 below). The prophets who ministered in the Northern Kingdom did largely prophesy to God's people, although Jonah delivered the Lord's words of reconciliation to the people of Nineveh, during a time of Assyrian weakness under Assur-Dan III (c. 771–754 B.C.).

Those who ministered in the Southern Kingdom had many more prophesies aimed at the foreign nations (e.g., Jeremiah 46–51), for they served the Lord during the periods of Assyrian dominance (from Tiglath-Pileser III, 745 B.C., to Assurbanipal III, 668–626 B.C.); that of Neo-Babylonian power (especially during the reign of Nebuchadnezzar II, 605–562 B.C.); and the coming of Persian international dominance, beginning with Cyrus the Great (559–529 B.C.) and lasting until nearly the close of the 5th century B.C. (especially with the reigns of Darius the Great [521–486 B.C.], Xerxes the Great [485–464 B.C.], and Artaxerxes Longimanus [464–424 B.C.]).

Those who ministered and wrote during the exilic period largely directed their words toward God's people: Haggai (520 B.C.), Zechariah in the late 6th century B.C. and following, and Malachi in the mid- to late 5th century B.C. Knowledge of the historical setting of the writing prophets is crucial to the understanding of their messages. The following chart lists these prophets in their chronological order.

2.2. WRITING PROPHETS AFTER THE DIVISION OF THE KINGDOM	
NORTH (ISRAEL) (793–722 B.C.)	
King	*Prophet*
Jeroboam II (793–753)	Hosea (c. 760–725)
Zechariah (753–752)	Amos (c. 760–750)
Shallum (752)	Jonah (c. 755–750)
Menahem (751–742)	
Pekahiah (741–740)	

Pekah (740–732)	
Hoshea (732–722)	
Fall of Samaria, Assyrian exile (722)	
SOUTH (JUDAH) (791–430 B.C.)*	
King	*Prophet***
Uzziah (791–740)	ISAIAH (c. 740–685)
Jotham (752–736)	
Ahaz ([743] 736–720)	Micah (c. 735–725; Israel/Judah)
Hezekiah (729–699)	
Manasseh (698–642)	Nahum (c. 660–645)
Amon (642–640)	Habakkuk (c. 640–635)
Josiah (640–609)	Zephaniah (c. 635–630)
Jehoahaz (609)	JEREMIAH (c. 626–586)
Jehoiakim (609–598)	DANIEL (c. 606–535)
Jehoiachin (598)	
Zedekiah (598–586)	EZEKIEL (c. 597)
Fall of Jerusalem (586)	Obadiah (after 586)
First return of exiles (536)	Haggai (c. 520)
Temple rebuilt (516/515)	Zechariah (c. 520)
Second return of exiles (458)	Malachi (c. 430)
Third return of exiles (445)	
*Major prophets in all caps **Dates for Joel are disputed; estimates range from 9th to 4th cent. B.C.	

SECOND TEMPLE PERIOD

Students of Scripture should not ignore the intertestamental period, or as it is more commonly called today, the Second Temple period (named after the time between the rebuilding of the first temple built by Solomon after the return from exile in 516 B.C. and its destruction by the Romans in A.D. 70). The world of the Gospels is very different from the one at the close of the Old Testament. Much has happened, and this interim period is attested to, not by biblical material but by extrabiblical literature (e.g., 1 and 2 Maccabees). Thus we encounter in the Gospels various Jewish sects—the Pharisees, the Sadducees, the Herodians, and the Zealots—whose roots lie in events that transpired in the centuries preceding the Incarnation, for the most part during the Maccabean revolt and its aftermath.

Hellenistic Period

Following periods of Babylonian and Persian rule, the Greeks (Alexander the Great) took over world domination at the battle of Issus in the year 333. Alexander's acquisition of Palestine in the following year (332) had far-reaching impact on the Jews owing to his policy of Hellenization, that is, the spread of Greek language and culture. Long after the Greeks had been defeated by the Romans, the reach of Hellenistic culture continued. The Romans essentially adopted the Greek pantheon (spectrum of gods). The Greek translation of the Old Testament, the Septuagint (LXX), prepared in the third century B.C., became the version used by the early Christians and most frequently cited by the New Testament writers (cf. *The Letter of Aristeas*). The New Testament would be written, not in Hebrew or Aramaic, but in Greek. Several of Jesus's disciples, such as Philip or Andrew, though from Galilee, had Greek names. Even the name of the Jewish ruling council, "Sanhedrin," is a transliteration of the Greek word for "gathering."

After Alexander's death in 323 B.C., his empire was divided, ushering in two major dynasties: the Ptolemies in Egypt and the Seleucids in Mesopotamia and Syria. After a century-long struggle for control of Palestine between these two empires, the Seleucids (Antiochus) seized control in 198. Things came to a head during the reign of Antiochus Epiphanes IV (175–164 B.C.), whose radical Hellenization program culminated in the erection of a statue of Zeus and the sacrifice of a pig in the Jerusalem sanctuary, an act that stirred Jewish outrage and galvanized national resistance led by Mattathias and his five sons Judas (Maccabeus; 166–160 B.C.), Jonathan (160–143 B.C.), Simon, John, and Eleazar, known as the Maccabees or the Hasmoneans.

Maccabean Period

The Maccabean revolt succeeded in reversing Antiochus's policy. The temple was rededicated in 164 B.C. (the Feast of Dedication; see John 10:22), and again in 142 B.C. Judah became independent until the Romans conquered Palestine under Pompey in 63 B.C. The second century B.C. was a period of considerable ferment in Jewish life. Nationalism was rife, and several movements emerged that continued to exist until the time of Jesus, such as the Sadducees (aristocracy) and the Pharisees (religious reformists, persecuted by Alexander Jannaeus who ruled 103–76 B.C.). The Dead Sea community likewise arose during the mid-second century B.C., rejecting what it considered to be the corrupt Jerusalem priesthood (led by the "Wicked Priest") and rallying around the enigmatic "Teacher of Righteousness."

2.3. BIBLE CHRONOLOGY: 333 B.C.–A.D. 37

DATE	PERSON/EVENT	SIGNIFICANCE
333 B.C.	Alexander the Great seizes world domination	Hellenization
198 B.C.	Seleucids seize control of Palestine	Hellenization (continued)
175–164 B.C.	Antiochus Epiphanes IV rules Palestine, radical program of Hellenization	"Abomination causing desolation"
164 B.C.	Maccabean revolt, rededication of Temple	Feast of Dedication
142 B.C.	Judah becomes independent	Rise of Sadducees, Pharisees, Dead Sea community
63 B.C.	Roman general Pompey conquers Palestine	Roman vassal rulers in charge of Palestine at time of Christ
31 B.C.–A.D. 14	Emperor Augustus presides over "Golden Age" of Rome	Roman peace (*Pax Romana*; compared with Christ; Luke 2:1)
6 or 5 B.C.	Birth of Christ	Virgin birth
4 B.C.	Death of Herod the Great	Slaughter of infants, head of Herodian dynasty
A.D. 14–37	Emperor Tiberius	Ruled when Jesus began ministry and when he was crucified

Roman Period

After Pompey's conquest of Palestine in 63 B.C., a series of local rulers were put in charge of the provinces of Palestine. At the time of Jesus's birth in 6 or 5 B.C., Herod the Great ruled the region, though he died soon afterwards (4 B.C.) and was succeeded by Archelaus. In Jesus's day, Herod Antipas was in charge of Galilee (Mark 6:14; Luke 13:32). The great Emperor Augustus (31 B.C.–A.D. 14) presided over a golden period of peace (the *Pax Romana*) and prosperity (as well as rising corruption and decadence), which provided a poignant counterpoint to the humble birth of Christ (Luke 2:1). When John the Baptist and Jesus commenced their ministries, the rule had passed to Emperor Tiberius (14–37; cf. Luke 3:1) who was still in charge at the time of Jesus's crucifixion in the spring of 33, with Pontius Pilate serving as the procurator or prefect of Judea.

NEW TESTAMENT PERIOD

Jesus

For the purpose of interpreting the New Testament, a brief discussion and survey of its underlying chronology is helpful. Especially important is the dating of the life of Jesus, in particular the crucifixion, and the life of Paul and related events. The two major questions with regard to the chronology of Jesus's life pertain to the dating of his birth and death.

Regarding his birth, the most likely date is 6 or 5 B.C. Herod's death in 4 B.C. provides the latest possible date. A medieval computation error in the reckoning of time is responsible for the fact that Jesus's birth does not fall in the year A.D. 1, as might be expected, but is dated 6 or 5 B.C.

2.4. CHRONOLOGY OF JESUS'S LIFE

EVENT	APPROXIMATE DATE	SCRIPTURE REFERENCE
Jesus's Birth	6 or 5 B.C.	Matt. 1:18–25; Luke 2:1–20
Death of Herod the Great	April/March 4 B.C.	Josephus, *Ant.* 17.6.4 §167

Beginning of John the Baptist's Ministry	A.D. 29	Luke 3:1–3.
Beginning of Jesus's Ministry	Fall 29	John 1:19–51
Jesus's First Passover	Spring 30	John 2:13–22
Jesus's Second Passover	Spring 31	Synoptics
Jesus at Feast of Tabernacles	Fall 31	John 5
Jesus's Third Passover	Spring 32	John 6
Jesus at Feast of Tabernacles	Fall 32	John 7–8
Jesus at Feast of Dedication	Winter 32	John 10:22–39
Final Passover, Crucifixion, Resurrection, Ascension, Pentecost	Spring 33	Gospels passion narratives; Acts 1–2

Luke (3:1) writes that John the Baptist began his ministry in the fifteenth year of Tiberius Caesar's reign (A.D. 14–37), which places the beginning of the Baptist's, and of Jesus's, ministry at A.D. 29. If Jesus was born in 6 or 5 B.C., he would have been about 33 years old when he started his public ministry, which coheres with the statement in Luke 3:23 that Jesus was "about thirty years old" when he appeared on the scene.

A date of 29 for the start of Jesus's ministry, in turn, requires a date of 33 for the crucifixion, since the Gospels record Jesus attending at least three or four Passovers (John mentions three Passovers; the Synoptics, that is, Matthew, Mark, and Luke, most likely add a fourth; see chart above). Of the two major possibilities suggested for the dating of Jesus's ministry, 26–30 or 29–33, the latter date is preferred.

Early Church and Paul

The book of Acts, on a canonical as well as a historical level, provides an excellent transition between the life of Jesus (the Gospels) and the New Testament Epistles, most notably the 13 letters of Paul. The following chart represents an effort to construct a Pauline chronology on the basis of the book of Acts, Paul's epistles, and extrabiblical data—a helpful tool in interpreting Paul's letters within their proper historical framework.

2.5. CHRONOLOGY OF PAUL'S LIFE AND LETTERS		
EVENT	**APPROXIMATE DATE**	**SCRIPTURE REFERENCE**
Paul's Birth	Around the turn of the era	
Jesus's Crucifixion, Resurrection, Ascension, and Pentecost	Spring 33	Gospels passion narratives; Acts 1–2
Paul's Conversion	34	Acts 9:1–19
First Missionary Journey	47–48	Acts 13–14
Authorship of **Galatians**	48	
Jerusalem Council	49	Acts 15
Second Missionary Journey Antioch to Corinth **Thessalonian Letters** from Corinth 18-Month Stay in Corinth Appearance before Gallio	49–51	Acts 16–18 Acts 18:11 Acts 18:12
Third Missionary Journey 3-Year Stay in Ephesus "Severe letter" **1 Corinthians** "Sorrowful letter" **2 Corinthians** (from Macedonia) Stay in Corinth **Romans** (from Corinth)	51–54 53/54 54/55 55	Acts 19–21 Acts 20:31 1 Cor. 5:9, 11 Acts 19:10 2 Cor. 2:4; 7:8 Acts 20:1–2 2 Cor. 13:1–2 Rom. 16:1–2, 23
Jerusalem Arrest	55	Acts 21–23 Acts 21:27–40
Imprisonment in Caesarea Defense before Felix, Festus, Agrippa	55–57	Acts 24–27
Journey to Rome Voyage and Shipwreck Winter in Malta	57–58	Acts 27 Acts 28:1–10

2.5. CHRONOLOGY OF PAUL'S LIFE AND LETTERS (CONTINUED)		
EVENT	**APPROXIMATE DATE**	**SCRIPTURE REFERENCE**
First Roman Imprisonment Prison Epistles: **Colossians, Philemon, Ephesians, Philippians**	58–60	Acts 28:11–30
Paul's Release	60	
Further Travels **1 Timothy** **Titus**	60–66	
Great Fire of Rome, Persecution of Christians under Emperor Nero	64	
Paul's Arrest and ***Second Roman Imprisonment*** **2 Timothy**	66	
Paul's and Peter's Martyrdoms	66/67	
Outbreak of Jewish War	66	
Destruction of Jerusalem	70	

Rest of the New Testament

The above two charts cover Jesus and the Gospels, the book of Acts, and Paul's Epistles (it should be added that the Synoptic Gospels were most likely written prior to the destruction of the temple in the year A.D. 70, while John dates in all probability to the 80s or early 90s). A framework for the rest of the New Testament writings is also needed.

James, a Jewish-Christian work written by one of Jesus's half-brothers, the head of the Jerusalem church, was likely written around the time of the Jerusalem Council in the early 50s. The epistle of Jude, authored by James's brother and half-brother of Jesus, may also be dated to the 50s. Jude, in turn, was possibly used by Peter in 2 Peter 2, which, among other factors, suggests dates in the 60s for Peter's two epistles.

The book of Hebrews was almost certainly composed prior to the destruction of the Jerusalem temple in the year 70. It is hard to imagine why the author would not have mentioned the temple's destruction if it had already taken place by the time of writing, since this would have provided strong support for his contention that old-style Judaism had now been superseded—and fulfilled—in Jesus and the Christian faith.

The Johannine writings, finally, consisting of the Gospel, John's three epistles, and the book of Revelation, most likely written in this order, cluster around the 80s and 90s, with Revelation closing the entire canon of Scripture. Thus the scriptural framework for New Testament interpretation spans from the Gospels to the historical narrative of Acts to the Epistles and to the concluding Apocalypse (see chapter 4 below).

Having secured a firm historical foundation by surveying the biblical chronology of the Old Testament, the Second Temple period, and the New Testament, we now move on to another important ancillary discipline that is relevant for biblical interpretation, namely archaeology. We will look at important archaeological discoveries which pertain to Old and New Testament interpretation in turn.

ARCHAEOLOGY

Old Testament

Archaeology has steadily increased the understanding of ancient Near Eastern history and culture beginning with the decipherment of the *Rosetta Stone* in the nineteenth century. This amazing discovery provided the key to the ancient Egyptian language and gave the impetus for further unraveling the tangled strands of the history of the ancient Near East. Building on several significant discoveries in the early twentieth century, the quest for knowledge of the ancient Near East blossomed between the first two world wars. Steady progress continues up to our own time.

Archaeology has contributed significantly to the understanding of the biblical record. Some of these contributions have been mentioned above in the discussions of the patriarchal period, the era of the exodus, and the time of the judges. With regard to the time of the united monarchy, the biblical description of Solomon's Temple finds confirmation in the excavation of similarly laid-out *temples of ancient Syro-Palestine*. Further information concerning Solomon's building activities comes from the excavations at Hazor, Megiddo, and Gezer.

With regard to the time of the divided monarchy, numerous discoveries aid in the fuller understanding of the biblical record in this period (931–841 B.C.). In the first part of this era, Pharaoh Shishak invaded Israel (1 Kgs. 14:25–26), and his own account has been found in the great temple at Karnak. In it he lists more than 150 Palestinian cities that he attacked and despoiled.

In the middle period of Old Testament history (841–640 B.C.), the Assyrian King Shalmaneser III (859–825 B.C.) records the capitulation of King Jehu of Israel on his well-known *Black Obelisk*: "The tribute of Jehu, son of Omri." This information supplements that which the biblical record provides concerning Jehu's reign (2 Kgs. 9:1–10:36). The familiar account of King Sennacherib of Assyria's siege of Jerusalem in which he lost 185,000 men due to the Lord's intervention (2 Kgs. 19:35–36) also falls into this period. Sennacherib's version of this event during his third campaign attempts to paint a more positive picture by claiming that Hezekiah paid him a heavy tribute in order to get him to leave Jerusalem. Concerning Hezekiah, Sennacherib declares, "As for Hezekiah, the Jew . . . Him, like a caged bird, in Jerusalem, his royal city, I shut up."

One further example of the contribution of archeology relates to Daniel's mention of King Belshazzar of Babylon (Daniel 5). This was considered by previous generations to be one of the most obvious errors in the Bible, for ancient historians mentioned Nabonidus as Babylon's last ruler. Yet subsequent information discovered in the *Babylonian clay tablets* proved not only the existence of Belshazzar, but also indicated that because Nabonidus, his father, was absent for long periods from Babylon, he left the affairs of state to Belshazzar. Critical denial of the existence of Belshazzar has now largely disappeared.

Confirmation of the biblical record for the third period (640–586 B.C.) concerning the scriptural record of Daniel's captivity at the hands of King Nebuchadnezzar II of Babylon in 605 B.C. comes from the *Babylonian chronicles*. In that year after his victory over the Assyrians and Egyptians at Carchemish, Nebuchadnezzar swept westward, but due to the death of his father Nabopolasser he returned to Babylon to secure the throne. Having done so, he rejoined his troops and marched "unopposed through

Hatti Land." Such data harmonizes well with the biblical accounts in Daniel 1:1–2 and 2 Chronicles 36:6–7.

New Testament

In recent years archaeology has also made a significant contribution to a better understanding of various geographical and topographical features of the New Testament, and detailed archaeological information is available regarding many sites mentioned in the New Testament. This section briefly addresses relevant historical, cultural, and archaeological issues for New Testament interpretation pertaining to the life of Jesus, Paul, and the New Testament writings.

The most important contributions made by archaeology to Jesus research are as follows:

1. Archaeological evidence that Jesus was crucified on the rock now seen inside the *Church of the Holy Sepulchre*

2. The *remains of a crucified first-century man* named Jehohanan

3. The *Praetorium*, the official residence of the Roman governor: Pilate's dwelling was probably in the Upper City and not in the Fortress of Antonia

4. The *Pool of Bethesda* described in John 5:2–9

5. The *Temple Mount*: monumental pre-70 structures located south of the southern retaining wall of the Temple

6. The *walls and gates of Jerusalem*

7. Pre-70 *synagogues* at Gamla, Masada, and the Herodium, and possibly at Jericho

Other important discoveries include the Pilate inscription ("Pontius Pilate, prefect of Judea") discovered in 1961 in Caesarea Maritima; the tombs of Annas and Caiaphas and the Caiaphas ossuary (bearing the name of Joseph Caiaphas); the James ossuary (bearing the inscription

"James, the son of Joseph, the brother of Jesus"); and the Alexamenos graffiti ("Alexamenos worships his god"). Though archaeologists do not always agree on the way in which they interpret archaeological findings and their relevance to Jesus, no archaeological discovery has disproved any information concerning Jesus that is found in the four canonical Gospels.

With regard to Paul and the New Testament writings, major excavations have been conducted in many of the cities where Paul ministered and where the early Christian mission unfolded. This includes important sites such as *Ephesus* and *Corinth*. Particularly important is the "Gallio Inscription," which allows us to date Gallio's governorship in the province of Achaia to between the summer of the year 51 and the summer of 52. Most likely, therefore, the Jews brought charges against Paul in the summer or fall of the year 51 per Acts 18:12. With Paul's ministry in Corinth spanning 18 months (Acts 18:11) and his departure from Corinth taking place sometime after the Gallio incident, Paul's arrival in Corinth can be dated to early 50. Thus the "Gallio Inscription," as one of the few reasonably fixed dates in New Testament history, provides an anchor for an absolute chronology of Paul's life, letters, and ministry (see chart 2.5 above).

CONCLUSION

Christianity is a historical religion, and Scripture presupposes that God revealed himself in human history. This requires that Bible students be sensitive to historical factors, whether chronological timelines, archaeological discoveries, or historical-cultural customs that have a bearing on biblical interpretation. Many helpful tools can assist in this endeavor, from technical commentaries to Bible handbooks to the more recent genre of Bible background commentaries.

While studying historical-cultural customs is of great value, often the Bible student is faced with the important question of whether a given biblical pronouncement is culturally relative or normative. How should the modern interpreter understand and apply biblical injunctions that are given in the context of social norms that may no longer be in effect? Grant Osborne (2006: 166) describes the interpreter's task in assessing the ancient historical-cultural background as follows:

> Therefore, the task of the receptor in the modern cultural framework is to recapture the total framework within which the sacred writer communicated and to transfer that message to our own day. The cultural aspects presupposed in the passage help interpreters get behind the words to the underlying message, understood by the original readers but hidden to the modern reader.

The interpreter may well ask, "Were these customs meant to be permanently binding or not?" The answer is not always readily apparent, and often there is a certain amount of diversity of opinion among biblical interpreters. We suggest the following three general guidelines.

1. Some cultural matters mentioned in the Old Testament clearly are limited in application and are not repeated in the New Testament. In other cases, the New Testament explicitly sets aside certain portions. For example, the book of Hebrews makes clear that the entire Old Testament sacrificial system and the Levitical priesthood found their fulfillment in Christ.

2. Some Old Testament cultural standards are repeated later on in the Bible and thus continue to be valid. The Ten Commandments, for example, are repeated in the New Testament (except for the Sabbath commandment) and for this reason continue to apply, though they are deepened by the New Testament. Or take the repeated Old Testament commands to show concern for the poor (Lev. 23:22; cf., e.g., 1 Cor. 16:1; 1 Tim. 5:3).

3. In many cases, biblical customs contain an underlying principle that remains applicable today. The biblical custom of employing a kiss as a conventional greeting, for example (see, e.g., Gen. 33:4; 2 Sam. 19:39; Luke 7:35; Rom. 16:16), may find application in today's handshake or hug. In these cases, we seek to discern and apply the underlying principle involved in the cultural expression.

GUIDELINES FOR INTERPRETING HISTORICAL-CULTURAL BACKGROUND

1. Determine the scope of the historical account. Look for links with other scriptural passages, especially those relating to the same event(s).

2. Compare the biblical record with external data for additional information and illumination.

3. Consider the author's purpose(s) in recording the event(s) he has selected.

4. Remember that historical events are descriptive of morality and conduct but not always prescriptive.

5. Make appropriate application(s) of the underlying lesson or principle involved in the event or custom recorded in the text.

6. Recognize that the biblical historical and cultural accounts are sacred and trustworthy records of what actually occurred.

7. Consider the important biblical witness on ethical issues.

8. Let clearer passages help illuminate ones that are less clear.

KEY WORDS

Gallio Inscription, Hellenism, Herodians, Maccabeans/Hasmoneans, Ossuary, Pharisees, Sadducees, Sanhedrin, Second Temple period, Septuagint, Zealots.

ASSIGNMENTS

1. Engage in a study of the relevant historical-cultural background for interpreting John 2:13–3:21.

2. Produce a chart relating Paul's letters to his ministry as narrated in the book of Acts.

KEY RESOURCES

Arnold, Clinton E., ed. *Zondervan Illustrated Bible Backgrounds Commentary: New Testament*. 4 vols. Grand Rapids: Zondervan, 2002.

Walton, John H., ed. *Zondervan Illustrated Bible Backgrounds Commentary: Old Testament*. 5 vols. Grand Rapids: Zondervan, 2009.

PART 2

LITERATURE

UNIT 1: CANON

CHAPTER 3 OBJECTIVES

1. To set forth three key themes, which provide a proper orientation to the Law, Prophets, and Writings of the Old Testament.

2. To discuss the nature and culmination of the law in the new covenant.

3. To trace the concept of redemption in the exodus event and discuss its contribution to the new covenant.

4. To discuss the God-man relationship in the Old Testament covenants and the culmination of the covenants in the new covenant.

5. To show the sovereign rule of God in relation to the people of Old Testament times and the importance of the promise of a coming Messiah and his relation to the new covenant.

6. To impart a perspective on the Old Testament that serves as preparation for understanding the New Testament revelation.

CHAPTER 3 OUTLINE

A. Introduction

B. Law

C. Exodus

D. Covenant

E. Coordinating Old Testament Themes

F. Key Words

G. Assignments

H. Key Resources

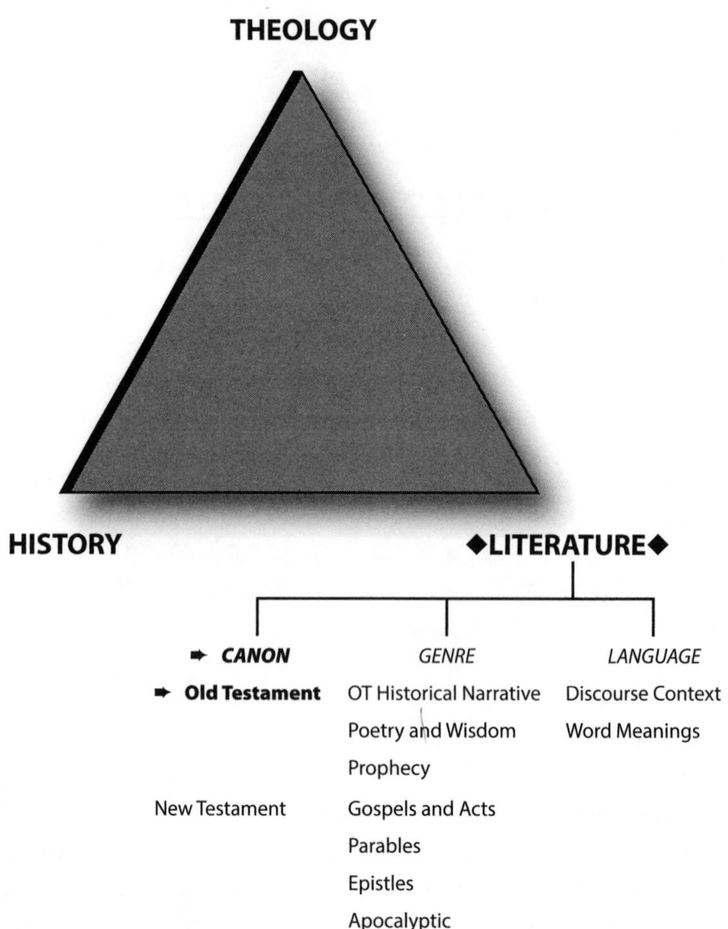
THEOLOGY
HISTORY
◆LITERATURE◆
➡ CANON
➡ Old Testament
New Testament
GENRE
OT Historical Narrative
Poetry and Wisdom
Prophecy
Gospels and Acts
Parables
Epistles
Apocalyptic
LANGUAGE
Discourse Context
Word Meanings

Chapter 3

OLD TESTAMENT CANON: LAW, PROPHETS, AND WRITINGS

INTRODUCTION

NOW THAT WE HAVE PROPERLY grounded our study of Scripture in an investigation of its historical setting, we are ready to turn to an exploration of the second element of the hermeneutical triad: literature. The study of the literary dimension of the biblical text will constitute the major focus of our interpretive journey. In keeping with the bedrock hermeneutical principle of interpreting the parts in light of the whole, we will proceed from the larger biblical framework to the literary genre including specific linguistic features of various passages of Scripture.

In this chapter, we will consider the three major parts of the Old Testament revelation: the Law, the Prophets, and the Writings. Although the Old Testament grew gradually over more than a millennium, when the individual writings were completed, they were often immediately recognized and accepted as divinely authoritative (e.g., Exod. 24:3–4,7; Deut. 4:1–2; 31:9–11, 24–26; Josh. 1:7–9; 8:35). Time and again, the prophets claimed that they had received a divine revelation and declared that they spoke for the Lord (e.g., 1 Kings 17:13–14; Isa. 1:1; 6:1–13; Jer. 1:4–19; Ezek. 2:1–3:4; Jonah 1:1; 3:1; Hab. 1:1; Zech. 1:1; Mal. 1:1; etc.). Many recognized the Old Testament writings as authoritative (1 Kings

16:34; 2 Kings 14:6, 25; 23:1–3; Ezra 5:1–2; Neh. 9:30; Isa. 34:16; Dan. 9:2), including Jesus (Matt. 5:17–20; 23:34–35), the apostles (e.g., Acts 2:17–21, 25–26, 34–35; Rom. 1:2–3; 11:2; 2 Pet. 1:19–21), and others in the New Testament (e.g., Luke 1:1–4; 24:27, 32, 45; Heb. 2:6–9; 5:5–6; 8:8–12; etc.).

Moreover, it may be safely said that careful historical inquiry and research have demonstrated that at each step of its formation the Old Testament accurately represents the area and era with which it is concerned. Its truthfulness in the case of data that can be verified further suggests that where it claims to be the word of the Lord, the Old Testament can be trusted. It is also of interest to note that phrases such as "thus says the Lord" and "God/the Lord said" occur thousands of times. When one adds to this the fact that individuals responding positively to the Bible's teachings and standards experience a life-changing spiritual condition, this indicates that the Old Testament books transcend mere human invention.

LAW

As the interpreter comes to the books of Exodus through Deuteronomy, he or she must remember that the word translated "law" (Hebrew "Torah") means basically "instruction." The Hebrew Torah includes Genesis through Deuteronomy and is also known as the five books of Moses. Genesis thus provides a narrative background not only for the four books that follow, but its message is also foundational for the whole Old Testament. As we examine the traditional three portions of the Old Testament (the Law, the Prophets, and the Writings), we will return to the teachings of Genesis on multiple occasions.

In the following discussion, we will consider three primary themes that form the basic focal points of the Old Testament: God's law, the exodus, and covenant. These three major concepts embody the principles of righteousness, redemption, and the believer's relationship to God. Indeed, it is these three themes that God brings together at Mount Sinai (Exod. 19:3–6) and that Moses later charges the Israelites to remember and pass on to subsequent generations (Deut. 6:4–12). Moses sums them up as follows:

> In the future, when your son asks you, "What is the meaning of the stipulations, decrees and laws the LORD our God has commanded you?" tell

> him: "We were slaves of Pharaoh in Egypt, but the LORD brought us out of Egypt with a mighty hand. Before our eyes the LORD sent miraculous signs and wonder—great and terrible—upon Egypt and Pharaoh and his whole household. But he brought us out from there to bring us in and give us the land that he promised on oath to our forefather. The LORD commanded us to obey all these decrees and to fear the LORD our God, so that we might always prosper and be kept alive, as is the case today. And if we are careful to obey all this law before the LORD our God as he has commanded us, that will be our righteousness" (Deut. 6:20–25).

The applicability of Old Testament law to New Testament believers is one of the most controversial issues in biblical theology. Questions such as, "Is the Old Testament law still in effect?" and, "How much of it, if any, is still binding on Christians?" continue to occupy believers today. We shall begin to address these issues by examining the law's Old Testament setting.

Types of Law

The Old Testament laws covered virtually every aspect of human conduct. For example, various laws concerned matters such as the needs of special classes in society (e.g., Exod. 22:22–24; Lev. 19:9–10, 33–34; Deut. 23:15–16), business dealings (e.g., Deut. 23:19–21), agriculture (e.g., Exod. 23:9–10; Lev. 25:1–24), and land and property rights (e.g., Deut. 19:14; 25:5–10). Laws of a religious or ceremonial nature were also included, such as regulations concerning the Sabbath (e.g., Exod. 31:12–17), sacrificial offerings (Leviticus 1–7), stated feasts (Num. 28:11–15; Deut. 16:1–15), and places of worship (Deut. 12:1–14). In addition, there were laws governing the personal lives of the people (e.g., Lev. 12–15; Deut. 12:15; 14:3–21). All these laws were designed to remind the Hebrews that they were a people specially chosen by God and that they were called to be a holy, just, and morally responsible people of God (Deut. 14:1–2).

Traditionally, some have classified these laws as to whether they are moral, civil, or ceremonial in nature. Others have classified them as to whether they are laws based upon legal precedents (casuistic laws) or laws prescribing absolute religious and moral standards for the smooth running of society (apodictic laws). The difficulty of assigning individual laws to specific categories has made scholars consider an alternative approach.

Increasingly, they are beginning to view Old Testament laws in relation to the narrative context in which they are found.

Therefore, rather than reading Old Testament laws in order to decide to which category they belong or which of these laws are absolute and universally binding standards or which are ethically and historically limited to Israel, the careful interpreter should see them as part of the broad narrative in which they are found (Exod. 12:1; Deut. 34:12). Viewed in this context, all the laws are to be treated as the expression of the will and high moral standards of a sovereign and holy God. They are designed for a redeemed people specially chosen to represent him and reflect his character in their lives (Lev. 19:1). In addition, their narrative setting places them in juxtaposition with our other two focal themes, the exodus event and covenant stipulations (cf. Exod. 19:1–6).

Terms for the Law

The law of Israel was known by several different terms, such as: "law of the Lord" (Exod. 13:9); "book of the law of God" (Josh. 24:26); "law of Moses" (2 Kings 23:25); "book of the law of Moses" (2 Kings 14:6); "the law which Moses set" (Deut. 4:44); "book of the law" (Josh. 1:8); and "the law" (Deut. 1:5) or "this law" (Deut. 31:9). Whatever the precise term, the teachings of the law were to be passed on and read regularly and obeyed (Deut. 31:10–13; Josh. 1:6–9).

Transmission of the Law

The Old Testament Scriptures point out that the law was read and transmitted to those who remained faithful to the Lord and to the spirit of the law (e.g., Josh. 8:31–35; 2 Kings 23:1–3, 24–25; Ezra 8:1–3; Neh. 9:6–15). Accordingly, the importance of the law (as well as of the exodus and covenant) is stressed in the poetic writings (e.g., Psalms 78; 119). Note, for example, the following texts:

> The law of the LORD is perfect,
> reviving the soul.
> The statues of the LORD are trustworthy,
> making wise the simple. (Ps. 19:7)

> Where there is no revelation, the people cast off restraint,
> But blessed is he who keeps the law. (Prov. 29:18)

The prophets also stressed the importance of remembering and keeping the law, as well as the danger of transgressing it (e.g., Isa. 42:20–25; Jer. 7:21–24; Hos. 8:12; Amos 2:4). But it is Jeremiah who in introducing the message of the new covenant (Jer. 31:31–34), encapsulates both the importance of the law and its relation to the other two basic Old Testament themes (the exodus and covenant). In this text, Jeremiah prophesies that although the Torah will find continuity in the future, its provisions will be written on the heart rather than serve as an external law code. Moreover, Jeremiah hints that what was unique to Israel will be universally available and applicable. At that point, there will be an intimacy of fellowship unmatched in previous times. Since this is an internal rather than external reality, Jeremiah makes it clear that it is the theological principles inherent in the specific laws that are in view.

Applicability of the Law

To be sure, the law was originally designed for Israel. Yet the realization that its theological and moral principles are embedded in the new covenant puts the applicability of the law into proper perspective. For Christ, the mediator of the new covenant, stressed the importance of the principles of the law for the believer's life. Also, it is he who supplies the ability to keep and apply the law to believers under the terms of the New Testament revelation. Nevertheless, although the old Mosaic law has been superseded by a new covenant (cf. Jer. 31:31–37; Ezek. 37:24–28; with Gal. 2:15–16), the underlying theological and moral principles are timeless and continue to be in effect (cf. Matt. 5:17). Thus the applicability of the law for Christians is channeled through the light of the new covenant established by Christ.

It is important for us to note that where the New Testament deals with specific Old Testament laws, they are to be given special regard. Even here, as elsewhere, however, the teachings inherent in the Old Testament law must be viewed through the lens of the New Testament revelation. It is important for the student of Scripture to realize that the whole Bible, including the Old Testament law, has much to teach us concerning Christian living.

A case in point is the Ten Commandments. Although written specifically for Israel, the theological principles in them are implicit in texts that antedate the revelation at Mount Sinai and are found in various places in the New Testament. Note the following selective chart of relevant texts:

3.1. THE TEN COMMANDMENTS AND UNDERLYING PRINCIPLES			
COMMANDMENTS			**PRINCIPLES**
Exodus	**Deuteronomy**	**Pre-Sinai**	**New Testament**
Exod. 20:2–3	Deut. 5:6–7	Gen. 17:1; Exod. 3:14	Acts 14:10–15; 1 Cor. 8:4
Exod. 20:4–6	Deut. 5:8–10	Gen. 35:3–4	2 Cor. 6:16; 1 John 5:20–21
Exod. 20:7	Deut. 5:11	Gen. 24:3	Matt. 6:5–13
Exod. 20:8–11	Deut. 5:12–14	Gen. 2:2–3	1 Cor. 16:2
Exod. 20:12	Deut. 5:16	Gen. 46:29; 50:1–5	Matt. 19:18; Eph. 6:1–3
Exod. 20:13	Deut. 5:17	Gen. 4:6–12, 15; 9:5–6	Matt. 19:19; Rom. 13:9
Exod. 20:14	Deut. 5:18	Gen. 39:9	Matt. 19:18; Rom. 13:9
Exod. 20:15	Deut. 5:19	Gen. 27:36; 31:5	Matt. 19:18; Rom. 13:9; Eph. 4:28
Exod. 20:16	Deut. 5:20	Gen. 39:16–18	Matt. 19:18; Rom. 13:9; James 4:11–12
Exod. 20:17	Deut. 5:21	Gen. 26:10	Rom. 7:7; 13:9–10

GUIDELINES FOR APPLYING THE OLD TESTAMENT LAW

1. As with any biblical text or passage, determine what the law meant to its original hearers or readers.

2. Determine the theological and moral principles inherent in the particular law.

3. Determine whether the law has been commented on by Jesus or the New Testament writers. If so, how has the law been modified (e.g., the Sabbath vs. Sunday worship)?

4. Granted the underlying theological or moral intention of the law and its New Testament application (if any), determine how this law applies to contemporary culture (e.g., the issues of slavery, business practices, women's dress, etc.).

5. Make proper personal application relying on the Holy Spirit's guidance.

THE EXODUS

By referring to the exodus as part of an event, we are emphasizing that Israel's deliverance out of Egypt was but the first part of a whole movement that took God's people from Egypt to the Promised Land (Exod. 3:16–17).

Setting of the Exodus

Israel's exodus from Egypt forms the climax of the contest between Moses and the Egyptian pharaoh (Exod. 3:1–12:36). The account of Israel's deliverance from Egypt is told in a well-structured narrative that portrays the various stages of Israel's journey: from Egypt to Succoth (Exod. 12:37–13:19); from there through the Re(e)d Sea (Exod. 13:20–15:21); and on in succession to the oasis at Elim (Exod. 15:22–27); to the Desert of Sin (Exod. 16:1–36); to Rephidim (Exod. 17:1–18:27); and on to Mount Sinai (Exod. 19:1–2).

The account of the events during the encampment before Mount Sinai (Exod. 19:3–Num. 10:10) forms a pivotal episode in the narrative of the exodus. For it was there that the stipulations of the law were delivered to Israel (cf. Exod. 20:1–17). As noted, however, the exodus would not be complete until God brought his people through the wilderness and into the Promised Land (Num. 10:11–Josh. 21:43). The full narrative thus ends only when Israel has entered and taken possession of the land of Canaan.

Rather than viewing the law or the exodus as isolated accounts that have been pieced together at some late date, understanding both as part of one complete narrative allows the interpreter to see the importance of each as well as to realize that the value of the whole narrative is greater than the sum of its individual parts. In fact, details regarding God's covenant act are also pertinent to the story of the giving of the law, which in turn forms part of the exodus account (cf. Exod. 19:1–6). We will consider this aspect of the narrative later in the chapter.

Transmission of the Exodus Account

Various aspects of the exodus narrative have come down to us in individual remembrances recorded in the Old Testament as part of the completed canon. Thus details may be gleaned from passages such as Exodus 15:1–18, 21; Deuteronomy 33:2; Judges 5:4-5; Psalms 18:7–15 (cf. 2 Sam. 22:8–16); 68:5–7; 77:16–20; 144:5–6; and Habakkuk 3:3–15. The antiquity of these texts is attested in that all of them are told in early Hebrew poetry. In these texts special attention is called to God's provision of victory for Israel over the Egyptians at the Re(e)d Sea and the successful crossing of the Jordan River (e.g., Exod. 15:1–18, 21; Ps. 77:16–20; Hab. 3:3–15).

God instructed the people that specific details of the story of the exodus out of Egypt were to be remembered and passed on to subsequent generations (cf. Exod. 13:1–13). Later writers also often commented on God's deliverance of his people in the exodus, sometimes as mere historical fact (e.g., Num. 1:1; Josh. 24:5–13) and at other times as a witness of the people's ingratitude and infidelity (e.g., Num. 21:5; Hos. 11:2–3; Mic. 6:1–5), for which God's judgment must surely come (e.g., Amos 2:6–16). On some occasions, the Lord called attention to the exodus while delivering specific stipulations of the Law to his people (e.g., Lev. 23:43; 25:54–55). The remembrance of the exodus also served as a source for spiritual instruction in various matters (e.g., Deut. 6:20–25) as well as in challenges to live righteously before the Lord (e.g., Deut. 6:2–12; 1 Sam. 12:6–8).

God's faithful believers often remembered the Lord's provision in the exodus in their praises (e.g., Pss. 66:3–6; 114; 135:8–9) and prayers to God (2 Sam. 7:23; Isa. 63:7–15; Hab. 3:2). Unfortunately, the exodus was also transmitted in warnings to the people of impending judgment for their failure to remember God's past deliverances and goodness to them (e.g., Jer. 2:5–9; 7:21–29; 11:14–17). Nevertheless, God assured his people that after the threatened judgment that would come in the form of expulsion from the Promised Land by way of captivity, with humble repentance and surrender to God there would come restoration to God's favor and a return to the land (e.g., Isa. 61:1–4; Jer. 16:14–15; Ezek. 20:32–38). Thus the exodus motif becomes a message of comfort to God's people and hope (e.g., Isa. 40:1).

Culmination of the Exodus in the New Covenant

Like the law, the exodus finds its climax in the new covenant (cf. Jer. 31:31–37). Although there were exoduses in historic Old Testament times (Ezra 1:1–2:70; 8:31–36), the thrust of the exodus as wedded to the new covenant involves a greater future exodus of God's people from the entire world. The temporal setting points toward the end times. It will indeed be an even greater exodus than that original one (Jer. 23:7–8) and involve the release of God's people from all lands (Isa. 43:5–7). God himself will go before them and provide for them (Isa. 43:16–21; 52:12). His ransomed people will return with singing (Isa. 35:10) to enjoy everlasting gladness in full fellowship with the Lord in the ancient land of promise (Isa. 65:17–25). As a restored, faithful, and blessed people they will be an avenue of salvation for all people (Isa. 49:6). Thus the exodus motif finds its full significance in being wedded to the new covenant.

Applicability of the Exodus

The initial exodus event bore witness to God's redemptive power. During the exodus, God, Israel's Redeemer, brought his people to himself. As wedded to the new covenant, the exodus prepares the readers of Scripture for the New Testament message of redemption by which all people may experience an exodus from the realm of sin and darkness in order to enter the realm of light and God's saving grace (Col. 1:12–14).

The exodus message of hope finds its fulfillment in the inauguration of the new covenant mediated by Jesus Christ (Matt. 26:27–29; 2 Cor. 3:6; Hebrews 8) and its ultimate reality in the end times as reflected in the imagery and symbolism of the Apocalypse (e.g., Rev. 14:1–5).

GUIDELINES FOR UNDERSTANDING THE EXODUS

1. Examine the story of Israel's deliverance from Egypt in the light of the full narrative of the exodus event.
2. Note the transmission of the exodus and its culmination in the new covenant.
3. Note the importance of the exodus in the teachings inherent in the law and the covenant structure of the Old Testament.
4. Take notice of the underlying theological principle of redemption in the exodus and its importance to the new covenant.
5. Note the importance of the exodus event as wedded to the new covenant as a preparation for the New Testament revelation.
6. Apply the principles inherent in the exodus to the Christian message and the missionary responsibility for all believers.

COVENANT

The concept of "covenant" is an old one in the ancient Near East stretching back nearly five millennia. It is inextricably bound to the needs of treaty-making and law.

Covenant Types

The information gained from historical inquiry enables us to isolate two basic types of treaties that have important ramifications for their interpretation in the covenantal conventions of the Old Testament. The first of the two prevalent types of covenants is known as the Suzerain Treaty. In it, the enacting party imposes covenant stipulations upon the vassal state. Several elements are standard in this form: (1) a title/preamble naming the parties involved; (2) a historical prologue tracing past relations between the covenanting parties; (3) the basic stipulations to be kept by the vassal; (4) a statement concerning the deposition of the covenant in an appropriate place as well as the periodic reading of the covenant; (5) a list of the witnesses who attend the making of the treaty/covenant; and (6) the sanctions to be imposed by the superior party, including revocation of the covenant, should the vassal fail to keep its terms. This type of treaty/covenant also contained a list of blessings and curses attendant to its ratification and maintenance by the vassal.

The suzerainty-type treaty is found in the Old Testament in connection with the Sinaitic (or Mosaic) covenant and its renewal in Deuteronomy and in Joshua 24. Many scholars have pointed out that the most fully developed example of a suzerainty-type treaty may be seen in the Book of Deuteronomy. Here most of the covenant elements are clearly present: (1) preamble (1:1–5); (2) historical prologue (1:6–3:29); (3) basic (4:1–11:32) and specific stipulations (12:1–26:19); (4) covenant sanctions in the forms of blessings and curses (chap. 28); (5) instructions concerning the reading and deposition of the covenant (31:9–13, 24–26; cf. 32:44–47); and (6) statements as to the witnesses to the covenant (31:19–22; 32:1–43).

It is crucial for the interpreter of suzerainty-type covenants to understand that all such covenants depict God as the sovereign regulator of the covenant. The covenant was also conditional, its continuity as well as the blessings and curses embedded in it being contingent upon the people's response and obedience to the terms of the covenant. It is important, too, to see that the sovereign God who affixed the covenant was not an overbearing despot but a gracious Lord who was providing a means for blessing his people. Their keeping of the terms of the covenant was not only for God's glory and as a testimony to his redemptive grace, but was intended for their good (Exod. 19:4–6; cf. Deut. 5:23–33).

A full understanding of the nature and provisions of the suzerainty treaty/covenant will enable you to grasp the difference between this type of covenant and the other major type that God made with his people: the royal grant type. Recent research concerning covenant and treaty forms in the ancient Near East has discerned two types of royal grants. In the first type, a beneficent king would often freely bestow certain privileges or benefits to a vassal or servant for faithful and loyal service. In the second, which could be termed a reconfirmation grant/treaty/covenant made by the king or his successor(s), continued compliance with the terms of the original grant was obligatory for the grant to remain in effect in order to be beneficial for the grantee and/or his heirs. As we will see, some effect of the difference between these two types of royal grants may be seen in the Old Testament covenants.

A royal grant covenant traditionally contained the following elements: (1) a preamble noting the parties involved; (2) a statement of the covenant's provisions or promises; (3) certain stipulations for the full enjoyment of the benefits of the covenant; and (4) a record of covenant enactment and/or oaths taken while putting the covenant into force. A covenant sign could also accompany the making of the covenant. Several royal grant types are found within the pages of the Old Testament (e.g., Gen. 9:1–17; 15:1–21; 17:1–16; 2 Sam. 7:8–16).

It is crucial for the interpreter to grasp the basic distinction between the suzerainty (conditional) and royal grant (unconditional) types of covenants. For only then will he or she come to realize the exceedingly great provisions and promises God has granted to his own. One other formal distinction between these two types of covenants is found in the formulae used in relation to them. Thus in the suzerainty type, the customary formula is "cut a covenant" (e.g., Deut. 5:3), while in the royal grant type verbs such as "set/establish/confirm/make" a covenant are typically found (e.g., Gen. 9:12, 17; 17:2).

Doubtless the grandest of all of the royal grant types is the new covenant (Jer. 31:31–37). Here we also see the typical elements inherent in such covenants: (1) the parties involved (v. 31); (2) covenant provisions (vv. 32–34); (3) covenant enactment (v. 33); and (4) a sign of the covenant (vv. 35–37). The terms or provisions of the new covenant are repeated in Jeremiah 32:36–44, where Jeremiah earlier was instructed to enact a sign of the validity of God's good intensions toward his people by purchasing his cousin's field on the eve of Jerusalem's captivity (Jer. 32:6–15).

As we have seen, the culmination of the law and exodus also takes place in the new covenant. We will now examine how both suzerainty and royal grant covenant types are brought together in the provisions of the new covenant.

Key Chain of Covenants Culminating in the New Covenant

Although both suzerainty and royal grant covenants held distinctive purposes for Israel, it is the latter that particularly directs our attention to the central emphasis of the completed Old Testament canon. For the royal grant covenants contain the Lord's unconditional, gracious promises for believers of all ages. For example, the Lord promised aged Abram a son and heir who would grow into a great number of descendants (Gen. 15:1–5; cf. Gen 12:1–3), and in response, "Abram believed the LORD, and he credited it to him as righteousness" (Gen. 15:6). This promise was subsequently reinforced by a theophany, which served as a sign guaranteeing the fulfillment of God's word (Gen. 15:17–21).

In the details of the covenant in Genesis 17, however, elements of conditionality may be seen, for it is stipulated that Abraham must continue in faithfulness to Yahweh and his heirs must do so also (vv. 2, 9). The promises in the original details of the Abrahamic covenant were not made by an earthly ruler, but by God whose word and faithfulness are certain (Ps. 100:5; 119:89–90). Indeed, the Lord assures Abraham that the covenant he is making with him is an "everlasting covenant between me and you and your descendants after you for the generations to come, to be your God and the God of your descendants after you." (Gen. 17:7).

It is imperative, therefore, for the interpreter to see both the perpetuity and inviolability of the Abrahamic covenant. For its remembrance continued down into New Testament times, where applications of its further benefits were made by Jesus (Matt. 22:32); the virgin Mary (Luke 1:55); John the Baptist's father Zechariah (Luke 1:72–75); Stephen (Acts 7:30–32); and Paul (Gal. 3:29).

Although the Abrahamic covenant was to remain in effect in perpetuity, it was channeled through a specific heir—King David (2 Sam. 7:11–16; 1 Chron. 17:10–14). Through the prophet Nathan God gave words of assurance reminiscent of the Abrahamic covenant that he would establish David's line and kingdom as an everlasting reality (2 Sam. 7:16). In so doing, the Lord declared that David's heir would enjoy a filial relationship with God.

That David understood that his covenant with God would extend into the future is certain in his reaction to God's promise: "You have spoken concerning the future of the house of your servant" (2 Sam. 7:19; cf. vv. 27–29). David goes on to remark, "And this is a revelation [or instruction/

law] for mankind, LORD God" (v. 19b; HCSB). Later he would declare: "Is not my house right with God? Has he not made with me an everlasting covenant, arranged and secured in every part?" (2 Sam. 23:5). Such would also be confirmed by the author of Psalm 89 (vv. 28–29, 35–37). It is also instructive to note that, like the Abrahamic covenant, David's heirs could forfeit the benefits of the Davidic covenant, yet the covenant itself would remain in force (Ps. 89:30–34). Many of David's royal heirs would fail, as would the nation they ruled, but ultimately the divine promise will prevail.

The ancient Abrahamic covenant, now channeled through the line of David, Judah's heir, was yet to be wedded to another all-embracing covenant. The themes of the law and the exodus event find their culmination in the new covenant (Jer. 31:31–37). These themes were also linked to the theme of covenant earlier (e.g., Exod. 19:3–6; Deut. 6:1–22). It is significant to note that Israel's deliverance out of Egypt and the subsequent giving of the Mosaic covenant/law are implicitly linked with the Abrahamic covenant in the term "house of Jacob" (Exod. 19:3). Therefore, it comes as no surprise to see that all of the above themes that we have studied come together under one grand new covenant.

The new covenant, however, is not limited to Jeremiah 31:31–37. It is found also in Jeremiah 32:36–44 and Jeremiah 33:14–26, where the Lord's promises in the new covenant include the terms and provisions of the Davidic covenant. Ezekiel likewise prophesies regarding a new exodus for God's people (Ezek. 34:11–14) and regarding the role of David's heir (vv. 22–24), as well as the establishing of a new covenant with Israel (vv. 25–30) God promises that in connection with the new covenant he will give Israel "a new heart and put a new spirit in you" (Ezek. 36:26) in order that they will be able to keep his laws (vv. 27–29; cf. Jer. 31:33–34). All of this comes together most clearly in Ezekiel 37. In this passage, Ezekiel prophesies that in the days of the new covenant there will be a new exodus (v. 21) and return to the land (vv. 22–23) in fulfillment of the promises in the Abrahamic covenant (v. 25). Moreover, as in the Davidic covenant, David's heir will rule over God's people (vv. 24–25) and "they will follow my laws and be careful to keep my decrees" (v. 24). Then they will enjoy everlasting gladness of life and worship in God's presence forever (vv. 26–27).

Clearly, then, just as the law and the exodus event find their culmination in the new covenant, so also does the covenant concept. Not only does the Abrahamic covenant remain in effect with its provisions for blessings for all of God's people, but the principles of the Sinai covenant will be lived out from the heart of redeemed new covenant believers (Ezek. 37:21–23). In accordance with the provisions of the Davidic covenant, God's people will once again live in the land, as was promised in the Abrahamic covenant, where the king who is David's heir now rules (v. 25). The new covenant is also called a "covenant of peace" (Isa. 54:10; Ezek. 34:25). In accordance with its name it will be a time of great universal peace (cf. Isa. 2:2–4; Ezek. 37:26) and security (Ezek. 34:27), and God's people will live in fellowship with God (Jer. 31:34; Ezek. 37:23) and enjoy his blessings (Isa. 61:8–9) forever (Ezek. 27:26). Here we see the outworking of God's plan for humanity as expressed in the Abrahamic covenant (Gen. 12:3).

Truly, the new covenant is the capstone of all the previous covenants, as well as the culmination of the provisions in the law and the principle of redemption resident in the exodus event. Yet even here, as we will see below, there are further features to examine, which will make the new covenant the stepping stone to the New Testament revelation.

3.2. MAJOR BIBLICAL COVENANTS

COVENANT	FUNCTION	TYPE	CONTENT
Noahic	Universal	Royal grant	No more universal flood
Abrahamic	Foundational	Royal grant	Land, seed, blessing
Mosaic	Conditional	Suzerainty treaty	Blessings and curses
Davidic	Royal, messianic	Royal grant	Built on Abrahamic covenant
New	Culmination	Royal grant	Predicted by prophets

Applicability of the Covenants

What significance do covenants have for today's believers? The theological principles that undergird the law as found in the conditional Mosaic (or Sinai) covenant still have validity today. This is because they have been transmitted by way of the new covenant into the teachings of the New Testament. Moreover, Jesus declared that he came to fulfill the law (Matt. 5:17). By this he meant that in himself the law and Mosaic covenant find their full meaning. Its principles therefore become realized because today's believers have been taken into union with Christ, enabling them by the power of the indwelling Christ to live in accordance with God's timeless standards (cf. John 17:22–23; Gal. 2:20; Col. 1:27).

As for the royal grant type of unconditional covenants, all people enjoy the provisions of the Noahic covenant in that they may be assured that God will not allow a worldwide flood to again cover the earth. The Abrahamic covenant remains in effect and has been incorporated into the new covenant; the same is true for the Davidic covenant. Thus both the Abrahamic and Davidic covenants find their development and culmination in the new covenant due to God's plan, which was progressively revealed across the centuries.

It is the new covenant, therefore, that brings together the essential provisions of the earlier covenants by incorporating their major planks into its finished construction. The new covenant is already in effect because of the finished work of Jesus Christ (Matt. 26:27–29; 2 Cor. 3:6; Hebrews 8). This does not mean, however, that all of the terms of the new covenant are completely fulfilled. Rather, some of its provisions, such as the rule of David's heir over a restored Israel, remain unfulfilled. Therefore, we may think of the new covenant as fulfilled in the New Testament revelation in the sense of being made fuller even though all of its provisions have not been totally met or brought to completion.

In every way, therefore, the message of the covenants is applicable to Christian living. For it reminds us of the need for faithful and obedient service (cf. Gen. 22:15–18) and the necessity of living holy and righteous lives (Gen. 17:1; Lev. 19:1; Deut. 5:6–21; 6:1–3) before the Lord with all our heart (1 Kings 2:1–4). As embedded in the new covenant, the promises, provisions, and theological truths inherent in the covenants find their richest relevance in Christ's provisions for the believer (Gal. 2:20). The blessings that the believer now enjoys, as well as those to which he looks forward in the culmination of the eschatological era, should also serve as a missionary imperative for sharing the gospel with a needy and lost world (2 Cor. 5:16–20).

GUIDELINES FOR UNDERSTANDING THE OLD TESTAMENT COVENANTS

1. Determine whether the covenant under consideration is conditional or unconditional.
2. Note the primary provisions within the covenant.
3. Take particular notice of the progressive revelation attached to the unconditional covenants, especially those with Abraham and David as incorporated in the new covenant.
4. Consider the role of the new covenant as preparation for the New Testament.
5. Make proper application of the theological principles in the covenants to today's Christian living.

COORDINATING OLD TESTAMENT THEMES

Rule of God and the Concept of Messiah

In drawing this chapter to a close, we return to an observation made in the introduction to this chapter. Although we have featured three primary themes that serve as important focal points for understanding the Old Testament revelation, it must not be forgotten that the most important figure and force in the Old Testament is God. As the Creator and Ruler of nature, as Job recognized long ago (Job 38–41; cf. Ps. 104:1–30), he is also the Ruler of mankind's history and the one who brings it to its final consummation (Isa. 46:10).

A corollary to this truth is the theme of God's plan through his Anointed, the coming Messiah. Although the presence of messianic themes has been the subject of great debate, it seems safe to conclude with Jewish tradition that there was an expanding message concerning a Messiah during Old Testament times. Certainly Daniel's reference to the Messiah, the Ruler (Dan. 9:25), establishes the reality of the messianic concept toward the end of the Old Testament.

If, then, the messianic ideal is part of God's plan for the outworking of earth's history, one would expect a gradual unfolding of that plan to be revealed. Although the term "Messiah" is not always present, such a concept may be found in the early days of man's and Israel's history (see Gen. 3:15; Num. 24:22; Deut. 17:15).

The role of a coming king/Messiah became a prominent theme in the first millennium B.C. It is found in many of the Psalms (e.g., Pss. 2:2, 4–7; 89:20–37; 110:1–2) and especially in the prophets (e.g., Isa. 7:13–17; 9:6–7; 11:1–9; 41:8–20; 42:1–7; 52:13–53:12; 61:1–3; Jer. 23:5–7; 33:15–18; Ezek. 34:20–31; 37:20–28; Dan. 7:13–14; 9:25–26; Zech. 12:10–14). Giving God his rightful place in the Scriptures is basic to proper interpretation. Seeing his plan to sum up all things in his sent one, the Messiah, is not only vital to understanding the Old Testament but also for viewing the Old Testament as preparation for the New Testament revelation.

Relation of God and of the Messiah to the Law, the Exodus, and the Covenants

The presence of the Lord permeates the Old Testament. It is he who is also the sovereign Ruler and providential Overseer of the themes we have examined earlier in the chapter. Thus the Lord is the author of the law, which he designed not only for the orderly regulating of society but for humankind's individual good (Exod. 19:5; 20:22–23:19; Num. 27:1–30:16; Deut. 5:32–6:2; 6:3–30:10).

Israel's exodus from Egypt demonstrated that God alone could accomplish its deliverance. A helpless Israel needed a redeemer. Its deliverance on the night of Passover was therefore evidence of the power and sovereign grace of God. As Israel's Redeemer, God delivered his people out of Egypt (e.g., Exod. 19:4; 20:2); led them on their journey from Egypt to Canaan (Exod. 40:36–38; Num. 10:11; 33:50; Josh. 1:1–3:17); and settled them in the Promised Land (Josh. 21:43–45). Not only was God Israel's national liberator but the Redeemer of each believing Israelite (cf. Job 19:23–27; Jer. 31:31–34) as well.

As we have seen, the theological principle underlying the exodus event was that of redemption. We have stressed repeatedly the central significance of the new covenant as the culmination of the law and exodus event. It was God who authored and entered into covenants with his people, whether in terms of a conditional covenant (Exod. 19:3; Deut. 6:13–25) or as a freely given unconditional grant in perpetuity (e.g., Gen. 9:12–17; 17:1–8; 2 Sam. 7:11–16; Ps. 89:27–19:23–27; Jeremiah 29, 35–37; Isa. 54:10; Jer. 31:31–37; 33:13–22; Ezek. 34:23–31; 37:20–27). The plan of God to rule through the Messiah is also a significant feature of the new covenant. In fact, the themes of law, exodus, and covenant all come to their climax in the new covenant. We have also noted that the promised Messiah plays the key role in the realization of the new covenant. Therefore, it may be expected that he bears some relation to those themes that find their culmination in it.

The same is true of God's covenants with Israel. Here again the importance of God's redeeming work is felt, for under the terms of the new covenant the Lord will again redeem his people from slavery in foreign lands (cf. Isa. 61:3, 11-12). The role of the Messiah is particularly significant here. He who was destined to be Israel's restorer (Isa. 49:5) would become its Redeemer (Isa. 61:1–3). In accordance with the terms of the new covenant, therefore, the Messiah would be a royal Redeemer. He will restore and comfort his people, defeat all his foes (Zech. 14:1–5) and establish his universal kingdom (Dan. 7:13–14; cf. Ps. 2:7–9; 110:1–2).

Relation of Old Testament Messianism to the New Testament

The climax of God's plan for the consummation of earth's history as contained in the new covenant, whose central figure is the Messiah, provides the grand perspective for viewing the New Testament revelation. It is the person and work of Messiah in terms of the new covenant which serves to prepare New Testament readers for the person and work of Jesus Christ.

In the New Testament, Jesus Christ is declared to be the long-expected Messiah. This is seen from the very outset. Thus the angel announced to the virgin Mary that Jesus "will reign over the house of Jacob forever; his kingdom will never end" (Luke 1:33). John the Baptist's father Zechariah declared that God "has raised up a horn of salvation for us in the house of his servant David . . . to show mercy to our fathers and to remember his holy covenant, the oath he swore to our father Abraham" (Luke 1:69–73).

The subsequent New Testament revelation reinforces that understanding repeatedly (e.g., John 1:41; Rev. 11:15). Christ, mankind's Redeemer, is indeed the central figure of the New Testament revelation in fulfillment of God's plan for the redemption of humankind through his atoning death and resurrection, as well as for the consummation of all things (Col. 1:15–20; (Heb. 1:1–3).

As those who have enjoyed an "exodus" from their old life of slavery to sin and entered into a new relation under terms of the new covenant, today's believers have a double assurance: because the principles of God's law are written within them (Jer. 31:33–34), and because Christ in whom the law finds its fulfillment has taken them into union with himself, they have the ability to live in accordance with the principles of God's high moral standards. What is more, as those united with Christ (Gal. 2:20) they have the privilege of being his ambassadors to people who are yet in bondage to sin (2 Cor. 5:17–21). Like Jesus's disciples whom he commissioned and sent out to carry on the message of redemption (John 20:21–22), we are to "go and make disciples of all nations" (Matt. 28:19).

GUIDELINES FOR UNDERSTANDING THE RELEVANCE OF MESSIANISM

1. Determine which passages contain a messianic relevance. Look for relevant terminology or the presence of thematic connections with biblical references to the Messiah.

2. Evaluate the passage's contribution to God's plan in accordance with the coming of Messiah under the terms of the new covenant.

3. Note the distinctive forms of the Messiah's ministry and compare them to the earthly ministry of Jesus.

4. Avoid the temptation to be overzealous with finding the preincarnate presence of Christ in the Old Testament, such as in every place the term "the angel of the Lord" occurs.

KEY WORDS

Covenant, Exodus, Law, Messiah, New covenant, Old Testament canon, Royal grant treaty, Suzerainty treaty.

ASSIGNMENTS

1. Discuss the importance of the new covenant to the basic Old Testament themes of law, exodus, and covenant. How is this applicable to normal Christian living?

2. Identify key passages in each of the three sections of the Old Testament—Torah, Prophets, and Writings—concerning the coming Messiah.

KEY RESOURCES

Kitchen, Kenneth A. *On the Reliability of the Old Testament*. Grand Rapids: Eerdmans, 2003.

Wegner, Paul D. Pp. 101–18 in *The Journey from Texts to Translations*. Grand Rapids: Baker, 1999.

CHAPTER 4 OBJECTIVES

1. To provide an assessment of the contribution of the Gospels, the Acts, the Epistles, and the Apocalypse to the New Testament canon.

2. To provide a synthesis of the theology of the New Testament, focusing on the fulfillment of biblical prophecy in Christ.

3. To provide a framework for the interpretation of individual New Testament passages by giving a sense of whole in which light to interpret any of the parts.

4. To instill confidence that there is underlying theological unity amidst the diversity of the biblical writers' witness.

CHAPTER 4 OUTLINE

A. Introduction

B. New Testament Canon

C. Gospels and the Gospel

D. Acts and the Early Church

E. Epistles, Christ, and the Churches

F. Apocalypse and the Revelation of the Word

G. Guidelines for Interpreting the New Testament

H. Key Words

I. Assignments

J. Key Resources

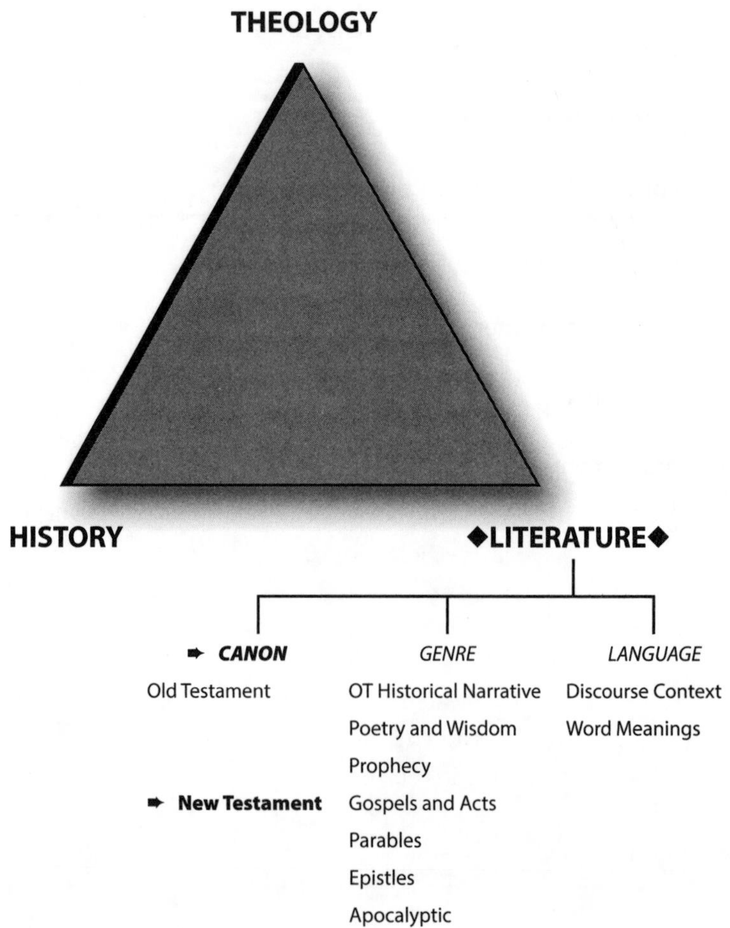
THEOLOGY
HISTORY
◆LITERATURE◆
➡ CANON
GENRE
LANGUAGE
Old Testament
OT Historical Narrative
Discourse Context
Poetry and Wisdom
Word Meanings
Prophecy
➡ New Testament
Gospels and Acts
Parables
Epistles
Apocalyptic

Chapter 4

NEW TESTAMENT CANON: GOSPELS, ACTS, EPISTLES, AND APOCALYPSE

INTRODUCTION

He said to them, 'How foolish you are, and how slow to believe all that the prophets have spoken! Did not the Messiah have to suffer these things and then enter his glory?' And beginning with Moses and all the Prophets, he explained to them what was said in all the Scriptures concerning himself. . . . They asked each other, 'Were not our hearts burning within us while he talked with us on the road and opened the Scriptures to us'?" Soon thereafter, "He said to them, 'This is what I told you while I was still with you. Everything must be fulfilled that is written about me in the Law of Moses, the Prophets and the Psalms.' Then he opened their minds so they could understand the Scriptures. He told them:

> This is what is written: The Messiah will suffer and rise from the dead on the third day, and repentance for the forgiveness of sins will be preached in his name to all nations, beginning at Jerusalem. You are witnesses of these things. I am going to send you what my Father has promised; but stay in the city until you have been clothed with power from on high (Luke 24:25–27, 32, 44–49; cf. Acts 1:4–8).

These passages from Luke provide us with the theology of the Bible in a nutshell: the Messiah spoken of in all the Scriptures as one who would suffer and rise on the third day, prophecies fulfilled in Jesus Christ, who in turn sent the Holy Spirit from the Father so that his followers could serve as witnesses from Jewish to Gentile territories, to the ends of the earth. Here is the heart of the theology of the Old Testament—the message about the Christ—and here is the heart of New Testament theology: the fulfillment of the Old Testament message about the Christ in Jesus of Nazareth, the Son of God.

The various parts of the Christian canon all cohere and contribute to this overall purpose of showing the fulfillment of the Old Testament hope and message in Christ: the Gospels narrate the life of Jesus of Nazareth, focused on his death and resurrection; the Book of Acts continues this narration by showing what Jesus continued to do in and through the mission of the early church (Acts 1:1); the Epistles flesh out the fulfillment of Christ's vision, "On this rock I will build my church" (Matt. 16:18); and the Apocalypse brings the canon to a glorious climax by focusing all eyes on the triumphant return of the Lamb of God—turned Lion of Judah—who judges the world and gathers believers to be with him in heaven forever.

NEW TESTAMENT CANON

The New Testament first features the Gospels, four documents presenting the one gospel according to four witnesses, Matthew, Mark, Luke, and John. The order should not necessarily be taken as an indication of the chronological order of writing, however. More likely, Matthew's Gospel was chosen to be first because it starts out with the genealogy of Jesus Christ and thus provides a fitting transition from the end point of the Old Testament and a proper entry point into the story of the New Testament, which is essentially the story of the Lord Jesus Christ.

John may have been placed last among the four Gospels in light of the fact that his Gospel was almost certainly the last Gospel to be written. As such, it is interposed between the two writings by Luke included in the New Testament, the Gospel of Luke and the Book of Acts. Cumulatively, the four Gospels—or the gospel according to these four witnesses—contribute to the New Testament canon its very foundation, the narrative of the birth, life, ministry, death, and resurrection of Jesus Christ. The early church's teaching, in turn, is inextricably rooted in the teaching and life of Jesus.

The book of Acts, then, presents the continuing mission of Jesus in and through the church in the power of the Holy Spirit (Acts 1:1; cf. John 14–16). The narration of the spread of Christianity in the book of Acts, in turn, encapsulates and provides the framework for the Epistles that follow. Peter, Paul, John, and James, all authors of New Testament letters, are featured in Acts, which provides the ministry setting for the later New Testament writings. Paul's ministry dominates the latter half of Acts, and it is letters to these very congregations Paul established that form the backbone of the Pauline corpus. This includes Paul's letters to the Galatians, Thessalonians, Corinthians, and Ephesians, as well as his letters to Timothy and Titus. It also includes the epistles written by James, Peter, and John.

This focus on the apostles as Jesus's appointed representatives proved decisive in the church's recognition of the New Testament canon. Matthew and John were accepted on account of their apostolic authorship, Mark and Luke-Acts on account of the authors' connection to leading apostles (Peter and Paul). Paul's letters were accepted on the basis of his apostolic office (as well as Hebrews). The Petrine and Johannine epistles, too, were recognized as apostolic, and the letters of James and Jude were penned by Jesus's half-brothers. Apostolicity, and, by extension, the "rule of faith" (i.e. the apostles' teaching), was the primary criterion by which the church recognized the divine inspiration and authority of the books that came to make up the New Testament.

This is true also for the last book of the New Testament, the Apocalypse, which purports to be from John "the seer," whom the early church took to be none other than John the apostle (the Gospel) and John "the elder" (the Epistles). Just as the Gospels in general, and Matthew in particular, provide a fitting entry point into the story of Jesus, so Revelation constitutes a fitting conclusion, depicting Jesus's glorious "Second Coming." Jesus's return, his subsequent judgment of the world, and his gathering of his covenant community to be with him forever provide proper closure to the biblical story which began with Creation and the Fall and concludes with the new creation and restoration of all things in Christ.

This summary of the coherent nature of the New Testament and the relationship of its various parts holds regardless of the specific ways in which the New Testament canon came to be officially recognized.

Traditionally, the canonical process has been conceived as a gradual process culminating in the fourth century. There is also evidence for an earlier compilation of the New Testament canonical books. In its current, final form, the canon of the New Testament with its 27 books constitutes a coherent and unified whole that serves as the proper overall frame of reference for the interpretation of individual New Testament passages.

GOSPELS AND THE GOSPEL

As mentioned, the four biblical Gospels all present the one gospel of salvation in Jesus Christ according to four major witnesses, Matthew, Mark, Luke, and John. All four Gospels root Jesus's mission in the Old Testament, which has important canonical implications. Consider the way in which the four Gospels open:

Matthew 1:1: A record of the genealogy of Jesus Christ the son of David, the son of Abraham . . .

Mark 1:1–2: The beginning of the gospel about Jesus Christ, the Son of God. It is written in Isaiah the prophet . . .

Luke 1:1–4 refers to previous accounts of the life of Jesus and relates Jesus's coming to David and Abraham (Luke 1:27, 54–55)

John 1:1–3: In the beginning was the Word, and the Word was with God, and the Word was God. . . . Through him all things were made . . .

Matthew begins with Jesus's family tree, with Abraham, David, and the exile as major junctures. Abraham and David are the major recipients of God's promises, while the exile marks Israel's failure to receive the blessings associated with these promises. Mark roots the coming of John the Baptist, Jesus's forerunner, in the prophetic message of Isaiah and Malachi. John is the God-appointed herald who prepares the way for Jesus the Messiah. Luke, like Matthew, anchors Jesus's coming in the Old Testament promises to Abraham and David; the Baptist is tied to Elijah (Luke 1:17). John reaches back all the way to creation through the pre-incarnate Word.

The same is true for the first letter in the New Testament, the book of Romans. There Paul speaks of "the gospel he [God] promised beforehand through his prophets in the Holy Scriptures regarding his Son, who as to his human nature was a descendant of David, and who through the Spirit of holiness was declared with power to be the Son of God by his resurrection from the dead: Jesus Christ our Lord" (Rom. 1:2–4). The important point Paul makes is that the gospel, rather than being a recent innovation, was promised beforehand through the prophets in the Old Testament.

The Apocalypse, too, presents Christ in keeping with Old Testament characters and imagery (e.g., Rev. 1:17–3:22).

When we read the Gospels, we are struck by the centrality of Jesus, particularly his crucifixion and resurrection. All four Gospels culminate in the Passion narrative, and concur in presenting Jesus's sacrifice as substitutionary and atoning. The Gospels thus form the perfect backdrop for Paul's statement in 1 Corinthians:

> For what I received I passed on to you as of first importance: that Christ died for our sins according to the Scriptures, that he was buried, that he was raised on the third day according to the Scriptures" (1 Cor. 15:3–4).

Not what the church believed about Jesus, but the person of Jesus himself is the towering presence in all four Gospels. Not only is Jesus called God (John 1:1, 18; 20:28; Phil. 2:6; Titus 3:4–5), both Paul and Peter apply Old Testament references to God unhesitatingly to Jesus. The author of Hebrews claims Jesus is not only the final revelation of God but also the exact representation of his being (Heb. 1:1–3).

With regard to Jesus's message, the theme that dominates is the kingdom of God (Mark 1:15; the kingdom parables). God's kingdom, in keeping with his promises to David (2 Sam. 7:14), represents a fulfillment of Old Testament promises to Israel. "Kingdom" also conveys the notion of God's reign or rule over his people, and in Jesus, God's kingdom is already present (Luke 17:21).

The Gospels provide the *complement to the Old Testament* and constitute the *foundation of the New Testament canon*. All four Gospels take their conscious point of departure from the Old Testament and from God's acts in history and promises to his chosen servants. The Gospels, in turn, constitute the quarry from which the early church, Paul, and the other New Testament authors draw their formulation of the Christian gospel (esp. Rom. 1:2–4; 1 Cor. 15:3–4). The book of Revelation shows that the kingdom of the world has now become the kingdom of God's Christ (Rev. 11:15).

ACTS AND THE EARLY CHURCH

The book of Acts not only sustains important links with the Gospel of Luke (cf. Acts 1:1), it also is founded on and continues the narration of Jesus's mission in the Gospels (cf. John 21:25 and Acts 1:1). Thus Acts registers the important claim that the life and mission of the early church is grounded in the life and mission of Jesus Christ himself. In this way, the various commissions of Jesus to his disciples recorded in the Gospels (Matt. 28:18–20; Luke 24: 46–49; John 20:21–22) result in the early church's mission (cf. esp. Luke 24:46–53 and Acts 1:1–11). This point is also integral to the structure of John's Gospel where Jesus is shown to anticipate his exalted status with God subsequent to the crucifixion and resurrection and speaks to his followers about their future mission (John 13–17).

The most important ingredients of New Testament theology contributed by the book of Acts are the following. First, the mission of the church is conducted in the power of the Holy Spirit subsequent to his coming at Pentecost (Acts 2). While the Holy Spirit is mentioned repeatedly in the Gospels, especially in the Gospel of Luke, these references are either focused exclusively on Jesus as the Spirit-anointed Messiah (e.g., Luke 4:18–19, citing Isa. 60:1–2) or anticipatory with regard to his future ministry in and through Jesus's followers (e.g., John 7:37–39; 14:16–18, 26; 15:26–27; 16:7–15; 20:22). The book of the Acts of the Apostles is in reality the book of the Acts of the Holy Spirit (cf. Acts 1:2, 5, 8, etc.).

Second, Acts also marks a new kind of relationship between believers and Jesus. Rather than fearing God (the Father) as Old Testament believers did, and rather than physically leaving their familiar surroundings and following Jesus during his earthly ministry as his first followers did, believers in the church age sustain a vital, organic relationship with God the Father and Jesus in and through the Holy Spirit (see John 14 and 15).

This scenario, in turn, involves *prayer* to the exalted Jesus in the church's pursuit of her mission (which continues to be Jesus's mission; cf. John 14:12–13; Acts 4:24–31). The fact that Jesus has not relinquished his mission but entrusted it to his followers under the direction of the "other helping presence," the Holy Spirit, means that they are to serve as his authorized and duly commissioned representatives—as his *witnesses* (Luke 24:48; Acts 1:8; John 15:26–27)—rather than exalt themselves as originators of the gospel message or set themselves off against Jesus in any way.

Third, the book of Acts is first and foremost about *mission*, about God's irresistible, inexorable pursuit of lost sinners with the gospel of forgiveness and salvation in the Lord Jesus Christ. Thus Acts marks the beginning of the fulfillment of Jesus's words that before the end would come the gospel must first be preached to all nations (Mark 13:13). In keeping with and in initial fulfillment of Jesus's words, Acts narrates the spread of the gospel from Jerusalem to Judea, Samaria, and the ends of the earth (Acts 1:8), culminating in Paul's preaching of the gospel in Rome, the empire's capital (Acts 28:30–31).

This, in turn, took place in fulfillment of the Old Testament prophetic vision (Acts 28:26–27, citing Isa. 6:9–10), according to which the gospel would spread beyond Israel to the nations (cf. Rom. 1:16). This movement is already evident in the Gospels in several ways:

1. within the Gospel of Matthew, there is a movement from Jew to Gentile (cf. Matt. 10:6, 15:24; 28:16–20);

2. from Matthew as focused on the fulfillment of Old Testament messianic predictions to Israel to the Gospels of Mark and Luke, both of which address a primarily Gentile audience;

3. the Gospel of John features Jesus's mission to the Jews, the Samaritans, and Gentiles in a nutshell in chapters 2, 3, and 4;

4. of all the Gospels, John is perhaps most keenly focused on the universal nature of the gospel and on the sole requirement of faith in Jesus as Messiah for salvation (John 3:16);

5. while the mission of Jesus in all four Gospels is limited to Israel (the exception being individual Gentiles taking the initiative in approaching Jesus), Acts shows that on the basis of Jesus's finished cross-work and resurrection, the gospel penetrates beyond its Jewish confines to the Gentile world, in fulfillment of the Abrahamic promise (Gen. 12:1–3; cf. Matt. 28:16–20); Paul makes this most explicit when he says that there is "neither Jew nor Gentile" in Christ (Gal. 3:26–28).

In light of these observations, it becomes clear that on a canonical level the mission of the early church is shown in Acts to be firmly grounded both in the Hebrew Scriptures and in Jesus's mission. Thus Acts provides a fitting continuation of the canonical story moving from God's promises to Abraham, the father of the Jewish nation, to Jesus, Abraham's offspring (Gal. 3:16), and through Jesus to all humanity, Jew and Gentile alike, through the instrumentality of Jesus's authorized and commissioned witnesses, the New Testament church.

EPISTLES, CHRIST, AND THE CHURCHES

The New Testament Epistles are living documents from the period of the early church's mission, providing a fascinating glimpse of the interaction between church-planting missionaries such as Paul and the churches he planted (or, in some cases, did not plant). In many (if not most) cases, Acts provides the canonical, historical, and logical foundation for reading the Epistles, setting forth the early days and years of the church from its inception and its missionary setbacks and successes, following a geographical pattern from Jerusalem to Rome and featuring the missionary work of Peter, Paul, and their associates.

The way in which the book of Acts serves as an essential background to our reading of the New Testament Epistles (especially those of Paul) can be illustrated by the following chart:

4.1. ACTS AS BACKGROUND OF EPISTLES

PASSAGE IN ACTS	BACKGROUND EVENT	NEW TESTAMENT LETTER
14; 16:6	Churches planted in Galatia	Galatians
15	Jerusalem Council	James
16:1–5	Paul and a disciple named Timothy	1–2 Timothy
16:11–40	Church planted in Philippi	Philippians

17:1–9	Church planted in Thessalonica	1–2 Thessalonians
18:1–17	Church planted in Corinth	1–2 Corinthians
19; 20:13–38	Church planted in Ephesus	Ephesians
28:30–31	Paul preaches the gospel in Rome	Prison Epistles

Beyond this, Acts also features the ministry of Peter and John, who wrote 1–2 Peter and 1–3 John, respectively. Aquila or another member of the Pauline circle is a possible candidate for author of the book of Hebrews, though this is uncertain.

With regard to a Pauline letter collection, there is some New Testament evidence that the Pauline corpus was formed very early, even while Paul's letters were still being written (2 Pet. 3:15–16). Not only this, they were regarded on par with the Old Testament, as were the Gospels (1 Tim. 5:18 possibly citing Luke 10:7 in conjunction with Deut. 24:5). There is also good reason to believe that Paul wrote 13 New Testament epistles: Galatians, 1–2 Thessalonians, 1–2 Corinthians, Romans, the Prison Epistles (Ephesians, Philippians, Colossians, and Philemon), and the letters to Timothy and Titus.

By Marcion's time, the Pauline corpus consisted of at least ten letters (including a letter to the Laodiceans, possibly Ephesians) and possibly 13 letters (including the letters to Timothy and Titus, whom Marcion may have rejected). This is confirmed by the papyrus manuscript $\mathfrak{P}^{46}$, which most date to around A.D. 200. The Muratorian canon, also dated to A.D. 180–200, lists 13 letters, and by the fourth century there is consensus that the Pauline corpus consists of 13 or 14 letters (depending on the authorship of Hebrews). Letters to congregations were placed before letters to individuals, and letters to the same church kept together. Perhaps Paul or a close follower such as Timothy or Luke (cf. Col. 4:14; Phlm. 24; 2 Tim. 4:11) may have had a part in collecting Paul's letters.

While Acts provides the foundation for our canonical reading of the New Testament Epistles, however, the latter go beyond a mere description of the progression of the mission of the early church. Each of the letters gives us an account of the problems and issues facing a particular church plus the New Testament writer's adjudication of these matters. This is perhaps most obvious in a letter such as 1 Corinthians, which, starting in chapter 7, deals with several matters the Corinthians apparently asked the apostle Paul to address (cf. 1 Cor. 7:1, 25; 8:1; 12:1; 15:1).

Let us remember, however, that the occasional nature of the New Testament Epistles does not necessarily imply that the New Testament authors' adjudications of the various matters addressed are likewise of a merely temporary nature. To the contrary, because of their apostolic nature, many of these adjudications should be expected to have permanent relevance, at least on a principial level (though at times cultural factors may necessitate a transposition of the principle to one appropriate in today's culture).

The New Testament Epistles also supply us with a more full-fledged theology of the implications of the work of Christ for the life of the believer, such as Paul's teaching of believers' union with Christ on an individual level and his teaching on the church as the body of Christ on a corporate level. In addition, the Epistles contain many other teachings which Paul wrestled to develop, including the nature of the resurrection body (1 Cor. 15:35–58), end-time events such as the rapture (1 Thess. 4:13–18), or the relationship between Gentiles and Israel (Romans 9–11). While at times Paul drew on Jesus's teaching, at other times Paul had to forge his own path in Spirit-led messianic application of the Hebrew Scriptures or other ways (cf. 1 Cor. 7:10, 12).

Thus, on a canonical level, the Epistles build on, and yet go beyond, the Gospels and Acts. In Acts, we read *about* Paul; in his Epistles, we hear *from* Paul directly. Conversely, in the Gospels, we hear *from* Jesus directly; in the Epistles, we hear *about* the ramifications of Jesus's work for believers. Both are necessary and complementary. In the end, the New Testament Epistles are a vital part of inspired Scripture and of authoritative divine revelation, communicated through the apostolic writers dealing with real-life issues in the various churches under their care.

While the book of Acts, as a historical narrative, tells us more overtly what *did* take place in the early church, the Epistles, as didactic material, focus more explicitly on what *should* happen in the church, both by way of direct pronouncement—e.g., "Forgive one another"—and case study or principle (e.g., exercising sensitivity toward others in the case of eating food offered to idols, 1 Corinthians 8; cf. Romans 14–15). This does not mean that every conceivable circumstance is dealt with in the Epistles.

Rather, representative instances serve as illustrations of how the Spirit led the church through God's authorized representatives in dealing with various challenges and opportunities. Within these scriptural parameters, the church today is to develop discernment and mature judgment—"the mind of Christ"—so that it may understand what the will of God is in whatever circumstances it faces.

One final observation pertains to the contribution of the Epistles to the New Testament canon. Just as the Gospels make reference to the towering figure of Jesus, and Acts records the things Jesus continued to do from his exalted position through the church in the power of the Holy Spirit (Acts 1:1), in the Epistles, likewise, Christ is at the center. Paul's letters in particular abound with references to "Christ," "Christ Jesus," or "the Lord Jesus Christ." The most basic early Christian confession was *Christos kyrios*, that is, "Christ is Lord" (e.g., Acts 2:36; Rom. 10:9; Phil. 2:11), and Paul taught that "there is but one Lord, Jesus Christ, through whom all things came and through whom we live" (1 Cor. 8:6). Paul also taught that Jesus himself is the head of his church (Eph. 1:22; 4:15; 5:23; Col. 1:18) and that he should have supremacy in everything (Col. 1:18). Thus Christ is at the very heart of the theology of the New Testament.

APOCALYPSE AND THE REVELATION OF THE WORD

The Apocalypse, the final book of the New Testament canon and of Scripture, provides the concluding bookend corresponding to Genesis in the Old Testament. The first book in the Bible tells us about creation (Genesis 1–2), the last envisions a new creation (Revelation 21–22). The first speaks of the fall of humanity (Genesis 3), the last of the curse being reversed, of sinful humanity and the devil and his minions being judged, and of a new humanity made up of the redeemed of all tribes, languages, and nations being restored (Revelation 4–5). The first book depicts the original state of humanity in an unbroken relationship with God, the last displays worship offered to God and to the Lamb, the Lord Jesus Christ.

As in the Old Testament (cf. Luke 24:25–27, 32, 44–49), and as in the other portions of the New Testament canon, so also in Revelation, Jesus is at the center—as the Lamb-turned-Lion (Revelation 4), as the Heavenly Warrior who defeats the Beast (Revelation 19), and as the End-time Judge (Revelation 20), Jesus utterly dominates the scene. The Apocalypse presents the consummation of the age and the fulfillment of God's plan for humanity and the cosmos in Christ (cf. Eph. 1:10, which portrays God's purpose as "bring[ing] all things back together under one head [*anakephalaioō*], even Christ").

In continuity with the Epistles, Revelation, too, includes seven epistles to the seven churches of Asia Minor (Revelation 2–3), including Ephesus, to which also one of Paul's letters is addressed. The concluding warning against adding to or taking away any words from the prophecy of the book extends at least to Revelation in its entirety and very likely on a canonical level to the entire canon of Scripture.

Notably, it is the same Jesus who is depicted as crucified and risen in the Gospels, who is cast as fueling and engineering the mission of the early church in the book of Acts, and who is presented as the Lord and Head of the church in the Epistles, who is also the Returning Glorious Conqueror, Supreme Ruler, and King of the Apocalypse (see esp. Rev. 19:16). Jesus is shown as defeating all the forces of darkness and as inaugurating the eternal state in which there is no more curse, no more night, no more death, mourning, crying, or pain, for the old order of things will have passed away forever (Rev. 21:4; 22:3–4).

There is also no more temple, for God himself will live among his people. "They will be his people, and God himself will be with them and be their God" (Rev. 21:3). Not only will Eden be restored, but the end will be even better than the beginning, for Jesus, the incarnate, suffering, resurrected, and triumphant Savior will be worshiped and adored by God's people for all eternity.

On a salvation-historical, as well as on a literary and theological level, the Apocalypse thus provides a satisfying conclusion to the New Testament and biblical canon. As in all of Scripture, this conclusion is Christ-centered. It also takes up and satisfactorily resolves all the various tensions of Scripture, including the believer's predicament of suffering persecution at the hands of the unrighteous and their cry for divine vindication. Theodicy, the vindication of God's righteous character and purposes, is thus at the heart of this final book of Scripture, and the Apocalypse fleshes out in eschatological terms Paul's pronouncement that "God was reconciling the world to himself in Christ" (2 Cor. 5:19).

GUIDELINES FOR INTERPRETING THE NEW TESTAMENT

1. Assign the passage you are studying to one of the following: Gospels/Acts, Epistles, or Revelation.

2. Understand the salvation-historical location of the book you are studying: in the Gospels, the earthly ministry of Jesus; in the book of Acts and the Epistles, the church age and the mission of the early church; in Revelation, the end times.

3. Be careful to observe how each of the respective portions of the New Testament complement and supplement one another and interpret them in proper relation to each other. For example, when studying Philippians, consult the account of the planting of the church of Philippi in the book of Acts.

4. Note any limitations that arise from the constraints of a given portion of the New Testament canon. For example, note how Jesus's pattern of training his disciples relates to Paul's teaching on the church as the body of Christ, made up of individual members with a unique set of spiritual gifts.

5. As relevant, carefully consider the New Testament use of the Old Testament (on which see more fully the chapter on Biblical Theology below).

6. Note not only the historical progression of New Testament teaching but also the topical interconnection between passages on similar or related topics, in keeping with the Reformation principle that Scripture is its own interpreter.

KEY WORDS

Eschatological, Eternal state, Rapture, Salvation-historical, Theodicy.

ASSIGNMENTS

1. Discuss how the book of Acts provides the basic framework for the New Testament Epistles.

2. Taking a given theme (e.g., discipleship, suffering, etc.), explain how each major block (Gospel, Epistle, Revelation) develops the theme.

KEY RESOURCES

Bartholomew, Craig G. and Michael W. Goheen. *The Drama of Scripture: Finding Our Place in the Biblical Story*. Grand Rapids: Baker, 2004.

Goldsworthy, Graeme. *According to Plan: The Unfolding Revelation of God in the Bible*. Leicester, UK: Inter-Varsity, 1991.

UNIT 2: GENRE

CHAPTER 5 OBJECTIVES

1. To discuss the nature, modes, and elements of Old Testament narrative.

2. To provide a survey of stylistic approaches within Old Testament narrative.

3. To provide a set of guides for interpreting Old Testament narrative and for determining word meanings in Scripture.

CHAPTER 5 OUTLINE

A. Nature of Biblical Narrative

B. Modes of Old Testament Historical Narrative

C. Elements of Old Testament Historical Narrative

D. Narrative Style

E. Guidelines for Interpreting Old Testament Narrative

F. Guidelines for Determining Word Meanings in Scripture

G. Key Words

H. Assignments

I. Key Resources

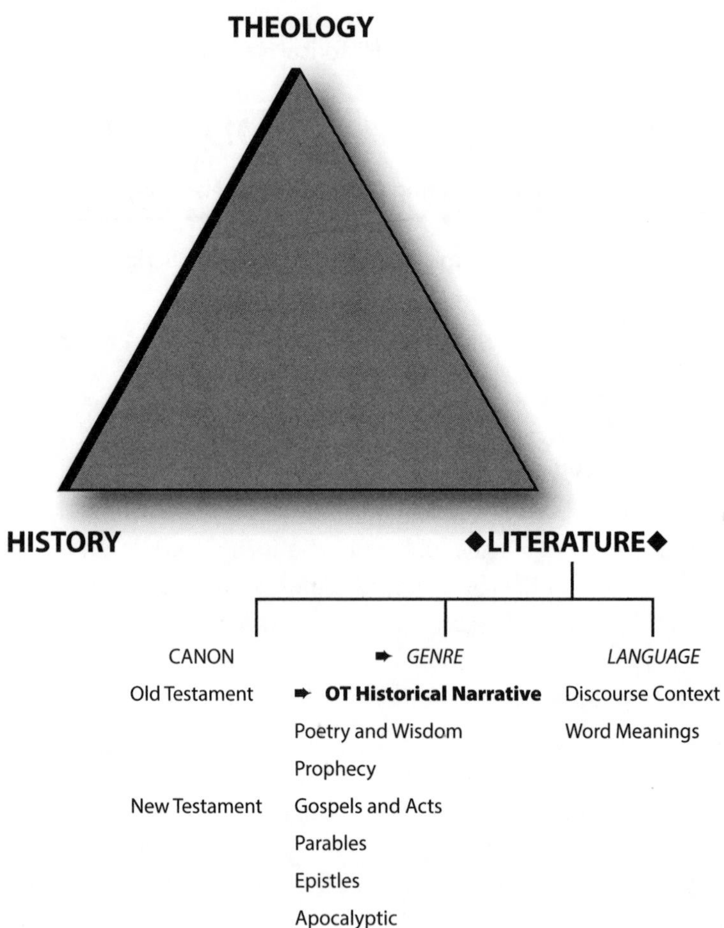
THEOLOGY
HISTORY
◆LITERATURE◆
CANON
➨ GENRE
LANGUAGE
Old Testament
➨ OT Historical Narrative
Discourse Context
Poetry and Wisdom
Word Meanings
Prophecy
New Testament
Gospels and Acts
Parables
Epistles
Apocalyptic

Chapter 5

ENJOYING A GOOD STORY: OLD TESTAMENT HISTORICAL NARRATIVE

NATURE OF BIBLICAL NARRATIVE

NOW THAT WE HAVE CULTIVATED a sensitivity to the historical dimension of the biblical landscape (in particular, the Old Testament), we are able to look around and familiarize ourselves with the various topographical features we encounter on our interpretive journey—the valleys, mountains, and plains, as it were. Applied to the interpretation of Scripture, these features (or genres) are historical narrative, poetry and wisdom, and prophecy in the Old Testament, and historical narrative, parable, epistle, and apocalyptic in the New. At the end of the chapter, we will also provide brief guidelines for determining word meanings in Scripture, since teachers may want their students to begin engaging in word studies.

But first our attention turns to the specific characteristics of each genre of Scripture. Some have compared interpreting types of literature such as narrative, epistle, or apocalyptic to playing various games such as baseball, basketball, or soccer. In each case, if you want to play the game, you must first acquaint yourself with the rules. If you don't know the rules, you'll most likely be unable to follow a game, much less play it. Similarly, when interpreting the various genres of Scripture, we must learn the "rules" that guide the interpretation of that particular biblical genre.

The present chapter explores the first such genre found in Scripture, Old Testament narrative. *Narrative* is a literary genre that builds its sentences and paragraphs around discourses, episodes, or scenes. Grasping the real nature of narrative is vital for accurate interpretation. Narrative texts can appear in three different shapes: stories, accounts, and reports. The ability to recognize the various ways a narrative can be presented is a necessary first step to its understanding.

Most often, narratives appear in dramatic form, that is, as *stories* that are presented by the biblical writer with a view toward driving home the significance of a given biblical event or series of events. In this regard, it is important to remember that these stories, in turn, typically contain historical *accounts* of speeches and dialogues that comprise the scenes or episodes which together make up the full story. Indeed, dialogues often form crucial points in a given narrative. In addition, a story may contain one or several *reports*.

MODES OF OLD TESTAMENT HISTORICAL NARRATIVE

Stories

Much of the historical information in the Old Testament is contained in narratives that are told in story form. Thus we gather details of Israel's early beginnings in the stories of the patriarchs found in the book of Genesis. We learn of events in the early days of Israel's occupation of the Promised Land through the stories about the various judges. Information concerning the establishment of the monarchy is often related in the form of tales concerning the exploits of David in the books of Samuel, while many events in the periods of the united and divided monarchies are told in the form of stories. For example, we learn of Solomon's fabled wisdom through the stories recorded in 1 Kings 3 and 10:1–13. Conditions in the Northern Kingdom surface in the stories of the prophets Elijah and Elisha (1 Kings 17–19; 2 Kings 2–8; 13:14–21).

One important fact to keep in mind when speaking of "stories" is that "story" does not imply that the historical information conveyed is fictional. Certainly the stories of the Old Testament deal with real life, real events, and real people. Thus interpreters should not dismiss the great stories of the Old Testament as of doubtful historical value. Rather, they should be aware that these stories carry the historical narrative along even while helping the reader to see the true nature of conditions in the larger context. At the same time, interpreters should learn to distinguish stories which are grounded in history from straight historical accounts and reports.

One of the major ingredients in many stories contained in the Old Testament is embedded oral discourse. For example, much of the patriarchal story of Joseph's adventures hinge upon *speeches* and *dialogues*. Joseph's reporting of his two dreams provokes his brothers to taking him captive and selling him into slavery in Egypt. Details in Joseph's early life in Egypt likewise turn on speeches and dialogues. Thus in Genesis 39 the narrator gives details of Joseph's social life as the manager of Potiphar's household (vv. 1–6). In time, he is faced with the advances of Potiphar's wife. The ensuing dialogue reveals the nature of both characters involved: her lust and Joseph's purity:

> After a while his master's wife took notice of Joseph and said, "Come in bed with me." But he refused. "With me in charge," he told her, "my master does not concern himself with anything in the house; everything he owns he has entrusted to my care. No one is greater in this house than I am. My master has withheld nothing from me except you, because you are his wife. How then could I do such a wicked thing and sin against God?" (vv. 7–9)

The story turns and moves forward on Joseph's words and the next words of Potiphar's wife. Her speech to her husband then forces Potiphar's hand—he must send Joseph to prison.

While in prison, it is Joseph's discussions with his fellow inmates, the cupbearer and the baker, in which he interprets their dreams that eventually bring him before the Pharaoh. Pharaoh has had two dreams and there is no one to interpret them. The cupbearer, now restored to Pharaoh's favor in accordance with Joseph's interpretation of his dreams, informs Pharaoh of Joseph's ability. Consequently, Joseph is brought out of prison to interpret the dreams. Here once again, the crucial points are reported in speeches (Gen. 41:9–36). Likewise, Pharaoh's putting Joseph in charge of economic affairs in Egypt is also given in direct speech (vv. 37–41). With the speeches and discourses duly reported, the narrator returns to a narrative account of subsequent events during Joseph's stay in Egypt.

Although Joseph's story could have been told in straightforward narrative, the speeches and dialogues make not only for dramatic effect but also provide deeper understanding of the character of those involved. The author has so developed the story that those speeches and dialogues provide turning points for events in the surrounding narrative. For this reason it is crucial for the interpreter to pause and focus on the oral discourses within the larger narrative. In so doing, they will not only increase their understanding of the character of the persons involved in the story but be caught up in the flow and actions of the whole context.

Another frequent ingredient in biblical stories is *description*. Here the emphasis is on the background of the narrative or on the characters involved. This includes descriptions of the various aspects of the setting of the story and other contextual indicators tying in the story with the preceding and following narrative. In addition, biblical stories often involve *commentary* provided by the biblical writer. In such cases the narrator supplies parenthetical information in order to clarify a given element of the story or comments on the significance of a character's actions or a certain event. In introducing the story of the Levite and his concubine, for example, the narrator discloses that "in those days Israel had no king" (Judg. 19:1), making mention of the unsettled state of affairs in the land. Similarly, later on in the story he observes, "In those days Israel had no king; everyone did as he saw fit" (Judg. 21:25).

It is also of interest to note that all or several of these elements—speeches or dialogue, description, and commentary—may be found in a single context. Thus after Israel's miraculous crossing of the Red Sea, we read of the following incident (Exod. 15:22–24):

Description: Then Moses led Israel from the Red Sea and they went into the Desert of Shur. For three days they traveled in the desert without finding water.

Narrative: When they came to Marah, they could not drink the water because it was bitter.

Commentary: (That is why the place is called Marah.)

Narrative: So the people grumbled against Moses, saying, "What are we to drink?"

Although not every narrative context will contain all of these story elements, it is important for the interpreter to recognize those that are there and interpret them correctly. We now turn to a consideration of accounts and reports before dealing with the external and internal elements of Old Testament historical narrative.

Accounts

Large sections of Old Testament narrative are written as historical accounts, including the Pentateuch and the so-called historical books (Joshua–Esther). Using selected facts of past events as material for building his perception of reality, the author arranges these into a coherent written history. In the case of the biblical author, he has the guidance and insight of the Holy Spirit in his choice of recorded events and oral tradition. Doubtless some of the author's material came from direct revelation.

While historical material included in Scripture provides factual information, it has several other purposes as well. First of all, it has a *theological* and *doxological* aspect (i.e., events are accomplished ultimately by God and to his praise). Second, it has a *didactic* dimension (i.e., it aims to teach proper response and conduct). And third, it has an *aesthetic* element as well (i.e., it is written in an artful manner that makes for a pleasing literary work). The result is an informative narrative of real events designed to provoke a proper response on the part of the reader. Such a response may be expected, therefore, because biblical historical narrative is more than a mere catalog of facts and record of events. It is *theological history*—designedly so. The book of Chronicles, for example, reflects a divine perspective and serves as a theological commentary on Israel's history.

Another example comes from Joshua 24 where Joshua, having gathered the leadership and citizens of Israel to Shechem, delivered his farewell address. First, he reviewed seminal events in Israel's history, including the call of Abraham, the exodus and the crossing of the Red Sea, the wilderness wanderings, and the conquest of the Promised Land (vv. 1–13). The emphasis throughout is on God's sovereign and gracious leading and on his provision for his covenant people. All that occurred in Israel's past was superintended by God and ultimately to his praise. The account is recorded in four aesthetically designed sections (vv. 2–4, 5–7, 8–10, 11–13), complete with a metaphor (the hornet) describing the stinging defeat God allowed Israel to achieve against the various people of Canaan (v. 12).

After this, Joshua moves on from information to motivation. God's dealings with Israel should cause them to respond in faithfulness to the Lord who has shown himself faithful to his people.

> Now fear the LORD and serve him with all faithfulness. Throw away the gods your forefathers worshiped beyond the River and in Egypt, and serve the LORD. But if serving the LORD seems undesirable to you, then choose for yourselves this day whom you will serve, whether the gods your forefathers served beyond the River, or the gods of the Amorites, in whose land you are living. But as for me and my household, we will serve the LORD. (vv. 14–15)

The historical narrative proceeds to record that the people responded favorably to Joshua's challenge (vv. 16–24), after which he led them in an act of covenant renewal (vv. 25–27).

The details of this historical narrative are designed not only for the purpose of recording the proper response of the people in Joshua's day but should have a similar effect on the part of the readers of Holy Scripture (2 Tim. 3:16). Just as Israel was incapable of serving the Lord in her own strength (Josh. 24:19–20), so God's people of all ages must have a genuine relationship with God that makes it possible for the Lord to live out his life through them to his glory and for their good. God alone must have first place in the believer's life (Deut. 6:4–5; Prov. 3:5–6; cf. Matt. 22:37–40).

To summarize, biblical historical narrative is more than an accurate account of past events; it is a *selective presentation of the facts designed to present a theological evaluation of that record—one that will bring about a proper spiritual and ethical response on the part of its readers.* The interpreter should therefore examine the historical accounts of the Bible with a view toward keeping all of this in balanced perspective.

Reports

Biblical narratives may also contain a report that provides information of a historical nature. Scripture contains many such instances. For example, the men who were sent to spy out the land of Canaan returned with the following report to Moses and the people:

> We went into the land to which you sent us, and it does flow with milk and honey! Here is its fruit. But the people who live there are powerful,

> and the cities are fortified and very large. We even saw descendents of Anak there. The Amalekites live in the Negev; the Hittites, Jebusites, and Amorites live in the hill country, and the Canaanites live near the sea and the Jordan. (Num. 13:27–29)

Old Testament narratives are replete with various reports (e.g., 2 Chron. 34:14–18; 1 Sam. 20:18–23, 35–42). In the prophetic genre, we find a special type of report known as a *vocation report* telling of the prophet's call and commission to the ministry. The Old Testament also contains numerous *battle reports* (e.g., Gen. 14:1–12; Josh. 10:1–15; 1 Sam. 31:1–7; 2 Sam. 1:1–10; 1 Kgs. 22:29–38; 2 Kgs. 25:1–21; etc.). There are also *census reports* (Num. 1:17–46; Num. 26:1–62; 2 Sam. 24:4–9), and other types of reports (e.g., 1 Kings 6–7; Ezra 5:6–17).

Closely related to these narrative reports are *lists or rosters*, which at times appear embedded within a historical narrative. For example, after David's last words (2 Sam. 23:1–7) and before the account of David's decision to take a census of his fighting men (2 Sam. 24:1–2), there is a roster of David's mighty men together with reports of some of their exploits (2 Sam. 23:8–36). To be noted also are the several lists of the tribes of Israel (Gen. 35:23–26; Exod. 1:1–4) and various other lists (1 Chron. 6:31–47; 23:1–32; etc.).

Significant also are *vision reports*. While these appear most prominently in the prophetic genre, they are also found in narrative literature. Customarily such visions came during the night (e.g., Gen. 46:2; 2 Sam. 7:4; Job 7:13–14; 20:8; 33:15; but see Ezek. 8:1–3). Vision reports take on special significance when they contain God's words of instruction to an individual (e.g., Gen. 15:1; 46:2; 2 Sam. 7:4) and are followed by reports of the addressees carrying out the divine command. Vision reports thus not only contain factual information and the effect that the vision had upon its recipient but report key events that move the narrative forward.

ELEMENTS OF OLD TESTAMENT HISTORICAL NARRATIVE

External Elements

Literary analysis commonly distinguishes three external elements: author, narrator, and reader. The author and reader are usually considered in the context of determining whether the real or implied author or reader is in view. The real author is the one who actually wrote the narrative or story. What we know of this person from the narrative or story is termed "the implied author." Thus we may not know the real author or all that he knows about the narrative, but we do know what he has written. From that we draw certain conclusions about the real author.

By the reader is meant the actual readers of the narrative; the "implied reader" is the one (or ones) for whom the author has composed his work. The readers may be the original audience, hence identical with the implied readers, or any who actually read the text including contemporary readers. It is crucial for the interpreter to place himself or herself as much as possible in the world of the implied reader so that he or she may make the proper transfer of application to the contemporary world.

A third distinction has to do with the one telling the story (the narrator) and the narratee—the one to whom it is told. In some literary compositions, an author will create a narrator who then tells the story. In Old Testament narratives, however, the narrator is usually the same as the implied author. The narrator may also take part in the narrative. At times, events may be told in the first person, as in the case of portions of Nehemiah. In any case, the narrator is always omniscient, even to the point of being able to inform his readers as to what the characters in the narrative are thinking. For example, in the account of Ben-hadad's challenge to King Ahab of Israel, we learn that the Aramaean king heard Ahab's proverbial reply to his challenge "while he and the kings were drinking in their tents" (1 Kgs. 20:12). The narrator also knows precisely the reasons for the fall of the Northern Kingdom (2 Kgs. 17:7–23).

The narratee may also be a part of the narrative. This phenomenon is particularly common in Old Testament prophetic literature (e.g., large parts of Obadiah and Nahum) where foreign peoples, citizens, or cities are addressed. In such cases, a distinction exists between the narratee and the implied reader. Although the narratees are those addressed, the implied readers are the people of Israel and/or Judah. In standard Old Testament narrative, however, no difference exists between the implied reader and the narratee.

This distinction is important for the student to understand. For prophetic passages do occur within historical narratives. For example, in the account of Sennacherib's siege of Jerusalem Isaiah sends a message from the Lord to King Hezekiah (the primary implied reader) but which is addressed to the king of Assyria (the narratee). Note, for example, the Lord's message through Isaiah in 2 Kings 19:22:

> Who is it that you have insulted and blasphemed?
> Against whom have you raised your voice
> and lifted your eyes in pride?
> Against the Holy One of Israel!

Doubtless Sennacherib never read these words.

In sum, in most Old Testament narrative accounts and stories the implied author and the narrator are one and the same, and the implied reader and the narratee are identical. As we have seen, however, distinctions do sometimes occur.

Internal Elements

Three internal elements provide the dynamic for the narrative: setting, plot, and characterization. The *setting* may include matters of physical location, time, or the cultural background of the narrative. *Plot* has to do with the arrangement of details in the narrative, while *characterization* considers the spiritual, moral, and psychological makeup of the characters of the narrative, as well as their role in the story.

Before the interpreter begins his examination of the narrative, he or she must determine the limits or boundaries of the narrative. An important Semitic compositional technique is particularly helpful here. An author often arranges his material in such a way that at the end of the narrative he will return to a theme, subject, or words mentioned at the beginning. This technique is known by such names as "book-ending" or *inclusio*. In addition, subunits in historical narrative accounts may be organized symmetrically as parallel sequences or in such a way that attention is called to the center of the account.

Parallel sequences (A B C, A' B' C') provide balance between the two subdivisions and stress the need for comparative examination of the details. First Kings 13:11–34 may serve as an example. The story has to do with the man of God and the old prophet, around whom the action proceeds. In part one, the old prophet (A) hears news of the man of God (v. 11); (B) speaks and has his son saddle his donkey (vv. 12–13); (C) finds the man of God and brings him back to his home (vv. 14–15); and (D) speaks God's message (vv. 20–22), which (E) is then fulfilled (vv. 23–24).

In part two the old prophet (A') hears news of the death of the man of God (v. 25); (B') speaks and has his sons saddle his donkey (vv. 26–27); (C') finds the man of God's body and brings it back home (vv. 28–30); and (D') confirms the Lord's message (vv. 31–32), which (E') serves as an example of the sin that will lead to the downfall of the dynasty of Jeroboam I (vv. 33–34).

Setting

Understanding the setting of a given narrative can be crucial to its interpretation. Interpreters should take note of several factors and ask themselves questions such as: Is the *physical location* significant to the action of the story? Surely such is the case in the account of the Battle of Taanach between the forces of the Hebrews under Deborah and Barak and those of the Canaanites led by Sisera (Judges 4–5). Sisera picked a place for battle in the wide expanse of the eastern Esdraelon Plain that would favor his iron chariots (Judg. 4:12–13). But recent rains had left the battlefield soggy and his chariots bogged down in the mire, leaving them virtually helpless (Judg. 5:19–22). At that moment, Barak swept down with his forces from his vantage point on Mount Tabor and "the LORD routed Sisera and all his chariots" (Judg. 4:15). Here the setting not only contributes to the understanding of the account but adds vividness to it.

Time may also contribute to the dynamics of the narrative. Thus Jacob, who was already apprehensive regarding his meeting with Esau, finds himself alone at night. In the pitch darkness, he has a physical encounter with one who proves to be the Angel of the Lord (Gen. 32:22–24). The night setting doubtless made the encounter more frightening for Jacob. The careful reader will not miss the drama of it all. Time of day and atmospheric conditions likewise play a role in Joshua's victory over the Gibeonites (Josh. 10:12–14).

Knowledge of the *cultural background* is especially important because of the great distance in time and differences between ancient and modern societies. Thus an understanding of culture is crucial to the proper interpretation of events in the story of Ruth, including Ruth's meeting at night with Boaz on the threshing floor (chap. 3) and such customs as conducting business at the city gate, redemption of property, and the institution of Levirate marriage (chap. 4).

Plot

By "plot" we mean the ordering of events in the story. Plot is concerned with the arrangement of details by which the story has a beginning, middle, and end. Each part of the story contributes to the fabric of the whole. The plot in biblical stories usually revolves around a *conflict* or *contest* (physical, psychological, or spiritual) and *suspense* (curiosity, dread, anticipation, or mystery). It is important for the interpreter to come to grips with these elements and to see the interrelationships between them.

The court tales of Daniel 2–7 provide excellent examples. In each chapter, there is a clear beginning or setting to the story. Trouble develops which the hero alone is able to resolve, resulting usually in reward—all of which is a testimony to God's working through his servant(s). Chapter 5 is a case in point. The story begins with Belshazzar giving a grand banquet for his nobles, during which they praise their gods while drinking from goblets taken from the temple in Jerusalem by Nebuchadnezzar II (vv. 1–4). A crisis develops when "the fingers of a human hand appeared and wrote on the plaster of the wall, near the lampstand in the royal palace" (v. 5). The phenomenon causes great panic among all who are present. Moreover, the hand has written something on the wall which none of Belshazzar's wise men can interpret (vv. 5–9). At this point, the story takes a decisive turn or what critics call "the crisis." The queen mother appears and suggests that Daniel be summoned (vv. 10–12) who then interprets the message on the wall (vv. 13–28). With the problem resolved, in an epilogue Daniel is rewarded and his interpretation of the words comes true in the fall of Babylon that very night (vv. 29–30).

Narrative plots may also take the form of *archetypal plot motifs*. By archetypal plot, we mean features or experiences that are common to humankind. It is helpful for the interpreter to be able to recognize certain of these types. Among the many that could be catalogued in the Bible, we note the following: the *quest*, in which a hero endures many obstacles and trials before achieving his desired or appointed goal (e.g., David); *tragedy*, in which matters begin well but then take a turn for the worse until the difficulties are overcome and end in success (e.g., Daniel 3, 6); and the *journey*, in which the hero faces dangers as he moves from place to place but which contribute to his personal character growth (e.g., Abraham).

Characterization

As the example in Daniel 5 demonstrates, there is a close association between plot and character in that it is often the character who generates the action that in turn makes up the plot. Yet the reader seldom receives a detailed description of a character's full nature or personality. Literary critics often describe a character as being *round*, *flat*, or simply an *agent*. A round character is more complex, less predictable, and therefore appears more real. A flat character, on the other hand, typically possesses only one trait and comes across as one-dimensional. Finally, an agent completely lacks personality and only moves along the story.

For example, in the stories concerning Elijah and Ahab in 1 Kings 18–22, both Elijah and Ahab may be described as "round," while Jezebel is "flat," and others are mere agents (e.g., Obadiah). Yet what we can know of individuals in the biblical stories is only that which the narrator directly reveals or by what that person does.

More basically, a biblical character is usually identified as to whether he or she is the *protagonist*, the main character of the story (e.g., Elijah, Ruth); the *antagonist*, the one who opposes the protagonist (e.g., Ahab); or simply a foil, one who provides a clear contrast to someone in the story (e.g., Obadiah, Jezebel). Events can also serve as literary foils in a story, such as Jacob's trickery in contrast to Esau's early impropriety (Genesis 25, 27). David's love for the Lord serves as a foil for all the kings who follow him.

The ability to recognize and utilize the above narrative elements will not only give the interpreter added insight into the intricacies of Hebrew accounts and stories but will also make his presentation of them more vivid and dramatic for his audience. Both biblical expositors and listeners or readers will thus be swept up in the dramatic effect. This can make the narrative more realistic. Biblical characters become not just long dead or idealized persons of the distant past but real persons who experienced life in a way that is instructive for all humankind.

NARRATIVE STYLE

Repetition

Biblical narratives are often filled with various types of repetition. Repetition may include plays on sounds or roots, keywords, themes, motifs, repeated dialogue, or repeated action sequences. Thus Abigail confirms that her husband Nabal is well named, for he is a fool (*nābāl*; 1 Sam. 25:25). The theme of the third day as a marker of some new spiritual emphasis is common to the Old Testament (e.g., Exod. 19:10–16). As we have seen in the previous chapter, the covenant theme and the exodus both constitute basic motifs common to both Testaments.

A characteristic of Semitic narrative is the repetition of speeches or dialogue. For example, Rehoboam repeated verbatim the advice of his younger counselors (1 Kgs. 12:8–14). Action sequences are often repeated in groups of three. Joseph's life story is centered on three dreams. The Lord called Samuel, who reported to Eli, three times before Eli realized that God was speaking to the lad (1 Sam. 3:1–9). Israel repeatedly apostatized in the sight of the Lord (Judg. 3:7, 12; 4:1; 6:1; 10:6; 13:1).

Another way in which the narrator often calls particular attention to some detail or character trait in the individual in the story is *highlighting*. Thus Joseph's purity is underscored throughout the accounts of his life, as is David's having a heart for God, and Daniel's commitment to the Lord. Ahab is consistently portrayed as a selfish, even evil, person.

Irony

Irony has to do with the reversal of what is said or expected. Old Testament narratives are filled with many such instances. For example, Job's wife tells him, "Bless God and die" (Job 2:9). She really means, "Why not curse God and get it over with?" Indeed, although the Hebrew word literally means "bless," translators uniformly render the sense of the context, rendering the word as "curse." The expression is thus taken as a euphemism said in irony. In the book of Esther, Haman is hung on the gallows he had prepared for Mordecai!

There is also dramatic irony by which the narrator imparts to the reader a given piece of information that the characters in the narrative do not know. This phenomenon is common to both Testaments. For example, throughout the historical narratives in Kings we learn that the seeming changes in the political climate among the nations were not chance happenings but were regulated by God himself. Although David is moved to take a census of Israel, we learn that which David and his followers do not know; it is Satan who actually incited him to do so (1 Chron. 21:1). In 2 Samuel 24:1, however, we also learn that "the anger of the Lord burned against Israel and he incited David against them, saying, 'Go and take a census of Israel and Judah.'" Thus the reader knows what none of the participants in the census knows: Satan, as permitted by God (cf. Job 1:12; 2:6), is the instigator behind David's decision to take a census.

Whenever the surface meaning of the text appears to be directly opposite to the context, we may suspect that the author intended the reader to understand that he is using irony.

Satire

Satire consists of an attempt to demonstrate through ridicule or rebuke the vice or folly of that which appears to be improper or ill-conceived. For example, in recounting the contest between David and Goliath, the narrator of Samuel exposes the giant's taunts as wrong-headed. What Goliath's gods and superior strength could not accomplish, a young, ill-equipped shepherd boy could do, with God's help. Not only did the mighty warrior have a great fall from sling and stone, but he was decapitated by his own sword (1 Sam. 17:41–51)!

Ahab's classic retort to the taunts of the Aramean king Ben-hadad drips with satire: "Tell him: 'one who puts on his armor should not boast like one who takes it off'" (1 Kgs. 20:11). Ahab's reply suggests that Ben-hadad ought not to boast of victory while he is putting on his armor. He may not live to take it off! Another classic case is the familiar contest between Elijah and the prophets of Baal on Mount Carmel. At the height of the contest, when Baal has failed to respond to his prophets, Elijah taunts them by saying, "Surely he is a god! Perhaps he is deep in thought, or busy, or traveling. Maybe he is sleeping and must be awakened" (1 Kgs. 18:27).

GUIDELINES FOR INTERPRETING OLD TESTAMENT HISTORICAL NARRATIVE

1. Determine the limits or boundaries of the narrative at hand, while recognizing its internal structural features.
2. Consider whether the narrative mode is direct, descriptive, dramatic, or commentary. Does the full context employ some combination of these?
3. Ask yourself whether the historical narrative functions basically as an account or report, or is it told in story form. Does more than one of these forms occur in the full context?
4. Come to grips with the respective roles of the author, reader, narrator, and narratee. Try to put yourself in the place of the narratee (or implied reader).
5. Examine the setting of the narrative. What do you learn from such features as geography, time, or culture within the narrative?
6. If the narrative is told in story form, look carefully for the flow of the story. Identify such features of the plot as its beginning, middle, denouement, resolution, and epilogue. Are there archetypal plot motifs present here? What biblical motifs and themes are resident in the full context?
7. In stories, identify the protagonist, antagonist, and what foils may be present.
8. Learn to appreciate the author's literary style, considering such features as dialogue, repetition, highlighting, irony, and satire.
9. Throughout the interpretive process employ sound exegetical procedures, noting the contributions of grammar, history, literary constraints, and theological emphases.
10. Drawing all of these data together, make a proper application to the contemporary situation. Ask how the narrative impacts the reader or hearer's spiritual life.

GUIDELINES FOR DETERMINING WORD MEANINGS IN SCRIPTURE

1. Select the word or words to be studied. This should be a word that is significant for the interpretation of a given biblical passage.

2. If possible, study a given Greek or Hebrew term or set of terms rather than the English one. This is important since, depending on the particular translation, a given Greek or Hebrew word will be rendered by several different English words and vice versa. Preferably, we want to study what a given word means in the original language. This is possible even for those who have not studied Greek or Hebrew through the use of tools such as Louw and Nida's *Greek-English Lexicon* and Köstenberger and Bouchoc's *The Book Study Concordance.*

3. Conduct a contextual study of all the relevant passages. In practical terms, one should start with passages for the target word. Lexicons and concordances can provide a quick overview of the semantic ranges for related words as well as furnish material for a more exhaustive (and sometimes exhausting) study.

4. Categorize the passages according to types of usage (i.e., word meanings). This will yield the semantic range of the word or words.

5. In light of this semantic range, return to your base passage and see how it fits within the overall semantic profile of your word and what it contributes to the overall theology or concept or theme in question.

KEY WORDS

Account, Antagonist, Archetypal plot motifs, Characterization, External elements of narratives, Highlighting, Implied author, Implied reader, Internal elements of narrative, Irony, Narrative, Plot, Protagonist, Real author, Report, Satire, Setting.

ASSIGNMENTS

1. Discuss Esther 4 first as a story and then as a historical account.
2. Discuss the use of repetition and highlighting in the following narratives:
    a. 2 Kings 1
    b. 2 Kings 2:1–18

KEY RESOURCES

Arnold, Bill T. and H. G. M. Williamson, eds. *Dictionary of the Old Testament Historical Books*. Downers Grove: InterVarsity, 2005.

Howard, David M. Jr. *An Introduction to the Old Testament Historical Books*. Chicago: Moody, 1993.

CHAPTER 6 OBJECTIVES

1. To discuss the nature and characteristics of biblical poetry.

2. To provide a survey of the chief structural patterns of biblical poetry.

3. To enable the interpreter to recognize the major stylistic devices found in biblical poetry.

4. To discuss the nature and types of wisdom literature.

5. To suggest prominent biblical texts for the study of poetry and wisdom.

CHAPTER 6 OUTLINE

A. Nature and Characteristics of Biblical Poetry

B. Poetry in the New Testament

C. Structural Devices in Biblical Poetry

D. Stylistic Devices in Biblical Poetry

E. Types of Figures of Speech in the Old Testament

F. Wisdom Literature

G. Guidelines for Interpreting Biblical Poetry

H. Guidelines for Interpreting Wisdom Literature

I. Key Words

J. Assignments

K. Key Resources

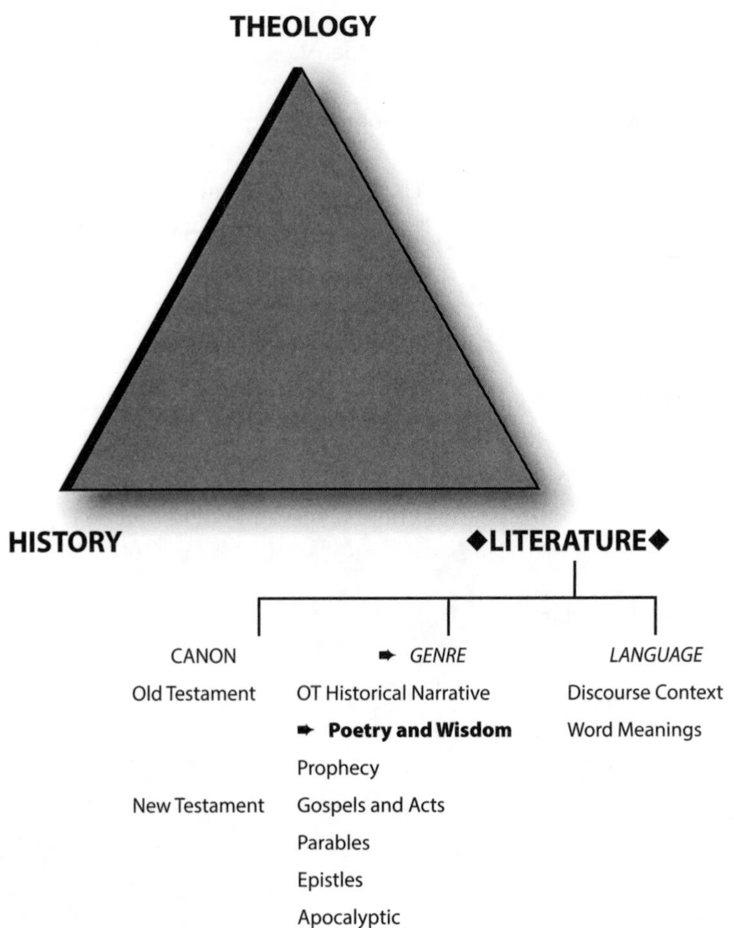
THEOLOGY
HISTORY
◆LITERATURE◆
CANON
➡ GENRE
LANGUAGE
Old Testament
OT Historical Narrative
Discourse Context
➡ Poetry and Wisdom
Word Meanings
Prophecy
New Testament
Gospels and Acts
Parables
Epistles
Apocalyptic

Chapter 6

A WORD FROM THE WISE: POETRY AND WISDOM

NATURE AND CHARACTERISTICS OF POETRY

FOLLOWING OLD TESTAMENT NARRATIVE, THE next genre we encounter on our canonical journey through Scripture is that of poetry or wisdom. Although some have cast doubt on the accuracy of labeling any biblical text as poetry, it is generally agreed that poetry does occur in the Bible. In addition to a host of positive features that distinguish poetry from prose, certain prominent features that occur frequently in prose are rarely found in poetry. Granted the broad consensus concerning the parameters of biblical poetry, we will suggest guidelines for its interpretation.

Parallelism

In contrast to prose, which constructs its sentences and paragraphs around narrative discourse, episodes, or scenes, poetry is built around individual lines, which commonly feature the heightened use of imagery and figurative speech. Although the basic unit of thought remains the individual line, the most recurring feature of Hebrew poetry is repetition. This can be seen especially in the poet's use of parallelism, the practice of using similar language of approximately the same number of words and length, and containing a corresponding thought, phrase, or idea over succeeding lines. Parallelism may occur in various patterns and be used for different purposes.

Similar Parallelism

The most common use of parallelism is to provide a closeness of thought and expression over parallel lines. Yet even here we should guard against the idea that the poet is simply saying the same thing in two different ways. Thus where similar parallelism does occur, there is often a heightening or intensifying of meaning from the first line to the second. Note, for example, Psalm 19:1:

> The heavens declare the glory of God;
> the skies proclaim the works of his hands.

In this example, the subject and verb of each line are clearly paralleled with nearly synonymous meaning, but the object in the second line moves beyond that of the first. The two lines display similar deliberately schematic features, yet there is a clear advance in the second. The combined effect of the two lines brings a new dynamic to the whole thought. Thus the heavens testify not only to the glory of God but to his creative work, here stated anthropomorphically as having been done by God's own hands.

Such instances could be greatly multiplied. Consider the following examples:

> If you have been trapped by what you said,
> ensnared by the words of your mouth. (Prov. 6:2)

> For he founded it upon the seas
> and established it upon the waters. (Ps. 24:2)

In both cases, we detect a similarity of grammatical structure and phraseology, but there is a change of imagery. In the first example, the one putting up security for the other runs the danger of being trapped by words spoken from his very own mouth. In the second, the imagery of God's creative work involving the seas is transferred to that of water in motion. Consider also the following words from Psalm 46:7:

> The LORD Almighty is with us;
> the God of Jacob is our fortress.

The careful exegete will ask himself, "What similarities and advance do I find here?" This illustrates the essence of understanding poetry. Poetry calls for the interpreter to enter into the world and thinking of the poet. In so doing, he or she reflects on the poet's experiences and mood in order to discern the poet's meaning and reasons for his choice of imagery. In reflecting on Psalm 46:7, ideas and images such as God's presence, provision, and protection will come readily to mind as well as scriptural passages reflecting God's care for his own.

Some similar parallel structures are presented with an inversion of grammatical structure. We may call these *inverted similar parallelisms.* Note, for example, Psalm 78:10:

They did not keep God's covenant
and refused to live by his law.

Unfortunately, such cases are not always evident in English translations. Thus the Hebrew here would be better rendered:

They did not keep God's covenant
and in his law refused to walk.

By juxtaposing "covenant" and "law," the effect of the inversion in the parallel lines is to call attention to the seriousness of deliberate covenantal failure while changing the thought of personal conduct to that of the familiar biblical image of walking (cf. Gen. 17:1; Ezek. 18:9). In other passages, the movement from the first line to the second may involve (1) a change from a general location to a specific one (Ps. 78:43) or (2) from a personal name to one's patrilineage (Num. 23:18) or (3) from a personal name together with one's patrilineage to an individual's distinctive characteristic (Num. 24:3):

The day he displayed his miraculous signs in Egypt,
his wonders in the region of Zoan.
Arise, Balak, and listen;
hear me, son of Zippor.
The oracle of Balaam son of Beor,
the oracle of one whose eye sees clearly.

All such examples may be listed under the general heading of *similar parallelism* with epithet in the second line.

Antithetic Parallelism

Rather than similarity of thought, some parallel lines may display a sharp contrast:

Righteousness exalts a nation,
  but sin is a disgrace to any people. (Prov. 14:34)

In addition to the just-noted simple parallelism over two lines, some contrast may be compounded over several lines. Note, for example, Isaiah 1:3:

The ox knows his master,
  the donkey his owner's manger,
but Israel does not know,
  my people do not understand.

The example contains poignant imagery. In contrast to dumb animals who recognize who their master is and where their daily provision comes from, God's people fail to understand that they belong to God and that everything they have is due to him.

Progressive Parallelism

With progressive parallelism, a succeeding line (or lines) supplements and/or completes the first line. Psalm 57:1 is a representative example:

Have mercy on me, O God,
  have mercy on me,
  for in you my soul takes refuge.

Here, the reason for the Psalmist's urgent cry is spelled out clearly in the closing line. We should note, however, that a causal particle is not always present in a parallel line. Consider Psalm 98:2:

The LORD has made his salvation known
  and revealed his righteousness to the nations.

Although there is a similarity of structure here, clearly the second line completes the thought of the first. The psalmist touches on two matters here: God's deliverance of his people, which in turn serves as a testimony of his righteousness to the surrounding people. That two groups are being considered is evident from the context, for the new song (v. 1) contains imagery of God's deliverance drawn from Exodus 15:11–12 (his right hand and his holy arm) while verse three commemorates God's covenant love and faithfulness toward Israel in his deliverance which the nations have clearly seen. Contextually, therefore, verse two displays a clear progression of thought that is only completed with both lines.

Special types of progressive parallelism may also be differentiated. In *staircase parallelism*, succeeding lines begin with similar phraseology leading to a completion of the thought in the first line.

> Sing to the LORD a new song;
> sing to the LORD, all the earth.
> Sing to the LORD, praise his name;
> proclaim his salvation day after day. (Ps. 96:1–2)

Here, the repeated call for singing God's praise leads to the celebration of his name (his established character and reputation) and is climaxed by the call to proclaim God's daily saving acts. Thus the new song of verse one is seen to be not only new in time with each day's passing but qualitatively new in accordance with God's continued blessings.

A type of staircasing is known as *terrace pattern parallelism*. In such instances, the progression is facilitated by repeating at the beginning of the second line the words or phraseology at the ending of the first. Note, for example, Psalm 96:12–13:

> Then all the trees of the forest will sing for joy;
> they will sing before the LORD, for he comes,
> he comes to judge the earth.

A variation of this arrangement is to omit one of the words or phrases so that a single element appears in one of the two lines but is to be understood in both. We can demonstrate this by comparing the words of Psalm 96:13 with those of Psalm 98:7–8:

Let the rivers clap their hands,
  let the mountains sing together for joy;
let them sing before the LORD,
  for he comes to judge the earth.

By comparing the phrase "for he comes" in Psalm 96:13 with that in Psalm 98:8 we can see that its single occurrence in the latter is intended to do double duty as a hinge connecting two parallel lines. We may term this type of parallelism *hinge terrace parallelism.*

Progression is at times indicated by utilizing a numerical sequence known as *ladder parallelism.* In these cases, the second line contains the next highest or corresponding digit. Consider the following two examples:

There are three things that are too amazing for me,
  four that I do not understand:
The way of an eagle in the sky,
  the way of a snake on a rock,
the way of a ship on the high seas,
and the way of a man with a maiden. (Prov. 30:18–19)

Saul has slain his thousands,
  and David his tens of thousands. (1 Sam. 18:7)

In both cases, the numerical sequence directs special attention to the elements indicated by the higher number. Where a literal number is intended, it is always the higher number, and the items under consideration are spelled out as in the Proverbs example. Where a literal number is not intended, no further details are given, as in the citation from 1 Samuel 18. In both cases, the numerical sequence not only attracts the hearer or reader's attention but also serves as an aid to memorization.

Progression may also be accomplished by the formal means of beginning each succeeding line or set of lines with the next successive letter of the Hebrew alphabet. Psalm 119 is a well-known case. Other psalms include Psalms 25, 34, 37, 111, 112, and 145. An incomplete alphabetic acrostic has often been noted in the combination of Psalms 9 and 10. Acrostics serve not only as stylistic and memory devices but invite the reader to consider the effect of the whole composition.

One other type of clear progression has traditionally been known as *emblematic parallelism*. Here, the parallelism is accomplished by way of a simile. Thus Psalm 103:13 states:

> As a father has compassion on his children,
> so the LORD has compassion on those who fear him.

Not only is God's love illustrated by comparing it to that of a human father but the comparison also invites an argument *a fortiori* (from the lesser to the greater; lit. "to the stronger"). If a father can have compassion on his children, how much more can God feel compassion for his own? The effect in Psalm 103:13 is to underscore the emphasis begun in verses 11–12. *A fortiori* arguments may of course also be stated in formal parallel fashion:

> If the righteous receive their due on earth,
> how much more the ungodly and the sinner! (Prov. 11:31)

Terseness

A second characteristic of Hebrew poetry is its terseness. Poets have a way of stating their thoughts so concisely that the result is a polished and succinct presentation free of unnecessary details. Consider the dramatic effect of Nahum's description of the attack against Nineveh:

> The crack of whips,
> the clatter of wheels,
> galloping horses
> and jolting chariots!
> Charging cavalry,
> flashing swords
> and glittering spears! (Nah. 3:2–3)

Note as well Moses's tribute to Yahweh in his victory song after Israel's deliverance through the waters of the Red Sea:

> Yahweh is a man of war
> Yahweh is his name. (Exod. 15:3; Heb. text)

Here, we are presented in succinct fashion with the figure of the Lord as a conquering warrior with an established reputation as the sovereign God of all in the well-known theme of the Name.

Concreteness

A third feature of poetry is its concrete nature. Poetry allows the reader to experience the matter portrayed with his or her five senses. In this regard, the contrast between prose and poetry becomes pronounced. This may be seen in the dual accounts of the report of Sisera's death at the hands of Jael. The prose account details Sisera's flight from the Israelite army; his meeting with Jael and their conversation; Jael's killing of the now exhausted commander of the Canaanite army; and the subsequent arrival of Barak, the commander of the pursuing Israelites (Judg. 4:17–22). The poetic account, however, centers attention on Sisera's demise and reports with dramatic flair:

> He asked for water, she gave him milk;
>   in a bowl fit for nobles she brought him curdled milk.
> Her hand reached for the tent peg,
>   her right hand for the workman's hammer.
> She struck Sisera, she crushed his head,
>   she shattered and pierced his temple.
> At her feet he sank,
>   he fell; there he lay.
> At her feet he sank, he fell;
>   where he sank, there he fell—dead. (Judg. 5:25–27)

Here, one can almost see Jael as she takes the heavy iron tent stake, places it at sleeping Sisera's temple, and hammers it home. Jael has delivered the *coup mortel* to the mighty enemy commander who now lies dead at the feet of a simple Kenite wife. How the mighty have fallen!

Imagery

A fourth characteristic of poetry is its abundant use of imagery. Poets tend to think in images rather than abstractions. By using an image, a poet portrays reality or expresses it in more concrete terms that demand the interpreter's careful attention and interaction. On the whole, imagery tends to be concise, because it not only conveys information but evokes an emotional response as well.

Imagery makes frequent use of figurative language. Here, words take on a sense other than their literal meaning. Thus two dissimilar things are brought together in a comparative way. By using figurative language, the poet not only makes his work more striking and colorful but also invites the reader to observe and meditate more closely on what he is saying. At the same time, the compressed language of figures makes for a conciseness of expression that is more easily remembered.

As we noted in the previous chapter, a host of figures occurs in biblical poetry. Particularly plentiful are figures of comparison such as metaphor and simile. The Song of Solomon is replete with imagery employing metaphor and simile. Note, for example, the following:

> I am a rose of Sharon
>   a lily of the valleys.
> Like a lily among thorns
>   is my darling among the maidens (2:1–2).

Because many of these involve the person and work of God, it is important that the interpreter grasp the force of the figures. Consider the following:

> The LORD is my shepherd. (Ps. 23:1)

> As a shepherd looks after his scattered flock . . . ,
>   so will I look after my sheep. (Ezek. 34:12)

> Hear us, O Shepherd of Israel. (Ps. 80:1)

In turn, God is likened to a shepherd by the use of metaphor, simile, and *hypocatastasis*. In a metaphor, a given object is identified as another: the Lord *is* a shepherd. By way of a simile, one object is likened to another: the Lord is (acts) *like* a shepherd. By means of *hypocatastasis*, one object is called another: "O shepherd," "you shepherd." In each instance, the poet creates a visual image of a shepherd and his sheep. As a shepherd tends his flock, so the Lord cares for his people.

Some comparisons are not so complimentary while nonetheless presenting vivid pictures. Consider the following:

> Am I a dog that you come at me with sticks? (1 Sam. 17:43)

> As a dog returns to its vomit,
> so a fool repeats his folly. (Prov. 26:11)

> Dogs have surrounded me. (Ps. 22:16)

Here again, the careful observer will note the variation between the three figures mentioned above.

Anthropomorphisms ascribe human characteristics or qualities to God. Especially common are the various parts of the human body such as the face (Rev. 6:16), mouth (Isa. 1:20), tongue (Isa. 30:27), lips (Job 11:5), eyes (Ps. 33:18), ears (Ps. 71:2), feet (Ps. 18:9), hands (Isa. 64:8), arms (Isa. 51:5), fingers (Ps. 8:3), and heart (Jer. 32:41). Anthropopathisms ascribe human emotions such as compassion to God:

> How can I give you up, Ephraim?
> How can I hand you over, Israel?
> How can I treat you like Admah?
> How can I make you like Zeboiim?
> My heart is changed within me;
> all my compassion is aroused. (Hos. 11:8)

Similarly, God is often portrayed as repenting (Jer. 26:3) or relenting about performing a given action.

By the use of a zoomorphism, animal qualities are ascribed to God. Thus God's tender care of the believer may be likened to that of a bird, while his chastening power is compared to that of a lion:

> He will cover you with his feathers,
> and under his wings you will find refuge. (Ps. 91:4)

> For I will be like a lion to Ephraim,
> like a great lion to Judah.

I will tear them to pieces and go away;
    I will carry them off, with no one to rescue them. (Hos. 5:14)

The careful interpreter of God's Word will need to make the necessary comparative mental leap and visualize the poet's portrayal in these and the other figures detailed in Chapter 5. Coming to grips with the nature of the figures involved in context is crucial to proper interpretation. It can even be a means to avoiding improper theological conclusions. For instance, failure to recognize anthropomorphic descriptions of God could lead to viewing God in purely physical terms rather than as he is—an eternal, infinite, and perfect spirit (John 4:24).

POETRY IN THE NEW TESTAMENT

All the above examples have been taken from the Old Testament. Nevertheless, the principles involved are applicable in large measure where poetry exists in the New Testament. We will do well to remember that with the possible exception of Luke, the New Testament authors were all Jewish by background. When it came to poetry, therefore, they would likely think in terms of Old Testament precedents. This is easily missed in reading the New Testament, because our English translations often fail to present relevant passages as poetry.

For this reason the various parallel structures we have already noted can be encountered in the New Testament: (1) similar, (2) antithetic, and (3) progressive.

Consider the following examples:

(1) Ask and it will be given to you;
    seek and you will find;
    knock and the door will be opened to you. (Matt. 7:7)

(2) Likewise every good tree bears good fruit,
    but a bad tree bears bad fruit. (Matt. 7:17)

(3) Blessed are the merciful,
    for they will be shown mercy. (Matt. 5:7)

You will also find parallel structures such as (1) staircase parallelism, including (2) the terrace pattern, and (3) emblematic parallelism. Note the following examples:

(1) Whoever welcomes this little child in my name
welcomes me;
and whoever welcomes me
welcomes the One who sent me. (Luke 9:48)

(2) If anyone is to go into captivity,
into captivity he will go.
If anyone is to be killed with the sword,
with the sword he will be killed. (Rev. 13:10)

(3) As the Father has sent me,
I am sending you. (John 20:21)

Poetry may also be seen in the psalmic praises clustered around the nativity (Luke 1:47–55, 67–79), in many of the sayings of the New Testament (1 Tim. 3:16), and in its hymns and songs (Luke 2:14; Rev. 11:15; 15:3). Some passages are recorded as poetry in the New Testament (e.g., Phil. 2:5–11). It is of interest to note that it has often been suggested that one may detect here an earlier poetic saying around which Paul may have fashioned his full poem:

Being in the very nature of God,
made himself nothing;
being found in appearance as a man,
he humbled himself. (vv. 6–8)

New Testament poetry likewise features terseness and concreteness. Note the following examples:

(1) Everyone should be quick to listen, slow to speak
and slow to become angry. (Jas. 1:19)

(2) You are like whitewashed tombs,

which look beautiful on the outside
but on the inside are full of dead men's bones
and everything unclean. (Matt. 23:27)

Imagery may be found throughout the pages of the New Testament, especially in the sayings of Jesus. This may be seen, for example, in his parables but also in several of his extended discourses built around the "I am" sayings in John (6:25; 8:12; 9:5; 10:7, 11, 14; 11:25; 14:6; 15:1). Indeed, Jesus often taught in mind-engaging pictures.

By appreciating the poetic nature of relevant New Testament passages, the interpreter gains a new perspective. Even theological discourses become alive with new dramatic dimensions. Consider the effect of reading the familiar introduction to John's Gospel as a predominantly poetic portion opening the Johannine account. We note here only verses 1–5:

1 In the beginning was the Word,
and the Word was with God,
and the Word was God.
2 He was with God in the beginning.
3 Through him all things were made,
and without him nothing was made
that has been made.
4 In him was life,
and that life was the light of men.
5 The light shines in the darkness,
but the darkness has not overcome it.

In light of our earlier discussion of poetic features and Semitic compositional techniques, what types of parallel structure do you see here? What compositional techniques are in evidence? What is the impact of such imagery as life, light, and darkness? How does an appreciation of terseness and concreteness help you to understand and feel more deeply the theological concepts that John is communicating? We suggest that in asking yourself questions such as these you will gain a new perspective and appreciation of the poetic skill with which John opened his Gospel.

STRUCTURAL DEVICES IN BIBLICAL POETRY

Building Blocks

Quite obviously parallelism is both an essential feature of biblical poetry and also an important structural form. Here, however, we are thinking of the basic building blocks that comprise the full poem. Poetic structuring begins with the individual line known variously as a stitch (pronounced "stick"), verset, or colon. We shall adopt the term "colon" for our discussion.

A *monocolon* is an individual poetic line which does not combine closely with another colon. It can be used to introduce a unit or a subunit of thought. Note, for example, Psalm 18:1: "I love you, O LORD, my strength." Here the psalmist's testimony of his love for God stands independently from the following poetic lines even though it colors all that he has to say throughout his psalm of praise to the Lord. Similarly, Psalm 11:1 begins with the psalmist's declaration of his love for God, which in turn is to be understood (though not structurally connected) in the rest of the psalm.

A monocolon can also be found at the close of a psalm. Thus Psalm 2 ends with a final single line of tribute to the Lord: "Blessed are all who take refuge in him" (Ps. 2:12). Occasionally, a monocolon functions as a sudden break in the flow of thought or structure. For example, in the midst of his description of eschatological military preparations Joel exclaims, "Bring down your warriors, O LORD!" (Joel 2:11). The individual line here serves not only as a sudden break in the description of events but constitutes an apostrophe or direct address to someone as though he were present. Not only people, but also things may be addressed as though they were present in the form of an apostrophe: "O land, land, land, hear the word of the LORD!" (Jer. 22:29).

Parallel thought over two successive lines is commonly known as a *bicolon*. We have noticed such examples in the preceding discussions, for it is perhaps the most common of all poetic structural devices. It is especially present in wisdom poetry. Consider the following:

My mouth will speak words of wisdom;
  the utterance from my heart will give understanding. (Ps. 49:3)

The fear of the LORD is the beginning of knowledge,
  but fools despise wisdom and discipline. (Prov. 1:7)

A *tricolon* consists of three lines that form a distinct unit. It, too, is extremely common in biblical poetry. Although tricola may occur anywhere in a psalm (e.g., Ps. 10:9), they frequently stand at the head of a unit or subunit of poetry. Note the following examples:

The LORD is my rock, my fortress and deliverer;
  my God is my rock, in whom I take refuge.
He is my shield and the horn of my salvation, my stronghold. (Ps. 18:2)

Listen to my prayer, O God,
  do not ignore my plea;
  hear me and answer me. (Ps. 55:1–2a)

Tricola may also be found at the end of a unit or subunit. Psalm 16 ends with these words:

You have made known to me the path of life;
  you will fill me with joy in your presence,
  with eternal pleasures at your right hand. (Ps. 16:11)

Psalm 18 concludes by saying,

He gives his king great victories;
  he shows unfailing kindness to his anointed,
  to David and his descendants forever. (Ps. 18:50)

Bicola and tricola are at times interchanged to indicate structural boundaries of units or subunits of thought.

Four-line cola (*tetracolon or quatrain*) and five-line cola (*pentacolon*) are rarer. Each, however, is attested. Psalm 114 is composed of four quatrains while Psalm 9:13–14 is structured by means of a pentacolon.

In poetry, the various line types are gathered together into larger units. Although different terminology is used among scholars, a full poem may be divided into successively smaller units known respectively as a *stanza* and a *strophe*. Moving from smallest to largest, the various cola discussed above may form a strophe. One or more strophes may constitute a stanza, and stanzas are combined to make up the full poem.

Ideally, poems of some length consist of several stanzas, which are further subdivided into strophes consisting of one or more cola. Thus the psalm of Habakkuk (3:3–15) may be diagrammed as follows:

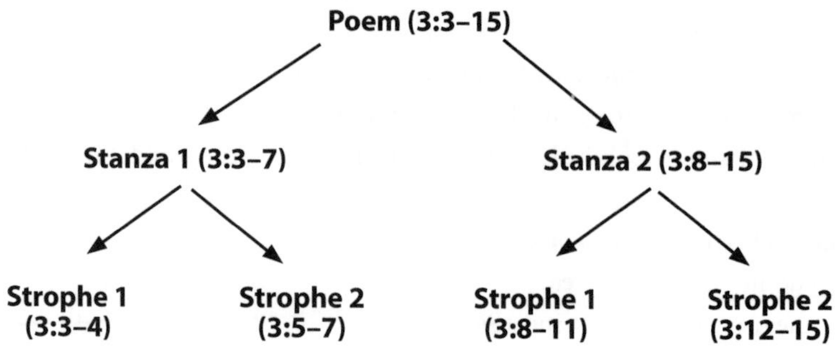

The various strophes are composed of alternating bicola and tricola lines of poetry.

Structural Indicators

It is one thing to be aware of the building blocks of poetry; it is another to recognize them. In determining distinct subunits of a given poetic piece, such as a psalm, we should keep in mind the various compositional techniques mentioned in Chapter 5 which will be covered more fully in the following chapter in connection with the guidelines for interpreting prophecy. Here we note in particular *bookending* (or *inclusio*) and *stitching*, both of which are extremely common in biblical poetry.

Bookending entails the technique of returning at the end of a unit to a theme, subject, or word(s) mentioned at the beginning of that section. The result of the *inclusio* thus formed is to enclose the intervening material so as to form a distinctive section of thought, much as a collector places a series of similar books between two bookends. Poets at times employ bookending to enclose whole poems. Thus Psalm 103 begins and ends with a call, "Praise [lit. bless] the LORD, O my soul" (vv. 1, 22). Individual subunits may similarly be detected. For example, Nahum's prediction of the Lord's judgment against Nineveh is enclosed by the theme of wickedness (Nah. 1:11, 15). The psalmist condemns the folly of amassing wealth apart from godly living by employing words for riches (Ps. 49:16, 20).

Poets also made use of *stitching*. By stitching, we mean the author's practice of linking successive units or subunits of a poem by means of repeating a word, phrase, or idea. Whole psalms may be linked together in the canon by such means. For example, Psalm 135 picks up the emphases on praise and ministry in the house of the Lord expressed in Psalm 134 (cf. Ps. 134:1 with 135:1–2). In turn, Psalm 135 prepares the reader for Psalm 136 with its emphasis on God's goodness (cf. Ps. 135:3 with Ps. 136:1). Psalm 135 also serves as a hinge (a third compositional technique) between the two surrounding psalms.

Stitching between units of a poem is extremely common. We may take Psalm 146 as an example. Here the words "river" and "stream" of the second stanza (vv. 4–7) provide stitching to the theme of water (v. 3) in the first stanza (vv. 1–3). Likewise, the idea of God as a refuge and strength (v. 1) provides further stitching for the thought of God being with his people as a fortress (v. 7). In turn, stanzas two and three are stitched together by words such as "nations" (vv. 6, 10) and "fortress" (vv. 7, 11), and the thought of the Lord Almighty being "with us" (vv. 7, 11).

We noted above that Psalm 135 serves as a hinge (or bridge) psalm between Psalms 134 and 136. A single verse can also stand as an independent unit of thought which, though forming a transition between two sections, also partakes in some measure of the two it connects. Thus Zephaniah 3:8 picks up the theme of judgment/justice and the nations (vv. 1–7) and prepares the reader for the theme of the eschatological day in verses nine through twenty. Verse eight also links together the emphasis on the city of Jerusalem common to both the preceding and following sections (cf. vv. 1, 7, with 11, 16). Even the prophets could express themselves in finely structured poetry.

Several other structural indicators may also be noted. Introductory particles, words, or phrases often reflect the fact that the poet has moved on to a new topic or unit of thought. In Psalm 46, the transition from the poet's praise and confidence in God in the first two stanzas to a new emphasis is marked by his invitation to "come and see the works of the LORD" (v. 8). Such invitations are not uncommon (e.g., Ps. 34:11; 66:5, 16; Isa. 1:12). Similarly, transitions to new units of thought are accomplished in Psalm 17 by the psalmist's renewed call to hear and answer his prayer (v. 6) and his further plea for the Lord's deliverance, confident of God's action (v. 13). Also, poets often begin units by expressing the Lord's condemnation using words such as "woe" (e.g., Nah. 3:1; Hab. 2:6, 9, 12, 15; Zeph. 3:1).

A clear change of subject matter may also indicate a new poetic unit. Such is common enough in literature. By way of illustration, note the flow of thought in Psalm 18. David's praise to God for the Lord's answering his call for deliverance from great trouble (vv. 4–6) is followed by words drawn from the historical record of Israel's deliverance during the exodus event (vv. 7–15; cf. Exod. 15:14–16; Judg. 5:4b–5; Ps. 68:8–9; 77:16–18; 144:5–6; Hab. 3:8–15). David then returns to testifying of God's delivering him out of great distress (Ps. 18:16–18). The implication is that the same great power God used in liberating Israel has been exercised on David's behalf. Note that although there is a change of subject matter in successive units of thought, there is coherence in the overall portrayal. The interpreter therefore needs to look not only for the shifting emphases of thought and subject matter in successive sections but to discern how each part contributes to the total picture that the poet wishes to convey.

Grammatical change may also signal the start of a new unit. In Zephaniah 3, there is distinct verbal variation from God's rehearsal of his past dealings with Israel (vv. 6–7) to the above-mentioned hinge verse which contains an imperative (v. 8). This is then followed by appropriate verbs indicating God's future plans (vv. 9–20). Grammatical patterning also at times indicates change of subject matter. For example, Psalm 73 begins with the psalmist's opening statement of confidence in the Lord ("surely"; v. 1) and is followed by a statement of his past problem ("but as for me"; v. 2). The poet then states the cause of his problem: the success of the wicked, which includes expressions of their attitude and actions (introduced by the word "therefore"; vv. 6, 10). The poet's past problem is rounded out by means of another "surely" expressing his resultant feelings concerning their success despite their godless behavior (vv. 13–17). The latter parts of the psalm also show similar, though not identical, patterning (vv. 18–28).

Structural change may also include the use of the refrain. For example, consider these words in Psalm 42:5, 11:

Why are you downcast, O my soul?
  Why so disturbed within me?

Put your hope in God,
  for I will yet praise him,
  my Savior and my God.

This twice-recurring refrain also appears in Psalm 43:5. Along with other data, this has suggested to many that originally the two psalms were one composition. Among other poetic refrains, we may note the following examples:

> Be exalted, O God, above the heavens;
> let your glory be over all the earth. (Ps. 57:5, 11)

> O my Strength, I watch for you;
> you, O God, are my fortress, my loving God. (Ps. 59:9; cf. v. 17)

Chiastic Structure

In *chiastic structure*, the second half of a composition takes up the same words, themes, or motifs as in the first half, but in reverse order. Often these two parts are united around a common core that can form the most prominent idea or intended emphasis of the author. The chiasm may cover two lines or three lines or even more. For example:

> A Wait for the LORD;
> B be strong and take heart
> A' and wait for the LORD. (Ps. 27:14)

Whole compositions can also be written in the form of a chiasm. Thus in Psalm 70, the psalmist's prayer for deliverance (vv. 1, 5) encloses a central core in which he asks for his enemies defeat (vv. 2–3) and God's blessing upon the righteous (v. 4).

One must avoid the temptation, however, to find chiastic structure almost everywhere. Some have gone to great lengths to reconstruct poetic pieces built around the slimmest of evidence such as a single word. To be sure, the A B A' pattern is attested even in the earliest literature of the ancient Near East, but this does not give precedent for ingeniously finding or creating a chiasm where it does not exist.

STYLISTIC DEVICES IN BIBLICAL POETRY

In addition to characteristics such as terseness, concreteness, and the poet's skillful use of figures of speech and imagery, there are miscellaneous features of style. Two such devices are rhyme and rhythm. Unfortunately, unless one is dealing with the original text, rhyming is not always apparent in biblical translations. Too often we miss this nice touch of the literary artist. For example, consider Nahum 1:15:

> Celebrate your festivals, O Judah,
> and fulfill your vows.

The parallel Hebrew words translated "festivals" and "vows" both end in *-ayik* but this is not apparent in our English translation. If one wished to reflect the sound pattern of the Masoretic Text, he could render the bicolon in question as follows:

> O Judah, observe your celebrations,
> fulfill your sacred declarations.

When we think of rhyme, however, we must not consider the intricate patterns of western poetry. Most commonly Hebrew rhyming is a matter of repeated similar endings. Thus in Isaiah 33:22, the fourfold repetition of the personal plural pronominal suffix *-nû* forms a clear rhyming pattern, which is missed in translation.

Not to be forgotten also is the more common rhyming which consists of two-word patterns as in the well-known *tōhû wābōhû* (formless and empty, Gen. 1:2). Similar *assonance* is common enough. *Assonance* and *alliteration* are also very common in the Hebrew Old Testament. Both devices made for ease of memorization.

Another literary device of poetry is the use of synonyms in successive poetic lines. For example, note Habakkuk 3:8:

> Yahweh, were you angry with the rivers,
> or was your wrath against the streams
> or your fury against the sea?

Here, three sources of water are heaped up to call dramatic attention to the Lord's triumphs at the Red Sea and the Jordan River.

Several other poetic devices are also worthy of mention. The poet will often use an unusual *word order* to draw attention to a particular item. Consider Psalm 63:8. Although not rendered adequately in English translations, the poet's great pleasure because of God's sustaining him is expressed in the placing of the direct object "me" as the first word in the parallel line of the bicolon:

> My soul clings to you;
> me your right hand upholds.

The effect is to underscore the intimate relationship between David and his Lord. A similar effect is felt in Jeremiah 2:13 where in succeeding lines Jeremiah rehearses the Lord's deep disappointment over his faithless people: "Surely my people have committed two evils; me they have forsaken." Not only is the direct object placed first in the clause for emphasis, but in the original text it is preceded immediately by "my people" as the final words in the previous clause. The effect is to juxtapose the words "my people" and "me."

Another poetic device is *allusion.* Thus in his condemnation of the people's pursuit of the god Baal (Jer. 2:33), Jeremiah points out that the people have abandoned the true baal (= husband). The imagery of Yahweh as a husband versus the false god Baal forms an allusion which can be felt throughout the second and third chapters of Jeremiah (e.g., 2:2, 22; 3:14; see also Jer. 31:22). Allusion is common in both prose and poetry but is particularly efficient in poetry. Thus one can hear an allusion to Genesis 49:10 in Ezekiel's mournful dirge where the phrase "to whom it rightfully belongs" (Ezek. 21:27) is an echo of Jacob's blessing on Judah, which is usually translated simply as "Shiloh" (lit. "the one whose it is").

Still another poetic device is *ellipsis*, the deletion of a word present only in one parallel line of poetry even though it is to be understood in both. Consider the following examples:

> Sound the trumpet in Gibeah,
> the horn in Ramah. (Hos. 5:8)

> He shot arrows and scattered the enemies,
> bolts of lightning and routed them. (2 Sam. 22:15)

In both cases, the verb of the first parallel line is absent in the second line, though felt in both lines.

Other examples demonstrate yet another poetic device known as a *ballast variant*. In cases where a major variant in one line is not attested in the parallel line, one or more words tend to be longer than the counterpart in the other line. Note the following examples:

God came for Teman,
the Holy One from Mount Para. (Hab. 3:3)

Balak brought me from Aram,
the king of Moab from the eastern mountains. (Num. 23:7)

While our focus here is on the Old Testament, it should be briefly noted that the New Testament writers used some of these same devices to convey their thoughts. Thus Paul used rhyme and word pairs in the creedal hymn in 1 Timothy 3:16 and assonance and alliteration in his admonition in Philippians 4:4. Set word pairs and phrases are also found in the title "King of Kings and Lord of Lords" (1 Tim. 6:15; cf. Rev. 19:16).

Apart from understanding structural and stylistic devices in biblical poetry, it will also be helpful to be acquainted with some of the more common types of figures of speech in Scripture.

TYPES OF FIGURES OF SPEECH IN THE BIBLE

Anthropomorphism

Anthropomorphism is the ascription of human characteristics to God. For instance:

The eyes of the LORD are on the righteous
and his ears are attentive to their cry;
the face of the LORD is against those who do evil,
to cut off the memory of them from the earth. (Ps. 34:15–16)

In this reference, the writer indicates God's regard for his people and rejection of the unrighteous. In verse 15, "the eyes" indicate God's active protection of his people, and "the ears" represent his responsiveness to their cries. In verse 16, "the face" signifies God's whole person in opposition to the unrighteous people who do evil. In all three anthropomorphisms, God is given human characteristics, with the result that his different attitudes toward the righteous and the unrighteous are made personal—and pointed.

Euphemism

Euphemism is the substitution of a less offensive term for an offensive one. The classic example of euphemism is Elijah's taunt of the prophets of Baal at Mount Carmel. When Baal does not answer his prophets' petitions, Elijah mocks, "At noon Elijah began to taunt them. 'Shout louder!' he said. 'Surely he is a god! Perhaps he is deep in thought, or busy, or traveling. Maybe he is sleeping and must be awakened'" (1 Kgs. 18:27). Here, the reference to Baal's being "busy" is a polite way of saying that he is "relieving himself" (in fact, this is the way in which the term is rendered in the ESV).

Hypocatastasis

Hypocatastasis is a device in which the comparison is implied by direct naming. In the prophet's taunt song against Nineveh in the book of Nahum, the vulnerability of the soon-to-be-defeated Ninevites is expressed in the hypocatastasis of the lions' den (Nahum 2). The lion was Nineveh's symbol. In saying that the lions' den is ravaged, the prophet mocks the Ninevites at their proudest point.

Image

Image is a word picture that makes an abstract idea concrete and reified. The imagery in the first chapter of the book of Revelation is a prime New Testament example. Here the golden lampstands and the Son of Man among them represent the glory and truth of the glorified churches in the presence of Christ. The effect of the imagery is to create awe. An Old Testament image is that of the four living creatures in the opening chapter of Ezekiel. The four faces, each one in itself symbolic, represent the omniscience of God, the wings and feet their ability to carry out God's commands, and the "appearance . . . like burning coals of fire or like torches" (Ezek. 1:13) the holiness and glory of God. It is appropriate that the writings of the prophets contain so many images, for imagery makes the abstract concrete and brings the eternal into the temporal.

The prophecies in the Old Testament and in the New Testament Apocalypse would not be nearly as accessible to us, were it not for the figures of speech they employ.

Metaphor

Metaphor is the imaginative identification of two distinct objects or ideas. The psalmist's declaration, "For the LORD God is a sun and shield" (Ps. 84:11), is an example of a double metaphor. The Lord is compared to the sun which provides life; the psalmist conveys the same idea explicitly in the same verse in saying that God "bestows favor and honor" and withholds "no good thing" from his people. As for the shield, no explanation is necessary; not only does God provide, he protects.

Metonymy

Metonymy is the substitution of one word for another. The great wedding song in Psalm 45 contains a vivid metonymy:

> Your throne, O God, will last for ever and ever;
> A scepter of justice will be the scepter of your kingdom. (Ps. 45:6)

There are actually two metonymies in this verse. The first is "the throne of God," for "throne" represents the rule of a king. Thus this metonymy reminds us of God's eternal reign or authority over all things. "The scepter" is the second metonymy, referring to the power of the king. In ancient cultures, the scepter represented authority—as, for instance, in Esther's case (Est. 5:1–3). Here, the scepter of God's authority is his righteousness, or holiness—his essential attribute. In two brief metonymies, the psalmist expresses something of the majesty and dominion of God.

WISDOM LITERATURE

Nature of Wisdom

In approaching the literature traditionally termed as wisdom, the interpreter must first come to terms with its nature. Although the books of Job, Proverbs, and Ecclesiastes are commonly known as the books of wisdom, wisdom literature may be found in many places in both the Old Testament and New Testament. Accordingly, it is important to recognize wisdom as a genre and become acquainted with its chief characteristics.

One may gain insight into the biblical concept of wisdom by noting the words used to express wisdom. Among the many biblical terms are "insight," "prudence," "understanding," and "resourcefulness." Of central importance is the notion of the skill and expertise born of virtue to apply godly wisdom properly. Common themes in wisdom literature such as genuine piety, morality, and proper thinking provide additional insight.

Although human wisdom that is traditional (e.g., Job 15:8–10) and/or purely humanistic wisdom (e.g., Isa. 29:14; 1 Cor. 1:20; 2:6) are acknowledged in the Bible, genuine wisdom is rooted in God, humanity's Creator (Job 28:25–28). True human wisdom finds its norm in the wisdom by which God created and orders his universe (Deut. 4:6; Prov. 8:22–31). It includes not only the accumulation of knowledge, but above all, the skill to discern how to apply the principles of godly wisdom to specific situations (e.g., 1 Kgs. 3:7–10, 16–28; cf. Dan. 5:14). These include interaction with human institutions (cf. Matt. 19:1–12), whether legal or cultural standards, and with the created order, whether the world of creatures or the physical world (cf. Gen. 3:27–30; 1 Kgs. 4:29–34; Job 38–41; Prov. 3:19–24).

The roots of wisdom are in the fear of the Lord (Ps. 111:10; Prov. 1:7). This involves understanding God as the Creator who controls all things and consummates history (Ps. 104:24–32) and as the one with whom we all have to do (Eccl. 12:13–14). Where these principles are taught as keys to godly living, they belong to the genre of wisdom literature. All wisdom literature is basically instructional in nature, with the author attempting to impart wise observations on the meaning of life and the proper conduct necessary to enjoy life to the fullest.

Wisdom literature may appear in many types. It may involve precepts or instructions intended to give advice for living the successful and happy life. These are often delivered in the form of proverbs, at times expressed as the teaching of a father to a son or of a teacher to his students. Treatises or essays provide a discourse on the meaning of life. Wisdom may be expressed in the form of a disputation in which one takes up the merits or demerits of one's opponent. Some wisdom literature is pessimistic or devoted to a denunciation of the evils of society. Still other wisdom literature may occur as a lamentation due to the punishment society has incurred because of ungodly or immoral conduct. Much of wisdom literature is couched in imagery, as figures of speech are designed to provoke thinking and reflection on the nature of its teaching. Literary devices such as satire, sarcasm, riddles, parables, and allegories are often found in wisdom literature as well.

Proverbs

When we think of wisdom literature, our minds are immediately drawn to the book of Proverbs. Proverbs are short memorable statements of the true state of things as perceived and learned by human observations over extended periods of experience. In terms of the biblical book of Proverbs, this refers to an apophthegm (a short, witty, and instructive saying) that has currency among those who fear the Lord. The proverbial literature found here thus exists in short pithy statements, but it may be found in the more extended instructional saying as well. When reading Proverbs, the interpreter should also keep in mind the principles of poetry discussed earlier in the chapter.

Biblical proverbs may be categorized in various ways. One such way is to classify the proverbs in chapters 10:1–22:16 and chapters 25–29 as to whether they deal with wisdom and life (A), society at large (B), or the individual (C). Type A deals with general wisdom designed to give practical suggestions for a successful and harmonious life. Type B discloses behavior that has a distinct effect on society, while Type C features moral truths intended for personal piety and purity as standards for personal behavior (though there is some overlap).

Some proverbs may be classified as either descriptive or prescriptive. *Descriptive proverbs* may be presented as a portrait of a way of life:

> The sluggard says, "There is a lion in the road,
>   a fierce lion roaming the streets!"
> As a door turns on its hinges,
>   so a sluggard turns on his bed."
> The sluggard buries his hand in the dish;
>   he is too lazy to bring it back to his mouth.
> The sluggard is wiser in his own eyes,
>   than seven men who answer discreetly. (Prov. 26:13–16)

Sometimes proverbs such as these take the form of a short sketch such as a discussion on the exemplary ways of the ant.

> Go to the ant, you sluggard;
> consider its ways and be wise!
> It has no commander,
> no overseer or ruler,
> yet it stores its provision in summer
> and gathers its food at harvest. (Prov. 6:6–8)

Still other descriptive proverbs are extended into short narratives such as that of the adulterous woman (Prov. 7:6–23) or wisdom's preparing a feast (9:1–6).

The aim of *prescriptive proverbs* is motivational. Good standards and habits thus have their own reward:

> The fear of the LORD is a fountain of life,
> turning a man from the snares of death. (Prov. 14:27)

Other proverbs may be viewed as comparative or contrastive. *Comparative proverbs* may be expressed as one thing being better than another or being likened to another. Note the following examples:

> Better a dry crust with peace and quiet
> than a house full of feasting, with strife. (Prov. 17:1)

> Like one who seizes a dog by the ears
> is a passer-by who meddles in a quarrel not his own. (Prov. 26:17)

Such proverbs attempt to point out the superiority of one manner of living to another, as well as suggesting the benefits of the superior way.

Contrastive proverbs likewise point to a better course of living but do so by presenting diametrically opposed settings. These may apply to the individual or corporate situations. Note the following:

> Pride only breeds quarrels,
> but wisdom is found in those who take advice. (Prov. 13:10)

> Righteousness exalts a nation,
> but sin is a disgrace to any people. (Prov. 14:34)

Conditional proverbs deal with the consequences of a person's actions. Consider the following:

> If a man pays back evil for good,
> evil will never leave his house. (Prov. 17:13)

> If a man digs a pit, he will fall into it;
> if a man rolls a stone, it will roll back on him. (Prov. 26:27)

In some cases, this type of proverb will contain an *a fortiori* argument (argument from the lesser to the greater).

> If the righteous receive their due on earth,
> how much more the ungodly and the sinner! (Prov. 11:31)

Declarative proverbs are primarily designed to make a statement. Consider the following examples:

> An unfriendly man pursues selfish ends;
> he defies all sound judgment. (Prov. 18:1)

> Before his downfall a man's heart is proud.
> But humility comes before honor. (Prov. 18:12)

Although all proverbs provide insight into wise living, some may be specifically classified as *instructional proverbs.* These characteristically have a distinctive structure, which contains an imperative plus motivation and/or accompanying conditions. The imperative may be single (positive: 3:9; negative: 23:9), double (positive: 4:24; negative: 22:24), or mixed (positive and negative: 1:8; 3:1). Reasons for the imperatives may be experience (23:20–21), theological principle (3:11–12), or negative consequences (3:2).

Numerical proverbs are cast in the form of *staircase parallelism*, a feature we noted earlier in the chapter. As a further example, consider Proverbs 30:15–16:

There are three things that are never satisfied,
  four that never say, "Enough!"
The grave, the barren womb,
  land, which is never satisfied with water,
  and fire, which never says, "Enough!"

This type of proverb usually contains wise observations on the way things appear to be, sometimes with a touch of satire as in the previously cited example from Proverbs 30:18–19. Other examples include Proverbs 6:6–11; 26:14–15; 30:21–23.

An interesting feature of biblical proverbs is that at times they appear to give directly contradictory advice or observations. For example, consider Proverbs 26:4–5:

Do not answer a fool according to his folly,
  or you will be like him yourself.
Answer a fool according to his folly,
  or he will be wise in his own eyes.

The contradiction may be more apparent than real, however. Thus in the above example, further reflection makes it clear that one is not to let the remarks of a fool go unchallenged but in answering him the respondent is not to stoop to his level by using unfit language or improper reasoning.

Short narrative passages also occur in the book of Proverbs. Although all of these are intended for wise reflection, their understanding varies in accordance with their purpose. Thus the autobiographical account concerning wisdom (chap. 8) is instructional in nature. So also are the contrasting instructional narratives concerning wisdom (9:1–12) and folly (9:13–18). Stories or vignettes may be intended as examples, whether positive (31:10–31) or negative (24:30–34). Because these are intended to motivate the hearer or reader to right conduct, they commonly conclude with a moral or lesson to be learned.

Charm is deceptive and beauty is fleeting;
  but a woman who fears the Lord is to be praised. (Prov. 31:30)

A little sleep, a little slumber,
  a little folding of the hands to rest—

and poverty will come on you like a bandit
  and scarcity like an armed man. (Prov. 24:33–34)

The perceptive interpreter has doubtless noticed that the various examples set out above are at times capable of being assigned to more than one class of proverb. Indeed, hard and fast distinctions are not always possible. Due to the popular nature of a proverb, it may often be viewed from more than one angle—perhaps even designedly so. It is therefore amenable to multiple insights that serve as guides for proper conduct and personal welfare.

The categories mentioned above do not necessarily exhaust all classes of proverbs. For example, the book of Proverbs also contains extended sayings (e.g., chaps. 30–31). These are usually intended for instruction or admonition. Yet the careful interpreter will find our general classifications to be helpful in interpreting the proverbial collection in general.

Ecclesiastes

The Book of Ecclesiastes speaks of the value of wisdom:

Wisdom, like an inheritance, is a good thing
  and benefits those who see the sun.
Wisdom is a shelter
  as money is a shelter,
but the advantage of knowledge is this:
  that wisdom preserves the life of its possessor. (Eccl. 7:11–12)

In reading Ecclesiastes, interpreters will encounter many of the same literary devices that we have already presented in our previous discussions. Written for the most part as poetry, Ecclesiastes contains the usual features of poetry such as various types of parallelism as well as terseness, concreteness, figures of speech, and abundant imagery. Its pages are filled with literary features such as lyric poems (e.g., 3:1–8; 12:1–7) and proverbs (e.g., 7:1–2). An unusual feature of Ecclesiastes is the author's double approach in searching for ultimate reality. Along the way, we find both positive and negative attitudes, as well as contrasting observations held in tension (e.g., 5:10–20). Thus, in 3:19–22 one may note a satirical tone in the author's negative conclusion, which is then followed by a more positive outlook.

> Man's fate is like that of the animals; the same fate awaits them both. As one dies, so dies the other. All have the same breath; man has no advantage over the animal. Everything is meaningless. All go to the same place; all come from dust, and to dust all return. Who knows if the spirit of man rises upward and the spirit of the animal goes down into the earth?
>
> So I saw that there is nothing better for a man than to enjoy his work, because that is his lot. For who can bring him to see what will happen after him?

This holding of negative and positive approaches is in keeping with the author's instructional goals (e.g., 12:9–10). Therefore, the perceptive interpreter must hold both negative and positive portions in tension until he or she is swept along in the flow of the author's thinking to the final conclusion (12:13–14). Premature judgment can easily lead to finding Ecclesiastes to be basically pessimistic and cause the interpreter to make an unwarranted application of a given text. Careful attention to both near and remote contexts is crucial for understanding the message of Ecclesiastes.

An added feature of Ecclesiastes is its abundant use of repetition such as the repeated emphasis upon meaninglessness and the phrase "under the sun." The inserting of repeated positive ideas may well supply a key to the author's designed structural division (e.g., 2:24–26; 5:18–20; 8:15–17; 11:9–12:8; 12:9–14). In short, rather than being overwhelmed by the shifting themes and observations of the author, the reminder that much of Ecclesiastes is poetry, and an awareness of the author's purpose and strategy will enable the interpreter to enjoy one of the richest literary masterpieces of wisdom literature ever written.

Job

Job is yet another important work in the corpus of biblical wisdom literature. In accordance with other biblical wisdom literature, Job examines the role of God in human affairs. Whereas the theme of Ecclesiastes centered on a search for the ultimate good, Job is concerned with the sufficiency of God. Can he be trusted for every situation in life?

Understanding the basic theme of Job is crucial to the book's interpretation. Although many have sought the basic genre of Job in theodicy—justifying the ways of God—or have held that the book is primarily concerned with why the righteous suffer, understanding the basic purpose of Job as a demonstration of the sufficiency of a sovereign God provides a balanced perspective on the book's message.

Like the Psalms, Proverbs, and the majority of Ecclesiastes, Job is written in poetry. Therefore, the interpreter will find that the conclusions we have reached thus far in the chapter will be largely applicable to the book of Job. Although many genres are present in the book, Job is chiefly an example of disputation literature, containing lengthy *disputation speeches* in which Job's friends debate the cause of Job's plight. Along the way, Job not only carries on a dispute in dialoguing with his friends, but even complains against God (e.g., 10:2–3, 18; 19:7–12; 23:13–17; 30:19–23). To be noted also is Job's autobiographical account of his life prior to his testing (chaps. 29–30).

In the pages of Job, the reader encounters many literary devices. Of particular note are psalmic materials (e.g., 9:5–10; 12:13–28; 37:21–24), many proverbs (e.g., 5:6; 8:11; 12:11–12; etc.), biting satire (12:1–2; 17:10), and the abundant use of rhetorical questions. Recurring motifs (e.g., the call/answer motif; 5:1; 13:22; 14:14–15; 19:26–27; 27:9–10) and themes such as righteousness and justice (about five dozen times), the problem of suffering, and the need for an intermediary (3:23–25; 5:2; 6:13; 9:32–33; 16:18–21; 19:25–26; 33:26–28), as well as the hope for immortality (14:14–15; 19:24–27) fill the pages of Job. Not to be overlooked is the wide-ranging use of imagery throughout the book, including mythopoeic language (language related to myth; e.g., 3:8; 5:7; 7:12; 9:8, 12–14; 18:13–19; 26:12).

As befitting a piece of wisdom literature, the subject of wisdom figures prominently throughout the book, whether the traditional human quest for wisdom (e.g., 8:8–10; 12:12; 15:17–19), acquired specially revealed wisdom (e.g., 4:12–21; 33:14–22), wisdom instruction (32:13–22; 33:31–33), divine wisdom (38:36–41), or even a long treatise on the subject (chap. 28). Structurally, the book of Job is composed around Job's experiences in suffering. The book has a clear plot line beginning with a prologue dealing with Job's testing (chaps. 1–2). The plot develops around the examination of reasons for Job's condition by means of Job's lament (chap. 3) followed by a long section of dialogue in which Job enters into disputation with his three friends who have come ostensibly to comfort him (chaps. 4–27). A movement toward solving the problem of Job's suffering (denouement) begins with Job's speeches concerning his condition (chaps. 28–31) and is continued when a young man named Elihu enters into the discussion with Job (chaps. 32–37). The resolution comes with God's arrival and his revelation to Job of what it means to be God (chaps. 38–41), to which Job responds in repentance and is restored to a happy life before God (chap. 42).

The fact that Job is presented as a story points to the need for employing the features that make up a story such as setting, plot, and characterization. Only then will the interpreter gain a full appreciation of what the author is conveying. When all of this is taken into account, the interpreter will find Job to be not only a rich source of biblical truth with strong advice for godly living but also a literary masterpiece that is thoroughly enjoyable reading.

Wisdom Elsewhere in the Old Testament

Although certain Old Testament books are generally classified as belonging to the genre of wisdom literature, examples of wisdom literature may be found throughout the pages of the Old Testament. Thus wisdom may be seen in the blessings of the patriarchs (e.g., Gen. 49:1–27). Wisdom may also be found in the historical books (e.g., Judg. 5:29–30; 14:14; 1 Sam. 10:12; 24:13; 2 Sam. 12:1–4; 1 Kgs. 3:16–28; 20:11; 2 Kgs. 14:9) and the prophetic books (e.g., Isa. 5:1–7; 10:15; 28:24–29; Hos. 7:8–10; Amos 3:3–8; 6:12).

Likewise, several of the psalms are appropriately designated as wisdom psalms (e.g., Psalms 1; 33; 49; 73). Such psalms exalt God-given wisdom as the key to successful living in the face of life's problems. Addressed to God, the tone of these psalms is declarative, hortatory, and reflective. Proverbs, figures of speech, and imagery as well as illustrations from life and nature are utilized in an effort to get the psalmist's hearers/listeners to heed his advice. Wisdom psalms feature themes such as righteousness versus wickedness, the importance of God's Word, the problem of why the wicked seem to prosper, and the importance of a trust in God that results in a faithful and obedient life. Note, for example, the psalmist's conclusions to an examination of the seeming prosperity of the wicked in Psalm 73:27–28:

> Those who are far from you will perish;
>   you destroy all who are unfaithful to you.
> But as for me, it is good to be near God.
>   I have made the Sovereign Lord my refuge;
>   I will tell of all your deeds.

The above examples suggest that the interpreter must be aware of noting and understanding the many occurrences of wisdom pieces throughout the Old Testament.

Wisdom in the New Testament

People in New Testament times were heirs of a long wisdom tradition. Jesus, of course, was the wise teacher par excellence. His sayings often contained wise observations about life and reality. Thus he contrasts earlier pronouncements and standards with newer, wiser ones (e.g., Matt. 5:21–48; Mark 2:15–17; 8:35–36). Note, for example, Matthew 5:38–42:

> You have heard that it was said, "Eye for eye, and tooth for tooth." But I tell you, do not resist an evil person. If someone strikes you on the right cheek, turn to him the other also. And if someone wants to sue you and take your tunic, let them have your cloak as well. If someone forces you to go one mile, go with him two miles. Give to the one who asks you, and do not turn away from the one who wants to borrow from you.

Jesus's teachings (e.g., Matt. 5:13–14; 7:13–14, 18; 6:24; Luke 12:34) and parables are often interlaced with proverbial material (e.g., Matt. 13:34–35; Luke 14:11, 34; 18:14). Likewise, Jesus's "I am" metaphors speak the language of wisdom (John 6:48; 8:12; 10:7, 9, 11; 11:25; 14:6; 15:1).

Wisdom literature may be noted in the teachings (e.g., Gal. 4:21–31; 6:7; 2 Tim. 2:11–13), parables, and aphorisms of the Epistles (e.g., 1 Cor. 15:33; Phil. 1:21; 1 Tim. 6:10). The book of James bears many of the marks of wisdom (e.g., Jas. 1:17, 19, 22; 2:20–24; 4:13–17; 5:16b). Particularly apropos is James's teaching concerning wisdom (3:13–17), which is concluded with the words, "Who is wise and understanding among you? Let him show it by his good life, by deeds done in the humility that comes from wisdom" (Jas. 3:18). The above examples are but samples of the frequent use of wisdom literature by the writers of the New Testament.

The careful interpreter must therefore be alert to the presence of wisdom not only in the wisdom books of the Old Testament but throughout the Scriptures. This is especially true of proverbial wisdom.

GUIDELINES FOR INTERPRETING BIBLICAL POETRY

1. Note the author's use of parallelism in accordance with the type employed.
2. In psalms and extended poetic pieces, read the entire passage.
3. Look for logical and formal structural devices.
4. Learn to appreciate the author's use of imagery and figures of speech.
5. Look for the author's unifying theme and consider carefully the flow of thought throughout the piece.
6. Using sound exegetical procedures relative to poetic medium, make proper application to the contemporary situation. Consider the impact of the author's emphases to the spiritual life of the reader or hearer.

GUIDELINES FOR INTERPRETING WISDOM LITERATURE

1. Determine the central purpose of any wisdom piece.
2. In Proverbs, note the type involved and the specific advice for godly living in its teaching.
3. Evaluate the general maxims of Proverbs in the light of the proverb's ancient setting as well as in comparison with other scriptural teachings.
4. Remember that proverbs are designed to be general guidelines and are not always applicable to every situation and circumstance.

5. Where instruction is the proverb's chief goal, take seriously the truths and moral standards it is teaching.

6. When interacting with Ecclesiastes, the interpreter should take careful note of both the positive and negative teachings of the book, balancing each in the light of the book's central purpose.

7. In Job, the interpreter must come to grips with the central message of the book and evaluate the contribution of each part to the book's ultimate purpose.

8. In Job, the interpreter should be careful to apply the rules of interpretation relative to storytelling such as setting, plot, and characterization. He should seek to determine what lessons are to be learned from the standpoint of each portion in the dialogue.

9. The interpreter should be alert to occurrences of wisdom throughout the pages of the Bible. Especially to be noted are the teachings of Jesus. One should pay close attention to the theological and moral truths embedded in his teachings as crucial for the development of Christian character and conduct.

10. In every wisdom piece of literature, determine the chief goal of the instruction. Be careful to evaluate it in the light of the total scriptural revelation in order that proper application of its truths and moral lessons may be applied properly to contemporary living.

KEY WORDS

A fortiori argument, Alliteration, Allusion, Antithetic parallelism, Anthropomorphism, Apophthegm, Assonance, Bicolon, Bookending, Chiasm, Concreteness, Denouement, Ellipsis, Emblematic parallelism, Hypocatastasis, *Inclusio*, Ladder parallelism, Monocolon, Parallelism, Progressive parallelism, Proverb, Similar parallelism, Staircase parallelism, Stanza, Stitching, Strophe, Terrace pattern parallelism, Terseness, Theodicy, Tricolon, Zoomorphism.

ASSIGNMENTS

1. Identify the types of parallelism in the following Psalms:
   a. Psalm 1
   b. Psalm 96:1–3, 7–9, 11–13

2. Conduct a basic interpretation of the book of Job. Discuss any historical details, sketch literary features such as setting, plot, and characterization, and explore the theology (teaching about God) provided in this book.

KEY RESOURCES

Bullock, C. Hassell. *An Introduction to the Poetic Books of the Old Testament*. Chicago: Moody, 1979.
Estes, Daniel J. *Handbook on the Wisdom Books and Psalms*. Grand Rapids: Baker, 2005.

CHAPTER 7 OBJECTIVES

1. To discuss the nature of the prophet and his role.
2. To introduce and survey the various subgenres within prophecy.
3. To suggest tools for determining the overall framework of a given book of prophecy as well as the make-up of individual units.

CHAPTER 7 OUTLINE

A. Nature of Prophecy

B. Subgenres of Prophecy

C. Prophecy Outside of the Old Testament Prophetic Books

D. Guidelines for Interpreting Prophecy

E. Key Words

F. Assignments

G. Key Resources

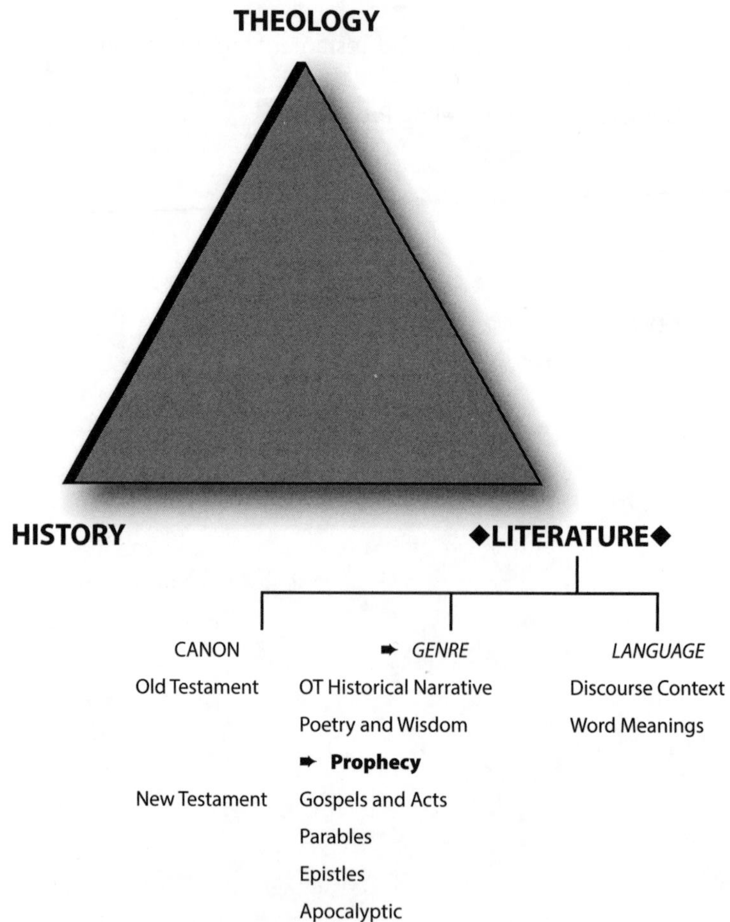
THEOLOGY
HISTORY
◆LITERATURE◆
CANON
Old Testament
New Testament
➨ GENRE
OT Historical Narrative
Poetry and Wisdom
➨ Prophecy
Gospels and Acts
Parables
Epistles
Apocalyptic
LANGUAGE
Discourse Context
Word Meanings

Chapter 7

BACK TO THE FUTURE: PROPHECY

NATURE OF PROPHECY

WE ARE MAKING GOOD PROGRESS in our interpretive journey through the canonical landscape. We have already gotten acquainted with sound principles for interpreting Old Testament historical narrative as well as poetry and wisdom literature. The last major portion of the Old Testament is made up of almost a dozen and a half prophetic books: the four major prophets (Isaiah, Jeremiah/Lamentations, Ezekiel, and Daniel), and the twelve so-called "Minor Prophets" (Hosea, Joel, Amos, Obadiah, Jonah, Micah, Nahum, Habakkuk, Zephaniah, Haggai, Zechariah, and Malachi; for the historical setting of individual prophetic Old Testament books, see chart 2.2. in chapter 2 above).

The understanding of prophecy, particularly the Old Testament prophetic books, seems at first a daunting task. The English reader is confronted with a literature that has no direct parallels in his own language. Moreover, interpreters are introduced to a large and seemingly bewildering array of material to assimilate. They can encounter obscure messages concerning people and places with strange names and customs. They are called on to grapple with texts utilizing a rich kaleidoscope of literary figures, motifs, themes, and symbols.

Although the message the interpreter reads can be written in either prose or poetry, the fact that it was first delivered orally is reflected in the elevated and at times impassioned language. There is also an urgency of tone and theme. Accordingly, some have gone so far as to say that prophecy is basically poetic. Perhaps this is only natural due to the fact that the biblical prophets were people called of God to proclaim his messages. Indeed, the most common word for "prophet" carries with it the sense of his call. Also, the common terms for his task emphasize his mission as a proclaimer of God's message.

As noted, the prophet's message was originally delivered orally. Therefore, those of us who now read the inscripturated written messages must attempt to *hear* as well as *read* what the prophet has said, which involves not only the eye but the ear and the heart. This is because we have entered the ancient world of the spoken word. Some prophecies even have a setting that involves people and times that lie in the future from the vantage point of the prophet's own day. This, in turn, adds a further dimension for the interpreter, who must look for the full meaning of the passage in a subsequent fulfillment.

Although all of this presents many challenges to us as readers of prophecy, the realization that these prophets were real people sent by God to people in a real (albeit ancient) world gives us assurance that the understanding of their messages is a realizable goal. The prophetic word was designed to be relevant to everyday life. Even more importantly, it was and is God's Word, which is designed to instruct people concerning his nature and standards for human conduct. Therefore, it has application for readers of every age. Understanding and effectively communicating biblical prophecy therefore requires a strategic grasp of the relevant principles related to interpreting this challenging, but rewarding genre of Scripture.

SUBGENRES OF PROPHECY

Many types and forms make up the genre of biblical prophecy. Great fluidity and some overlap exist. Therefore, the assigning of a specific subgenre label to a given portion of prophecy may lack absolute precision. In addition, a passage may include more than one type of subgenre. In every case, we must determine the basic subgenre on the basis of both form and the identification of the author's primary purpose in the full context.

Comparison with other prophecies of a similar nature may also help. Such beginning steps in approaching a particular passage are necessary ones.

There is wide agreement that the two most prominent subgenres of prophecy are those dealing with judgment and salvation. Because in our view prophecy consists basically of proclamation, we shall use the terms "announcements of judgment" and "salvation oracles."

Announcements of Judgment

General Characteristics

Announcements of judgment account for the preponderance of Old Testament prophecy. The pronouncing of judgment can also be embedded within other subgenres that we will consider. Formal announcements of judgment consist of two main elements:

1. *accusation*, stating the Lord's charges for which judgment must come
2. *announcement of a specific judgment* to be levied

Amos 2:6–16 may serve as an example. Here the Lord lists the various charges he has against his people (vv. 6–12) and then warns them of impending doom to come (vv. 13–16). Announcements of judgment may also include a call to hear the word of the Lord (e.g., Amos 3:1; 5:1). Note the following example:

7.1. PROPHETIC ANNOUNCEMENT OF JUDGMENT	
Call	Hear this word
Accusation	You cows of Bashan on Mount Samaria, you women who oppress the poor and crush the needy and say to your husbands, "Bring us some drinks!"
Announcement	The Sovereign LORD has sworn by his holiness: "The time will surely come when you will be taken away with hooks, the last of you with fishhooks, you will each go straight out through breaks in the wall, and you will be cast out toward Harmon," declares the LORD. (Amos 4:1–3)

Other features can include a plea for repentance and the rewards of God's blessings for doing so. Thus the prophet Joel warned the people of his day that the present disastrous conditions in the land due to the locust plague were but a precursor to a more serious invasion of the land (1:1–2:11). He therefore called on the people to repent (2:12–14). Then, having further urged the people to call a formal ceremony of repentance and reconsecration to the Lord (vv. 15–17), he enumerated the resultant blessings of the Lord for doing so (vv. 18–27).

Such themes appear abundantly throughout the prophets as they called God's people to vital religion in the face of God's threatened judgment. Duvall and Hays (2005: 373) point out that prophetic messages "can be boiled down to three basic points, each of which is important to the message of the prophets:

1. You have broken the covenant; you had better repent!

2. No repentance? Then judgment!

3. Yet, there is hope beyond the judgment for a glorious, future restoration."

The prophets also have messages of judgment for other nations. For example, note Nahum's strong denunciation of the Assyrian capital of Nineveh:

Woe to the city of blood, full of lies,
  full of plunder, never without victims!
The crack of whips, the clatter of wheels,
  galloping horses, and jolting chariots!
Charging cavalry, flashing swords and glittering spears!
Many casualties, piles of dead,
bodies without number,
  people stumbling over the corpses
all because of the wanton lust of a harlot,
  alluring, the mistress of sorceries,
who enslaved nations by her prostitution
  and peoples by her witchcraft. (Nah. 3:1–4)

Nahum goes on to deliver the Lord's message of severe judgment against the city (vv. 5–7). Basically, the foreign nations are condemned for two reasons: (1) their treatment of God's people, a crime that constituted an attack against the Lord himself; and (2) their inhumane treatment of many nations (e.g., Isa. 14:12–17; Nah. 3:19).

Prophecies relative to the foreign nations are often gathered in large collections (e.g., Isa. 13–23; Jer. 46–51; Ezek. 25–32; Amos 1:3–2:5; Zeph. 2:4–15). In some cases, these are arranged geographically in relation to the land of Israel. For example, Zephaniah's prophecies move from west of Judah (Philistia) to the east (Moab and Ammon), then south and north (Cush, Assyria). Ezekiel inverts Zephaniah's order, moving from east (Transjordan) to west (Philistia) and then north to south (Phoenicia, Egypt).

Woe Oracle

A specific type of an announcement of judgment involves the woe oracle. Woe oracles were traditionally made up of three elements:

1. invective (the pronouncement of woe)
2. threat (the details of coming judgment)
3. criticism (the reason for the coming judgment)

Typical examples may be found in Habakkuk 2:6–20. Note Habakkuk's opening taunt against the Chaldeans (or Neo-Babylonians):

7.2. WOE ORACLE	
Invective	Woe to him who piles up stolen goods and makes himself wealthy by extortion! How long must this go on?
Threat	Will not your debtors suddenly arise? Will they not wake up and make you tremble? Then you will become their victim.
Criticism	Because you have plundered many nations, the peoples who are left will plunder you. For you have shed man's blood; you have destroyed lands and cities and everyone in them. (Hab. 2:6–8)

Lament

Another subgenre is the lament. Lament can be understood in two ways. On the one hand, it involves prayer to God (e.g. Psalm 22; Habakkuk 1–2). On the other hand, lament constitutes a statement of distress or mourning, with the latter type being the one further discussed here. In addition, laments are found not only in prophetic literature but also in the Psalms and wisdom literature such as the book of Job, and in portions of the New Testament (such as the Gospels), as well.

Amos 5:1–17 is clearly labeled as a lament. Here the judgment of Israel is pronounced as though it had already happened—it is an accomplished fact (vv. 1–2). The threatened judgment is amplified with the prediction of how that judgment will play out (v. 3). There follows a long list of accusations against God's people for which their punishment must come, together with a plea for repentance (vv. 6–15). The prophet then returns to the prediction of judgment (vv. 16–17).

Another classic case of lament occurs in Ezekiel 19. Here the call to lament precedes a catalogue of accusations against Judah's leadership for which judgment had come. The judgment in this case is not represented as something certain to happen in the future but as a past reality resulting in the present misery. Nevertheless, the elements of accusation and announced judgment are still present even though the judgment is past.

Covenant Lawsuit

Another type of judgment speech is the covenant lawsuit, in which God summons his people to appear before him for covenant violations. Such announcements of judgment usually contain the summoning of witnesses, a list of the charges against the accused (or indictment), and an announcement of punishment (or sentencing). Micah 6:1–16 provides an excellent example. Here, the Lord initiates a case against his people, summoning the mountains to serve as a witness:

> Listen to what the LORD says:
> "Stand up, plead your case before the mountains;
> let the hills hear what you have to say.
> Hear, O mountains, the LORD's accusation;
> Listen, you everlasting foundations of the earth.

For the LORD has a case against his people;
He is lodging a charge against Israel." (Mic. 6:1–2)

He then launches into a long list of charges against his people, in which he reminds them of his past goodness to them and calls attention to their present unfaithfulness (vv. 3–12). In so doing, he even includes a short imagined dialogue in which the people's projected response is given together with God's answer (vv. 6–7). A final divine sentence of judgment follows (vv. 13–15), accompanied by a concluding summation (v. 16):

You have observed the statutes of Omri
and all the practices of Ahab's house,
and you have followed their traditions.
Therefore I will give you over to ruin
and your people to derision;
you will hear the scorn of the nations.

Salvation Oracles

The second most prominent subgenre of prophecy revolves around those prophecies that deal with God's saving work. You will note that in many of the cases cited here judgment and salvation occur side by side. Moreover, a great many of these deal with Israel's projected final state.

Promise of Deliverance

Salvation prophecies customarily deal with God's deliverance after a time of experiencing his judgment. Frequently, you will detect a pattern of sin, judgment, repentance, and restoration. For example, Ezekiel informs his hearers that they have suffered the judgment of captivity and exile because of Israel's sin. Yet God will restore his people to their land and give them a new heart to serve the Lord (Ezek. 11:14–21).

Somewhat earlier, Jeremiah warned of the arrival of desperate circumstances (Jer. 16:1–9). God's coming chastisement would involve going into captivity because of the people's long-standing flirtation with various sinful practices (vv. 10–13). Nevertheless, there would come a time when their punishment would end and God would restore them to the Promised Land:

> "However, the days are coming," declares the LORD, "when men will no longer say, 'As surely as the LORD lives, who brought the Israelites up out of Egypt,' but they will say, 'As surely as the LORD lives, who brought the Israelites up out of the land of the north and out of the countries where he had banished them.' For I will restore them to the land I gave their forefathers." (vv. 14–15)

Here we see that the promise of deliverance/salvation is wedded to the motif of the new exodus (cf. Isa. 43:16–21; 48:20–21). It should be noted that not only is the exodus motif prominent in the Old Testament, it culminates in a new, greater exodus. Such a promise may be found, as in the Jeremiah passage just cited, in many Old Testament prophecies as well as in numerous New Testament texts. In most cases, the historical exodus from Egypt serves as an assurance of future similar instances of divine deliverance. Often it is difficult to know whether a given text speaks of a future that is close at hand or distant or both (e.g., Isa. 52:4–13). Often near and distant futures blend into one another (see also Isa. 61:1–3; Ezek. 20:32–38). Note for example, as in Jeremiah 16:14–15 above.

Kingdom Oracles

A great many salvation oracles look to the distant or end-time future, including those featuring the new exodus motif (e.g., Isa. 51:4–11; Jer. 23:3–8; Ezek. 37:18–20). We call such prophecies "kingdom oracles," for they deal with the establishment of Israel's final kingdom. Kingdom oracles not only tell of Israel's great future deliverance and return to the land but contain an announcement of universal judgment. These judgments often deal with the future in such a way that they predict a series of judgments. The last judgment completes the series and serves to prepare for the final era of blessing.

This judgment differs from other announcements of judgment in that it is universal in scope and features such dramatic details as cataclysmic phenomena in the natural world and widespread devastation on earth. Typical of these is Joel 3:9–21. Here the prophet proclaims the need for the nation to prepare for war (vv. 9–11). It is no less than the time of God's great judgment on rebellious earthly forces (vv. 12–13). Through the clamor of war and natural upheaval God will deliver his people (vv. 14–17). He will then dwell in their midst and bring in everlasting peace and prosperity (vv. 18–21).

Other prophets give a similar picture of these great events. Zephaniah calls this era the great "day of the LORD" (Zeph. 1:14–18). It is a time for God's great judgment against this wicked world (Zeph. 3:8). He will initiate a final new exodus of his people, restore them to the land, bless them, and bring in everlasting happiness:

> "At that time I will gather you; at that time I will bring you home. I will give you honor and praise among all the peoples of the earth when I restore your fortunes before your very eyes," declares the LORD. (Zeph. 3:20)

The careful student of prophecy can recognize kingdom oracles by the presence of both announcements of judgment and promises of salvation blended together in a future, universal setting. He can also recognize that at times details of the Lord's predicted judgment may have an anticipatory fulfillment somewhere within a series of God's future judgments without exhausting the full prediction. Because of this, God's people can find applications to various events in relation to the culmination of the full prophecy in the end times. In any case, even though kingdom oracles apply primarily to the distant future, they provide an admonition to believers of all ages to live holy lives in anticipation of God's final consummation of earth's history.

Apocalyptic

Kingdom oracles have also been noted for their inclusion of dramatic events, which often record phenomena of a cosmic dimension accompanied by a sudden drastic divine intervention. In such cases, the text reads much like the apocalyptic literature that became so prominent in the period after the completion of the Old Testament.

John Collins (1984: 4) penned the classic definition of *apocalyptic* as "a genre of revelatory literature with a narrative framework, in which a revelation is mediated by an otherworldly being to a human recipient, disclosing a transcendent reality which is both temporal insofar as it envisages eschatological salvation, and spatial insofar as it involves another, supernatural world." Among the many features of apocalyptic, these are especially prevalent:

1. This present world is evil and without hope and can be remedied only by sovereign divine intervention.

2. The issue of the ages is essentially a spiritual battle between good and evil.

3. The Lord's intervention will entail catastrophic events.

4. Following the time of God's universal judgment, a final new age of peace, prosperity, and righteousness will be ushered in.

Apocalyptic literature customarily is presented via visions of the future and contains graphic images, fantastic other-worldly settings and scenes, and an abundant use of symbols, such as the use of numbers, colors, and animals.

Daniel (especially chapters 7–12) is commonly considered the apocalyptic book of the Old Testament. Fully developed apocalypses, however, appeared after the Old Testament era. They were especially prominent from the second century B.C. to the early second century A.D. Unlike standard biblical prophecy, apocalypses were written in prose rather than poetry. By this time, their use of the special characteristics mentioned above enables us to think of apocalyptic as a distinct literary genre. Representative examples include 1 and 2 Enoch, 2 and 3 Baruch, 4 Ezra, and the New Testament book of Revelation.

We consider apocalyptic here because some have suggested that apocalyptic and apocalypses occur in the Old Testament. Frequently mentioned passages include Isaiah 24–27, Ezekiel 38–39, Daniel 7, Joel 2:28–32; 3:9–17, and Zechariah 1–6; 12–14. Even a casual glance at several of these texts confirms that they contain some of the features found in classic apocalyptic literature. Old Testament prophecies betray a gradually increasing use of such features, especially toward the end of the Old Testament canon (e.g., Ezekiel 38–39; Daniel 7; Zechariah 1–6, 14). It is safe to conclude, therefore, that the apocalyptic genre, which was based upon Old Testament precedents and came into full bloom subsequent to the Old Testament era, was largely of Hebrew origin and had its beginning in Old Testament kingdom oracles.

Because the Scriptures contain both a distinct apocalypse (the book of Revelation) and passages that utilize apocalyptic language both in the

Old Testament (e.g., Daniel 7) and New Testament (e.g., Matthew 24), the student of prophecy needs to have a basic acquaintance with the nature and features of the apocalyptic genre if he or she is to interpret the text correctly. We suggest the following guidelines:

1. Acquaint yourself with the characteristics of the apocalyptic genre.
2. Note the setting of the passage both in its historical dimension and contextual orientation.
3. Distinguish carefully the use of symbols, themes, and figures of speech from their standard literal sense.
4. Determine the author's purpose in using apocalyptic features.
5. As with other types of prophecy, try to place yourself in the oral setting of those who first heard the message. Use historical imagination and engage not only your mind but also your heart and affections.
6. In teaching the passage to others, be sure to emphasize the spiritual component of its message, particularly in the ultimate resolution of the divine purpose it presents.
7. Above all, make the application of the passage relevant to the lives of those whom you are attempting to reach.

Instructional Accounts

You've probably noticed that in the two subgenres we've considered there was often an element of instruction. Here again, we note that prophetic speeches are not always one-dimensional. God's prophet may weave two or more literary types together in achieving his purposes. Therefore, the interpreter should not be surprised to find diverse types embedded within the basic type of prophecy. We examine here those passages where instruction is clearly the main feature and general purpose of the context.

Disputation

We turn, first of all, to the disputation. The most common elements of disputation speeches are: declaration, discussion, and refutation. Of the several examples that could be cited (e.g., Ezekiel 18; Amos 3:3–8), perhaps Malachi is best known for using this literary device. Nearly the whole of his prophecy is presented as a disputation between the Lord and his people. Here, the dispute takes the form of an imagined dialogue between them. Note the following portion from the first chapter of Malachi:

7.3. DISPUTATION	
Discussion	"A son honors his father and a servant his master. If I am a father, where is the honor due me? If I am a master, where is the respect due me?" says the LORD Almighty.
Declaration	"It is you, O priests, who show contempt for my name."
Refutation	"But you ask, 'How have we shown contempt for your name?'" (Mal. 1:6–7)

The passage goes on with discussion, refutation, and counter-refutation and is concluded with the lesson to be learned: only pure offerings are acceptable and honoring to God's great name. Note, for example, the Lord's words through his prophet in verse eleven:

> "My name will be great among the nations from the rising to the setting of the sun. In every place incense and pure offerings will be brought to my name, because my name will be great among the nations," says the LORD Almighty.

In keeping with his presentation, Malachi often uses a satiric tone to accomplish his objectives. We will shortly say more concerning satire.

Exhortation/Warning Speeches

We turn next to prophecy in which an exhortation toward repentance or reform occurs. Here the hearers or readers are urged to follow the Lord and his standards. These instructional messages can be introduced with a call to hear the word of the Lord and contain motive, which encourages a favorable response. The motive may be positive (reward) or negative (warning of the consequences of the present lifestyle).

An example of the former case is Isaiah's message of exhortation to the exiles (Isa. 55:1–5):

7.4. POSITIVE EXHORTATION	
Call	Come all who are thirsty, come to the waters; And you who have no money, come buy and eat! Come, buy wine and milk without money and without cost.
Exhortation	Why spend money on what is not bread, and your labor on what does not satisfy? Listen to me, and eat what is good, and your soul will delight in the richest of fare.
Call	Give ear and come to me; hear me, that your soul may live.
Motive	I will make an everlasting covenant with you; my faithful love promised to David. (Isa. 55:1–3)

The blessings attended to that covenant continue as added incentive in verses four and five.

Jeremiah 44:24–28 serves as an example of the negative response. Here, however, the exhortation is implied in the satire of verse twenty-five:

7.5. NEGATIVE EXHORTATION	
Call	Hear the word of the LORD, all you people of Judah in Egypt.
Exhortation	This is what the LORD Almighty, the God of Israel, says: "You and your wives have shown by your actions what you promised when you said: 'We will certainly carry out the vows we made to burn incense to and pour out drink offerings to the Queen of Heaven.'" Go ahead then, do what you promised! Keep your vows! But hear the word of the LORD, all Jews living in Egypt: "I swear by my great name," says the LORD, "that no one from Judah living anywhere in Egypt will ever again invoke my name or swear, 'As surely as the LORD lives.'" (Jer. 44:24–25)

The motive follows in a warning as to the tragic consequences of Israel's past worship practices. Worst of all, the Jewish exiles in Egypt would die with only a small remnant ever able to return to Judah (vv. 26–28).

Both reward and warning may be present in a single context. Typical of this is Jeremiah 7:2–7a:

7.6. REWARD AND WARNING EXHORTATION	
Call	Hear the word of the LORD, all you people of Judah who come through these gates to worship the LORD.
Exhortation	This is what the LORD Almighty, the God of Israel, says: "Reform your ways and your actions, and I will let you live in this place. Do not trust in deceptive words and say, 'This is the Temple of the LORD, the Temple of the LORD!'
Motive	If you really change your ways and your actions and deal with each other justly, if you do not oppress the alien, the fatherless or the widow and do not shed innocent blood in this place, and if you do not follow other gods to your own harm, then I will let you live in this place, in the land I gave your forefathers forever and ever."

The discourse that follows contains instructions concerning the objectionable nature of their present behavior (vv. 7b–11). Similar to Shiloh (vv. 12–15), the inhabitants of Jerusalem ought not to assume that they can carry on their abominable syncretistic worship and still expect to escape God's judgment.

The interpreter should note that in these verses, prophetic instruction and judgment speeches are combined with disputation and satiric tone. The goal is to motivate the people toward genuine repentance and reformation. Such a mixture of literary devices is common enough in Old Testament prophecy (e.g., Isa. 42:18–25; Ezek. 18:25–32; Mic. 3:1–4).

Instructional messages of exhortation or warning may be directed toward individuals, even kings (Jer. 22:1–6). Messages to false prophets (Jer. 29:20–23) or decadent priests (Amos 7:16–17) are delivered with strong words of warning. Often, the motivation toward reformation is omitted, for the individuals are so guilty that they are doomed to judgment.

Satire

Satire can be thought of as containing four basic elements:

1. an object of attack—whether a particular thing, position, person, or the ills of society in general;

2. a satiric vehicle—ranging anywhere from a simple metaphor to a full-blown story;

3. a satiric tone—displaying the author's attitude toward the object of his attack; and

4. a satiric norm—a standard, whether stated or implied, by which the author's criticism is being applied.

As mentioned, you can discern satiric elements in a great many of the prophetic messages. This is especially true of announcements of judgment and instructional accounts. Satire occurs in virtually every prophetic book. It is perhaps erroneous to speak of satire as a subgenre of prophecy. Most concede that formal satire originated with the Romans, but elements of satire already figure prominently in the account of Jonah's spiritual odyssey (particularly, chaps. 1 and 4).

No less than Jonah, Amos is replete with satire. Amos even includes an obituary notice of the northern kingdom before its fall: "Fallen is virgin Israel, never to rise again, deserted in her own land, with no one to lift her up" (Amos 5:2). Not to be forgotten is Malachi's abundant use of satire in his disputation with an apostate society (e.g., 1:6–14; 2:7–9, 13–14, 17; 3:13–15).

In each case, satire is most at home in contexts dealing with judgment. The widespread presence of satire in prophecy should alert interpreters that they must come to grips with its purposes to grasp the full force of the context.

Wisdom Sayings

Instruction may also take the form of proverbial wisdom. In criticizing Assyria's arrogance at thinking that it had been able to spread its power across the Near East by virtue of its own strength, Isaiah delivers God's judgment by way of a wise saying:

> Does the ax raise itself above him who swings it, or the saw boast against him who uses it? As if a rod were to wield him who lifts it up, or a club brandish him who is not wood! (Isa.10:15)

The Assyrian king needed to understand that his success came only through the power of Israel's God.

Jeremiah and Ezekiel chide their people for suggesting that their punishment is due to the sins of those who went before them rather than their own. For example, Ezekiel reports that the people were saying, "The fathers eat sour grapes, and the children's teeth are set on edge" (Ezek. 18:2). Apart from containing a proverbial wisdom component, the statement also drips with satire and irony. Hosea concludes his prophecy with a challenge to walk before God with words reminiscent of Proverbs 10:29:

> Who is wise? He will realize these things.
> Who is discerning? He will understand them.
> The ways of the LORD are right;
>   the righteous walk in them,
>   but the rebellious stumble in them. (Hos. 14:9)

Here, as in Jeremiah 21:8, we see a reflection of the familiar proverbial teaching of the two ways (cf. Prov. 4:14–19). The theme of the two ways became a well-known biblical motif (cf. Deut. 30:19; Psalm 1) and was also used by the sect at Qumran (e.g., 1 QS 3:20–22), and even Jesus (Matt. 7:13–14), as well as the early Christian church (e.g., *Didache* 1–6).

The prophets often used wise sayings in their admonitions. Thus they appear in exhortation or warning speeches to encourage God's people to righteous living and to impress on them the dangers of disobedience. The godless were warned of certain judgment should they continue in their present course of action.

Prophetic Narratives

The prophetic books include several types of narrative accounts. These give details of the prophet's life and work. Two types have been suggested.

The first are *vocation reports* (e.g., Jer. 1:4–19; Amos 7:14–17), telling of the prophet's call and commission to the prophetic office. These serve to inform and assure hearers that the prophets have an authentic role as God's spokespersons. The variation in the call of individual prophets serves to illustrate the different callings extended to God's servants throughout the ages.

A second type includes *biographical* (e.g., Jeremiah 26–29; 34–45) and *autobiographical* (cf. Ezek. 24:15–27) details concerning the prophet's life. They provide further instruction to God's servants as to what they may face during their ministry.

Although traditionally not reckoned among the prophetic books, the prophet Daniel obviously had the gift of prophecy. The first six chapters of the book of Daniel give details of Daniel's being carried away captive and his life at a foreign court. These court narratives are of two types: (1) the court contest—in which Daniel's wisdom is demonstrated as superior to the king's advisors (chaps. 2, 4–5); and (2) the court conflict—in which Daniel's three friends retain their spiritual purity in the face of formal opposition (chaps. 3, 6).

Three other types of prophetic narratives may be noted. In some situations, a prophet is called upon to *dramatize his message by way of symbolic acts.* For example, Isaiah went about naked and barefoot for three years to signify the defeat of Egypt and Ethiopia (Isaiah 20); Jeremiah walked the streets of Jerusalem with a yoke around his neck to symbolize the Babylonian conquest of the nations, including Judah (Jeremiah 27–28). Ezekiel performed numerous symbolic acts (Ezek. 3:15; 4:1–17; 12:1–70), and Hosea was even instructed to marry a prostitute as part of his prophetic calling (Hosea 1–3).

Occasionally, we meet the so-called *prophetic confessions* in which a prophet acknowledges his own or his people's sins. Thus Daniel prays:

> O LORD, the great and awesome God, who keeps his covenant of love with all who love him and obey his commands, we have sinned and done wrong. We have been wicked and have rebelled; we have turned away from your commands and laws. We have not listened to your servants the prophets, who spoke in your name to our kings, our princes and our fathers, and to all the people of the land (Dan. 9:4–6).

Not to be forgotten are the *historical narratives telling of outstanding public events* during the prophet's time of ministry (e.g., Isa. 36–39; Jer. 39–44; 52; Ezek. 24:1–2). In a sense, all of these prophetic narratives may be viewed as subtypes of instructional accounts designed to provide spiritual instruction for God's servants.

Miscellaneous Subgenres

Vision/Dream Reports

Several other subgenres remain to be considered. Vision reports are instances in which the prophet receives God's message in a vision, which he in turn is to proclaim to his people. At least three types can be discerned.

1. We have noted previously that some kingdom oracles contain elements that partake strongly of the apocalypses that would become so prominent in the post Old Testament era. Here God's plans for his people and earth's future history are delivered in a vision that contains much symbolism and often fantastic imagery (e.g., Daniel 7).

2. Some vision reports deal with predictions of the less distant future (e.g., Daniel 8) or give much-needed instruction for God's people (e.g., Zechariah 1–6). On the basis of two visions, Amos warns the people of his day concerning the certainty of God's imminent judgment (Amos 7:1–6; 7:7–9; see also Jer. 42:7–12).

3. Isaiah (chap. 6) and Ezekiel (chaps. 1–3) both receive their calls to the prophetic ministry through a vision. Some vision reports feature the presence of angelic intermediaries (e.g., Dan. 8:13–27; Zechariah 2–6).

Prophetic Hymns/Songs

The prophetic books also frequently contain distinctive poetic pieces (e.g., Isa. 5:1–2; 12:4–6; 42:10–12; 52:7–10; Jer. 20:13; 31:7; 33:11; Dan. 2:20–23; Amos 4:1–3; 5:8–9). Poetic songs could comprise extensive portions, (e.g., Isaiah 26; Habakkuk 3). Habakkuk includes a long epic section telling of Israel's exodus from Egypt (Hab. 3:3–15).

Prophetic Prayers

The third chapter of Habakkuk is termed a prayer, and the subscription indicates that it has been set to music for liturgical purposes. You will also be able to identify several other prayers among the prophetic books (e.g., Isa. 37:14–20; 38:2; Jer. 32:16–25; Dan. 9:4–19; Jonah 2:1–9).

Prophetic Letters

In a few cases, we possess records of letters within the prophetic corpus (e.g., Jer. 29:24–28, 29–32). Such cases need to be interpreted in accordance with the normal principles of epistolary literature including careful regard to content and context.

PROPHECY OUTSIDE OF THE OLD TESTAMENT PROPHETIC BOOKS

In the Old Testament

Before moving on to list some specific principles for interpreting prophecy, we should point out that prophecy can be found in the Bible outside the books of the classical prophets. Indeed, in the Hebrew canon the books from Joshua to Kings are termed the Former Prophets. Accordingly, the interpreter may expect to find prophetic messages in the pages of these books. Here, we meet many prophets such as Nathan, Elijah, and Elisha. Nathan conveyed God's intention to David that the Lord would establish David's lineage as a royal dynasty in perpetuity (2 Samuel 7:11–16). Elijah and Elisha delivered many messages from the Lord, in addition to performing miraculous deeds.

Prophecy was known even before the Former Prophets. Among the many examples that could be cited, we note just three. In blessing his sons, Jacob prophesied their future. Especially well known is his prediction that "the scepter will not depart from Judah, nor the ruler's staff from between his feet, until he comes to whom it belongs" (Gen. 49:10; cf. Ezek. 21:27).

Within the oracles of Balaam found in Numbers 23 and 24 is the prophecy that "a star will come out of Jacob, a scepter will rise out of Israel" (Num. 24:17; cf. Matt. 2:2; Luke 1:78; Rev. 22:16).

Moses delivered God's promise to raise up a prophet who would speak the very words of the Lord (Deut. 18:15–18). By this prophecy, Moses predicted the coming of a series of prophets culminating in the Messiah, the greatest of all prophets.

The existence of these and other passages outside of the prophetic books (the so-called Latter Prophets) demonstrates that the interpreter should not only be aware of their existence but be prepared to interpret them in accordance with the normal subgenres and principles of prophecy.

In the New Testament

The literature of the New Testament mentions the existence and ministry of many prophets or persons engaging in prophetic ministry or conveying prophetic utterances. Examples include Elizabeth (Luke 1:41–45), Zechariah (Luke 1:67–69), Simeon (Luke 2:25–35), Anna (Luke 2:36–38), Agabus (Acts 11:27–28; 13:1; 21:10), Judas and Silas (Acts 15:32), and the daughters of Philip (Acts 21:9). Prophecy was considered an important gift in the early church (cf. 1 Cor. 12:28; Eph. 2:20; 3:5; 4:11). John the Baptist was recognized as a prophet by his contemporaries (Matt. 11:9; 14:5). Like the Old Testament prophets, he employed instructional prophecy, exhorting his hearers to repent and warning them of impending judgment should they fail to do so (Matt. 3:1–12).

Jesus was the prophet *par excellence* (Matt. 21:10–11; John 6:14; 7:40, 52; Acts 3:19–23), yet his speeches were not collected into a book of prophecies. The major theme in his prophetic pronouncements was his teaching concerning the kingdom, which he viewed as entailing both a present and a future dimension. With his presence among the people, the kingdom was now already here, but in its full realization it was yet to come (Mark 1:15; 8:38; John 4:23; 5:24–29; 16:25–26, 32). Jesus also put greater emphasis on the universality of the kingdom over against the strict exclusivity of Israel (Matt. 21:43–44; Luke 12:8–10; John 3:14–21). In this, we see the outworking of the age-old promise to Abraham (Gen. 12:3).

Another important aspect in Jesus's teaching pertained to life in the kingdom (Matt. 5:43–44; Luke 17:33; 22:26–27; John 4:23; 12:24–25). Jesus taught the need for essential righteousness, and thus the need for repentance (Matt. 5:20, 48; 6:33). Where repentance was lacking, judgment lay imminently in the future (Matt. 12:26–37). In such teachings, Jesus at times employed the familiar "woe formula" in announcing judgment. For example, in his warning to the cities of Chorazin, Bethsaida, and Capernaum he used the typical elements of invective, criticism, and threat (Matt. 11:21–24). Like the Old Testament prophets, Jesus's prophetic utterances included elements of forth-telling (present pronouncements) as well as a foretelling (future predictions).

Similar to the message of the Old Testament prophets, Jesus's teaching concerning the kingdom at times focused on the coming of the future kingdom. Of particular importance in this regard is his Olivet Discourse (Matt. 24:3–44; Mark 13; Luke 21:7–33). In this discourse, the emphasis is on judgment blended with apocalyptic-type events such as cataclysmic disasters, worldwide war, terrible tribulation, and the glorious return of Christ.

Although no precise salvation and end-time blessing is included here as in the Old Testament kingdom oracles, such features are found elsewhere in Jesus's teaching (e.g., Matt. 11:25–29; 19:28–29; 22:1–14; 25:21; Luke 22:29–30).

Among his announcements of judgment, Jesus also predicted the destruction of Jerusalem (Matt. 23:37–39; Luke 13:34–35). Not only will you find here the standard elements of judgment: address/call, accusation, and announcement, but in addition the prophecy has the form of a lament. This, of course, is another familiar subgenre of announcements of judgment. It should be noted that Jesus predicted his own suffering, death, and resurrection, as well as his return (e.g., Matt. 16:21–28; Mark 8:31–9:1; Luke 9:22–27). In these predictions, the interpreter may discern many Old Testament motifs such as the suffering Messiah, the third-day theme, the reality of resurrection, and the establishment of the final kingdom.

Although he did not claim to be a prophet, the apostle Paul also exercised the prophetic gift. Paul was certainly aware of the fact that he had the gift of prophecy (e.g., 1 Cor. 14:37–38; 2 Cor. 12:9). In a sense, Paul's whole ministry was akin to that of the Old Testament prophets. Thus he, too, engaged in both forth-telling and foretelling. With regard to the former, Paul's writings are closely related to the Old Testament instructional subgenres that emphasized exhortation or the giving of assurance. For example, Paul instructed the believers in Rome regarding the inclusion of Gentiles in God's plan of salvation (Rom. 11:25–26). At times, Paul issued warnings concerning the expected results of ungodly behavior (Gal. 5:21; 1 Thess. 4:2–8). This included Christians associating with those whose conduct was disruptive (2 Thess. 3:6). Paul also engaged in predictive prophecy, foretelling matters such as his persecution and sufferings (1 Thess. 3:4), details regarding believers' future resurrection (1 Cor. 15:50–57), and the circumstances and conditions in the last days (1 Tim. 4:1–5; cf. 2 Tim. 3:1–9).

Whether in forth-telling or foretelling, Paul's prophetic words contain a great deal of information and instruction, which is aimed at encouraging his fellow believers. Indeed, there is a strong hortatory element in Paul's prophetic speeches. Much like the Old Testament autobiographical accounts, Paul often reports instances in which God revealed to him what lay before him in his future ministry (e.g., Acts 18:9–10; 23:11; 27:23–24).

Several distinctions between Old and New Testament prophecy remain.

First, there is a more universal element in New Testament prophecy than in Old Testament prophecy. We have observed this phenomenon in Jesus's teaching concerning the kingdom as well as in Paul's end-time teachings.

Second, while there are common elements between Old Testament prophetic genres and New Testament prophecy, the latter tends to be far less structured.

Third, outside of the ministry of Jesus, New Testament prophetic speeches are more difficult to identify than their Old Testament counterparts. They may be instances of prophetic speech distinctly attributed to a supernatural being, or predictive material that a writer such as Paul could not have known by ordinary means, and be indicated by the presence of an identifying prophetic phrase.

Fourth, we should pay close attention to discerning those Old Testament predictions that find their realization in New Testament prophecy and events.

GUIDELINES FOR INTERPRETING PROPHECY

1. Select and determine the boundaries of the prophecy.

2. Understand the specific type of subgenre to which the passage belongs and apply its rules carefully.

3. Investigate the historical and cultural contexts of the passage. For the New Testament, this involves correctly assessing both the relevant Old Testament and extrabiblical data.

4. Interpret the passage carefully in accordance with sound grammatical exegesis.

5. Observe the literary features of the passage, considering the prophet's use of figurative language, imagery, motifs, themes, and symbols. Try to determine the meaning or emphasis that the figure is conveying.

6. Be sensitive to the theological truths conveyed by the passage. Note whether the prophet is building on previously revealed theological principles or is presenting new truths. Keep in mind that Jesus's prophetic perspective was especially concerned with the Kingdom of God.

7. Determine whether the prophecy applies to the prophet's day or to a future time, or both. Keep in mind the distinction between forth-telling and foretelling. Prophets were usually concerned primarily (though not necessarily exclusively) with conditions in their own day.

8. Determine whether the prophecy's future orientation looks to the near, short term, or to the more distant future, whether to the New Testament era or to the end of the age. Also seek to

ascertain whether the prophecy as given was conditional or unconditional in nature.

9. In the case of the New Testament, remember that some prophecies were fulfilled in part, but their fulfillment was not exhausted in the New Testament era. Determine also whether the prophecy has been literally fulfilled or whether the New Testament writer was applying the prophecy in a non-literal manner.

10. Make judicious application of the prophecy to the modern situation. Be careful to ask how the prophecy impacts your spiritual life or the spiritual condition of your church or the church as a whole.

KEY WORDS

Announcement of judgment, Apocalypse, Apocalyptic, Covenant lawsuit, Disputation, Exhortation speech, Instructional account, Lament, Prophetic narrative, Salvation oracle, Satire, Vision or dream report, Woe oracle.

ASSIGNMENTS

1. Investigate the historical setting, literary structure, and theological message of the Old Testament prophetic book of Nahum.

2. By comparing Peter's address on Pentecost (Acts 2:14–36), evaluate Joel 2:28–32 as an example of a prophecy that is fulfilled but not completely exhausted. What basic genre is best assigned to Joel's prophecy?

KEY RESOURCES

Bullock, C. Hassell. *An Introduction to the Old Testament Prophetic Books*. Chicago: Moody, 1986.

Sandy, D. Brent. *Plowshares & Pruning Hooks*. Downers Grove: InterVarsity, 2002.

CHAPTER 8 OBJECTIVES

1. To provide a discussion of the nature, genre, and origins of the Gospels.

2. To set forth general hermeneutical principles related to the Gospels and Acts.

3. To delineate the overall arrangement and structure of the Gospels and Acts.

4. To provide the student with a set of guidelines for interpreting the Gospels and Acts.

CHAPTER 8 OUTLINE

A. Nature of the Gospels

B. Genre of the Gospels and Acts

C. Origins of the Gospels

D. General Hermeneutical Principles

E. Guidelines for Interpreting the Gospels and Acts

F. Key Words

G. Assignments

H. Key Resources

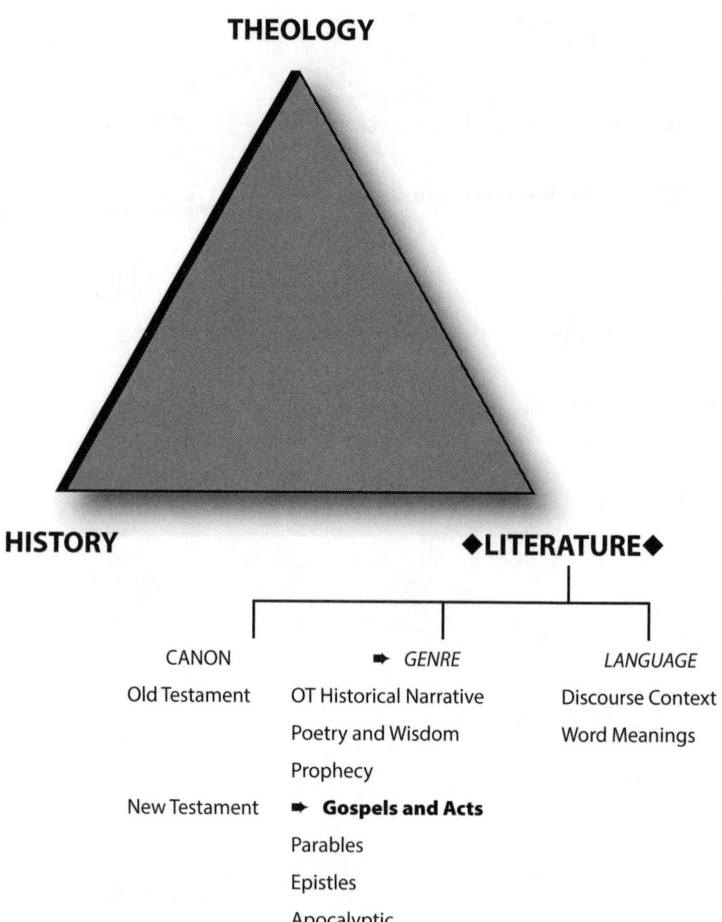
THEOLOGY
HISTORY
◆LITERATURE◆
CANON
Old Testament
New Testament
➨ GENRE
OT Historical Narrative
Poetry and Wisdom
Prophecy
➨ Gospels and Acts
Parables
Epistles
Apocalyptic
LANGUAGE
Discourse Context
Word Meanings

Chapter 8

HEARING THE GOOD NEWS: NEW TESTAMENT HISTORICAL NARRATIVE (GOSPELS AND ACTS)

NATURE OF THE GOSPELS

As we continue to travel through the canonical landscape, we now cross the threshold from the Old to the New Testament. The Gospels make up the first four books of the New Testament, bearing the titles "The Gospel according to Matthew, Mark, Luke, and John," respectively. While these titles were attached to these documents by the early church, most likely in the decades following the composition of the Gospels by the original authors, only Mark uses this self-designation in the text of his Gospel (Mark 1:1). Originally, the word "Gospel"—which literally means "good news," from the Greek prefix *eu-*, "good," and the noun *angelion*, "news" or "message"—was used for oral rather than written communication.

Since the Gospels are narratives that focus on the earthly life and ministry of Jesus, all four Gospels share common characteristics in both form and content. Luke is unique in that his Gospel is part of a two-volume work that consists of the Gospel and the book of Acts. The importance of Luke-Acts is further underscored by the fact that in terms of length, Luke's writings make up a quarter of the entire New Testament corpus. In what follows, we will take a closer look at the nature, genre, and origins of the Gospels. We will also develop an acquaintance with the pertinent general interpretive principles and close with guidelines for interpreting the Gospels and Acts.

GENRE OF THE GOSPELS AND ACTS

One of the major issues in Gospels studies is the genre of the four canonical Gospels. Not only do these works display similarities with other early Christian writings, they also reflect aspects of their Greco-Roman literary setting, particularly that of Greco-Roman *biography* (*bios*). At the same time, the Gospels constitute in some ways a distinct literary genre. Scholars have categorized the Gospels variously as biographies of Jesus, memoirs of the apostles, aretalogies (strings of "I am" statements), comedies, tragedies, or theological biography. The genre most commonly proposed today is that of Greco-Roman biography.

Indeed, a comparison between the particular characteristics and features of the Gospels and Acts on the one hand and Greco-Roman literature on the other reveals numerous similarities. For instance, the formal preface of Luke (Luke 1:1–4; cf. Acts 1:1) closely resembles the introductions of Greco-Roman literary works. There are also similarities in thematic emphasis and content. Popular Greco-Roman biographies tended to promote a particular hero or important person. Similarly, the Gospels may be said to promote a "hero," Jesus Christ, setting forth his deeds and activities and presenting him as the Savior of humanity. The inclusion of a vindication scene, in the case of the Gospels Jesus's post-resurrection appearances, was also a common device in Greco-Roman literature. In addition, we find literary similarities such as the use of genealogies (Matt. 1:1–16; Luke 3:23–38) and chronologies (Luke 2:1–2; 3:1–2). Finally, in terms of narrative technique, the anecdotal style shows close affinities with Greco-Roman literary techniques. These and other similar characteristics and features may indicate that the Gospels and Acts belong to the genre of Greco-Roman biography.

Despite these similarities, however, there are sufficient differences to suggest that the canonical Gospels constitute a unique genre. A common objection to classifying the Gospels as biography relates to the lack of comprehensive biographical detail regarding Jesus. The absence of a consistent chronological order in the four Gospels is noted as well. While each of the four Gospels devotes considerable space to the final days of Jesus's life, we know little of the events prior to the inception of his ministry. Only Matthew and Luke include the birth narrative (Matt. 1:1–25; Luke 2:1–20); only Matthew recounts the flight to Egypt and the subsequent return to Nazareth during Jesus's childhood (Matt. 2:13–23); and only Luke records the temple incident during Jesus's twelfth year (Luke 2:41–51). Apart from these accounts, little is known about Jesus's early life, and neither Mark nor John has any additional information about Jesus's childhood or early adulthood. However, Greco-Roman biographies likewise did not necessarily provide complete biographical details. Only those segments that were viewed as pertinent to the telling of a given story were included.

In addition, there are other significant differences that distinguish the Gospels from Greco-Roman biographies. Of the four Gospels, only Luke has a formal literary preface (though John's introduction is highly literary in nature as well). Moreover, unlike their Greco-Roman counterparts, all the Gospels are formally anonymous. Another important difference lies in the evangelists' intended audience. All the Gospels, as well as the book of Acts, were written for a Christian audience. For this reason, these works served a different purpose than the literature of the day and were intended to achieve a different response from the readers. After all, no ordinary hero could compare with Jesus Christ.

In light of these similarities and differences, it seems preferable to view the Gospels and Acts as a subgenre of *historical narrative*. Like the Old Testament historical narratives, the Gospels and Acts do not merely report facts. The evangelists carefully selected and arranged material that most effectively conveyed God's message. They used a Christ-centered approach that presented a theologically motivated account of the life and work of Jesus and significant events in the life of the early church. Their accounts represent God's saving activity in history and demand a faith response from readers. In their presentation, the Gospels and Acts reflect a close connection with the literary forms, vocabulary, and themes of Old Testament historical narrative.

The literary style of all four Gospels and the book of Acts, for example, is very similar to that of Old Testament historical narratives. Luke, in particular, displays a style that reveals the influence of the Hebrew Scriptures and reflects self-conscious patterning of his account after Old Testament models. John, likewise, from his opening introduction features salvation-historical points of reference in presenting his Gospel. Also, all four Gospels as well as Acts feature numerous direct Old Testament quotations and allusions. In many cases, these are used in contexts indicating the fulfillment of prophecy. Matthew, for instance, cites Isaiah 7:14, indicating the fulfillment of Isaiah's prophecy that a virgin would be with child and give birth to a son (Matt. 1:22–23).

The four modes of narrative identified earlier in this volume are all present in the Gospels and Acts (i.e., reporting of events, dramatic mode, pure description, and commentary). The account of the birth of Jesus (Matt. 1:18–19) emphasizes both *setting and character*:

Setting: "This is how the birth of Jesus Christ came about: His mother Mary was pledged to be married to Joseph, but before they came together, she was found to be with child through the Holy Spirit."

Character: "Because Joseph her husband was a righteous man and did not want to expose her to public disgrace, he had in mind to divorce her quietly."

Like the Old Testament historical narratives, the Gospels and Acts have their fair share of *dialogue*. The speeches and dialogues in the narrative provide dramatic effect and a deeper understanding of the characters involved. For instance, the conversations between Jesus and the Jewish authorities in John are a window into their unbelief and rejection of his revelation (John 8:48–51):

The Jews: The Jews answered him, "Aren't we right in saying that you are a Samaritan and demon-possessed?"

Jesus: "I am not possessed by a demon," said Jesus, "but I honor my Father and you dishonor me. I am not seeking glory for myself; but there is one who seeks it, and he is the judge. I tell you the truth, if anyone keeps my word, he will never see death."

There are also numerous instances of *explicit commentary.* In Mark's account of the raising of Jairus's daughter (5:21–43), the evangelist inserts the explanatory statement, "She was twelve years old." In the earlier example given of the use of chronologies, Luke inserts an editorial comment:

> In those days Caesar Augustus issued a decree that a census should be taken of the entire Roman world. (*This was the first census that took place while Quirinius was governor of Syria.*) (Luke 2:1–2)

These and numerous other characteristics found in Old Testament historical narratives can be identified in the Gospels. Rather than suggesting that the Gospels and Acts constitute a new genre altogether or are to be identified with Greco-Roman popular biography, it seems best to understand them as belonging to the genre of historical narrative. This requires the interpreter to be familiar with the features of Old Testament historical narrative, both external characteristics (author, narrator, reader) and internal characteristics (setting, plot, characterization, style), discussed in chapter 5 above.

ORIGINS OF THE GOSPELS

Why Four Gospels?

While the Gospels are very similar in content and tone, they are not identical. The differences raise the issue of why four canonical Gospels were needed to tell the story of Jesus. The issue also has implications for the Gospels' historical reliability and has caused some to question the integrity of the Gospel accounts. In the days of the early church, the diversity found in the four Gospels led to attempts to reconcile these differences. The second-century church father Tatian combined all four Gospels in his *Diatessaron* (Grk. "through four"), the first known harmony of the Gospels. Later, Augustine wrote a treatise entitled *The Harmony of the Gospels*.

Why, then, did the early church see fit to include four Gospels in the Christian canon? One of the reasons for the need for multiple canonical Gospels is a simple and pragmatic one. Each Gospel was originally written to address the concerns of a particular community or group of believers, and since such concerns differed, the Gospels could not for that reason be identical. Thus there arose the need for several different Gospels serving

Christian communities in various geographical locations. At the same time, all four canonical Gospels were intended for a broad readership not limited to a particular locale.

The significance of the diversity of the Gospels for interpretation cannot be overstated. While the four Gospels all focus on the story of Jesus, each Gospel has a unique contribution to make, so that what emerges is a composite, multi-faceted picture of Jesus. The cumulative effect resulting from reading all four Gospels is that readers attain a more comprehensive understanding of the story of Jesus than if they were only reading one of these Gospels. For instance, reading the Gospel of John on its own apart from the Synoptic Gospels may lead to the conclusion that Jesus never taught in parables or performed exorcisms; however, when we read Matthew, Mark, and Luke, we learn that much of Jesus's teaching was given in parables and that Jesus performed a fair share of exorcisms. Reading Mark's Gospel on its own—a much shorter account—for its part may raise questions about gaps in the story of Jesus. For example, unlike Matthew or Luke, Mark does not begin with a birth narrative, but having established that the Gospel is about Jesus Christ the Son of God (Mark 1:1) Mark immediately moves on to an account of Jesus's baptism (Mark 1:9–11). Here, the more extensive accounts provided by Matthew and Luke fill in some of the gaps in Mark's shorter presentation.

Understanding that each evangelist had his own unique purpose in writing his Gospel and that the needs of the readers differed, the perceptive interpreter will be careful to read each Gospel in its own right ("vertically") while paying careful attention to the distinctive story line and theological emphasis of the respective Gospel. At the same time, the other Gospels should not be ignored because they serve to enhance the overall understanding of the story of Jesus; thus you should also read across all four Gospels ("horizontally"). Not only do the Gospels share the same overall genre in continuity with Old Testament historical narrative, all four Gospels have as their primary subject the life, death, and resurrection of Jesus Christ and the training of his followers, the new messianic community.

John and the Synoptics

The nature of the relationship between John and the Synoptics is difficult to determine. The common material is limited to the feeding of the five thousand, the anointing, and the passion narrative. In addition, John features extended discourses, such as Jesus's encounters with Nicodemus and the Samaritan woman (John 3–4), the "Good Shepherd discourse" in John 10, or the "Farewell Discourse" in John 13–17 including Jesus's discourse on the vine and the branches (John 15). Also included are several startling "signs" (messianic manifestations including, but not limited to, miracles) of Jesus, most notably the raising of Lazarus (John 11).

The degree of difference between John and the Synoptic Gospels suggests that John probably wrote his Gospel independently of the other three, although it is likely that he was aware of their existence (see, e.g., the reference to Andrew as "Simon Peter's brother" in John 1:40; the reference to "the village of Mary and her sister Martha" in John 11:1–2 [cf. Luke 10:38–42]; or the reference to "the Twelve" in John 6:67, 71, even though they were not previously mentioned in John's Gospel). These connections suggest that John wrote his Gospel with an awareness of the Synoptic Gospels while pursuing his own unique purposes, modifying some of their themes much like a composer might transpose a melody into a different key. That said, the relationship between John's Gospel and the other canonical Gospels is considerably more complex than can be discussed here.

Historical Reliability of the Gospels

Another issue that arises in the study of the Gospels relates to the fact that the narration of one and the same event resulted in different versions. Rather than doubt the credibility of the Gospels and Acts, the judicious interpreter will evaluate these documents with an understanding of the literature of their day. Students of the Gospels ought not to force modern conventions onto the Gospels but must understand that the use of paraphrase and the telescoping of events were legitimate devices in ancient historiography.

In addition, given that there were four different writers involved, one cannot expect them to feature identical translations from the original Greek and Aramaic nor should one expect a given event to be recounted in an identical fashion. That said, there is sufficient agreement in the relating of accounts and the placement of events to engender confidence in the evangelists' credibility. Consequently, any approach to the interpretation of the Gospels must begin with the presumption that the Gospels are historically accurate and contain reliable eyewitness testimony.

GENERAL HERMENEUTICAL PRINCIPLES

Characteristics of the Gospels

Grant Osborne (2006: 203) notes that the "interpretation of narrative has two tasks: poetics, which studies the artistic dimension or the way the text is constructed by the author; and meaning, which recreates the message that the author is communicating." Both poetics and meaning can be understood from a study of the following major characteristics of the Gospels:

1. historical context;
2. literary context; and
3. arrangement.

These three elements provide us with a vital interpretive tool for understanding the message of the Gospels and Acts.

We have noted previously that the Gospels and Acts are narratives that tell the story of the life, death, and resurrection of Jesus Christ and the training of his followers, the new messianic community. This shared subject necessarily means that the Gospels share certain material in common and concur in placing primary emphasis on the significance of Jesus. In telling this story, the evangelists used certain literary techniques. Thus the Gospels should be read as integrated narratives with all the various component parts contributing to the overall story.

At the same time, while the *literary* elements of a narrative are important, the *historical* and *theological* elements must also be given their proper place in the interpretive task (the hermeneutical triad). In telling the story of Jesus and the early church, the evangelists wrote from a particular historical perspective and were theologically motivated to highlight the significance of Jesus. But in so doing, they used the literary forms and conventions of their day. Our task as interpreters is to study the text before us with these three elements—history, literature, and theology—always in mind.

Historical Context

Historical context provides us with vital background information necessary for understanding the purpose of a given text and aids in reconstructing the particular situations that generated the need for it. For instance, the footwashing scene of John 13 brings to the fore the importance of understanding cultural practices during the time of Jesus. Footwashing was a task customarily done by non-Jewish slaves and never by a superior to his inferior. In taking on this menial stance, Jesus provides an example of true service, the kind he expected of all his followers.

Without the understanding that this task was considered too demeaning for disciples or even Jewish slaves, the significance of Jesus's action would be lost or at least much less apparent. The areas that yield the most useful data for reconstructing historical context include geography, politics, economics, military and war, cultural practices, and religious customs. Bible dictionaries, encyclopedias, atlases, and so on are valuable resources for uncovering this data. In addition, allusions to the Old Testament and parallels with Jewish and Greco-Roman sources should not be ignored.

The historical context of the Gospels operates on two levels: the life setting in Jesus's day and the life setting of the church at the time of composition. Because the Gospels are about Jesus, they record events that happened during his earthly life. This means that his teachings and actions were given and took place in a particular historical context. As these stories and sayings were passed on from community to community, the original context gradually receded into the background and the accounts were adapted for the needs of the respective audiences of the individual Gospels.

In this regard, knowledge of the ways in which particular evangelists adapted given stories in the life of Jesus proves useful. For instance, Mark's emphasis on the disciples' fear and misunderstanding is most likely intended to reassure and encourage a Gentile Christian audience, possibly in Rome, at a time when imperial persecution against Christians intensified. Luke wrote, at least in part, to defend Christianity against Jewish charges that the movement was politically subversive, which may explain his extensive account of Paul's trials before various Roman officials in the final chapters of the book of Acts.

Literary Context

Klein, Blomberg, and Hubbard (2004: 214) note that a "basic principle of biblical hermeneutics is that the intended meaning of any passage is the meaning that is consistent with the sense of the literary context in which it occurs." The literary context refers to the place of a given unit in the context of any one of the Gospels. The material that comes before and after it forms its literary context. Reading the Gospels *vertically* and *horizontally*, as mentioned, means that in cases where a similar incident is recorded in all four Gospels or in the Synoptics, the first step is to determine what the passage means in the context of the Gospel in which it is found (the "vertical" reading). Only after this is done is it appropriate to compare a given textual unit with parallels in the other Gospels (the "horizontal" reading). Note, for instance, the literary contexts within which the four evangelists chose to fit their feeding accounts in the following horizontal comparison:

8.1. LITERARY CONTEXT OF THE FEEDING ACCOUNTS IN THE GOSPELS

Matthew	Mark	Luke	John
14:1–12	6:14–31	9:1–9	5:31–47
John the Baptist beheaded	John the Baptist beheaded	Jesus sends out the twelve	Testimonies about Jesus
14:13–21	16:32–44	9:10–17	6:1–15
Feeding account	Feeding account	Feeding account	Feeding account
14:22–36	6:45–56	9:18–27	6:16–24
Jesus walks on water	Jesus walks on water	Peter's confession of Christ	Jesus walks on water

Whereas Matthew and Mark include the passage on John the Baptist's beheading (in form of a flashback) just prior to the feeding incident, Luke and John feature the sending out of the twelve and testimonies about Jesus, respectively. Matthew, Mark, and John place the incident of Jesus walking on the water after their accounts of the feeding, while Luke follows up the feeding narrative with Peter's confession of Jesus as the Messiah. Each of the accounts, while relating the same incident, must be interpreted within the framework of the literary contexts in their respective Gospels in light of the author's purpose as far as it can be determined. After this, it is appropriate to consult the other three Gospels. This is best done by consulting a synopsis or harmony of the Gospels.

Arrangement

The arrangement of the four Gospels and Acts also provides us with an important interpretive tool for understanding the message conveyed by the four evangelists. In some situations, a Gospel may reflect a chronological as well as a topical arrangement. The two are not necessarily mutually exclusive. In other instances, the same event may be narrated in the context of differing chronological presentations.

The principle of arrangement, selectivity, and adaptation applies also to structure. The evangelists chose to organize their accounts differently, both at the macro- and the micro-level. An understanding of how the evangelists chose to structure their message is important because it provides the reader with clues about the focus of the author. Before one can identify the author's focus, the plot and the structure must first be clarified. Structure therefore provides us with an important interpretive tool for understanding the message of the author.

In what follows, we will discuss the basic arrangement and structure of each of the four Gospels and discuss the major theological themes found in Matthew, Mark, Luke, and John. We reiterate that with regard to structure, in keeping with our "hermeneutic of perception," what we are after is not *our own* outline of a given book but rather *the author's* literary structure and presentation. You will best be able to discern this structure by paying close attention to the transitional phrases, literary *inclusios*, and other textual markers found in these documents.

Matthew

Matthew's Gospel shows clear evidence of the evangelist's arrangement of his material for stylistic, theological, and thematic reasons. The Gospel is structured thematically around five discourses found in chapters 5–7; 10:5–42; 13:1–52; 18:1–35; and 24–25, identified by the concluding transitional markers that more or less conform to the following formula: "When Jesus had finished saying these things . . ." (Matt. 7:28; 11:1; 13:53; 19:1; 26:1).

In certain instances, Matthew chose not to arrange his material in a chronological manner because apparently his authorial purpose was better served by a thematic approach. In keeping with numerical symbolism (five "books of Jesus" corresponding to the five books of Moses, the Pentateuch), Jesus is in varying ways presented as the "new Moses." Note also the pattern of narration that oscillates between narrative and discourse:

INTRODUCTION (1:1–4:11)

I. JESUS'S GALILEAN MINISTRY (4:12–18:35)
   A. First Part of Galilean Ministry (4:11–25)
      DISCOURSE #1: SERMON ON THE MOUNT (5–7)

   B. Second Part of Galilean Ministry (8–9)
      DISCOURSE #2: INSTRUCTION OF THE TWELVE (10)

   C. Third Part of Galilean ministry (11–12)
      DISCOURSE #3: KINGDOM PARABLES (13)

   D. Galilean Ministry Extended to the North (13:53–17:27)
      DISCOURSE #4: KINGDOM PARABLES (18)

II. JESUS'S JUDEAN MINISTRY AND HIS PASSION (19–28)
   A. Judean Ministry (19–20)

   B. Final Ministry in Jerusalem (21–23)
      DISCOURSE #5: OLIVET DISCOURSE, KINGDOM PARABLES (24–25)

   C. The Passion, Resurrection, and Great Commission (26–28)

The most significant theological theme in Matthew's Gospel is that *Jesus is the Messiah* predicted in the Hebrew Scriptures. This is highlighted especially in chapters 1–4 in form of several "fulfillment quotations." At the very beginning, Matthew presents Jesus as the son of David and the son of Abraham (Matt. 1:1–18). Jesus is also the new Moses, who in his "inaugural address" in the Gospel, the Sermon on the Mount, ascends a mountain and instructs his followers in his new Law (chaps. 5–7). Another major motif is that of the kingdom of God, which forms the subject of several series of parables (chaps. 13, 18, 25).

Mark

Overall, Mark presents Jesus's ministry along a geographical pattern from Galilee to Jerusalem. The watershed or turning point in the narrative is marked by Peter's confession of Jesus as Messiah at the midway point of the Markan narrative (Mark 8:29).

While Mark largely follows a chronological approach, there are times when his Gospel, like Matthew's, is arranged thematically. For instance, in chapters 4–5 Mark demonstrates Jesus's authority over four different entities: (1) nature (Mark 4:35–41); (2) demons (Mark 5:1–20); (3) death (Mark 5:21–24, 35–43); and (4) sickness (Mark 5:35–43).

Throughout his Gospel, Mark features selected references to Jesus as Son of God peaking with the centurion's confession in Mark 15:39. The basic structure of Mark's Gospel presents itself as follows:

I. INTRODUCTION (1:1–15)
II. JESUS'S MINISTRY IN GALILEE (1:16–8:26)
   A. First Part of Galilean Ministry (1:16–3:12)
   B. Second Part of Galilean Ministry (3:13–5:43)
   C. Third Part of Galilean ministry (6:1–8:26)
III. THE WAY TO THE CROSS (8:27–16:8)
   A. The Way of Suffering and Glory (8:27–10:52)
   B. Final Ministry in Jerusalem (11:1–13:37)
   C. The Passion and the Empty Tomb (14:1–16:8)

The preeminent theological theme in Mark's Gospel is that *Jesus is the miracle-working, authoritative Son of God*. Strategic references to Jesus as the Son of God are found at the following locations in Mark's Gospel:

8.2. STRATEGIC REFERENCES TO JESUS AS THE SON OF GOD IN MARK

I. Introduction			II. Galilean ministry			III. The way to the cross		
1:1	1:11	3:33	5:7	9:7	12:6	13:32	14:61	15:39
Mark	God	Demons	Demons	God	Jesus	Jesus	Caiaphas	Centurion

The chart indicates that this theme forms the all-inclusive bookend of the Markan narrative. The evangelist frames his narrative in terms of Jesus being the Son of God in the opening verse and the climactic reference in 15:39 features the Roman centurion—no coincidence, since Mark's audience was the church in Rome—uttering the final reference to Jesus as Son of God in the Gospel.

In between, Jesus is declared by the heavenly voice to be the Son of God at his baptism (1:1) and at the Transfiguration (9:7). Apart from Jesus's two self-references (12:6; 13:32) and Caiaphas's question at Jesus's trial (14:61), the only other characters in Mark's Gospel who acknowledge Jesus as Son of God are demons (though see Peter's confession of Jesus as the Messiah in 8:29, which, however, is at once revealed as lacking full understanding, 8:31–33). Remarkably, demons are the only ones to acknowledge Jesus as God throughout his entire Galilean ministry narrated in 1:16–8:26.

This indicates that in Mark's Gospel, no one—other than God and Jesus, and demons!—understands that Jesus is the Son of God prior to the crucifixion. This, in turn, works hand in hand with two other major Markan themes, the so-called *"messianic secret"* and the *"discipleship failure"* motif. Another important Markan topic is the *kingdom of God*, which is proclaimed by Jesus (1:15), featured in several parables (4:11, 26, 30), and addressed in the form of entrance requirements (9:47; 10:14–15, 23–25; 11:10; 12:34; see also 9:1; 14:25; 15:43).

Luke/Acts

Luke's Gospel is organized around a geographical motif with an emphasis on Jerusalem. At the heart of Luke's narrative is the extended Lucan "travel narrative," which shows Jesus journeying toward Jerusalem on his way to the cross for the better part of ten chapters in the Gospel (Luke 9:51–19:27). After narrating Jesus's passion in Jerusalem at the end of his Gospel, Luke's second volume, the book of Acts, takes its point of departure from Jerusalem. From there the gospel moves outward to Judea, Samaria, and finally to the Gentile nations (Acts 1:8). This movement is also characteristic of Paul's mission and is shown to fulfill Old Testament prediction (Acts 13:47 citing Isa. 49:6; Acts 28:26–27 citing Isa. 6:9–10).

Luke/Acts is a two-volume work (Acts 1:1) centered on Jesus's journey to Jerusalem ushering in his crucifixion (vol. 1, Gospel of Luke) and on the church's spread from Jerusalem to the ends of the earth (vol. 2, book of Acts; see Acts 1:8). In his preface, Luke frankly acknowledges his reliance on a variety of sources in compiling his account (Luke 1:1–4). In fact, his overall chronology is similar to Mark's and Matthew's in that it first records various rounds of Jesus's ministry in Galilee and subsequently presents Jesus's journey to Jerusalem. In Luke's narrative, however, this "travel narrative" is considerably more extensive and includes much material unique to Luke.

I. INTRODUCTION (1:1–4:13)
   A. Preface (1:1–4)
   B. Jesus's and the Baptist's Birth and Jesus's Boyhood (1:5–2:52)
   C. Preliminaries to Jesus' Ministry (3:1–4:13)
II. JESUS'S GALILEAN MINISTRY (4:14–9:50)
   A. First Part of Galilean Ministry (4:14–7:50)
   B. Second Part of Galilean Ministry (8:1–39)
   C. Third Part of Galilean Ministry and Withdrawal (8:40–9:50)
III. JESUS'S JOURNEY TO JERUSALEM AND HIS PASSION (9:51–24:53)
   A. The Lucan Travel Narrative (9:51–19:27)
   B. Final Ministry in Jerusalem (19:28–22:38)
   C. Jesus's Crucifixion, Resurrection, and Ascension (22:39–24:53)

In contrast to Matthew who presents Jesus first and foremost as the Jewish Messiah, Luke's Gospel focuses on Jesus as *"the son of Adam, the son of God"* (Luke 3:37). Throughout the Gospel, Jesus is shown to engage in fellowship with people viewed as "sinners" by the Jewish religious establishment. He is presented as *a friend of sinners* and as a *compassionate healer,* who is guided by a concern for those who are socially disenfranchised and of low status, including the poor, the Gentiles, women, and children. Perhaps Jesus's mission according to Luke is best summarized by Jesus's statement in Luke 19:10, "For the Son of Man came to seek and to save what was lost."

The book of Acts, as mentioned, narrates the *spread of the gospel from Jerusalem all the way to the ends of the earth* (Acts 1:8). Jesus, through the *Holy Spirit*, is shown to lead the church as it bears *bold witness to the resurrection* and *overcomes a variety of external and internal obstacles*. This includes legal challenges before Roman government officials, which remain unproven and inconclusive, amounting to a vindication of Christianity as "not guilty" of the political charges brought against it. In the end, nothing is shown to stop the irresistible spread of the gospel on its march to the capital of the Roman Empire, and the book concludes with reference to Paul's free and unhindered proclamation of the good news there (Acts 28:15–31).

I. FOUNDATIONS FOR THE CHURCH AND ITS MISSION (1:1–2:41)
   A. Preface (1:1–5)
   B. Jerusalem: Waiting for the Spirit (1:6–26)
   C. Pentecost: The Church is Born (2:1–41)

II. THE CHURCH IN JERUSALEM (2:42–6:7)
   A. The Early Church (2:42–47)
   B. A Miracle and its Aftermath (3:1–4:31)
   C. Trouble Within and Without (4:32–6:7)

III. WIDER HORIZONS FOR THE CHURCH: STEPHEN, SAMARIA, AND SAUL (6:8–9:31)
   A. Suffering: One of the Servants Arrested and Martyred (6:8–8:1a)
   B. Palestine and Syria: Philip, Saul, and Peter (8:1b–9:31)

IV. PETER AND THE FIRST GENTILE CONVERT (9:32–12:24)
   A. Peter Heals and Raises Woman from Dead (9:32–43)
   B. Peter Visits Cornelius in Caesarea (10)
   C. Peter Reports to Jerusalem Church (11:1–18)
   D. The Church in Antioch (11:19–29)
   E. James Martyred, Peter Imprisoned, and Herod's Ignominious End (12:1–24)

V. PAUL TURNS TO THE GENTILES (12:25–16:5)
   A. First Missionary Journey (12:25–14:28)
   B. Jerusalem Council (15:1–35)
   C. Second Missionary Journey Begins (15:36–16:5)

VI. FURTHER PENETRATION INTO THE GENTILE WORLD (16:6–19:20)
   A. Second Missionary Journey (16:6–18:22)
   B. Third Missionary Journey (18:23–19:20)

VII. ON TO ROME (19:21–28:31)
   A. From Ephesus to Jerusalem (19:21–21:16)
   B. Paul's Final Visit to Jerusalem and His Removal to Caesarea (21:17–23:35)

C. Paul's Defenses before Felix, Festus, and Agrippa (24:1–26:32)
D. Paul's Trip to Rome (27:1–28:31)

The book of Acts continues and completes Luke's two-volume work. While Jesus in volume 1 (the Gospel) is presented as the Crucified and Risen One, he appears in volume 2 (the book of Acts) as the One Exalted to God's right hand who directs the church's mission through the person of the Holy Spirit (Acts 1:1; see also the logic underlying Peter's Pentecost sermon in Acts 2). Peter in the first half and Paul in the second half of the book are the key figures who advance the gospel following a geographical pattern from Jerusalem and Judea to Samaria and to the Gentile world.

John

The pattern of John's Gospel is chronological. John arranges his material around his presentation of seven messianic signs of Jesus, revealing him as the Messiah and Son of God (John 20:30–31). These messianic signs, spanning from John 2 to 11, are part and parcel of Jesus's ministry to the Jews. They are designed to convince the Jewish people that Jesus is the messianic Son sent by God the Father. Though crucified, Jesus was nonetheless God in the flesh and the Savior of the world. The second half of John's Gospel anticipates Jesus's exaltation with God and shows Jesus preparing his new messianic community—the Twelve minus Judas—for their mission subsequent to Jesus's crucifixion, resurrection, and ascension (his "glorification").

John's Gospel is carefully structured, as is evident from the outline below. The Gospel breaks down symmetrically into a corresponding introduction and epilogue and two equal halves. The introduction sets the entire Gospel in perspective as Jesus is presented as *the pre-existent Word* that was *made flesh* and definitively revealed God the Father. The remainder of the narrative is thus to be read as *Jesus's revelation of God in word and deed* (including the cross). The first major half sets forth *seven selected signs of Jesus*, startling works that display his messianic status to the Jewish people. The second half first presents Jesus's *cleansing and instruction of his new messianic community* and subsequently narrates his *passion and resurrection appearances*. In the purpose statement, John affirms that all those who believe in Jesus will have eternal life.

- I. INTRODUCTION: THE WORD MADE FLESH (1:1–18)
- II. THE BOOK OF SIGNS: THE SIGNS OF THE MESSIAH (1:19–12:50)
  - A. The Forerunner, Jesus's Inaugural Signs & Representative Conversations (1:19–4:54)
  - B. Additional Signs amidst Mounting Unbelief (5–10)
  - C. Final Passover: The Climactic Sign and Other Events (11–12)
- III. THE BOOK OF EXALTATION: THE NEW MESSIANIC COMMUNITY (13–20)
  - A. Cleansing and Instruction of the New Covenant Community (13–17)
  - B. Passion Narrative (18–19)
  - C. Jesus's Resurrection, Appearances, and Commissioning of Disciples (20:1–29)
  - D. Purpose Statement (20:30–31)
- IV. EPILOGUE: COMPLEMENTARY ROLES OF PETER AND BELOVED DISCIPLE (21)
  - A. Jesus's Third Appearance, to Seven Disciples in Galilee (21:1–14)
  - B. Jesus and Peter (21:15–19)
  - C. Jesus and the Disciple Jesus Loved (21:20–25)

The introduction presents Jesus as the pre-existent Word through whom God created the world and who, made flesh, made known the Father (see esp. 1:1, 14, 18). The entire subsequent Gospel narrative, both Jesus's works and his words, is thus cast in terms of revelation of God, including the cross where God's love for the world was made manifest and salvation was made available for those who believe. Virtually all the major theological themes of John's Gospel are featured in the purpose statement in 20:30–31: (1) Jesus's signs; (2) the need to believe that Jesus is the Messiah and Son of God; and (3) eternal life for those who place their trust in him.

GUIDELINES FOR INTERPRETING THE GOSPELS AND ACTS

1. Before you interpret your passage, have a general understanding of the *background issues* related to the book you are studying. Identify the purpose of the book as well as its major themes.

2. Based on the *arrangement and structure* of the entire narrative, determine the boundaries of the textual unit you are studying. Make sure that you correctly identify transitional phrases, literary inclusions, and other textual markers.

3. Identify the *literary context* of your passage. Take note of how a given evangelist may have adapted his material from the available sources (which may include one or several of the other Gospels).

4. In light of the particular genre characteristics of the Gospels and Acts, identify how the *external elements* (author, narrator, and reader) function in the narrative. Also clarify any issues related to narrative mode, commentary, and point of view.

5. Identify the *internal elements* and how they function in the narrative. These include the setting, plot, characterization, literary style, and narrative time (order of events, passage of time covered by events).

6. Take note of the *historical-cultural context*. Keep in mind that the Gospels have two levels: the life setting in Jesus's day and the life setting of the church at the time of composition.

7. Keep in mind that the entire interpretive process should be based on *sound exegetical procedures*. Take note of the meaning

of significant words and the contribution of grammar and syntax.

8. Draw all your findings together and *summarize the meaning* of your passage. Ensure that this is consistent with authorial intent.

9. Finally, *apply* this passage to the contemporary situation.

KEY WORDS

Aretalogy, Diatessaron, Horizontal reading, Narrative time, Narrator, Synoptic Gospels, Vertical reading.

ASSIGNMENTS

1. Using a Harmony of the Gospels, compare the accounts of Jesus's feeding of the 5,000 in all four Gospels. Note similarities and differences in wording and presentation and develop a hypothesis of Gospel relationships based on the observations from your study of this unit of text.

2. Analyze the account of Jesus's healing of the paralytic in Mark 2:1–12. Identify the setting, plot, characters, and other stylistic features in this passage and discuss how an analysis along these lines enhances your understanding of the deeper spiritual meaning and message of this passage in Mark's Gospel.

KEY RESOURCES

Blomberg, Craig L. *The Historical Reliability of the Gospels.* 2nd ed. Downers Grove: InterVarsity, 2007.

Köstenberger, Andreas J. *Encountering John.* 2nd ed. Grand Rapids: Baker, 2013.

CHAPTER 9 OBJECTIVES

1. To impart a basic knowledge of the style of Jesus's teaching including parables.

2. To provide a set of guidelines for interpreting Jesus's parables.

CHAPTER 9 OUTLINE

A. Style of Jesus's Teaching

B. Parables of Jesus

C. Guidelines for Interpreting the Parables

D. Key Words

E. Assignments

F. Key Resources

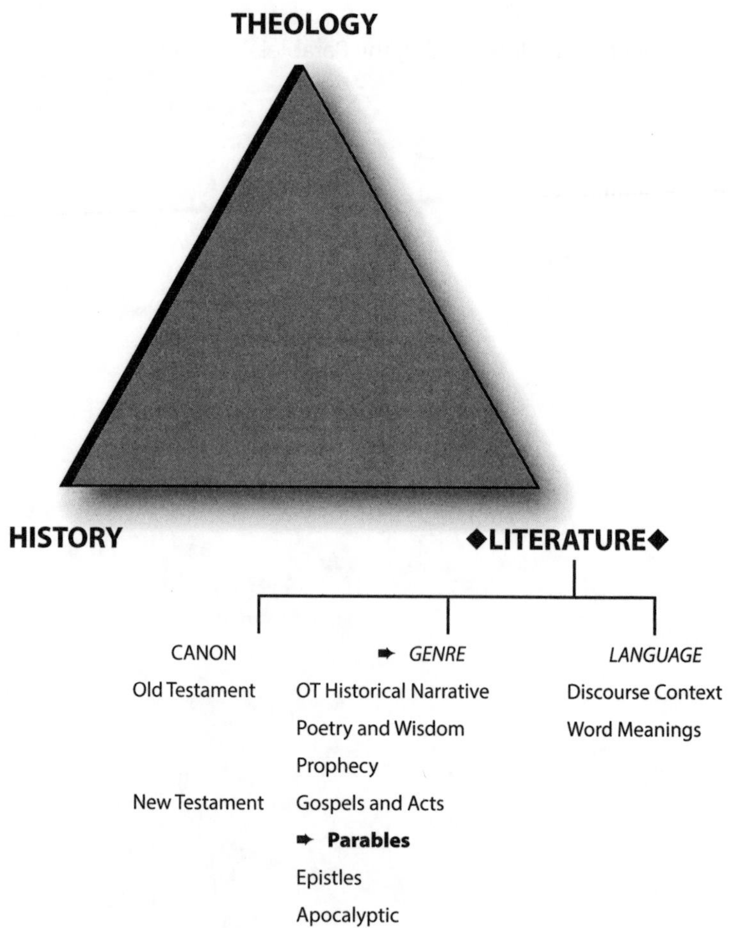
THEOLOGY
HISTORY
◆LITERATURE◆
CANON
Old Testament
New Testament
➡ GENRE
OT Historical Narrative
Poetry and Wisdom
Prophecy
Gospels and Acts
➡ Parables
Epistles
Apocalyptic
LANGUAGE
Discourse Context
Word Meanings

Chapter 9

CALLING FOR DISCERNMENT: PARABLES

STYLE OF JESUS'S TEACHING

BEFORE WE MOVE ON TO the next major body of literature in the New Testament—the Epistles—let's take some time to look at a fairly subtle genre represented in the Gospels, the parable. Our study of Jesus's parables, in turn, is best set within the larger framework of Jesus's teaching as a whole. Preachers often struggle with interpreting parables, either because they tend to treat them as historical narratives or because they unduly spiritualize every element of a given parable. In this chapter, we set forth principles that will help students of Scripture steer clear of either extreme and develop growing sensitivity to this attractive, yet at times treacherous, feature of the biblical landscape.

A look at any of the Gospels reveals that Jesus engaged in extensive teaching activity. In order to understand *what* Jesus taught, it's important to understand *how* he taught, while at the same time recognizing that the "how" is simply a medium for the message and not the message itself. His teaching method reflects his familiarity with and indebtedness to the wisdom tradition of the Old Testament. This can be clearly seen in the beatitudes, admonitions, parables, and his longer discourses. Approximately one-third of Jesus's teaching is given in form of parables. Before we turn to a study of parables, it should be noted that Jesus also taught in a variety of other ways. The fact that Jesus was not confined to one style or method of teaching made his teaching even more effective. Robert Stein (1978: 7–33) identifies the following forms and techniques used by Jesus in his teaching.

Overstatement. Overstatement involves the exaggeration of a point or the heightening of a truth in order to capture the attention of one's audience. This technique was not unique to Jesus; it was a general characteristic of Semitic speech. Its aim was to communicate to the listeners the need to get rid of sinful attitudes and behavior in their lives. In these statements, it is the meaning underlying the actual words that needs to be discerned if one wants to understand the essential message.

> "If your right eye causes you to stumble, *gouge it out and throw it away.* It is better for you to lose one part of your body than for your whole body to be thrown into hell. And if your right hand causes you to stumble, *cut it off and throw it away.* It is better for you to lose one part of your body than for your whole body to go into hell." (Matt. 5:29–30)

> "If anyone comes to me and does not *hate* father and mother, wife and children, brothers and sisters—yes, even their own life—such a person cannot be my disciple." (Luke 14:26)

Hyperbole. The use of hyperbole is closely related to overstatement, and it is sometimes difficult to differentiate the two. The difference lies in the fact that the degree of exaggeration is more pronounced in the case of hyperbole and the fact that, unlike overstatement, a literal fulfillment or portrayal is impossible.

> "Woe to you, teachers of the law and Pharisees, you hypocrites! You give a tenth of your spices—mint, dill and cumin. But you have neglected the more important matters of the law—justice, mercy and faithfulness. You should have practiced the latter, without neglecting the former. You blind guides! *You strain out a gnat but swallow a camel.*" (Matt. 23:23–24).

> "Why do you look at the *speck of sawdust in your brother's eye* and pay no attention to the *plank in your own eye*? How can you say to your

> brother, 'Let me take the speck out of your eye,' when all the time there is a plank in your own eye? You hypocrite, first take the plank out of your own eye, and then you will see clearly to remove the speck from your brother's eye ." (Matt. 7:3–5)

> But Jesus said again, "Children, how hard it is to enter the kingdom of God! It is *easier for a camel to go through the eye of a needle* than for someone who is rich to enter the kingdom of God." (Mark 10:24b–25)

Pun. A pun is a play on words in which one word may have more than one meaning, or two like-sounding words (homonyms) may be intentionally used to suggest two or more different meanings. Often the reader misses the use of puns by Jesus. While they are obvious in the original language (Aramaic or sometimes the written Greek), Bible translations are not always able to transmit them intact. Note, for instance, the following pun in Matthew 23:23–24, originally spoken by Jesus in Aramaic:

> "You blind guides! You strain out a gnat (*galma*) but swallow a camel (*gamla*)."

Another well-known example in the Greek text of Matthew's Gospel is Jesus's reference to Peter and his confession as a rock on which he would build his church:

> "And I tell you that you are Peter (*Petros*), and on this rock (*petra*) I will build my church, and the gates of Hades will not overcome it." (Matt. 16:18)

Simile. A simile is a figure of speech that compares two things that are essentially like each other. It uses connectives such as "like," "as," or "than" or a verb such as "seems." In its simplest form, a simile identifies a single correspondence between two items in a sentence. When extended into a picture, it is known as a similitude. When expanded into a story, it becomes a story parable.

> "I am sending you out *like sheep among wolves*. Therefore be as *shrewd as snakes* and as *innocent as doves*." (Matt. 10:16)

> "For *as Jonah was three days and three nights in the belly of a huge fish, so the Son of Man will be three days and three nights in the heart of the earth*." (Matt. 12:40)

> He replied, "If you have faith *as small as a mustard seed*, you can say to this mulberry tree, 'Be uprooted and planted in the sea,' and it will obey you." (Luke 17:6)

> "Jerusalem, Jerusalem, you who kill the prophets and stone those sent to you, how often I have longed to gather your children together, *as a hen gathers her chicks under her wings*, and you were not willing." (Luke 13:34)

Metaphor. A metaphor, like a simile, also compares two things that are essentially different, but that share one thing in common. Like similes, they may also occur in series and in extended form.

> Then he said to his disciples, "The *harvest is plentiful* but the *workers are few*. Ask the *Lord of the harvest*, therefore, to *send out workers into his harvest field*." (Matt. 9:37–38)

> "Be careful," Jesus warned them. "Watch out for the *yeast of the Pharisees and that of Herod*." (Mark 8:15)

> "Everyone will be *salted with fire*. Salt is good, but if it loses its saltiness, how can you make it salty again? *Have salt among yourselves*, and be at peace with each other." (Mark 9:49–50)

> At that time some Pharisees came to Jesus and said to him, "Leave this place and go somewhere else. Herod wants to kill you." He replied, "Go tell *that fox*, 'I will keep on driving out demons and healing people today and tomorrow, and on the third day I will reach my goal.'" (Luke 13:31–32)

Proverb. A proverb is a succinct, pithy statement that conveys truth in a memorable manner. In his use of proverbs, Jesus displayed his continuity with Israel's wisdom tradition. In a broad sense, this category also includes maxims and aphorisms.

> "Put your sword back in its place," Jesus said to him, "for *all who draw the sword will die by the sword.*" (Matt. 26:52)

> Jesus said to them, "*A prophet is not without honor* except in his own town, among his relatives and in his own home." (Mark 6:4)

> Jesus replied, "*No one who puts a hand to the plow and looks back is fit for service in the kingdom of God.*" (Luke 9:62)

***A fortiori* statement**. An *a fortiori* statement, arguing from the lesser to the greater, is a type of argument in which the conclusion follows with even greater necessity than an already accepted fact or conclusion.

> "And why do you worry about clothes? See how the flowers of the field grow. They do not labor or spin. Yet I tell you that not even Solomon in all his splendor was dressed like one of these. *If that is how God clothes the grass of the field, which is here today and tomorrow is thrown into the fire, will he not much more clothe you*—you of little faith?" (Matt. 6:28–30)

> "Which of you, if your son asks for bread, will give him a stone? Or if he asks for a fish, will give him a snake? *If you, then, though you are evil, know how to give good gifts to your children, how much more will your Father in heaven give good gifts to those who ask him!*" (Matt. 7:9–11)

Irony. Narrowly conceived, irony is a literary device that intends a statement to be understood in a manner that is opposite its literal meaning. It is often placed in a context in which there is a feigned sense of ignorance. The most basic definition of irony recognizes that this device contrasts appearance and reality.

> He replied, "When evening comes, you say, 'It will be fair weather, for the sky is red,' and in the morning, 'Today it will be stormy, for the sky is red and overcast.' *You know how to interpret the appearance of the sky, but you cannot interpret the signs of the times.*" (Matt. 16:2–3)

> And he told them this parable: "The ground of a certain rich man yielded an abundant harvest. He thought to himself, 'What shall I do? I have no place to store my crops.' Then he said, 'This is what I'll do. I will tear down my barns and build bigger ones, and there I will store my surplus grain. And I'll say to myself, "You have plenty of grain laid up for many years. Take life easy; eat, drink and be merry."' But God said to him, *'You fool! This very night your life will be demanded from you. Then who will get what you have prepared for yourself?'*" (Luke 12:16–20)

Questions. Jesus frequently used questions to make a point and to impress a truth more effectively upon his listeners.

> Jesus and his disciples went on to the villages around Caesarea Philippi. On the way he asked them, *"Who do people say I am?"*
>
> They replied, "Some say John the Baptist; others say Elijah; and still others, one of the prophets."
>
> *"But what about you?"* he asked. *"Who do you say I am?"*
> Peter answered, "You are the Messiah." (Mark 8:27–29)

Jesus's preferred questioning style involved the use of rhetorical questions which were intended to produce an effect in his hearers.

> So Jesus called them over to him and began to speak to them in parables: *"How can Satan drive out Satan?"* (Mark 3:23)
>
> "Or suppose a woman has ten silver coins and loses one. *Doesn't she light a lamp, sweep the house and search carefully until she finds it?*" (Luke 15:8)

Jesus also employed the device of counter-question, particularly in hostile situations.

> They arrived again in Jerusalem, and while Jesus was walking in the temple courts, the chief priests, the teachers of the law and the elders came to him. "By what authority are you doing these things?" they asked. "And who gave you authority to do this?"

> Jesus replied, "I will ask you one question. Answer me, and I will tell you by what authority I am doing these things. *John's baptism—was it from heaven, or of human origin?* Tell me!" (Mark 11:27–30).

Parabolic or figurative actions. In some instances, Jesus used nonverbal teaching techniques in which the action itself made a specific point. In such cases, a verbal commentary may have followed, explaining the significance of Jesus's actions.

> The evening meal was in progress, and the devil had already prompted Judas, the son of Simon Iscariot, to betray Jesus. Jesus knew that the Father had put all things under his power, and that he had come from God and was returning to God; so he got up from the meal, took off his outer clothing, and wrapped a towel around his waist. After that, he poured water into a basin and began to wash his disciples' feet, drying them with the towel that was wrapped around him. . . .
>
> When he had finished washing their feet, he put on his clothes and returned to his place. "Do you understand what I have done for you?" he asked them. "You call me 'Teacher' and 'Lord,' and rightly so, for that is what I am. Now that I, your Lord and Teacher, have washed your feet, you also should wash one another's feet. I have set you an example that you should do as I have done for you. Very truly I tell you, no servant is greater than his master, nor is a messenger greater than the one who sent him. Now that you know these things, you will be blessed if you do them. (John 13:2–5, 12–17)

Poetry. The Gospels reflect a number of instances in which the sayings of Jesus are mediated through poetry (remember that Semitic poetry involved parallel ideas, not rhyme as in English). There are numerous examples of poetry in the sayings of Jesus in the Gospels.

> "Ask and it will be given to you;
> seek and you will find;
> knock and the door will be opened to you." (Matt. 7:7)

> "Love your enemies,

do good to those who hate you,
bless those who curse you,
pray for those who mistreat you." (Luke 6:27–28).

PARABLES OF JESUS

Definition and Purpose of Parables

Definition of Parable

A parable is a short narrative that demands a response from the hearer. Parables are true-to-life or realistic stories. They differ from historical narrative in that they are not true stories, though they are told with verisimilitude. At the same time, parables don't include fanciful elements as do fables, legends, or other mythical stories. Since they are not historical narratives, the characters and the story are created for the purpose of teaching a particular spiritual lesson. For instance, there probably was no historical innkeeper or "good Samaritan." Although most focus on the story parables, there are a variety of other forms as well.

In keeping with the genre's Semitic origin, there is a range spanning from extended similes (e.g., "the kingdom of heaven is like a merchant looking for fine pearls"; Matt. 13:45) to full-orbed story parables. This spectrum from short and simple to more extensive and complex can be diagrammed as follows:

9.1. EXTENDED FIGURE OF SPEECH TO FULL PARABLE			
Short Simile or Metaphor			**Long Allegory**
Similitude	Short parable	Story parable	Allegorical parable
Matt. 13:33	Luke 17:7–10	Luke 15:11–32	Mark 12:1–12

The various forms of parables found in Scripture should be understood along the continuum depicted above, though the distinctions between these categories are often fluid. While similitudes and short parables are similar in that they stress comparisons, a *similitude* is more straightforward and uses the present tense while a *short parable* is indirect, shaped in narrative form, and uses the past tense. A possible example of a similitude is the parable of the yeast in the dough (Matt. 13:33; Luke 13:20–21).

There are many examples of *story parables* in the Gospels. One that is familiar to many readers is the parable of the Good Samaritan (Luke 10:25–37), which is a story with a plot and active interaction of characters.

Perhaps the most difficult distinction to be made is that between parables and allegories. *Allegories* are a series of related metaphors. An easily identifiable allegory in the Gospels is that of the sower in which Jesus himself identifies the seed and the soil as representing the Word of God and a person, respectively (Matt. 13:2–23; Mark 4:1–20; Luke 8:4–15). Again, the distinction between parables and allegories may be fluid at times.

A case in point is the parable of the Royal Wedding Feast in which many of the details in the story are representative of something else (Matt. 22:1–14). The king refers to God, the servants to the prophets, and the son to Christ. Another example of an allegorical parable is that of the Wicked Tenants (Matt. 21:33–44; Mark 12:1–11; Luke 20:9–18). However, although a parable may in some cases resemble an allegory, parables are not allegories, because the two have differing functions.

Purpose of Parables

Parables serve a didactic purpose. They are designed to teach a particular spiritual or moral lesson to a particular audience. In this sense, they are similar to fables. However, the means by which they teach the lesson is different. Jesus himself commented on the purpose of his parables in the Parable of the Sower (Mark 4:10–12; Matt. 13:10–15; Luke 8:9–10). When asked by the disciples why he used parables, Jesus responded with the words of Isaiah 6:9–10:

> so that "they may be ever seeing but never perceiving,
> and ever hearing but never understanding;
> otherwise they might turn and be forgiven!"

This seems to suggest that Jesus's parables were spiritually appraised in such a way that precluded understanding by those who rejected his messianic claim and proclamation of the kingdom of God.

The key to understanding Jesus's statement is to be found in the context. Note that this parable is told in response to the phenomenon of

Jewish unbelief and rejection. Jesus's use of an Old Testament text that stresses the same motif clarifies that his particular emphasis is on unbelief. The unbelieving reception of Jesus by the Jews parallels the unbelief with which the people of Isaiah's day received his message. Thus, the Parable of the Sower emphasizes the fact that the lack of people's response to Jesus's words was in continuity with how people responded to God's message in Old Testament times.

At other times, Jesus used parables in order to challenge individuals to respond to his message or to instruct them in some other way (e.g., Matt. 24:32–25:46; Luke 7:40–43; 10). Osborne's statement (2006: 294) encapsulates well the purpose of parables:

> It seems clear that Jesus did indeed have a larger purpose in using the parable form. Parables are an "encounter mechanism" and function differently depending on the audience. . . . The parables encounter, interpret and invite the listener/reader to participate in Jesus's new world vision of the kingdom. They are a "speech-event" that never allows us to remain neutral; they grasp our attention and force us to interact with the presence of the kingdom in Jesus, either positively (those "around" Jesus in Mark 4:10–12) or negatively (those "outside").

Understood as "encounter mechanism," the purpose of Jesus's parables was not limited to instruction but also served to engage his hearers' value systems, priorities, and ways of thinking. When Jesus told a given parable, he aimed not merely at imparting information but sought to effect a change in people's perception and a reversal in their values and world view. In essence, parables were Jesus's preferred teaching tool for producing in his listeners a proper alignment with God's values which characterized the kingdom Jesus had come to inaugurate and proclaim.

Interpreting Parables

How should we view parables in order to bring out their intended meaning as accurately as possible? Most importantly, the parables should be viewed as *authentic teaching of Jesus.* Although some have questioned the authenticity of the parables of Jesus in the Gospels, there is ample reason for confidence in the parables' ability to provide some of the most authentic and reliable teaching from Jesus. One of the proofs of this authenticity is the closeness in language and content to other attested sayings of Jesus.

In addition, while not falling back on the pattern of extreme allegorization and subjectivity that dominated the interpretation of the church for so long, some parables may be more *allegorical in character* than is generally acknowledged. However, one should interpret a parable allegorically only if the text warrants the use of symbols by the original speaker. On the basis of the literary and the historical contexts, the interpreter should learn to distinguish between local color and details that are meant to convey allegorical significance. Parables are human interest stories with a spiritual lesson attached to them, but they are not necessarily allegories.

Finally, parables often *make more than one point*. One should not confine a parable to one point if it is evident that more than one truth is being conveyed. Recent parable studies have come to the conclusion that approximately two-thirds of Jesus's stories are triadic in structure. That is, they represent three main characters or groups of characters: a master figure (king, master, father, shepherd) and two contrasting subordinates (servants, sons, sheep). The implication of this is that the perspectives of the main characters reflect different parts of the overall meaning of the parable.

An approach in keeping with the hermeneutical triad that seeks to balance the historical, literary, and theological dimensions in parable interpretation is the most appropriate.

Jesus's Parables in the Synoptic Gospels

While parables abound in the Synoptic Gospels (especially Matthew and Luke), there are no parables in a more narrow sense in John's Gospel (though see the parabolic element in John 9:39–41 and the symbolic discourses in John 10:1–5 and 15:1–8). The parables in the Synoptic Gospels are frequently arranged thematically to highlight certain theological emphases. Note, for instance, the surrounding contexts of the Parable of the Wicked Tenants, a parable found in all three Synoptic Gospels. Whereas Mark and Luke place their version of the parable in the context of Jesus's authority, Matthew accentuates more keenly Israel's rejection. It is more than likely that Jesus retold some of these parables, which may explain the different variations encountered.

9.2. SYNOPTIC COMPARISON OF THE PARABLE OF THE WICKED TENANTS		
MARK	**MATTHEW**	**LUKE**
Mark 11:27–33	Matthew 21:28–32	Luke 20:1–8
The authority of Jesus questioned	The parable of the two sons	The authority of Jesus questioned
Mark 12:1–12	Matthew 21:33–46	Luke 20:9–19
The wicked tenants	The wicked tenants	The wicked tenants
Mark 12:13–17	Matthew 22:1–14	Luke 20:20–26
Paying taxes to Caesar	The parable of the wedding banquet	Paying taxes to Caesar

Most of Matthew's parables are found in three of his five discourses in Matthew 12–13, 18, and 24–25. In conformity with his overall theological thrust, Matthew groups the kingdom parables in Matthew 13; parables on his "ecclesiastical discourse" in Matthew 18:10–14, 21–35; those on Israel's rejection in Matthew 21:28–22:14; and seven more related to the end times in Matthew 24:32–25:46. At least twelve parables are unique to Matthew.

With regard to story parables, Mark has the fewest, featuring only four, with three of these being found in chapter 4 (the Sower; the Secretly Growing Seed; and the Mustard Seed) and one in chapter 12 (the Wicked Tenants). Matthew and Luke have all these except for the Secretly Growing Seed; they also share the parables of the Leaven and the Lost Sheep. Luke places most of his parables in his travel narrative (Luke 9:51–19:27). At least fifteen parables are unique to him.

Jewish Background and Parallels

Jesus did not invent the parable teaching form. The background of parables is found in the wisdom tradition of Israel (Heb. *mašal*; Grk. *parabolē*). *Mašal* encompasses forms as diverse as "saying," "proverb," or "wisdom saying." While commonly associated with teachers of wisdom (1 Kgs. 4:32; Prov. 26:7, 9; Eccl. 12:9), its most general usage is in describing a popular saying or maxim whose origins have been lost in antiquity (cf. 1 Sam. 24:4). From its more popular meaning of proverb, it came to be used as a technical term for wisdom teaching until eventually it was taken to encompass a wide range of terms including prophetic proverbs, parables, riddles, and symbolic action.

Salvation History and the Life Setting of Jesus

An important interpretive issue with regard to parables has to do with understanding the life situation of Jesus. You should ask the question: "Is there anything significant about the particular juncture in Jesus's ministry in which the parable was told?" In order to answer this question, you must understand Jesus's ministry in terms of its place in salvation history. Whereas God is active in all of history in general, his redemptive activity in the history recorded in Scripture is unique. This "salvation history" is intimately tied up with God's revelation of himself. Of great significance is his ultimate self-revelation through his Son Jesus Christ.

Hence, the Parable of the Sower (Mark 4:1–9, 13–20; Matt. 13:1–9, 18–23; Luke 8:4–8, 11–15), which describes the reception of a seed by four different kinds of soils, anticipates the rejection that Jesus would eventually face. Whereas all four soils received the same seed, only one bore fruit. This parable demonstrates, among other things, that although obedience in faith is the right response to the revelation that has come in Jesus Christ, not all who hear will respond positively. In Matthew's context, the parable concludes with the following words: "He who has ears, let him hear." All three evangelists place this parable in contexts in which the Jewish leaders express their rejection of Jesus and his message. Thus, this parable serves the purpose of explaining to the hearers—particularly Jesus's disciples who by this time were surely wondering why people's response to Jesus was not more positive—why people didn't respond in larger numbers to Jesus and his message.

Likewise, the allegorical Parable of the Wicked Tenants must be understood from a pre-Christian vantage point (Mark 12:1–11; Matt. 21:33–44; Luke 20:9–19). The owner of the vineyard represents God; the first group of tenants represents Israel's leaders; and the second, those who replace this original, corrupt group. Both God's patience and his judgment on these wicked people come to the fore in this parable. The focus in the parable is on the son, who is symbolic of Jesus himself. Arising from a context in which Jesus's authority is in question, this parable exposes the eventual rejection of Jesus by the Jews and anticipates his death. This comes into sharper focus from a post-resurrection perspective.

Characteristics of Parables

In order to interpret parables effectively, it is important to recognize that parables have certain defining characteristics. Identifying these characteristics and understanding what role they play in the parable is crucial for correct interpretation. Osborne (2006: 296–302) identifies the following ten characteristics of parables.

Earthiness: Almost all the parables are told within a setting in which the images in the parables are supported by earthy details. Understanding these details is crucial to understanding the parable itself.

> "Listen! A farmer went out to sow his seed. As he was scattering the seed, some fell along the path, and the birds came and ate it up. Some fell on rocky places, where it did not have much soil. It sprang up quickly, because the soil was shallow. But when the sun came up, the plants were scorched, and they withered because they had no root. Other seed fell among thorns, which grew up and choked the plants, so that they did not bear grain. Still other seed fell on good soil. It came up, grew and produced a crop, some multiplying thirty, some sixty, some a hundred times." (Mark 4:3–8)

Conciseness: Unlike complex narratives that have numerous characters and a detailed plot, parables are simple and uncomplicated.

> "Again, the kingdom of heaven is like a merchant looking for fine pearls. When he found one of great value, he went away and sold everything he had and bought it." (Matt. 13:45–46)

Major and minor points: This is one of the issues in parable research that has yet to be settled. Many modern interpreters tend to emphasize a "one-point" approach. However, most parables have one major point as well as one or more secondary points. Note, for example, that the Parable of the Prodigal Son appears to come to a conclusion in Luke 15:24:

> "But the father said to his servants, 'Quick! Bring the best robe and put it on him. Put a ring on his finger and sandals on his feet. Bring the fattened calf and kill it. Let's have a feast and celebrate. For this son of mine was dead and is alive again; he was lost and is found.' So they began to celebrate." (Luke 15:22–24)

However, perhaps surprisingly, Jesus is not yet done. He continues,

> "Meanwhile, the older son was in the field. When he came near the house, he heard music and dancing. So he called one of the servants and asked him what was going on. 'Your brother has come,' he replied, 'and your father has killed the fattened calf because he has him back safe and sound.' The older brother became angry and refused to go in." (Luke 15:25–28)

Jesus proceeds to drive home a lesson for his original audience (represented in the parable by the older brother), which corresponds to the setting narrated at the outset of the parable:

> Now the tax collectors and sinners were all gathering around to hear Jesus. But the Pharisees and the teachers of the law muttered, "This man welcomes sinners and eats with them." (Luke 15:1–2)

Repetition: In telling his parables, Jesus sometimes used repetition to stress the climax or the major point. An example is the twofold confession of the prodigal son:

> "When he came to his senses, he said, 'How many of my father's hired servants have food to spare, and here I am starving to death! I will set out and go back to my father and say to him: *Father, I have sinned against heaven and against you. I am no longer worthy to be called your son*; make me like one of your hired servants.' So he got up and went to his father.
>
> But while he was still a long way off, his father saw him and was filled with compassion for him; he ran to his son, threw his arms around him and kissed him.
>
> "The son said to him, '*Father, I have sinned against heaven and against you. I am no longer worthy to be called your son.*'" (Luke 15:17–21)

Conclusion: In most instances, Jesus used a terse dictum to conclude a parable. Note, for instance, Luke 12:21:

> "This is how it will be with anyone who stores up things for himself but is not rich toward God."

In others, he used the technique of questions or even interpreted the parable himself.

> Then Jesus said to them, "Don't you understand this parable? How then will you understand any parable? The farmer sows the word. Some people are like seed along the path, where the word is sown. As soon as they hear it, Satan comes and takes away the word that was sown in them. Others, like seed sown on rocky places, hear the word and at once receive it with joy. But since they have no root, they last only a short time. When trouble or persecution comes because of the word, they quickly fall away. Still others, like seed sown among thorns, hear the word; but the worries of this life, the deceitfulness of wealth and the desires for other things come in and choke the word, making it unfruitful. Others, like seed sown on good soil, hear the word, accept it, and produce a crop—some thirty, some sixty, some a hundred times what was sown." (Mark 4:13–20)

Whereas the conclusion generally provides the main point, it may in some instances apply to the broader situation.

Listener-relatedness: The main purpose of parables is to elicit a response from the listener, either positive or negative. An example of this is the Parable of the Good Samaritan. When the expert in the law, "wanted to justify himself" and asked Jesus, "And who is my neighbor?" (Luke 10:29), Jesus told a story in which a man traveling from Jerusalem to Jericho fell into the hands of robbers. Three men—a priest, a Levite, and a Samaritan—pass by, but only the Samaritan helps the man. Then Jesus asks the expert in the law:

> "Which of these three do you think was a neighbor to the man who fell into the hands of robbers?"
>
> The expert in the law replied, "The one who had mercy on him."
>
> Jesus told him, *"Go and do likewise."* (Luke 10:36–37)

Reversal of expectation: Parables frequently contain unexpected elements that force the hearer to reconsider a course of action or an attitude. They frequently promote norms that run counter to those listening. Without an understanding of the historical context, it is impossible to grasp this reversal. For instance, "good Samaritan" was considered an oxymoron in Jesus's day, for Jewish relations with Samaritans were strained (cf. John 4:9). Only by understanding the hatred that existed between the Jews and the Samaritans of Jesus's times can one begin to understand the point of the parable.

Kingdom-centered eschatology: The thread that ties the parables together is the kingdom of God. They reflect the reality of the kingdom as present, as well as future, since the kingdom is an expression used for God's power and rule. At the same time, they are christological in focus since they center on Jesus Christ as the one who brings this kingdom into being. A classic example is the Parable of the Ten Virgins in which Jesus is represented by the bridegroom:

> "At that time the kingdom of heaven will be like ten virgins who took their lamps and went out to meet the bridegroom. Five of them were foolish and five were wise. The foolish ones took their lamps but did not take any oil with them. The wise ones, however, took oil in jars along with their lamps. The bridegroom was a long time in coming, and they all became drowsy and fell asleep.
>
> At midnight the cry rang out: 'Here's the bridegroom! Come out to meet him!'
>
> Then all the virgins woke up and trimmed their lamps. The foolish ones said to the wise, 'Give us some of your oil; our lamps are going out.'
>
> 'No,' they replied, 'there may not be enough for both us and you. Instead, go to those who sell oil and buy some for yourselves.'
>
> But while they were on their way to buy the oil, the bridegroom arrived. The virgins who were ready went in with him to the wedding banquet. And the door was shut.

> Later the others also came. 'Lord, Lord,' they said, 'open the door for us!'
>
> But he replied, 'Truly I tell you, I don't know you.'
>
> Therefore keep watch, because you do not know the day or the hour." (Matt. 25:1–13)

Kingdom ethics: Since the kingdom is present and not just future, there is a demand for higher ethical standards. This has important implications for discipleship. Such standards often involve a reversal of the values and priorities of this world.

> At that time the disciples came to Jesus and asked, "Who, then, is the greatest in the kingdom of heaven?"
>
> He called a little child to him, and placed the child among them. And he said: "Truly I tell you, *unless you change and become like little children, you will never enter the kingdom of heaven. Therefore, whoever takes the lowly position of this child is the greatest in the kingdom of heaven*. And whoever welcomes one such child in my name welcomes me" (Matt. 18:1–5).

God and salvation: The parables reflect the fact that God, in all the guises in which he is represented (king, father, landowner, employer, judge), is a gracious God who offers forgiveness and salvation. All that is required is repentance and a positive response to his offer. This is epitomized in the father of the Prodigal Son:

> "But *while he was still a long way off, his father saw him and was filled with compassion for him; he ran to his son, threw his arms around him and kissed him*.
>
> The son said to him, 'Father, I have sinned against heaven and against you. I am no longer worthy to be called your son.'

But *the father said to his servants, 'Quick! Bring the best robe and put it on him. Put a ring on his finger and sandals on his feet. Bring the fattened calf and kill it. Let's have a feast and celebrate. For this son of mine was dead and is alive again; he was lost and is found.'*" (Luke 15:20b–24a)

GUIDELINES FOR INTERPRETING THE PARABLES

1. Determine the *structure* of the parable. Make note of plot development, literary style, and narrative flow. Ensure that you correctly identify transitional phrases, literary inclusions, and other textual markers. Note the crucial pointers that constrain the purpose of the parable.

2. Determine the *literary context* of the parable. Investigate how the parable fits with the theological emphasis of the particular evangelist.

3. Establish the *historical context* and note other aspects of the setting that may contribute to an understanding of the parable. Always keep in mind the two-level nature of the parables.

4. Make careful note of the *points of reference*, that is, those items with which the hearer is to identify, and the *climax* of the narrative. Remember that the point of the parable is often found in the response elicited by the parable.

5. Determine the *main point* of the parable as well as any *secondary points*. Avoid placing too much significance on surrounding details and allegorize only if the text warrants it.

6. Determine the *original intent* of the parable. What is the function of this parable in terms of Jesus's kingdom teaching and the message of the evangelists? What theological message does it convey? Ensure that you clarify any doctrine with other parts of Scripture.

7. Keep in mind that the entire interpretive process should be based on *sound exegetical procedures*. Take note of the meaning

of significant words and the contribution of grammar and syntax.

8. Draw all your findings together and *summarize the meaning* of your parable. Ensure that this is consistent with authorial intent.

9. *Apply the central truth(s)* of this parable to the contemporary situation.

KEY WORDS

Allegory, Hyperbole, Life Setting, Parable, Pun, Simile, Similitude.

ASSIGNMENTS

1. Keeping in mind the classification of various types of parables provided in the course text, classify the Parable of the Tenants in Mark 12:1–12. Provide a basic interpretation of the parable and discuss its significance within the plot and theological message of Mark's Gospel.

2. Discuss Jesus's three parables on "lost things" in Luke 15, focusing on the Parable of the Prodigal Son. Identify the historical setting of the parable and show how it organically fits within Luke's Gospel and theological message.

KEY RESOURCES

Blomberg, Craig L. *Interpreting the Parables*. Downers Grove: InterVarsity, 1990.

Stein, Robert H. *The Method and Message of Jesus's Teachings*. Philadelphia: Westminster, 1978.

CHAPTER 10 OBJECTIVES

1. To acquaint the interpreter with the genre of the New Testament Epistles by reference to ancient epistolary conventions.

2. To provide a discussion of the most salient features of the Pauline Epistles.

3. To introduce special issues pertaining to individual New Testament letters.

4. To discuss general hermeneutical issues related to the Epistles.

5. To provide the interpreter with a set of guidelines for interpreting the Epistles.

CHAPTER 10 OUTLINE

A. New Testament Epistles and Ancient Epistolography

B. Pauline Epistles

C. General Epistles

D. General Hermeneutical Issues

E. Guidelines for Interpreting Epistles

F. Key Words

G. Assignments

H. Key Resources

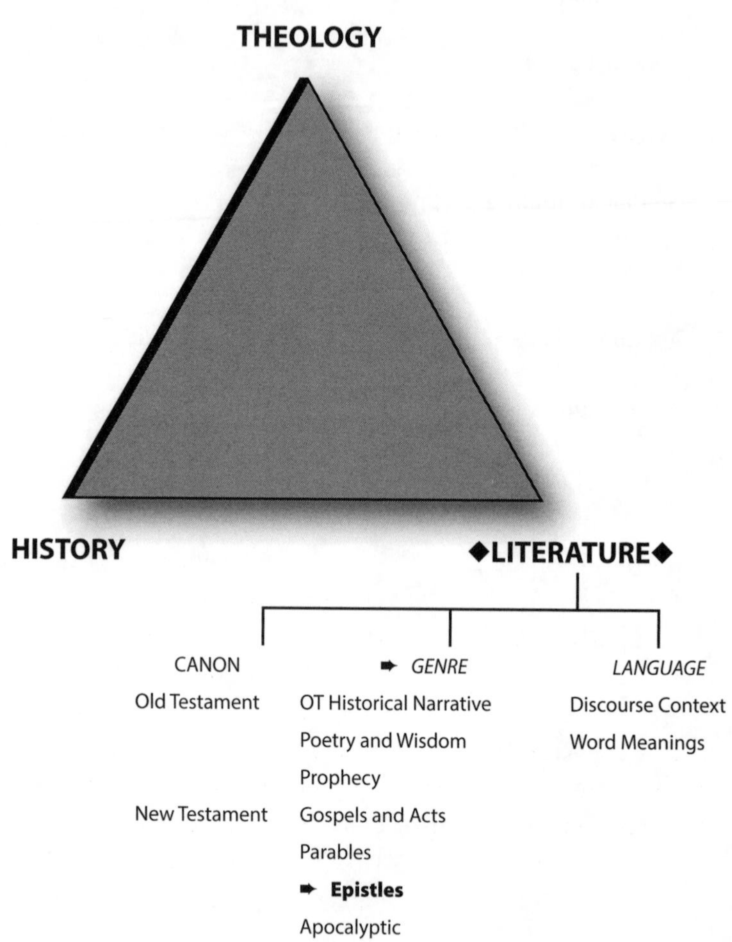
THEOLOGY
HISTORY
◆LITERATURE◆
CANON
Old Testament
New Testament
➨ GENRE
OT Historical Narrative
Poetry and Wisdom
Prophecy
Gospels and Acts
Parables
➨ Epistles
Apocalyptic
LANGUAGE
Discourse Context
Word Meanings

Chapter 10

GOING BY THE LETTER: EPISTLES

THE NEW TESTAMENT EPISTLES AND ANCIENT EPISTOLOGRAPHY

Introduction

As we continue our interpretive journey through the canonical landscape, we turn next to an investigation of the epistolary genre. It is hard to exaggerate the importance of the New Testament letters; it is here that we find the bulk of the instruction as to how we should live our lives as believers today. This explains why many preachers spend a considerable amount of time expounding the Epistles.

Although Epistles make up a considerably larger portion of the New Testament, several letters are also embedded in various books of the Old Testament. These include several found in narrative and prophetic literature, many of them quite short (2 Sam. 11:14–15; 1 Kgs. 21:9–10; 2 Kgs. 5:6; 10:2–3, 6; 19:10–13 [= Isa 37:10–13]; 2 Chron. 2:11–15; 21:12–15; Neh. 6:6–7; Ezra 4–5; Jer. 29:4–23, 26–28). Official letters were dispatched to report various military or other matters to a king or other superior (e.g., 1 Kgs. 5:8–9; 2 Chron. 2:3–15).

Readers of the New Testament will quickly discover that the majority of the books making up the New Testament (21 out of 27 books) have the superscript "Epistle." This designation, though not part of the original documents themselves, nonetheless identifies correctly the genre of these writings. In fact, the designation "epistle" can be found in several of the

New Testament letters (e.g., Rom. 16:22; 2 Cor. 7:8; Col. 4:16; 1 Thess. 5:27; 2 Thess. 3:14; 2 Pet. 3:1). It was Paul's custom to write to his churches in letter form (2 Thess. 3:17). His opponents acknowledged that he wrote "weighty and forceful" letters (2 Cor. 10:10), and Peter referred to Paul's letters as "hard to understand" (2 Pet. 3:16).

Since Paul is the author of the vast majority of the letters included in the New Testament—13 out of 21—our discussion of ancient epistolography will make reference mostly to his letters, though the insights gained concerning Paul's letters pertain to the other New Testament letters as well. After the discussion of epistolography with special focus on Paul's writings, we will address the other letters included in the New Testament.

Opening

The similarities between Paul's letters and ancient epistles are most clearly seen in the opening and closing sections of the letter. Typically, the ancient letters opened with an identification of the sender and the addressee, followed by a salutation or greeting (e.g., "Paul to Timothy, greetings"; cf. Acts 15:23; Jas. 1:1), and adding the element of prayer, which could contain a health wish (cf. 3 John 2) and/or a prayer to the gods on behalf of the addressee. It is important to observe how the writers of the New Testament letters, particularly Paul, followed these conventions and how they deviated from them, because the similarities and differences provide indications as to the occasion and circumstances surrounding the writing of a given New Testament letter.

Most of the New Testament letters identify in their opening section the sender. In addition, co-senders are mentioned in most of Paul's letters (except for Romans, Ephesians, and the letters to Timothy and Titus). These co-senders were not necessarily co-writers but were mentioned for various other reasons, such as to let the congregation know the whereabouts of the people with whom they were acquainted or to establish the authority of the carrier of a given letter.

Apart from the sender, the New Testament Epistles customarily mention the addressee. Most New Testament letters were sent to Christian communities. The designations used for the reader likewise have interpretive significance. In his first letter to the Corinthians, for instance, Paul adds "all those everywhere who call on the name of our Lord Jesus

Christ—their Lord and ours" (1 Cor. 1:2), most likely in order to remind his readers that they are not an isolated body of believers. In using the expression "the church of *God* in Corinth" (1 Cor. 1:2), Paul may be communicating the fact that the church belonged to *God* and not to Paul or Apollos.

The opening section of a Pauline letter also contains distinctive features in its salutation or greeting. A typical Hellenistic greeting was *chairein* ("greetings"; see Acts 15:23). Paul Christianized the term by changing the greeting to *charis* ("grace"). He also added the greeting that was usually present in the Aramaic or Hebrew letters (*shalom* meaning "peace"), which in Greek is *eirēnē*. The inclusion of both a Greek and Hebrew type of greeting may indicate the fact that Paul was writing to a mixed audience including both Jews and Gentiles, and thus suggesting that both groups had equal standing before God (cf. Gal. 3:28–29).

The prayer section in the Hellenistic letters addressed to the gods was likewise Christianized and presented in the form of a *thanksgiving*. Thus the occasion for the thanksgiving was no longer favor with the gods but salvation by Jesus Christ. This section also alerts the readers to *central themes* that the author will develop in the body of the letter. For instance, in his first letter to the Corinthians, Paul reminds them of spiritual gifts and blessings they possessed as a result of God's generous grace, gifts that gave rise to problems in the Corinthian church (1:4–9; cf. chaps. 12–14). Of Paul's letters, only Galatians and Titus lack a thanksgiving section.

Body

While the opening and the closing of Paul's letters reflect certain similarities with ancient Hellenistic letters, such similarities are less recognizable in the body of his letters. This may be due again to Paul's freedom in adopting and adapting the conventional forms in light of the exigencies that determined the writing of his letters. On the whole, ancient letters were fairly stereotypical, closely following epistolary conventions, while Paul's letters do not seem to conform to any one literary pattern and structure.

We will discuss the rhetorical structure of the Pauline epistles in more detail below; for now it will be sufficient to note that no consensus has been reached on the structure of Paul's letters. While Paul's letters exhibit a considerable degree of diversity, the body of his letters often begins with typical phrases, including: (1) a disclosure formula by which he seeks to inform the addressees about a certain subject—"I do not want you to be unaware" (Rom. 1:13; cf. 2 Cor. 1:18; Phil. 1:12; 1 Thess. 2:1); (2) a request formula which in Philemon is strikingly extended by Greek standards—"I appeal to you" (1 Cor. 1:10; cf. 2 Thess. 2:1); or (3) an expression of astonishment—"I am astonished that you are so quickly deserting the one who called you" (Gal. 1:6).

Closing

The apostle Paul typically included several items in the closing of his letters, apparently in no particular order, except for the benediction which always came at the end (Romans is an exception). Among the items Paul includes in the closing of his letters are: prayers (Rom. 15:33, 16:25–27; 1 Thess. 5:23; 2 Thess. 3:16); commendations of fellow workers (Rom. 16:1–2; 1 Cor. 16:10–12); prayer requests (Rom. 15:30–32; Col. 4:2–4; Eph. 6:18–20; 1 Thess. 5:25); greetings (Rom. 16:3–16, 21–23; 1 Cor. 16:19–21); final instructions and exhortations (Gal. 6:11–17; Col. 4:16–18a); references to a "holy kiss" (1 Cor. 16:20b; 2 Cor. 13:12a; 1 Thess. 5:26); autographed greetings (1 Cor. 16:21; Gal. 6:11; Phlm. 16); and a grace benediction (Rom. 16:20b; 1 Cor. 16:23–24; Col. 4:18b).

As might be expected, Paul Christianized the typical formula for closing a Hellenistic letter of the day with the word "farewell" (e.g., Acts 15:29) by using the word "grace" (*charis*). Likewise, we do not find in Paul's letters the wish for good health of the recipients which was typical of the Hellenistic letters, a formula that came to function as bidding farewell. Instead, Paul replaced such a wish with a *benediction* or *doxology*, which served as functional substitutes and had a similar effect. Thus Paul's letters are less bound by the conventional formulas of closing characteristics of Hellenistic letters.

Types of Letters

We have already mentioned the broad categories of private and official letters. Apart from these, there are other more specific types of letters in antiquity. Among them are letters of friendship, introduction, blame, reproach, consolation, criticism, censure, praise, interrogation, accusation, apology, and gratitude. While caution should be exercised in aligning

Paul's letters too closely with other ancient epistolary forms, it is worth mentioning here some of the features of the various types of ancient letters, since many of these are also present in Paul's letters.

First, many ancients preferred the plain, carefree speech rather than an elevated style, modeling the letter after the *everyday speech* of educated individuals. In this regard, the letter should not be too long, nor should the writer include frequent breaks in sentence structure, thus imitating conversation. One could thus almost speak of spoken letters. In our discussion of the rhetorical features of Paul's letters below, we will see that traits of oral presentation are present in his letters and that we get a sense at times that Paul is preaching as if he were with his readers in person.

Second, letters were intended to be *expressions of friendship*, or of one's friendly feelings, and were thus to be written more carefully than a dialogue since they formed a sort of literary present to their recipient and a picture of a writer's own soul.

The third feature is that of *literary presence*. A letter was intended to revive the existence of a friendship when the correspondents were physically separated. In this vein, Paul wrote letters usually as substitute communication. This is not to say that Paul always preferred bodily presence, for in some cases he deemed the writing of a letter as more expedient. For example, a personal visit to Corinth ended in disaster (2 Cor. 12:20–21) while the use of an envoy (i.e. Titus; 2 Cor. 7:5–16) and a painful letter (2 Cor. 2:4) proved to be more effective.

Finally, fourth, we may identify several specific types of letters that are found in the New Testament. One type is that of *diatribe*, which includes a series of questions and answers and which characterizes parts of Paul's Epistle to the Romans. Another epistolary subgenre is that of the apologetic letter of *self-commendation*, which was a well-known form of rhetorical self-defense (see especially 2 Corinthians 10–13). Yet another type of letter is that containing *exhortation* (paraenesis), a frequent feature in Paul's and other New Testament letters. After preparing his readers to receive his exhortation by commending them for their faith, godly example, or some other Christian virtue, the letter writer proceeded to the business at hand, whether the existence of divisions in the church, people's lack of humility, or some other problem or issue. Then there is the *letter of introduction or commendation*, which is exemplified particularly in Philemon.

Letter-Writing

Of importance here is the use of secretaries or amanuenses and dispatchers or carriers since Paul used both of these in the writing of his letters. There are three ways in which a *secretary* might have been used: (1) word-by-word dictation; (2) dictation of the sense of the message, leaving the formulation of the material to the secretary; and (3) instruction of a secretary to write in one's name, without indication of specific contents. It is beyond dispute that Paul used secretaries (see Rom. 16:22; 1 Cor. 16:21; 2 Thess. 3:17; Phlm. 19). In any case, Paul, before sending a given letter, doubtless made sure that what was written was exactly what he intended to communicate, the proof being his signature written with his own hand (e.g., Gal. 6:11).

The *dispatchers or carriers of letters* were very important. In antiquity, private letters were often entrusted for delivery to strangers passing through or stumbled upon in the marketplace. The only way a sender could exercise any control over the delivery of a letter was by sending his own servant, which implied some measure of wealth and social status. The writers of (official) letters would often send the real message by word because of the insecurity of the postal system and owing to political intrigue. Regardless of the system of delivery, the oral aspect of private letters was present, given several factors such as (1) that greetings at times were to be shared with others; (2) the possibility that the recipient was illiterate and thus the letter needed to be read aloud and before an assembled family, making the arrival of a correspondence a social event; and (3) the fact that letter carriers often waited for a reply before returning to the original writer. The oral aspect of official letters was also due to the general distrust of the written word and to the need for carriers to answer inquiries related to the letter's contents.

Paul's letters display the same characteristics when it comes to their delivery. In contrast to the dispatch of private letters through hired carriers or slaves or the chance of journeying of friends or strangers, Paul had trusted colleagues (e.g., his co-senders) who carried his letters and were invested with authority from Paul to interpret his letters upon arrival and to read out loud the content of his letters (Eph. 6:21–22; Col. 4:7–8; 1 Thess. 5:27). The carriers were thus his *surrogates*, his personal representatives. In light of these factors in the writing of a letter, one can easily see why the mention and the selection of the carriers of his letters were important for Paul.

Pseudonymity and Allonymity

Given the use of secretaries and carriers, one is confronted with the issue of pseudonymity and allonymity. *Pseudonymity* refers to a writing in which a later follower attributes his own work to his revered teacher in order to perpetuate that person's teachings and influence. Among the letters alleged to have been written by someone other than Paul are his letters to Timothy and Titus. One reason why some commentators claim pseudonymity for these letters is the distinctive vocabulary we find in these letters in comparison to the commonly acknowledged Pauline writings (such as Romans or Galatians). But this argument based on stylistic differences is of limited value when one takes into account the type of recipients for the letters to Timothy and Titus (i.e., individuals) in comparison with the recipients of Paul's other letters (i.e., public, with the possible exception of Philemon). Another argument is that 1-2 Timothy and Titus present a well-structured church organization based on a hierarchical model, a sort of "early Catholicism," which supposedly proves a second-century date. This argument, however, does not take sufficiently into consideration the fact that the appointing of elders and deacons was already a practice found in the church long before the writing of the letters to Timothy and Titus (Acts 14:23; 15:2; 20:28–31; 21:18). Most likely, Paul wrote these letters sensing an urgency to leave behind a clearly defined body of doctrine and instructions for church organization and leadership as he was nearing the end of his life.

At the core, pseudonymity is a historical matter. How is the alleged pseudonymity of the letters to Timothy and Titus or other New Testament Epistles supported from first-century usage and practice? The answer is, not very well at all. First, while pseudonymous writings in other genres (such as Gospels or apocalypses) were not uncommon, pseudonymous letters were exceedingly rare, if not completely unknown, apparently because letters in their very essence constitute a person-to-person or person-to-group communication. Second, in the apostolic era, far from a prevailing acceptance of pseudonymous epistles, there was actually considerable concern that letters might be forged (see, e.g., 2 Thess. 2:2). In the second century, Tertullian (*Bapt.* 17) reports that an Asian presbyter was removed from office for forging a letter in Paul's name. Serapion in A.D. 211 distinguished between apostolic writings and those that "falsely bear their name" (*pseudepigrapha*; cited in Eusebius, *Eccl. Hist.* 6.12.3).

Another difficulty with the supposed pseudonymous authorship of certain ones of Paul's letters (as well as Peter's; see below) is that this theory requires the assumption that scores of incidental details in Paul's, Timothy's, and Titus's life were invented by the alleged later pseudonymous author, all supposedly without deceptive intent. However, it is unclear what purpose such large-scale fabrication of fictional details would serve.

Finally, since pseudonymity was most likely not an accepted practice, some have claimed *allonymity* or *allepigraphy*, a mediating position, which holds that a later author edited what Paul wrote but attributed the writing to Paul or another person without intent to deceive. However, this view is problematic as well. A better hypothesis is frequently that the author (such as Paul) used an amanuensis, which may account for the distinct vocabulary, a practice attested in his other letters, as we have seen.

Conclusion

Paul was part of a culture that used letters for different purposes, from private correspondence intended to maintain friendship to official correspondence intended to establish authority. Paul inevitably followed some of the epistolographic conventions as is evident especially in the introduction and conclusion of his letters. But even here, we see Paul not only adopting but also adapting some of the forms in order to fit them to his purpose for writing. At times, he Christianized the secular terms and format while at other times he left out certain conventional phrases because of the exigencies that prompted him to write. Thus, we can see in Paul a level of freedom in structuring his letters, not bound to any one form. Even when we compare his letters with one another, we find that they display a natural diversity.

In content, many of Paul's Epistles deal with complex relationships among Christians rather than with cultivating friendly relations with outsiders. While the subject of his letters is more akin to official correspondence (e.g., establishing his authority as in Galatians), Paul sought to bring his addressees into richer experiences of their new-found relationship with Christ, not merely to move them to submission to his authority or to maintain friendly relations. Therefore, a student of Paul's Epistles will be wise to analyze each letter on its own terms, noting each detail in its introduction and conclusion in order to determine the purpose for writing and studying its contents in order to find out what clues it offers to the situation that gave rise to the writing of the particular letter.

PAULINE EPISTLES

Paul's Use of the Old Testament

One highly significant feature of Paul's letters is his extensive use of the Old Testament in constructing his arguments. We find quotations, paraphrases, and allusions in every Pauline letter with the exception of Philemon. These are introduced with the formula "it is written" or with some other introductory phrase. In addition, Paul's letters reflect Old Testament themes, structures, and theology. In fact, one could say that the Old Testament provided the framework and foundation for Paul's theology.

In interpreting Paul's explicit *quotations* of the Old Testament, there are several questions we must answer in order to determine their function in Paul's context more accurately:

1. What Old Testament text(s) is (are) being cited? Is it just one or a combination? If it is a combination, what is the contribution of each text?

2. Is the Old Testament citation part of a wider tradition or theology in the Old Testament? If it is, the citation may be alluding to a context much wider than the specific passage from which it has been taken.

3. How did various Jewish and Christian groups and interpreters understand the passage in question? And in what ways does the New Testament citation agree or disagree with the interpretations found in other ancient interpreters?

4. How does the function of the citation compare to the function of other citations in the New Testament writing under consideration?

5. Finally, what contribution does the citation make to the argument of the New Testament passage in which it is found?

When it comes to *allusions* and *echoes*, it becomes much harder to identify where Paul relies on the Old Testament text, theme, or theology.

We will take one example from the letter to the Philippians. In Philippians 1:19 ("what has happened to me will turn out for my deliverance"), Paul seems to allude to Job 13:16. While Paul's words are intelligible without reference to Job, an understanding of the context in Job helps us appreciate Paul's message more fully. Paul's citation of Job identifies him with the righteous sufferer who, like Job, will be vindicated by God before his interlocutors and rivals.

The greatest interpretive challenge may be to understand how Paul exegeted a particular Old Testament text or arrived at a certain interpretation of a given passage. What may aid us in understanding Paul's exegetical style is to look at the Jewish hermeneutical methods that most likely affected Paul. Another hermeneutical parallel exists with the interpretive practice known as *pesher* (i.e., verse-by-verse interpretation), in particular its end-time orientation. But the comparison is limited given the fact that Paul believed that with Christ the age to come had already arrived (cf. 1 Cor. 10:11).

More likely is an affinity with the rabbinic exegesis called *midrash*, which generally means "interpretation" or "commentary." While *pesher* pertains to the plain or obvious meaning, *midrash*, while including this meaning, at the same time transcends it. Early *midrash* is recognized by the seven rules (*middoth*) attributed to the famous first-century rabbi Hillel. We will mention here the three most often found in Paul. The first rule is *qal wahomer* ("light and heavy"), an argument from the lesser to the greater, that is, what applies in a less important case will certainly apply in a more important one (e.g., Rom. 5:10).

The second rule is *gezera shawah* ("rule of equivalence"), a method that states that passages that share similar vocabulary clarify each other (e.g., Rom. 4:7–10; 11:7–10). This is similar to the Reformation principle of Scripture interpreting Scripture and the parallel passage apparatus in many of today's Study Bibles.

The third rule is *kelal upherat* ("general and particular"), where a general principle may be deduced from a specific passage and vice versa (e.g., Rom. 13:8–10). But even these parallels must be drawn with great caution. Paul was surely immersed in Jewish culture and therefore most probably made use of its exegetical methods. However, the precise nature of Paul's dependence continues to be debated, since Rabbinic Judaism (from which we derive most data) developed only subsequent to the first century.

Moreover, some of the Jewish hermeneutical rules are general logical principles of arguing which reflects the general *a fortiori* ("from the lesser to the greater") argument used in different cultures.

Paul's use and interpretation of the Old Testament may at times be difficult to understand in light of our modern rules for determining meaning. But what may seem to us a strange interpretation may have represented conventional hermeneutical procedure to Paul's contemporaries. This is why Paul's interpretation of the Old Testament had considerable apologetic power and convinced many Jews to believe in Jesus as the fulfillment of Old Testament prophecy. Paul, like his contemporaries, sought to bring an Old Testament passage or prediction into a new historical and theological context, which involved some shift in meaning while remaining faithful to the message in its original context.

Paul's Use of Christian Traditions

Creeds or Hymns

In constructing his arguments in his letters, Paul made use of different Christian traditions. Among the most discussed are creeds or hymns. Creeds are usually contained in *hymns*, and therefore our focus here will be on the latter. It is usually possible to detect a hymn by the presence of strophes and/or rhythm, which marks the intrusion of poetic style into prose material. In this regard, these passages can be identified as traditional material, because they contain terminology uncommon to the Pauline letters as well as information that goes beyond the need of the immediate context. This is true particularly when it comes to major christological hymns (see esp. Phil. 2:6–11; Col. 1:15–20).

A quick look at Philippians 2:6–11 will help us to recognize some of the important aspects of Paul's use of traditional material. The text falls into two stanzas that describe the condescension vv. 6–8) and exaltation (vv. 9–11) of Jesus. The poetic structure is brought out well in versions such as the NIV:

> Who, being in very nature God,
>   did not consider equality with God
>   something to be used to his own advantage;
> rather, he made himself nothing
> by taking the very nature of a servant,

being made in human likeness.
And being found in appearance as a man,
he humbled himself
by becoming obedient to death—
even death on a cross!
Therefore God exalted him to the highest place
and gave him the name that is above every name,
that at the name of Jesus every knee should bow,
in heaven and on earth and under the earth,
and every tongue acknowledge that Jesus Christ is Lord,
to the glory of God the Father.

This symmetry shows that Paul most likely borrowed the tradition from its liturgical context with its emphasis on creed/doctrine, especially since the passage goes beyond the purpose of the immediate context: to exhort the Christians to humility for the sake of unity by giving the example of Christ. Even though it does not contribute much to his message, Paul leaves untouched the added information on Christ's exaltation, but he does include the phrase "even death on a cross" (at the end of v. 8) in order to emphasize the theological center of his preaching (cf. 1 Cor. 2:2).

Domestic Codes

Another example of Paul's use of Christian tradition is the *domestic/social/household codes.* Household codes deal with reciprocal responsibilities between the members of the household: husband/wife; parents/children; and master/slave. The household codes are found in some of the later letters of Paul (Eph. 5:22–6:9; Col. 3:18–4:1; Titus 2:1–10; cf. Rom. 13:1–7). Usually, these codes are identifiable by the presence of verbs conveying the notion of submission or obedience in the instructions Paul gives to individuals. While for us today such instructions of submission seem outdated given our culture's emphasis on the equality of individuals, not only in essence, but also in function, in Paul's day they most likely offered a clear alternative to the authoritarian-based society, since these instructions seem to place value on the submissive part in the relationship. Thus Paul's use of these codes had not only the purpose of regulating the social relationships within the church, but they also had an apologetic purpose—to show that Christianity was not subversive (1 Tim. 3:7, Titus 2:5, 8, 10; 3:10)—as well as a missionary/evangelistic purpose in a hostile world (1 Thess. 4:12).

Slogans

The book of 1 Corinthians presents us with yet another example of traditional material: *slogans.* First Corinthians is unique among the Pauline letters because it is clearly an epistle written in response to questions raised by the Corinthians (chaps. 7–16) in a letter that they sent through a carrier, as well as Paul's discussion of congregational issues reported by the members of Chloe's household (chaps. 1–6). The topics addressed by Paul in response to the questions raised by the Corinthians are usually marked by the phrase "now about" (7:1, 25; 8:1; 12:1; 16:1, 12). In discussing these topics, Paul usually quotes Corinthian slogans.

One such slogan is found in 1 Corinthians 6:12: "Everything is permissible for me" (cf. 1 Cor. 10:23). Many recent translations rightly put quotation marks around these words in order to show that they are slogans and not Paul's own words (see, e.g., the NIV: "'I have the right to do anything,' you say—but not everything is beneficial. 'I have the right to do anything'—but I will not be mastered by anything"). Paul uses this slogan in a context in which he discusses sexual sins such as incest (sexual activity between family members or close relatives) that was taking place in the Corinthian body. While Paul initially agrees with the Corinthian saying, he introduces qualifications by way of contrast ("but"). Thus the Corinthian church members have "liberty to do all things"—but not everything is helpful. "Liberty to do anything"—but I will not let anything take liberties with me.

It is thus important to differentiate between Paul's own words and the Corinthian slogans borrowed from the surrounding pagan culture so as not to develop a false theology from statements which Paul himself qualifies. As one may expect, slogans are typically short and concisely worded. Other likely slogans in 1 Corinthians are found in 6:13 ("Food for the stomach and the stomach for food"); 7:1 ("It is good for a man not to marry"); and 8:1 ("We all possess 'knowledge'").

Vice and Virtue Lists

The last example of preexistent material incorporated by Paul into his letters is the *vice and virtue lists.* The general purpose of including such lists in his letters is to point out the distinctiveness of the Christian community in contrast to the larger pagan society that condoned sexual sins, in particular, the lists have at least five functions.

First, these lists depict the depravity of unbelievers. In Romans 1:29–31, for instance, Paul describes the immorality of the Gentiles, though in chapter 2 he accuses the Jews of practicing the same sins. In 1 Corinthians 5:9–11, he lists sexual sins for the purpose of exhorting the believers to dissociate themselves from any Christian who still practices such sins, like the man in the Corinthian congregation involved in incest.

Second, and most importantly, Paul lists vices and virtues in order to encourage the believers to avoid the vices and practice the virtues (e.g., Gal. 5:19–23).

Third, in writing to Timothy, Paul lists vices in order for Timothy to clearly distinguish between true and false teachers (e.g., 1 Tim. 1:3–11; 6:4–5).

By contrast, fourth, Paul lists virtues that are required of the church leaders (e.g., 1 Tim. 3:2–13).

Lastly, Paul lists vices in his advice to Timothy in order to warn him of the sinful behavior of the people in the last times (2 Tim. 3:2–5).

You can find parallels of these lists, both of virtues and vices, in both Hellenistic Judaism and Greek literature. At the same time, you should be careful not to over interpret the vice list as being necessarily an exact depiction of the sins of the community Paul is writing to, though certainly some were characteristic.

GENERAL EPISTLES

Hebrews

Oral Nature of Hebrews

Hebrews is an unusual document, because it combines oral and written features. On the one hand, the document was known and circulated in the days of the early church in written form and at the end of the letter the author mentions that he has written to his readers briefly (Heb. 13:22).

On the other hand, there are also clear indications of the oral nature of the letter, which may suggest that it originated as a series of sermons that only later was written down and sent as a letter. One such indication may be the lack of a formal epistolary introduction (on which see below). Also, the author himself calls his communication a "word of exhortation" (Heb. 13:22), a phrase found elsewhere in the New Testament only in Acts 13:15 where synagogue officials invited Paul and Barnabas to give a "word of exhortation to the people." It appears that the author of Hebrews conceived of his communication primarily as a sermon of exhortation.

There are other aspects of the writing that indicate the essentially oral character of the epistle. The most important is the author's repeated use of the word "speak" (Heb. 5:11; 6:9; 8:1; 13:6). As mentioned above, New Testament letters were intended to be read aloud and therefore have oral features. The same is true with Hebrews. The author's use of the word "speak" clearly indicates that his letter is intended to be one end of a verbal communication. In Hebrews 5:11, he indicates that he wished to convey ("speak") to them deeper things but he is hindered from doing this because they have literally become "dull in the ears." This expression points to the oral nature of the communication intended for the ear. Also, the phrase "many words" is indicative of a lengthy speech (cf. Acts 15:32, 20:2) which in the present instance the speaker does not have the time to deliver.

In addition, there are also rhetorical devices used by the author that point to its oral nature. These stylistic features are part of any speech that seeks to convey a message to the audience clearly and to make a lasting impact on their minds and hearts. The author of Hebrews uses devices such as diatribe and rhythm that reflect the letter's oral character. Diatribe is a technique for anticipating objections to an argument, raising them in the form of questions, and then answering them. (Like rhetorical questions, a diatribe asks a question, but unlike rhetorical questions, whose answer is considered so obvious that it can afford to remain unstated, the diatribe provides the answer to the stated question.) The technique is found in letters (such as Romans) but is most effective in an oral presentation. The author of Hebrews uses this technique in several places. The most pertinent to our study is 3:16–18. Here the author uses the triple rhetorical question format which he answers with three more questions in order to warn against rebellion and unbelief and to point out the serious consequences as illustrated in the generation that perished in the wilderness.

Rhythm is usually found in poetical compositions, but the author of Hebrews uses it extensively in his writing, thus demonstrating some familiarity with Hebrew poetry besides the Greco-Roman rhetorical style.

One of the most famous instances of the use of rhythm in Hebrews is the first four verses of the book as they appear in the original, with its alliteration with the letter "p," assonance and its chiastic structure. Here is how the letter opens: "In the past God spoke to our ancestors through the prophets at many times and in various ways." Or, in the original Greek: (1) *Polymerōs kai* (2) *polytropōs* (3) *palai ho theos lalēsas tois* (4) *patrasin en tois* (5) *prophētais* (Heb. 1:1). As you can see, all the relevant words ("at many times," "in various ways," "in the past," "ancestors," "prophets") are alliterated (beginning with the Greek letter "p") to increase memorability. The texture of the text is so refined that we cannot avoid the conclusion that the author of Hebrews has taken great pains in making an impression on the ear of his readers. The oral style of his communication is not, however, employed just for the sake of aesthetic beauty but concords with his high christological message contained in these verses. Style does not overshadow the content but brings it to the forefront, so that the medium enhances the poignancy of the message.

In light of all these features, the conclusion is unavoidable that the letter of Hebrews has a distinctively oral character. We may thus speak of the letter as an adapted sermon or series of oral messages.

Literary Structure of Hebrews

Determining the structure of a book or its flow of argument is important for the interpretation of that book. The interpretation of each part is dependent on our understanding of the overall message. When it comes to Hebrews, however, apart from the uncertainty surrounding the issues of authorship and literary genre, discussion and debate have focused also on the literary structure of the letter. Some emphasize the formal aspects, while others stress the content of the book.

When seeking to determine the outline of the epistle to the Hebrews, we should keep in mind several prominent topics in the book. The outline, for instance, should reflect the important place that the warning passages have in the flow of the argument (i.e., Heb. 2:1–4; 3:7–19; 5:11–6:12; 10:19–39; 12:14–29). Likewise, chapter eleven, with its "Hall of Fame of Heroes of the Faith," should be given its due. Neither should one neglect the argument centering on the superiority of Christ or the author's repeated use of the phrase "greater than." Another relevant feature is the distinction between the doctrinal and the exhortation or ethical sections of the book. The author moves back and forth between doctrine and exhortation. He accomplishes this not, as Paul does in some of his letters, by dividing the letter into two parts, a doctrinal and an ethical one (see, e.g., Ephesians 1–3 and 4–6). Rather, his organization of material and the connection between units is signaled by way of "hook-words," such as the subject of faith that is predominant in several different sections of the book (see also the hook-word "Melchizedek" connecting 5:10 with 7:1). One must also pay close attention to transitional and summarizing elements such as in 8:1, "The point of what we are saying is this" (the dream of every exegete and listener to a sermon!), which serves the purpose of summarizing what has been said thus far and of transitioning to the next unit.

Space does not permit us to reproduce a detailed outline of the book. The macrostructure of the epistle to the Hebrews presents itself as follows:

Introduction: God Has Spoken to Us in a Son (1:1–4)

I. The Son Is Superior (1:5–4:13)

II. The Position of the High Priest in Relation to the Earthly Sacrificial System (4:14–10:25)

III. The Importance of Faith, Perseverance, and Obedience (10:26–13:19)

Benediction and Conclusion (13:20–25)

James

Jewish-Christian Nature of James

Doubtless James is a Jewish composition in the sense that it has its roots in Judaism and the Old Testament. For instance, James chooses Old Testament examples of faith such as Abraham (2:23), Rahab (2:25), Job (5:11), and Elijah (5:17–18) rather than Jesus as Peter does in his first letter (1 Pet. 2:21). Second, James demonstrates familiarity with some of the concepts of first-century Judaism such as *gehenna* (3:6). He is aware of rabbinic theological and psychological anthropology such as the belief in the two impulses within each one of us (1:14). In his advice for believers to be concerned for widows and orphans (1:27), he shows familiarity with the prophetic notion of justice.

Despite its lack of direct references to and mention of Jesus (except for 1:1 and 2:1), James does use Jesus as a source for his teaching, as we will see later. But evidence for the letter's Christian nature can be gathered also from noting the topical parallelism between James and the other writings of the New Testament.

We will give several examples, beginning with the *lexical* evidence. One of the surest signs of James's essentially Christian character is the absolute use of the word "name" in 2:7. Although its use is attested in the Greek translation of the Old Testament, the Septuagint (LXX; e.g., Exod. 20:7, 24), it is a specifically Christian designation used in reference to the power of the resurrected Jesus (e.g., Acts 5:40, 41; 9:14–15, 21). Likewise, the self-designation of James as "servant" parallels not only the use in the LXX by leaders such as Joshua (Josh. 24:30) and David (Ps. 88:4) but the term is used extensively by Christian leaders such as Paul (e.g., Rom. 1:1–2) and Peter (2 Pet. 1:1). Though James does not mention "hope," he does discuss at length the other two Christian virtues: faith (2:14–26) and love (2:8; cf. 1 Thess. 1:2–3; 1 Cor. 13:13; 1 Pet. 1:3–9). Another distinctively Christian feature of James is his use of end-time language. He talks about "the Lord's coming" in 5:7–8, a phrase never found in the LXX but a common phraseology for the return of Jesus (e.g., Matt. 24:3, 27, 37, 39; 1 Cor. 15:23; 1 John 2:28).

Apart from the lexical evidence, and more importantly the combination of terms that identifies the letter as having a distinctly Christian character within the Jewish literature of the first century, there is also *thematic* parallelism with other New Testament writings. For instance, both James 4:8–10 and 1 Peter 5:5–6 talk about "submission" and "lowliness of attitude" and cite Proverbs 3:34, though the target of their instruction is different. Therefore we conclude that James is just as Christian a writing as the other New Testament documents (though its Jewish Christian nature is unmistakable).

Jesus as a Source

The Christian nature of the letter of James can best be seen in James's dependence on Jesus's words. A remarkable feature of the epistle of James is that he borrows extensively from the teachings of Jesus, especially as expounded on in Matthew (e.g., the Beatitudes: Matt. 5:3–11). In fact, James's dependence on Jesus is not matched by any other New Testament author. This is remarkable in light of the fact that James does not quote Jesus (except in 5:12; cf. Matt. 5:33–37) and, even more strikingly, uses the name of Jesus only twice (1:1; 2:1).

Despite James's lack of reference to Jesus's deeds, he does show interest in Jesus's words. The parallelism between James and Jesus can be seen both at the linguistic and the thematic level. The topics he discusses in his letter as well as the approach, interpretation, and emphasis he gives to them resonate with Jesus's teachings and emphasis. It appears that James was so immersed in the teachings of Jesus that he subconsciously replicated them in his letter.

Here is a sample of the striking linguistic parallels between James and Jesus:

- believers are to rejoice in trials (1:2; cf. Matt. 5:12);
- believers are called to be perfect/complete (1:4; cf. Matt. 5:48);
- believers are encouraged to ask God, for God loves to give (1:5; cf. Matt. 7:7);
- believers should expect testing and be prepared to endure it, after which they will receive a reward (1:12; cf. Matt. 24:13);
- believers are not to be angry (1:20; cf. Matt. 5:22);
- actions are the proof of true faith (2:14; cf. Matt. 7:16–19);
- the poor are blessed (2:5; cf. Luke 6:20);
- the rich are warned (2:6–7; cf. Matt. 19:23–24);
- believers are not to slander (4:11; cf. Matt. 5:22);
- believers are not to judge (4:12; cf. Matt. 7:1);
- the humble are praised (3:13; cf. Matt. 5:3).

At the thematic level, the similarities are particularly seen in the shared theology of prayer with Matthew. There is thus no doubt that Jesus was a significant source for James and his teaching, both lexically and thematically.

Jude and Petrine Epistles

Relationship between Jude and 2 Peter

A cursory reading of Jude and 2 Peter will bring to light the close resemblance between the two. In light of the many similarities in terminology between the two letters, scholars have wondered whether there is any kind of literary relationship between the two or if each author independently used a common source. In fact, a comparison between Jude 4–19 and 2 Peter 2:1–3:3 yields a considerable number of parallels.

The following four hypotheses have been posited: (1) Peter used Jude; (2) Jude used Peter; (3) both independently used a common source; and (4) common authorship. Until the nineteenth century, the predominant view was that Jude used 2 Peter as a source, but more recently a consensus has emerged that 2 Peter used Jude. The third view is also possible in view of the lack of precise verbal links between the two, although literary dependence is preferred as a simpler hypothesis.

The more likely view is that Jude was written prior to 2 Peter and served as a source. This can be illustrated by the way in which these writings use Jewish apocryphal literature. Jude includes three such quotations or allusions: (1) to *The Assumption of Moses* in verse 9; (2) to *1 Enoch* in verses 14–15; and (3) to an otherwise unattested saying of the apostles in verse 18. All three quotations are lacking in 2 Peter. It seems more likely that Peter avoided reference to these apocryphal works than that Jude added these references on the assumption that Peter wrote first.

In addition to these remarkable *verbal* similarities, the two texts display a rather striking similarity in terms of the *sequential* development of the argument. In particular, Jude and Peter concur in their basic structure: angels—Sodom and Gomorrah—[archangel Michael]—Balaam. Beyond this, Peter (on the assumption that Jude served as his source) replaced his two negative examples, Cain and Korah, with two positive figures, Noah and Lot. While the similarity in structure could also be accounted for on the basis of a common source, it seems more probable that Peter used Jude directly and adapted his epistle to his own situation. If so, it is particularly conspicuous that Peter reworked Jude's letter in such a way that the sequence of his examples is in proper Old Testament chronological order while Jude uses a topical arrangement.

Despite the similarities between the two works and their interdependence, we should not assume that they are identical in purpose. Just as the chronicler used the material in 1 and 2 Kings and yet pursued a different purpose and Luke used earlier accounts of the life of Jesus (presumably including Mark) but had different audiences and purposes, so Peter's use of Jude must not be interpreted as a lack of distinctiveness. Both writings must be studied for what each contributes to the teaching and theology of the Bible.

Johannine Epistles

Oral Nature of 1 John

The fact that 1 John lacks a formal epistolary introduction and conclusion has led some to suggest that it is a general treatise, perhaps a pamphlet, a brochure, or an encyclical (circular letter). Others classify the document as a homily (sermon), given its strong hortatory style. The designation of "homily" points to the suggestion that the letter has an oral character. Evidence for this is the author's reference to traditional material. The author frequently appeals to what his audience has known "from the beginning" (1 John 2:13, 24; etc.). Like Hebrews, 1 John also functions as a word of exhortation (1 John 2:7–11), though the phrase itself does not appear in the letter. Nevertheless, there are clear indicators within the book that it is a written document. Most importantly, the author states 13 times that he is *writing*. Thus we are dealing with a literary document. This, however, does not preclude that the letter was experienced orally by its first readers, since letters were typically read aloud.

Literary Structure of 1 John

There is a lack of consensus on the literary structure of 1 John. The proposals fall into three categories: a division into two, three, or multiple parts. Those who advocate a twofold division argue that this is required for two reasons. First, the two declarations that John makes in his epistle (i.e., "God is light," 1 John 1:5; and "God is love," 1 John 4:6) are keys to its structure. Second, the similarities between John's Gospel and 1 John allegedly point to the Gospel as the structural model for the epistle. Those who hold to a multiple-part structure contend that there is no developing argument throughout the letter and no logical plan that is being followed. Most scholars, however, divide the letter into three parts, a structure that we will follow here, based on grammatical and semantic indicators. Such a structure takes into consideration both the form and the content.

Prologue: The Word of Life Witnessed (1:1–4)

I. The Departure of the False Teachers (1:5–2:27)

II. The Proper Conduct of God's Children (2:28–3:24)

III. The Proper Beliefs of God's Children (4:1–5:12)

Epilogue: The Confidence of Those Who Walk in God's Light and Love (5:13–21)

Typical Nature of 2 and 3 John

Matters are much more straightforward with regard to 2 and 3 John, both of whom fit the criteria for ancient letters. They each contain the conventional introduction and conclusion. Both are addressed specifically to a local church or a network of house churches (i.e., "the chosen lady and her children"; cf. 2 John 1) and to an individual (i.e. "Gaius"; cf. 3 John 1). The mention of the author ("the elder") and the addressees is followed by a greeting or a prayer for their well-being. Both letters also contain in their closing sections elements seen in the Pauline letters, such as an expression of the wish to visit soon and to communicate in person ("face to face") and a greeting. In this sense, these two letters resemble closely the personal type of ancient letters, especially given their reduced length. They fit easily on a single sheet of papyrus. They also clearly indicate that they are (inadequate, but for the time being necessary) substitutes for the author's physical presence. In this sense, 2 and 3 John are probably closer to the ancient personal/private letter form than any of Paul's epistles, with the possible exception of Philemon.

GENERAL HERMENEUTICAL ISSUES

Occasionality and Normativity

One of the basic characteristics of letters is that they are *occasional* or *situational*. This means that they were written to address situations and offer solutions to problems related to the author or (most often) to the reader(s). The ethical instructions that are offered in the New Testament letters in response to some of the problems that were faced by the audiences are thus situation-specific.

We can illustrate this by reference to 1 Corinthians, one of the most occasional letters in the New Testament. We have already noted that Paul organizes his material according to topics, which are answers to questions raised by the Corinthians in a letter (chaps. 7–16) and responses Paul gives to some of the problems in the Corinthian congregation he heard about from a report (chaps. 1–6). Among the topics he discusses in this letter is that of meat associated with idols in chapters 8–10, a topic introduced by the phrase "now concerning." It is obvious that in the idolatrous culture of Paul's day, when temples dedicated to pagan deities abounded and immorality was associated with sacrifices, people who turned from their pagan worship to the true God were wondering whether practices in which they had engaged while in their state of unbelief were compatible with their new life in Christ or not. One such issue was the meat associated with idol worship. There was a lack of consensus among the Corinthian Christians as to whether they should continue to consume such meat, the result being that some became a stumbling block to others by the way in which they related to this issue. Paul had to offer a solution to the specific issue. Examples such as this are what makes 1 Corinthians and the other New Testament letters situation-specific.

Faced with such specific situations that are time- and culture-bound, the interpreter has the responsibility to *reconstruct as precisely as possible the original situation* that gave rise to the problem which Paul addressed by looking into the social, historical, and cultural contexts of Corinthian Christianity. Without such information we will be in danger of misunderstanding what was at issue in the Corinthian church. But once we understand the original situation, the task of interpretation has just begun, for we are then faced with the question of its applicability and normativity for us. The question is whether a situational issue like the meat associated with idols has anything to teach Christians today who are not faced with debates surrounding pagan temple worship. Does 1 Corinthians 10–12 contain any binding principles for us today? Are Paul's instructions on meat associated with idols normative for us?

Put in more general terms, how do we distinguish between what is purely occasional and what is normative? Why, for instance, should the prohibition of stealing be normative for us today (e.g., Eph. 4:28) and wearing something on one's head be nonbinding for women (1 Cor. 11:2–16)? The issue is further complicated in cases where part of the original context cannot be easily reconstructed. For instance, who are the original readers of Hebrews and what were the reasons that prompted the author to write his letter? What was the heresy confronting the audience of 1 John? The difficulty of reconstructing the original situation thus complicates the question of normativity.

Another corollary to the issue of a situation-specific letter is that of *constructing a biblical and systematic theology for today.* Since the letters are occasional, they are not meant to be exhaustive dictionaries of Christian doctrine. Even if we can extract normative principles for today from a particular letter, we should beware of not thinking that what a letter teaches on a certain topic is all we need to know about that topic. In other words, we should not conclude too much from one letter. For instance, if we only had James, we might be led into thinking that works justify the one who believes. But Romans gives us the other side of the issue with its emphasis on justification by faith. For this reason, if we want to have a more complete and balanced view of a given issue, we must read all the letters—in fact, the entire New Testament and all of Scripture—that address situations that deal with similar or related problems.

Another aspect of which the interpreter must be aware when trying to determine the normative principle embedded in a text is the *distinction between primary and secondary issues* in a text. Most of the time, normativity is connected with the main topic discussed in the text rather than with secondary issues. In other words, the interpreter must be careful not to extract a principle or build a theology from a context in which the issue is not addressed as the primary topic. In building a theology, we must go to those passages that clearly touch on the issue and avoid drawing principles from obscure passages. This constitutes a general hermeneutical principle of avoiding teaching the right doctrine from the wrong text.

For now, it will suffice to state that the letters of the New Testament are occasional and that they address specific situations. At the same time, there is clear evidence that the authors believed that what they were communicating was normative at least for the original readers. What is more, in light of the fact that their instructions are always based on theological convictions, it is inevitable to conclude that the teachings offered to the churches facing certain circumstances are *applicable to any church or individual facing similar situations* throughout the ages. But what about teachings that are responding to circumstances that we might never face, such as meat associated with idols? Are there any normative principles to be drawn from such teachings? Our belief in the divine inspiration and authority of Scripture compels us to give an affirmative answer. Even in passages where the author deals with issues that are specific to a place, time, and culture, he offers general abiding principles.

For instance, in Paul's response to the issue raised by the Corinthians concerning meat sacrificed to idols, he discusses the issue of the believer's freedom and rights. Thus, in chapter 9, in what seems like a parenthesis, he offers the solution to the dispute by way of personal example: the giving up of his rights for the sake of winning others to Christ. While we may never be faced with the question of whether or not we can eat from meat associated with idols (though missionaries in some cultures will be), we are certainly faced all the time with the issue of how we may win our neighbor for Christ and not be a stumbling block to him.

In conclusion, the New Testament letters are *both occasional and normative*. The way in which we determine the normativity of a passage is by looking closely at the occasion of the writing and its social, cultural, and historical contexts and then trying to find the general principles that are transferable to us today. In so doing, we must ask ourselves questions such as: Is the topic from which we are drawing the principle the main one in the text? Is it clearly taught? What other passage(s) must we study to corroborate the teaching in order to get as complete a picture as possible concerning the entire biblical counsel on the topic? When answering such questions, we should guard ourselves from drawing out principles that are not in the text or not corroborated by the rest of Scripture.

Other Issues in Interpreting Epistles

There are many other relevant issues in interpreting the New Testament epistolary literature. Having outlined the most pertinent issue, namely that of the occasional and normative nature of New Testament Epistles, it will suffice to summarize briefly what are proper principles of interpreting and applying these letters. Essentially, the interpretive task, when reading the New Testament Epistles as well as other biblical books, includes the following four elements.

1. *Original Application:* What did the text mean to the original audience? In order to discover the meaning and application to

the original audience one must get as much information on the cultural, social, and historical background as possible. Another important element in determining the meaning for the original audience is looking at the literary context. Context is determinative for meaning, and without an understanding of the whole picture we will be in danger of misinterpreting the parts. We must make sure that we do not impose onto a passage a meaning that is not indicated by the context. For this, we must look at the textual connections and constructions.

2. *Specificity of Original Application:* What are the differences and similarities between the biblical audience and us? As already mentioned, if the situation faced by the original audience and our own circumstances are similar, the principles are transferable without modification or generalization. But in cases where letters are written to answer specific situations most churches today do not face (e.g., meat associated with idols) we must identify the differences between our situation and that of the original audience.

3. *Broad Principles:* What is the theological principle in the text? Once we've determined the meaning of the passage for the original audience and noted the similarities between our situation and that of the original audience, it's time to draw out general principles. These must be reflected in the text studied but at the same time not bound to the text and its situation. Thus they must be specific enough to apply to the situation in the text but general enough not to be bound to its time and culture. In this sense, these principles must correspond to the teaching of the rest of Scripture.

4. *Contemporary Application:* How should we apply the principles in our lives today? The application can take different forms, depending on the specific situation faced by the contemporary audience. We must differentiate between meaning and significance. While the text has one meaning (i.e., the original meaning), this meaning can be applied in different

ways depending on the situation. In order to apply correctly the general principles discovered in the text, however, we must be careful to apply them to contemporary situations that are equivalent to the original situation.

GUIDELINES FOR INTERPRETING EPISTLES

1. Find out as much as possible about the situation behind the writing of the letter. Corroborate the information found in the text with *background information* (i.e., historical, social, and cultural setting).
2. Discern the *major parts* of the letter (introduction, body, and conclusion) and their constitutive elements.
3. Look for the *conventional elements* that the letter-writer included and left out, especially in the introduction and conclusion. It is in these parts of the letter, especially in the introduction, that we can discern the major problem(s) that occasioned the writing of the letter.
4. Determine the *structure* and *argument* of the epistle by paying close attention to grammatical, semantic, and rhetorical elements. Above all, it is important for the structure to correspond as closely as possible to the flow of the argument.
5. Interpret each passage in light of the *message of the letter as a whole*. In other words, always interpret a passage in light of its larger literary context.
6. Seek to discern between what is purely *occasional* and what *normative principles* can be drawn out from the specific situation the writer is addressing. The normativity of a teaching is usually imbedded in the theological basis for the writer's ethical teaching.

KEY WORDS

Allonymity or allepigraphy, Amanuensis, Diatribe, Disclosure formula, Domestic code, *Gezera shawah*, Midrash, Pesher, Pseudonymity, *Qal wahomer.*

ASSIGNMENTS

1. Engage in a comprehensive study of the openings of all 21 letters included in the New Testament, both the 13 letters written by Paul and those written by others. Note the elements contained in the various introductions and compare and contrast the letter openings, noting any features that are theologically significant.

2. Do the same with the letter closings. Identify each of the 21 letter closings and provide a basic, initial study comparing and contrasting these closings. Discuss also what light these closings shed on the nature of the letter under consideration.

3. Engage in a close contextual study of Romans 7:14-25, pinpointing the historical setting, literary structure, and theological message of the passage. After you've done your own study, check at least two standard commentaries and one study Bible to compare your findings with the interpretation provided in these resources.

KEY RESOURCES

Carson, D. A. and Douglas J. Moo. "New Testament Letters." Pp. 331–54 in *An Introduction to the New Testament*. 2d ed. Grand Rapids: Zondervan, 2005.

Schreiner, Thomas R. *Interpreting the Pauline Epistles.* Guides to New Testament Exegesis. Grand Rapids: Baker, 1990.

CHAPTER 11 OBJECTIVES

1. To acquaint the interpreter with the most important characteristics of apocalyptic literature and to sketch the most significant issues with which he or she is faced when seeking to understand the Book of Revelation.

2. To equip the interpreter with knowledge of the most important historical background information, literary features, and theological issues involved in interpreting Revelation.

CHAPTER 11 OUTLINE

A. Introduction and Definition of Apocalyptic

B. Major Interpretative Approaches to the Study of the Book of Revelation

C. Historical Background

D. Literary Aspects

E. Guidelines for Interpreting Apocalyptic Literature

F. Key Words

G. Assignments

H. Key Resources

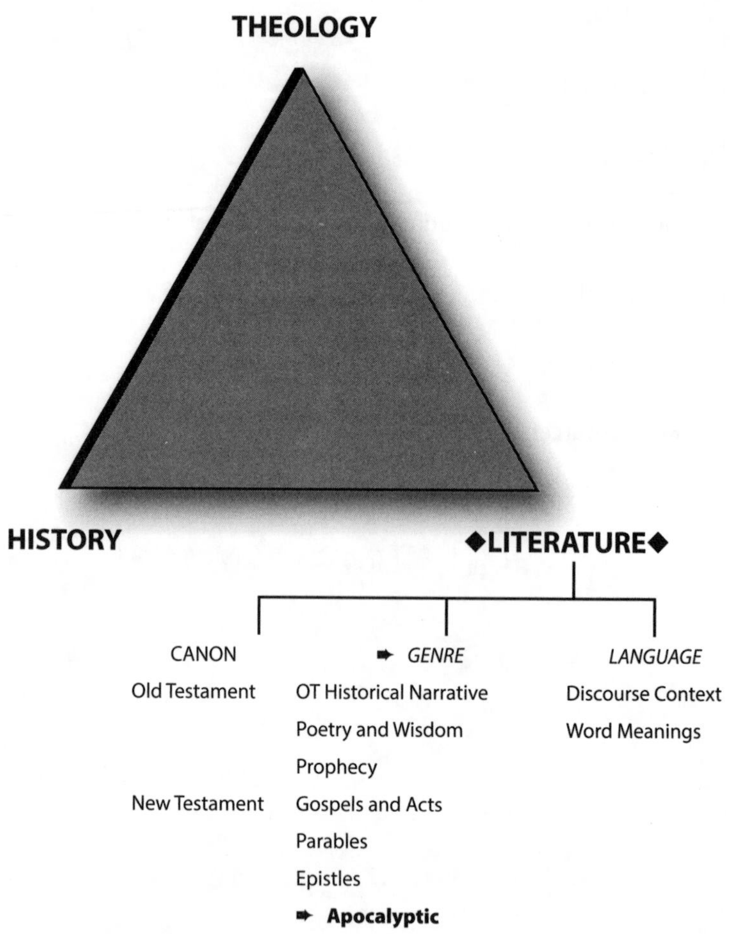
THEOLOGY
HISTORY
◆LITERATURE◆
CANON
Old Testament
New Testament
➡ GENRE
OT Historical Narrative
Poetry and Wisdom
Prophecy
Gospels and Acts
Parables
Epistles
➡ Apocalyptic
LANGUAGE
Discourse Context
Word Meanings

Chapter 11

VISIONS OF THE END: APOCALYPTIC LITERATURE (REVELATION)

INTRODUCTION AND DEFINITION OF APOCALYPTIC

Introduction

AT LONG LAST, WE HAVE arrived at the final leg of our canonical journey. Having encountered Old Testament narrative, poetry and wisdom, prophecy, as well as New Testament narrative (Gospels and Acts), parables, and Epistles, we must climb one final mountain: the tricky but exceedingly rewarding genre of apocalyptic. On this arduous journey, only well-prepared climbers will scale the heights, and challenges abound. In the following pages, we will first develop a definition of apocalyptic and survey the major approaches to interpreting Revelation. After this, we will discuss important historical background matters such as the "Nero *redivivus* myth" or the emperor cult and various relevant literary aspects that have a bearing on the interpretation of the book of Revelation. We will close with a list of guidelines for interpreting New Testament apocalyptic.

While there is no book in the Old Testament that is apocalyptic in its entirety, as mentioned in chapter 7 on prophecy, apocalyptic is a significant component of the Old Testament prophetic literature (e.g., Isaiah 24–27; Ezekiel 38–39; Daniel 7; Joel 2:28–32; 3:9–17; and Zechariah 1–6,

12–14). Together with promises of deliverance and kingdom oracles, we identified Old Testament apocalyptic as a subset of salvation oracles. At the same time, we noted that fully developed apocalypses did not appear until after the Old Testament era. This kind of literature flourished during the Second Temple period, especially between 200 B.C. and A.D. 200.

In terms of salvation-historical development, the arrival of Jesus the Messiah "in the fullness of time" indicated that certain eschatological expectations had come to fruition. Jesus announced the nearness and even (partial) arrival of God's kingdom (Mark 1:15; Luke 11:20). The presence of God's kingdom suggests the eschatological fulfillment of the prophetic promises regarding the son of David, the restoration of Israel, and the renewal of creation. Jesus inaugurated the end times with his resurrection followed by the outpouring of the Holy Spirit, but believers still expect a time of final consummation at the end of the age. This time between the ages is commonly viewed as the "already and not yet" of God's eschatological fulfillment. In this regard, the New Testament shares affinities with an apocalyptic worldview.

For this reason, we should not be surprised to find apocalyptic portions in various places of the New Testament. The Olivet discourse (Matt. 24:1–31; Mark 13; Luke 21:5–32), also known as "the little apocalypse," comprises Jesus's apocalyptic expectations in the Synoptic Gospels. Apocalyptic language and images appear scattered throughout the New Testament letters. The book of Hebrews, for example, exhibits an apocalyptic worldview, contrasting the temporary earthly institutions with eternal heavenly realities. Second Peter 3 also represents eschatological expectations expressed in terms of apocalyptic imagery (i.e., the earth and all the elements being consumed by fire).

Definition of Apocalyptic

In seeking to define "apocalyptic," we will do well to revisit and further extend the discussion of apocalyptic in chapter 7 on prophecy. The very word "apocalypse" conjures up a myriad of images. Scholars typically distinguish between (1) "apocalypse"; (2) "apocalyptic"; and (3) "apocalypticism." "Apocalypse" refers to a particular genre of literature written between approximately 200 B.C. and A.D. 200. The adjective "apocalyptic" is used when describing either the literary genre or the worldview. "Apocalypticism," finally, denotes a worldview, ideology, or theology merging the eschatological aims of particular groups into a cosmic and political arena.

The development of the definition for the apocalyptic genre has a long complex history. Early studies identified formal features such as pseudonymity, visionary accounts, and historical reviews, a doctrine of two ages, pessimism and hope, universalism, and imminent expectation of the end. John J. Collins (1979: 9), in conjunction with a group of scholars, developed the following classic definition:

> "Apocalypse" is a genre of revelatory literature with a narrative framework, in which a revelation is mediated by an otherworldly being to a human recipient, disclosing a transcendent reality which is both temporal, insofar as it envisages eschatological salvation, and spatial, insofar as it involves another, supernatural world.

This definition emphasized the *form* as a narrative framework involving an otherworldly mediator and the *content* as containing both temporal (eschatological salvation) and spatial (supernatural world) elements. The definition, however, lacked any reference to the *function* of an apocalypse. For this reason, a subsequent study group, led by Adela Yarbro Collins, David Hellholm, and David E. Aune (1986: 7), added an amendment which stated that an apocalypse is "intended to interpret present, earthly circumstances in light of the supernatural world and of the future, and to influence the understanding and behavior of the audience by means of divine authority."

This amended definition of the apocalyptic genre, then, pertains to its form, content, and function. The apocalyptic genre exhibits several *formal* features including visionary accounts, otherworldly mediators, and symbolic language. The apocalyptic genre also expresses *content* depicting temporal and spatial realities as a way to emphasize the heavenly realities and devalue earthly circumstances. Finally, the apocalyptic genre *functions* to encourage piety and faithfulness in the midst of suffering or during times of crisis (whether real or perceived).

These definitions broadly encompass all canonical, extrabiblical, rabbinical, and sectarian examples of apocalyptic literature. Not all apocalyptic writings necessarily exhibit every genre characteristic discussed in the above definition. This warrants a scaled-down assessment of essential elements attributed to the apocalyptic genre. The first essential element is that an apocalypse comprises a *visionary or revelatory means of communication*. Apocalyptic literature must reveal some heavenly or spiritual reality through the agency of a seer or prophet. Usually, the vision is autobiographical and expressed in a narrative framework. In addition, apocalyptic communication frequently employs the use of divine or angelic intermediaries as guides and interpreters. Embedded within this revelatory communication are prophetic exhortations for desired behaviors, choices, and responses from the recipients. Non-essential elements include pseudonymity and historical reviews (written in predictive form).

Second, apocalyptic literature is saturated with *symbolic, figurative, and metaphorical language*. Symbols and other figures constitute the common stock of apocalyptic writing. Human and angelic beings and even animals serve as symbolic representations of spiritual truths. Symbolic imagery may express historical, contemporary, or future events in cosmic terms. By using metaphors when describing cosmic scenarios, the author invests both current and anticipated earthly events with symbolic meaning.

A final element essential to the apocalyptic genre is the *dualism between earthly and heavenly realities*, usually steeped in eschatological significance. Earthly situations are depicted as temporary and transitory in light of the eternal realities of the spiritual world. This heavenly perspective dramatically contrasts the worldly scenarios facing the recipients. Although some scholars downplay the eschatological nature of the visions, apocalyptic literature provides a provocative and effective vehicle for communicating end-time expectations. The belief that God is sovereign over history permeates most apocalyptic writings, including the idea that he will radically intervene in the near future to consummate his plans for all creation.

MAJOR INTERPRETATIVE APPROACHES TO THE STUDY OF THE BOOK OF REVELATION

How you read the book of Revelation will largely depend on your approach to understanding the areas of history, symbolism, and eschatology. Interpreters differ in their view of the relationship between John's vision and history. Does the book of Revelation reflect past, present, or purely future events, or does the book feature events future to John but historical to modern readers? The way you answer these questions will significantly influence how you interpret the book.

No one doubts that Revelation is saturated with symbolism, but not all agree on what those symbols mean. Do they have literal referents or literary ones? Literal interpretations produce remarkably divergent meanings from those who follow more literary approaches. Finally, your eschatological perspective becomes the theological lense which influences how you answer the historical questions and how you interpret the book's symbols. There are four basic ways in which interpreters approach this complex work.

Preterist

The preterist position approaches the relationship of history and the Apocalypse from the vantage point that the events prophesied were fulfilled in the first century. One school of preterism interprets the book of Revelation as a message of judgment against apostate Israel for rejecting Christ by prophesying the destruction of Jerusalem in A.D. 70. Other preterist interpreters see the Roman Empire and the situation of Christians as the focus of John's vision prophesying the fall of Rome. The primary virtue of this approach is that it takes seriously the historical circumstances of the first-century audience of Revelation. On the negative side, the preterist position unduly diminishes the more remote future fulfillment of biblical prophecy.

Historicist

The historicist approach represented the most popular interpretive approach for the book of Revelation during the Middle Ages and throughout the Reformation. The historicists viewed John's vision as forecasting the course of history in Western Europe with particular emphasis on popes, kings, and wars. Thus Martin Luther, John Calvin, and other Reformers equated the Vatican with the harlot Babylon that corrupted and persecuted the true church. While this approach has been largely abandoned, one may detect modern variations in readings of Revelation as if it were being fulfilled through current events on the world's stage. A historicist approach is inadequate owing to its narrow focuses on Western history and its insufficient consideration of the first-century historical context of the churches to which the book of Revelation is addressed.

Idealist

The idealist, timeless, or symbolic approach sets aside the historical question altogether by positing that Revelation is not about events in the space-time continuum but rather symbolically portrays the spiritual and timeless nature of the battle between good and evil. Thus the vision and its symbolism are loosed from their historical moorings so that they represent a universal message to all believers about God's defeat of Satan and the spiritual victory of faith in Christ as the church contends with a world ruled by wicked potentates. Variations of this view are found in Origen, Dionysius, and Augustine.

On the positive side, this approach accounts for the symbolic nature of John's vision and underscores its universal relevance for believers throughout history. Negatively, the view does not adequately address the historical nature of Revelation. John writes to real churches facing specific circumstances. The allusions to the imperial cult, the Nero *redux* myth, and other first-century events indicate that the book's meaning is grounded in history. Also, this approach does not adequately explain the church's expectation of the consummation of God's plan in history with the return of Christ.

Futurist

The fourth major approach for interpreting Revelation contends that chapters 4–22 refer to future events. Early Christian writers such as Justin Martyr, Irenaeus, Tertullian, and Hippolytus held to a futuristic interpretation known as *chiliasm*. In modern times, the futurist position enjoys pride of place among most evangelical Christians. Not all futurists, however, agree as to how Revelation portrays the unfolding of future events, taking one of two basic forms: dispensational and modified or moderate futurism.

The hermeneutical hallmark of classic dispensationalism is a commitment to the literal interpretation of prophetic Scripture, a principle often expressed with the dictum, "When the plain sense of Scripture makes common sense, seek no other sense." This hermeneutical approach has resulted in a particular theological system that makes a strict and consistent distinction between Israel and the church and contends that Revelation focuses on the future of ethnic Israel.

Since the term "church" does not occur after Revelation 4:1, dispensationalists contend that God will rapture the church at the beginning of the tribulation in order to be able to deal with Israel. Thus, the tribulation and Christ's millennial reign have nothing to do with the church. Progressive dispensationalism, on the other hand, believes that the various dispensations overlap and that Jesus already began his reign as the Davidic king at the resurrection, his millennial reign constituting the complete fulfillment for Israel.

A second form of a futurist approach, modified or moderate futurism, is commonly associated with historical premillennialism because of its affinities with the *chiliasm* of the early church. The view is similar to dispensationalism in that it affirms a thousand-year reign of Christ on earth but it departs from the dispensational insistence on a strict literalism, the rigorous distinction between Israel and the church, the chronology of end-time events, and the belief in a pretribulational rapture.

While dispensationalists argue that the second coming of Christ will involve a *secret* return for the church prior to the tribulation followed by his *visible* return after seven years, modified futurists affirm *only one* return of Christ to earth allowing the church to persevere through the tribulation. This is largely due to the inauguration of the new covenant making all believers in Jesus the spiritual descendants of Abraham and therefore covenant members of the people of God—true Israel.

Modified futurism and historical premillennialism are appealing because they enable interpreters to maintain the future orientation of John's vision while avoiding the literalism of dispensationalism that limits the applicability of Revelation for today's church. In addition, there are various eclectic approaches that combine elements of each of the above-discussed positions in order to capitalize on the perceived strengths of given arguments while avoiding their weaknesses.

HISTORICAL BACKGROUND

There are several important background features that aid in interpreting the book of Revelation. The most relevant are the type of persecution faced by the readers, the imperial cult, and the "Nero *redivivus* myth."

Type of Persecution

For generations, tradition has maintained that the churches suffered from monstrous persecution at the hands of the tyrant Domitian who mandated obeisance throughout the Roman Empire. Until the late twentieth century, many scholars accepted Domitian as the second great persecutor of the church (Eusebius, *Eccl. Hist.* 4.26.9). Recent scholarship has altered this traditional view of Domitian by demonstrating the paucity of evidence supporting an official imperial persecution against Christians during his reign. In the wake of this reevaluation, scholars have sought to reconstruct the historical situation in terms of possible social crises, real or perceived, that left the churches in the dilemma of capitulating to sociocultural pressures or clinging to their faith in Christ. Believers in Asia Minor, however, did not merely imagine this crisis because they lived with the genuine threat of unjust treatment due to their faith in Christ.

John indicates that he was on Patmos owing to persecution related to his Christian witness (1:9) and associates his suffering with what the believers in Asia Minor will experience (6:9; 12:17; 20:4). He was on Patmos because of "the word of God and the testimony of Jesus" (1:9). This phrase occurs regularly throughout the book of Revelation in connection with persecution. This reading is supported by John's self-identification as a fellow participant with the churches in their hardships (1:9). The letters to the seven churches reveal various situations ranging from spiritual lethargy to external opposition. The Christians in Ephesus were commended for enduring hardships because of the name of Christ (2:3). The exact nature of their suffering, however, remains elusive. At least some of the hardships may have derived from internal conflicts with the Nicolaitans (2:6), but this does not rule out external opposition from non-Christian sources.

Conflict in Smyrna apparently arose from the Jewish community (2:9). Their suffering relates to unspecified tribulations, poverty, and slander from Jews. The forensic nature of this slander is confirmed by the reference to future imprisonment (2:10). Jewish hostilities against Christians in the form of legal denunciation commonly occurred in the early church. The situation for Christians in Smyrna also paralleled conditions in Philadelphia (3:8–9). In both cities, believers were few in number and poor but faced intentional, religious, and legal opposition from Jews who sought to decimate their number. In at least one case, this opposition escalated to the martyrdom of Antipas in the city of Pergamum (2:13).

The remaining visions either reflect or expect a time of intense persecution as believers engage in a spiritual battle with the forces of Satan (chaps. 12–13). The scenes depicted in Revelation 13:1–18 evoke images of forced participation in the imperial cult. That the hostility envisioned relates to a Roman threat is seen in the identification of Babylon as Rome (17:9). Throughout the vision, Christians are encouraged to remain faithful and endure patiently because one day God will vindicate them through judgment and renewal (20:4). While it is unlikely that believers in Asia Minor were currently experiencing this level of persecution, they lived at a time and in an environment that fostered hostility toward those who maintained exclusive religious devotion to Jesus Christ.

Emperor Cult

Another important background datum is the cult of the emperor. The imperial cult existed as part of Asia Minor's religious climate ever since the time of Augustus. Pergamum hosted the very first temple dedicated to Augustus and Roma for the entire province of Asia beginning in 29 B.C., which remained an active temple well past the reign of Hadrian. The cult's political purpose was to express just how grateful and loyal the provinces were to the emperor.

The cult used religious conventions for political purposes. From its inception, the emperor, along with the goddess Roma, was worshipped and honored for their benevolence toward the provinces. During the reign of Tiberius, the cities of Sardis and Smyrna competed for the right to host a second provincial imperial cult in Asia, which was won by Smyrna in A.D. 26. Then, during the reign of Domitian, the city of Ephesus erected an unprecedented third imperial temple in Asia Minor (A.D. 89/90). Some estimate that there were more than 80 smaller localized imperial temples in over 60 cities in Asia Minor. These cities and their citizens ensured the success of the imperial cult due to their enthusiastic participation in worshipping the divine Caesar.

The imperial cult, however, was much more than a mere political tool; it had an important religious dimension as well. Participants actually worshipped the emperor as divine. Inscriptional evidence demonstrates that the emperors Augustus and Gaius were considered gods. The use of the term *theos*, though rare, attests to the fact that worshipers esteemed emperors by elevating them to a status high above regular mortals. The cult employed all the trappings and paraphernalia of rituals common to other religious practices. Images of the emperor or his family members greeted worshippers in the form of massive statues. Adherents offered prayers to these statues and even carried smaller pocket-sized statues of imperial figures. Those who lived in a polytheistic culture easily adopted the imperial cult into their pantheon.

Domitian's religious devotion is beyond dispute and evidenced by the numerous temples that he constructed or renovated. In keeping with the Flavian tradition, he worshipped Jupiter and throughout his reign was portrayed as Jupiter's warrior vice-regent. The temple to Domitian in Ephesus represented the pinnacle of the imperial cult's popularity in Asia Minor during his reign. Here, worshippers would perform obeisance to Domitian and other members of the Flavian family. The colossal statue of Domitian, between twenty-two and twenty-six feet tall, was not only awe-inspiring but an object of worship. Thus, the second beast (13:11–15) that erects an image of the first beast and mandates everyone to worship it may correspond to the high priest of Domitian's imperial cult in Ephesus.

References to the imperial cult in the Apocalypse are unmistakable. Allusions to it occur frequently in the latter half of the second vision (13:4, 15–16; 14:9–11; 15:2; 16:2; cf. 20:4). John envisions a time when the imperial cult escalates to a point of universal mandatory participation. Significantly, the term "worship" is used in direct connection with the beast (13:4, 8, 12, 15); it was also a term commonly employed in the imperial cult. Thus, Christians abhorred the imperial cult as idolatry which was doubly evil due to the political ramifications associated with it.

"Nero **Redivivus** *Myth"*

Another piece of important background information for interpreting Revelation is the "Nero *redivivus* myth." Shortly after Nero committed suicide on June 9, A.D. 68, Roman historians recount how a belief emerged throughout the empire that Nero had not actually died but was going to return with the Parthian army (Suetonius, *Nero* 49.3). Even after his death, many people decorated Nero's statue "as if he were still alive and would shortly return and deal destruction to his enemies" (Suetonius, *Nero* 57.1). The fact that very few saw Nero's corpse, coupled with uncertainty regarding the location of his tomb, gave credence to this belief, which was further nourished and reinforced by at least three pretenders.

The Nero *redivivus* myth surfaced in several apocalyptic Jewish and Christian writings toward the end of the first century. The Christian apocalypses, likewise, associate Nero with Beliar and cast him as the paradigmatic persecutor of the church (e.g., *Ascen. Isa.* 4:2–4 [end of first century A.D.]). These writings indicate that toward the end of the first century, two distinct traditions developed regarding Nero's supposed return. One stemmed from the idea that Nero never died and that he was going to return with the Parthian army to conquer Rome. The other envisioned a demonically empowered Nero-like figure that would attack God's people.

The book of Revelation, according to many commentators, reflects an awareness of the return of Nero legend. Revelation 13 describes how the dragon gives rise to the beast and endows him with authority. In Revelation 13:3, one of the beast's heads receives a fatal head wound but is miraculously resuscitated. As a result, the entire world worships him as he proceeds to slaughter faithful Christians (13:4–10). Although Nero is not mentioned by name, the language in Revelation 13:1–7 suggests that John may have adapted the form of the Nero myth that alludes to the enemy of God's people in Daniel 7:2–25.

In addition, Revelation 17:10–12 reflects parallels with the other form of the Nero *redux* myth depicting Nero's attack on Rome. John's portrayal differs radically from the other expectations of Nero's return, because in the Apocalypse the beast actually rises from the dead (*redivivus*), whereas all the other examples assume Nero never died (*redux*). The reason John departs from the usual tradition is that in his vision the beast mimics Christ who died and rose again and will return to conquer the world's kingdoms.

LITERARY ASPECTS

Continuing the study of the book of Revelation along the lines of the hermeneutical triad, history, literature, and theology, it is vital to engage in a thorough investigation of the various literary aspects of the book. This will entail a study of the general and special literary features of Revelation.

General Literary Features

Genre

The book of Revelation constitutes one of the most unique biblical books, not only because it represents the concluding work of inspired revelation, but also because it is the only apocalyptic book of the New

Testament. Revelation exhibits elements consistent with the genres of apocalyptic, prophecy, and epistle. Some have maintained that the first word of the book, *apokalypsis*, suggests an immediate genre classification, especially given the use of apocalyptic language and imagery throughout the Apocalypse.

A more accurate genre designation, however, occurs in 1:3 and 22:7, 10, 18–19 (cf. 11:16; 19:10) where John identifies the book as a prophecy. This close association between apocalypse and prophecy is natural because the apocalyptic genre originated from and remained under the rubric of Old Testament prophecy. Apocalyptic writings derived from prophetic oracles, and therefore the lines of demarcation separating these genres are somewhat fluid. What is more, Revelation is addressed to specific congregations and thus also has certain epistolary features.

For these reasons, Revelation constitutes a mixed genre. The book falls into the overall genre of prophecy but corresponds to apocalyptic writings in many respects. The best overall assessment regarding the genre of Revelation is that the book constitutes a prophecy in apocalyptic form written down in form of a letter.

Setting

In addition to the historical setting, you should take careful note of the visionary setting of the book. Understanding that the book of Revelation presents a series of visions John saw will be vitally important in interpreting the book correctly and in understanding its structure. The book opens with John banished to the rocky isle of Patmos in the Aegean Sea (1:9b). There, he received his vision on the Lord's Day (1:10). John used the phrase "in the Spirit" to indicate the means of his vision, and this phrase occurs four times to signal a new vision (1:9; 4:2; 17:3; 21:10). In the first vision, John sees the exalted Christ standing among his churches and delivering messages to each of the seven churches (chaps. 1–3).

The setting changes, however, with the introduction to the second vision (4:1–2) when John is transported from the barren isle of Patmos to the heavenly throne room of God. This is followed by three series of sevens (involving numerical symbolism, the number seven conveying the notion of completeness and perfection): the breaking of the seven seals; the sounding of the seven trumpets; and the pouring out of the seven bowls. At the heart of each of these three series of sevens is God's judgment of the world which proves his righteous character and also serves as a vindication of believers who suffered persecution on account of their faith. Although the scenes in chapters 6–16 alternate between heaven and earth, John remains before the throne of God, giving him a heavenly vantage point.

In 17:3, John is transported in the Spirit from heaven into a desert in order to witness the judgment of "Babylon," signifying the perversion and corruption of the world apart from God, depicted as a seductive and lewd prostitute (Babylon had taken Old Testament Israel into exile and served as a common cipher of godless world empires in Second Temple Jewish literature).

After "Babylon" is judged and destroyed, John is once again transported in the Spirit to a great and high mountain (21:10). From this lofty height, John sees the New Jerusalem as a heavenly bride descending to earth where God will dwell with his people for all eternity.

Narrative Framework

Revelation represents an intricately woven literary masterpiece intended to convey a unified message. The book has a clearly delineated prologue (1:1–8) and epilogue (22:6–21). It is divided into four visions marked by the phrase "in the Spirit" (1:9; 4:2; 17:3; 21:10), and several series of sevens pervade the book (2:1–3:22; 6:1–8:1; 8:2–11:19; 15:1–16:21). In a "tale of two cities," the harlot city of Babylon (chaps. 17–18) is contrasted with the bride city of the New Jerusalem (chaps. 21–22).

The book of Revelation tells a story complete with characters, a variety of settings, a plot, and a climax. The narrative dynamic of Revelation centers on the opening of several heavenly scrolls. The first scroll contains Christ's prophetic message to the seven churches of Asia Minor at the time of writing (1:9–3:22). The bulk of the Apocalypse (4:1–22:5) revolves around the unveiling of the contents of the heavenly scroll by the slain Lamb of God, Jesus Christ. The seven seals are opened (5:1–8:1), followed by the seven trumpets announcing divine judgment (8:2–11:19), and a detailed description of the open scroll (12:1–22:5). The open scroll features several apocalyptic figures, including the woman and the dragon, the beasts from the sea and the earth, the Lamb, and the 144,000. At last, the seven bowls of judgment are poured out, and the judgment of the world and the victory of Christ ensue.

As mentioned, Revelation consists of four separate interrelated visions introduced by the phrase "in the Spirit," with each occurrence of the phrase locating the seer in a different place. The setting shifts from Patmos (1:9) to the heavenly throne room (4:1–2) into a desert (17:3) and finally to a high mountain (21:10). Moreover, the phrase "I will show you" occurs three times (4:1; 17:1; 21:9) in close proximity to "in the Spirit" (4:2; 17:3; 21:10), suggesting that these two phrases are used in conjunction with each other to signal major structural transitions. Interestingly, 4:1–2 also contains one of the three occurrences of the phrase "what must take place" (1:1; 4:1; 22:6), which stresses the future prophetic nature of 4:1–22:4.

Characterization

At the heart of the characterization of the book is *the Lord Jesus Christ* who is presented as risen and glorious, as the source of revelation regarding the state of the seven churches (chaps. 1–3) as well as regarding the final judgment (chaps. 4–18), and as the one who returns triumphantly at the end of time to establish his kingdom (chaps. 19–22). It is in this Christ that the other major themes in the book of Revelation find their integrative center.

John also features prominently in the book as the author and narrator. He identifies himself three times in the beginning and once at the end as the author (1:1c, 4a, 9a; 22:8a). The use of the first person, then, signals that John is the one narrating, seeing, and hearing the contents recorded unless it is attributed to another figure (i.e., Christ in 1:17–18; 2–3). The function of the first person is that it brings the narrative closer to the reader by conveying direct witness to the truth. In 1:1c, John testifies as an eyewitness to the veracity of the message handed to him by God. You can detect the eyewitness nature of the account by frequent references to seeing and hearing but also by John's active participation in events at various junctures of the vision (e.g., 1:17; 5:4; 10:8–11; 11:1; 19:10; 22:8–9). Thus John, as the narrator, guides the reader through all he saw, heard, and experienced.

Angels, both elect and evil, appear as significant characters throughout the book. Angelic beings come in all different shapes, sizes, and colors ranging from the four living creatures (4:4), to the colossal angel straddling earth and sea (10:1), to Satan as a great red dragon (12:3), to the locust demons ascending forth from the great abyss (9:2–11), and even demonic spirits that resemble frogs (16:13–14). Elect angels function as mediators of divine messages to the churches (2:1, 8, 12, 18; 3:1, 7, 14), and to the inhabitants of heaven (5:2; 14:15) and earth (8:13; 14:6–11). They continuously worship God declaring his worthiness and justice (5:11–12; 16:5). They function as the agents that carry out God's decrees, which involve the judgment of humanity (8:1–6; 15:1) as well as the protection of believers (7:1–3). They engage in war against Satan and the evil angels (12:7–9).

The *believers in the seven churches* are a final set of characters that are important to recognize when interpreting the book of Revelation. The book was written to the believers in the seven churches of Asia Minor, suggesting not only that they are the intended audience but that they serve as implicit characters as the people of God. They are addressed in the prologue and epilogue as "the one who reads" (1:3; 22:19), "those who hear" (1:3; 22:18), and those within the "seven churches" (1:4; 20; 22:16). They are also identified by a number of other terms to associate them with all Christian believers.

Minor Transition Markers

As you attempt to interpret a given passage in the book of Revelation and try to locate boundary markers for a given set of textual units, you will want to be sensitive to minor transition markers. Discerning these will help you identify correctly the microstructure and the macrostructure of the book. Minor visionary transitions within any one of the four visions featured in the book are often signaled by references to "seeing" or "hearing." The phrase "and I saw," in particular, acts as a marker within a given vision, signaling a minor transition. It demonstrates a progression within the narrative but does not necessarily introduce a new vision if the location of the seer remains the same. The effect of this narration would be like listening to someone excitedly share what he or she saw while sitting in a theater watching a play or movie, creating a flow similar to "I saw this and then I saw that, oh, and then I saw and heard such and such." While the phrase "in the Spirit" indicates the beginning of a new vision, therefore, the phrase "and I saw" conveys the series of images John sees in a given vision, similar to watching a movie or a play.

Series of Sevens and Relationship between the Sevens

Another significant structuring device is a series of sevens specifically enumerated as such. Within these series of sevens, schemes vary from six, seven, and eight septets. Although John demonstrates a proclivity for explicitly arranging his material into groups of sevens, only three or four septets are explicitly numbered. As mentioned, the number seven carries significant symbolic weight, indicating perfection or completion. Apart from the explicitly numbered septets, however, the effort to identify additional unnumbered series of sevens is precarious and often contrived.

The nature of the relationship between the seven seals, trumpets, and bowls has long confounded interpreters. There are three primary theories: (1) chronological succession; (2) recapitulation; and (3) telescopic progression. *Chronological succession* argues that the series of septets occur in strict chronological order without any overlap. The strength of this view is its simplicity. On the downside, however, such an approach does not sufficiently account for the many areas of overlap between the septets. *Recapitulation* holds that the each septet represents an intensification and closer look at the same material. In other words, the trumpets cover the same occurrences as the seals, and the bowls signify the same period as the seals and trumpets. While recapitulation allows for an intensification of severity with each successive septet and offers a viable explanation for the apparent overlap, it does not adequately account for the dissimilarities between each series of septets.

The *telescopic theory* (also known as "dove-tailing") maintains that the seventh seal contains the seven trumpets and the seventh trumpet comprises the seven bowls. It attempts to demonstrate the interconnectedness and overlap between the series of septets but also to account for the progression evident in each new septet. A progressive telescopic theory seems to offer the most satisfying explanation for the literary relationship between the septets. However, caution against too strict an application of these theories is warranted, because the Apocalypse exhibits both repetition and progression in the unfolding series of judgments revealed in the septets which culminate in the consummation of God's judgment and the establishment of his kingdom on earth.

Interludes

John incorporates several interludes interspersed throughout the seals, trumpets, and bowls. The first two emerge between the breaking of the sixth and seventh seals (7:1–17) and between the blowing of the sixth and seventh trumpets (10:1–11:14). These interludes appear in the narrative for theological reasons. They are bound to the preceding sections and provide answers for questions that the audience might be asking. The sixth seal (6:12–16) unleashes devastating catastrophes causing the earth's inhabitants to flee into caves praying to die. In their terror, they cry out concerning the wrath of God and the lamb, asking, "Who can stand?" The succeeding narrative (7:1–17) answers this question by depicting the protective sealing and salvation of God's people who are standing before the throne.

A similar pattern occurs when the fifth and sixth trumpets unleash horrible and devastating plagues upon the earth's inhabitants. Their response indicates a failure to repent from their sins. The succeeding narrative (10:1–11:14) not only provides justification for the plagues but also depicts the people of God in their role as prophetic witnesses before the nations. These interludes enable the hearers to identify their role within the narrative first as protected and then as prophetic witnesses. The purpose of the interludes, then, is to challenge the churches to remain faithful and to endure opposition because God will protect them and use them as witnesses.

The third interlude differs from the first two in that it occurs at the end of the seventh trumpet and precedes the introduction of the seven bowls. Revelation 12 represents a dramatic shift in the flow of John's vision narrative; it is introduced by the statement "A great and wondrous sign appeared in heaven" (12:1) followed by "Then another sign appeared in heaven" (12:3) and later with "I saw in heaven another great and marvelous sign" (15:1). As in John's Gospel, "sign" in the Apocalypse most likely points to something more significant than a given miracle itself. Thus this third interlude, in the form of a "signs narrative," occurs prior to the final outpouring of God's judgments.

As with other interludes, the signs narrative focuses on the role of the people of God concomitant with the series of judgments. The first interlude illustrates the protection and ultimate salvation of believers (7:1–17). The second interlude pictures their role as God's final prophetic witnesses (10:1–11:14). The third interlude (12:1–15:4) portrays believers as engaged in a holy war against Satan. Although the precise microstructure of this interlude proves elusive, the narrative falls into three natural divisions: (1) holy war in heaven (chap. 12); (2) holy war on earth (chap. 13); and (3) believers' vindication followed by the judgment of unbelievers (chap. 14). Amid the scenes of this cosmic spiritual warfare, John makes the purpose of this interlude explicit by interjecting calls for encouragement (12:10–12), patient endurance (13:9–10), and believers' ultimate vindication (14:6–13). Revelation 12:1–15:4 also provides the basis and justification for the severe and final nature of the judgments brought upon the inhabitants of the earth.

Special Literary Features

Assessing and Interpreting Old Testament Allusions

Because the issue of assessing Old Testament allusions remains rife with difficulties, we will need to probe this topic in some detail. To begin with, we will need to define some basic terms, namely "intertextuality," "allusion," and "echo." In distinction from allusions, intertextuality represents the rubric of all interaction between texts in general, whereas allusions represent the specific occurrences of an intentional appropriation of an earlier text for a particular purpose.

Allusion occurs when an author incorporates the language, imagery, and themes of another text without direct citation. Allusions are distinct from formal citations in that there is no introductory formula but the phrases are woven into the text and are often less precise in wording. Nevertheless, allusions still represent an intertextual reference. Allusions include both verbal and thematic parallels to words and themes. Authorial intention serves as the crucial criterion for distinguishing between allusions and echoes.

An echo may be present when a given text suggests to the reader that text B should be understood in light of a broad interplay with text A. This is predicated upon the notion that every text involves the interplay of other texts and so functions within a larger literary and interpretive network. Texts behave like echo chambers, so that even a word or phrase may resound as a faint trace of texts that may be unconscious but emerge from minds saturated with the Jewish scriptural heritage.

This methodology, in turn, should adhere to a hermeneutic that locates textual meaning in authorial intention. The almost continuous allusion to the Old Testament in the book of Revelation is not a haphazard phenomenon but reflects a pattern of deliberate allusion to certain Old Testament texts. The interpreter of Revelation is primarily concerned with what John intended the allusion to mean rather than with the original intent of the Old Testament writer.

Before we will be able to answer the question of what is intended by the author's use of the Old Testament, we will need to develop criteria for identifying allusions. In doing so, you can place all potential references along a sliding scale of three categories: (1) embedded allusion; (2) implied allusion; and (3) incidental allusion. Embedded allusions are clear, probable, and direct allusions. Implied allusions constitute cases where the potential allusion is indirect or demonstrated through logical necessity. Incidental allusions, including echoes, pertain to minor or subordinate cases of low probability.

The primary key to determining the presence of an allusion is authorial intention. There are five criteria for identifying and classifying allusions. In the chart below, we have placed allusions along the sliding scale of probability based on how many of the criteria they match. Allusions that fit four or five of the criteria are identified as embedded allusions. If the potential allusion only matches three or four criteria, it is ranked as an implied allusion. In cases where a possible allusion matches fewer than three criteria, it is classified as an incidental allusion.

11.1. SLIDING SCALE OF ALLUSION PROBABILITY

Embedded		**Implied**				**Incidental**	
Clear Allusion	Probable Allusion	Structural Allusion	Thematic Allusion	Typological Allusion	Conceptual Allusion	Loud Echo	Soft Echo

The first of the five criteria is that of *linguistic parallels*. Linguistic parallels represent the most crucial and visible of the criteria. *Lexical* indicators are verbal links between words in the primary text and a subtext. *Syntactical* indicators refer to grammatical phenomena that may signal shifts in the text to alert the reader to an Old Testament allusion. *Structural* indicators relate to instances when the patterns, ordering, and chronology of the primary text may be appropriated in the structure of a given text.

Theological significance constitutes the second criterion. This criterion refers to the impact of the potential allusion on the reading of the text. If the potential Old Testament reference does not contain any theologically significant dimension that accounts for its inclusion in the new context, its designation as an allusion remains in doubt.

The third criterion is that of *contextual consistency.* Contextual consistency pertains to the correspondence between the potential allusion and its consistency with the original Old Testament context. An intended allusion summons a specific Old Testament passage to the mind of the reader or hearer, which establishes a link between author and audience by appealing to shared knowledge.

The fourth criterion relates to the *transitivity* of the allusion from the author to the audience. Transitivity denotes the ability of the audience to comprehend the allusion and its source text. Is the alluded text something to which the original readers or hearers had access or with which they possessed a measure of familiarity? If they did not, a measure of doubt is cast upon whether or not the author would have alluded to something that would have been foreign to his audience.

The fifth criterion pertains to the *exegetical tradition* of an Old Testament text. This criterion examines the tradition of how the text of a potential Old Testament allusion has been interpreted in both inner- and extrabiblical exegesis. Tracing the interpretive history of a particular Old Testament passage enables you to identify certain traits of similarity and dissimilarity that may illuminate the potentiality of the allusion in Revelation. If other writings quote, cite, or allude to an Old Testament passage in a manner comparable to Revelation, this bolsters the probability of the allusion. Innerbiblical exegesis tracks the (re)interpretation of earlier Old Testament writings in later Old Testament documents. Extrabiblical exegesis, on the other hand, examines how Old Testament passages were interpreted in noncanonical Jewish writings.

These five criteria jointly serve as tools for adjudicating the probability of a potential allusion. In doing so, we should be careful to distinguish between the identification of allusions and their interpretation. Once you have successfully identified and classified a given allusion, you can proceed to interpret it.

The task of determining how John used the Old Testament allusion is challenging but also very rewarding. We can identify seven categories of usage: (1) *fulfillment of prophecy:* an Old Testament prophecy is presented as directly or indirectly fulfilled in John's vision; (2) *analogical use*: an Old Testament text is compared to an area such as judgment, persecution, false teachings, divine protection, etc.; (3) *indirect Old Testament typological prophecies:* parts of historical narratives (e.g., the plagues of the exodus) are presented in an escalated or universalized manner involving a climax of salvation history; (4) *inverted* or *ironic use of the Old Testament:* the Old Testament promise is applied to the church rather than Israel or universalized to include all nations; (5) *use of Old Testament themes:* passages that develop or continue important concepts that run throughout the Old Testament (e.g., creation and new creation, covenant, exodus, holy war); (6) *use of Old Testament as a literary prototype or model:* instances where the Old Testament influences the structure and language of significant portions of John's vision; (7) *stylistic use of Old Testament language:* observable by the numerous grammatical incongruities in the Greek language that result from the appropriation of the Hebrew text. These seven categories of John's use of the Old Testament provide a basic framework for interpreting the meaning of the allusions in the book of Revelation.

Types of Figurative Language

Figures of speech serve as devices of comparison. By using analogical language, figures of speech lead the reader from the known to the unknown, in the present case, future events. Thus, their use helps alleviate the difficulty of communicating a subject—the end times—that defies mere propositional or descriptive language.

As do all forms of human communication, figurative language operates within a particular context. In the case of Revelation, this context is essentially made up by Old Testament prophetic-apocalyptic portions. Since Revelation depicts *a series of real visions* experienced by the seer, John, it is only natural that this individual, steeped in the world of Old Testament depictions of the end, saw these visions *in terms reminiscent of these passages.* At the same time, this does not mean that his portrayal of these visions *slavishly* follows the original Old Testament context. Thus, Revelation ought to be interpreted not merely in literary terms as if the seer operated exclusively on a literary level, performing a series of cut-and-paste operations in working with various Old Testament antecedent passages.

Rather, these texts constitute *points of departure* that guided the seer in experiencing these visions but did not *limit* him in describing what he saw. Thus, the interpreter's work is not done once he or she has identified one or several possible Old Testament texts to which a given passage in Revelation may allude. In the end, it is the interpreter's goal to understand the visions depicted in Revelation *on their own terms* and to identify the real-life historical referents which form the point of reference for the various symbols and figures in a given passage in Revelation.

Symbolic Nature of Revelation

The book of Revelation presents the reader with a vast number of captivating images: the glorified Christ, the heavenly throne and those surrounding it, a slain lamb with seven horns and seven eyes, a woman crowned with twelve stars, a red dragon, a seven-headed beast, a great prostitute, and a host of awe-inspiring angelic beings. These highly symbolic images make Revelation a truly unique book and one that is highly controversial and frequently misunderstood. It is undeniable that the Apocalypse contains a legion of symbolic and metaphorical images, but interpretive approaches divide sharply as to how these symbols should be interpreted. Two major divergent hermeneutical positions have emerged in this regard: (1) primarily literal and secondarily symbolic; or (2) primarily symbolic and secondarily literal.

The first approach advocates interpreting Revelation primarily in a literal manner unless it is impossible to do so. This view is encapsulated in the hermeneutical dictum "When the plain sense of Scripture makes common sense, seek no other sense." While recognizing the presence of symbols, this view holds that we should identify a given term as symbolic only when it does not make sense to take it literally (e.g., Jesus does not have a literal sword protruding from his mouth). Interpreters such as these argue that nonliteral interpretations result in an unchecked multiplicity of meanings based on human imagination.

Many of those favoring literal interpretation maintain that the figures of speech (i.e., symbols) result from John attempting to describe future objects and scenarios from the limited framework of his ancient conceptions and language. The goal for interpreting these symbols, then, is to identify the one-to-one correspondence between his image and a modern parallel. On the positive side, this approach takes the text at face value, avoids reducing it to an extended allegory, and often produces a simple, straightforward interpretation. However, while the approach may work when interpreting narrative or texts, its application to highly figurative genres such as apocalyptic falls short.

What could be wrong with interpreting apocalyptic literature such as Revelation literally? The main problem with such an approach is that it inadequately considers that the literary genre of a given text establishes the rules for how it should be interpreted. Meaning is intrinsically bound up with genre. It follows that genre provides a context assigned by the author to communicate meaning. We have already shown that the genre of Revelation is prophetic-apocalyptic. The apocalyptic genre, by definition, is highly symbolic and not intended to be interpreted in a literal manner. For this reason, a rigid literal interpretation or literalism may actually obscure the author's intended meaning rather than expose it.

In this regard, it is important to distinguish between the literal sense and literalism. If Revelation is prophetic-apocalyptic in nature, ascribing literalism to its numbers, proper nouns, and other images may actually prevent a proper understanding of John's intended meaning. A more profitable hermeneutical approach is to reverse the interpretive order by placing the symbolic in the foreground while shifting the literal into the background. Rather than positing the dictum "When the literal makes sense, seek no other sense," we suggest that a better maxim in interpreting apocalyptic is "Start out with the assumption that a given statement or image is figurative rather than literal."

Interpreting Symbols in Revelation

How, then, should you interpret the symbolic language in the book of Revelation? The symbols of Revelation, although enigmatic, are intended to reveal meaning rather than conceal it. The interpreter's task is to determine how a given symbol functions in its context and what it signifies. To grasp the meaning of a symbol, you must recognize both the mental or conceptual idea and the image it represents. Visionary accounts represent a genre of biblical literature that employs the full arsenal of figurative language—similes, metaphors, and symbols—intended to communicate through the medium of symbolic images that burst with meaning. Symbols represent a type of metaphor in which a visual or linguistic sign of a known object or concept is used to express an unknown object or concept.

The symbols in the Apocalypse derive from John's visual experience as a means to express *in* words what cannot necessarily be expressed *with* words. This is rather unlike a historical narrative where the primary theological meaning corresponds rather straightforwardly to the events narrated. The symbolism in Revelation dominates in such a way that the passage expresses directly the theological significance and only indirectly points to the underlying event. John communicates through symbolic imagery so as to recreate the details of his vision, but the symbols point beyond the text to spiritual, theological, and also physical realities. We recommend the judicious use of the following interpretive steps to arrive at the most probable intended meaning for a given symbol.

1. *Recognize the symbolic imagery associated with the description of people and beings, colors, numbers, institutions, places, and events.* All too often interpreters fail to recognize that almost everything in Revelation resonates with symbolic connotations. Think of Revelation as an impressionistic painting instead of a video recording of the future world. John paints verbal pictures depicting the contents of his vision replete with symbolic hues and shades. His descriptions are intended to evoke a sense of wonder, awe, and worship, as well as to communicate prophetic eschatological expectations. This implies that most descriptions of people or beings, colors, numbers, institutions, places, and events carry a metaphorical or symbolic connotation. Therefore, read Revelation with an informed sensitivity to the symbolic nature of its language and imagery.

2. *Look for interpretations of those symbols within the vision.* Often the intended meaning of a symbol is explicitly provided by John or a heavenly being. These are fairly easy to identify because of the formula: *symbol + "is this" "these are" "which are" = identification.* While these self-interpreted symbols help to narrow the range of referents for a given symbol, they also create a whole new set of questions. At times, they interpret the symbol with another symbol. The following chart (11:2) illustrates self-interpreted symbols in the book of Revelation.

3. *Determine if the symbol stems from an allusion to the Old Testament.* The entire text of John's vision(s) is saturated with allusions to the Old Testament. John frequently uses the language and imagery of the Old Testament to provide his readers with a framework for understanding the significance of what he saw. This does not imply that John was performing an exegesis of the Old Testament, but rather that he borrowed the wording, images, themes, and eschatological expectations from the Old Testament. These allusions are pressed into the service of the textual imagery.

11.2: SELF-INTERPRETED SYMBOLS IN REVELATION:			
Reference	**Symbol**	**Interpretive Signal**	**Symbol Identified**
1:20	seven stars	"[they] are" (*eisin*)	the angels of the seven churches
1:20	seven lampstands	"[they] are" (*eisin*)	the seven churches
4:5	seven lamps before the throne	"these are" (*ha eisin*)	the seven spirits of God
5:6	seven horns and seven eyes of the Lamb	"which are" (*hoi eisin*)	the seven spirits of God sent out into all the earth
5:8	golden bowls full of incense	"which are" (*hai eisin*)	the prayers of the saints
7:13–14	the multitude in white robes	"these are" (*houtoi eisin*)	the saints who have come out of the great tribulation
11:4	the two olive trees and the two lampstands that stand before the Lord of the earth	"these are" (*houtoi eisin*)	the two witnesses
14:4	the 144,000	"these are" (*houtoi eisin*)	those who did not defile themselves with women and kept themselves pure
17:9	the seven heads of the beast	"[they] are" (*eisin*)	seven hills (Rome) and also seven kings (emperors?)
19:8	fine linen, bright and clean	"stands for" (*gar… estin*)	the righteous acts of the saints

The interpreter must first determine if the text alludes to an Old Testament subtext. After the allusion is verified, the interpreter should seek to understand the meaning of the Old Testament passage in its context. Next, you need to compare carefully the similarities and differences between the Old Testament and its allusion in Revelation. Once you have compared the texts, you will be able to see how John ascribes a particular meaning to the Old Testament language and imagery by using and reworking it into the account of his vision.

4. Compare the symbol with other apocalyptic writings to see if it is a common symbol with a relatively standard meaning. John primarily uses

Old Testament imagery, but he occasionally employs imagery belonging to the common stock of apocalyptic writings. Some images have no parallels in the text of the biblical canon. In these cases, a comparative reading of other apocalyptic texts and Jewish writings may shed light on Revelation. Before consulting these texts, a few caveats are in order. First, the existence of any parallels between Revelation and these writings does not necessitate, demand, or imply any form of literary dependence on the part of Revelation. Second, most of these are not exact parallels in that they rarely share identical wording. Third, the date of a given writing deserves serious consideration because if the other apocalyptic work postdates Revelation the symbolic parallel may derive from Revelation, indicate a shared tradition, or be unrelated.

5. *Look for any possible connections between the symbol and the cultural-historical context.* The fifth step looks beyond the text in an attempt to set the imagery within the cultural and historical context of first-century Asia Minor. Two thousand years of history separate modern readers of Revelation from the social, cultural, and political environment of the original recipients. Some of the confusion regarding the imagery of the Apocalypse derives directly from the fact that John wrote to people that all shared a common understanding of their surrounding culture within the Roman Empire. Images of beasts, kings, and cities wielding enormous military and political power over their citizens may seem strange and foreign to the modern reader living in America. A historically informed reading of the text will often clear up the haze of a given set of symbols. The mark of the beast in Revelation 13:18 provides an example of how some symbols are wedded to the historical context.

6. *Consult treatments of the symbol in scholarly commentaries and other works.* The sixth step is to see how scholars have interpreted the symbols. This step may actually occur in tandem with steps one through five. The complex nature of symbolism requires the mature insights of seasoned experts who have devoted serious time studying the text of Revelation. Keep in mind, however, that serious time and study does not guarantee that a given interpretation is plausible or probable.

7. *Remain humble in your conclusions.* Interpreting Revelation requires humility and an openness to return to the text again and again. Once you

have thoroughly studied the text, avoid thinking that you have now unlocked all the mysteries of the Apocalypse. Make studying the book of Revelation a lifetime pursuit. Repeat steps one through six on a regular basis. This will prevent you from falling into the temptation of thinking that you alone have the right interpretation of this mysterious and complex book. No one other than God has the final answer on the meaning of Revelation. While this is sobering, it will keep you humble and encourage you to keep studying God's Word.

Structure

While there are multiple proposals for the structure of the book of Revelation, one of the most plausible ways to outline the book focuses on the four visions "in the Spirit" that place John, the seer, in four different locations as indicated below.

- I. Prologue (1:1–8)
- II. Vision One (Patmos): The Glorified Christ and His Message to the Churches (1:9–3:22)
  - A. The Inaugural Vision of Jesus Christ (1:9–20)
  - B. The Messages to the Seven Churches of Asia Minor (2:1–3:22)
- III. Vision Two (Heaven): The Divine Court Proceedings and the Trial of the Nations (4:1–16:21)
  - A. Transition from Patmos to Heaven (4:1–2)
  - B. Worship around the Throne (4:3–11)
  - C. The Divine Courtroom (5:1–14)
  - D. Preliminary Investigative Judgments (6:1–17)
  - E. First Interlude: The Protective Sealing of God's People (7:1–17)
  - F. Eschatological Investigative Judgments (8:1–9:21)
  - G. Second Interlude: God's People as Prophetic Witnesses (10:1–11:19)
  - H. Third Interlude: God's People in Holy War (12:1–15:1)
  - I. Final Investigative Judgments: The Third Woe/Seven Bowls (16:1–21)
- IV. Vision Three (Desert): The Destruction of Babylon and the Return of Christ (17:1–21:8)
  - A. Transition: "Come, I Will Show You the Punishment of the Great Prostitute" (17:1–2)

- B. The Prostitute City Babylon Described (17:3–6)
- C. The Prostitute City Babylon as Rome (17:7–18)
- D. The Trial and Sentencing of Babylon (18:1–24)
- E. The Heavenly Celebration of Babylon's Destruction (19:1–10)
- F. The Divine Warrior and the Final Tribunal (19:11–20:15)
- G. The Renewal of Creation and the Arrival of the New Jerusalem (21:1–8)

V. Vision Four (Mountain): Believers' Reward and the Renewal of Creation (21:9–22:5)

- A. Transition: "Come, I Will Show You the Bride" (21:9–10)
- B. The Description of the New Jerusalem Descending from Heaven (21:11–27)
- C. The Paradise of God: The Renewal of Creation (22:1–5)

VI. Epilogue (22:6–21)

GUIDELINES FOR INTERPRETING APOCALYPTIC LITERATURE

1. Locate the historical setting of the book of Revelation.
2. Distinguish between intertextuality, inner-biblical exegesis, allusion, and echo.
3. Identify the type of allusion, whether embedded, implied, or incidental.
4. Identify the specific Old Testament passage(s) invoked in a given passage in Revelation.
5. Identify the plot and development of the book of Revelation and relate the specific passage to the overall plot.
6. Identify the major characters and their role in the narrative.
7. Identify the major theological themes in the book of Revelation.
8. Identify the way in which a given theological theme finds its culmination in Revelation.
9. Determine principles for godly living in view of the culmination of Christ's kingdom at his return.

KEY WORDS

Allusion, Apocalypse, Apocalyptic, Apocalypticism, Eclectic approach, Emperor cult, Futurist approach, Historicist approach, Idealist approach, Inaugurated eschatology, Interlude, Intertextuality, Millennium, Nero *redivivus* myth, Preterist approach, Progressive dispensationalism, Prophetic-apocalyptic, Transitivity.

ASSIGNMENTS

1. Discuss the basic structure and major theological themes in the book of Revelation.

2. Engage in a detailed, thorough study of Revelation 11:1-13, canvassing the likely historical setting, literary flow and structure, and theological message of the passage.

KEY RESOURCES

Pate, C. Marvin, ed. *Four Views on the Book of Revelation.* Grand Rapids: Zondervan, 1998.

Schnabel, Eckhard J. *40 Questions about the End Times.* Grand Rapids: Kregel, 2012.

Wilson, Mark. *Charts on the Book of Revelation: Literary, Historical, and Theological Perspectives*. Grand Rapids: Kregel, 2007.

UNIT 3: LANGUAGE

CHAPTER 12 OBJECTIVES

1. To address important grammatical and syntactical matters pertaining to the study of Scripture.

2. To introduce the interpreter to the analysis of biblical discourse.

3. To underscore the importance of interpreting smaller exegetical units in light of a book's overall structure.

CHAPTER 12 OUTLINE

A. Defining the Terms: Grammar, Syntax, and Discourse

B. Larger Syntactical Features and Sentence Structure

C. Discourse Analysis: Overview of Method

D. Discourse Analysis: Specific Examples

E. Guidelines for Outlining a Biblical Book or Interpretive Unit

F. Key Words

G. Assignments

H. Key Resources

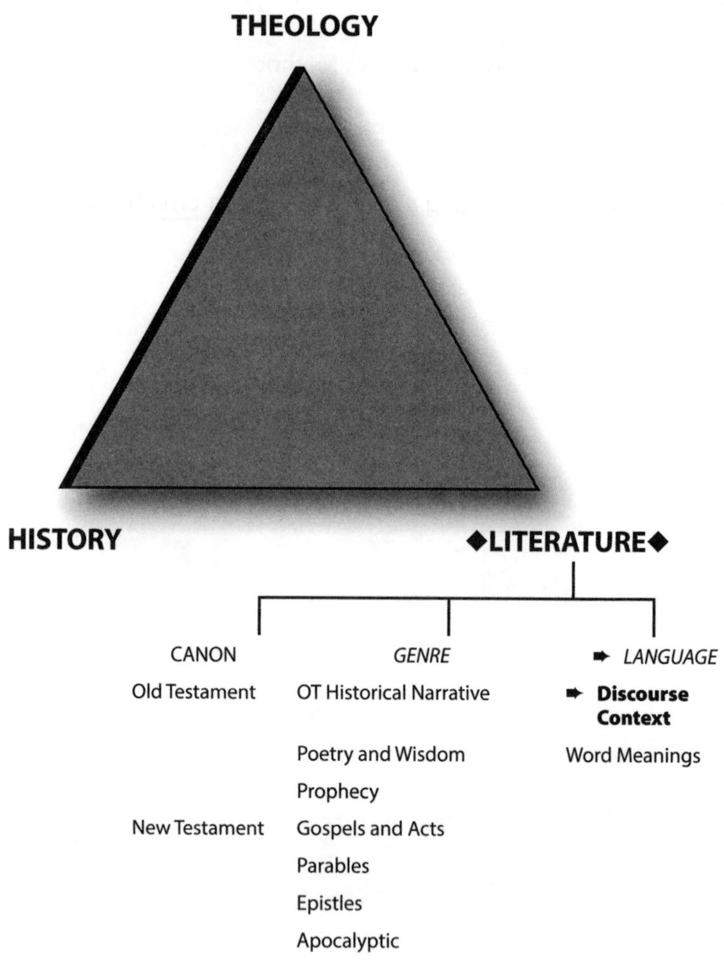
THEOLOGY
HISTORY
◆LITERATURE◆
CANON
Old Testament
New Testament
GENRE
OT Historical Narrative
Poetry and Wisdom
Prophecy
Gospels and Acts
Parables
Epistles
Apocalyptic
➨ LANGUAGE
➨ Discourse Context
Word Meanings

Chapter 12

CONTEXT IS KING: DISCERNING DISCOURSE STRUCTURE

DEFINING THE TERMS: GRAMMAR, SYNTAX, AND DISCOURSE

NOW THAT WE HAVE SURVEYED the canonical landscape and acquainted ourselves with the various types of literature found in Scripture, we will move from the level of the genres of biblical *literature* to the level of biblical *language*. Continuing to follow the principle of interpreting the parts in light of the whole, we will now attempt to come to terms with two important phenomena of the language of Scripture: (1) discerning the structure of the biblical text; and (2) determining the meaning of words with interpretive significance.

In interpreting any text of Scripture, context is extremely important. The proper textual unit at which meaning is to be discerned is not the individual word, the phrase, or even the sentence, but the larger discourse, that is, the paragraph level and ultimately the entire document of which a given word, phrase, or sentence is a part. This simple insight, amply confirmed by recent linguistic research, has the potential of revolutionizing your study of the biblical text.

Before moving on to the discussion, it will be helpful to define three major terms: (1) grammar; (2) syntax; and (3) discourse. There is no sharp distinction in definition and usage between the terms "grammar" and "syntax." If any distinction can be made at all, it may be said that *grammar* denotes specific features of syntax, such as a certain kind of genitive or participle (form), while *syntax* refers more broadly to relationships between words in the larger scheme of discourses and sentence structures. A distinction exists also between semantics and syntax. *Semantics* is concerned with the meaning of *individual words* (based on the recognition that word meaning is to be discerned in context), while *syntax* is concerned with *the relationship between words.*

Discourse

Before delving into the subject, it will be helpful to define several key terms, most importantly that of discourse itself. What is discourse? Essentially, *discourse* may be defined as any coherent sequence of phrases or sentences, whether a narrative, logical argument, or poetic portion of text. To be coherent and intelligible, all forms of extended human discourse must possess certain features that provide them with boundary markers, cohesion, prominence, relations, and situatedness. As will be seen, this is accomplished by a variety of linguistic means, such as initiatory phrases, topics or themes, logical connections, and a myriad of other linguistic, grammatical, and syntactical features.

An example of the relevance of discerning the boundaries of biblical discourse for interpretation is John's account of Jesus's encounter with Nicodemus. The chapter division suggests that the account commences with John 3:1. More likely, however, the unit starts with 2:23–25, which serves both as a conclusion to the temple clearing in 2:13–22 and as an introduction to the Nicodemus narrative. This is suggested by several instances of words occurring in both 2:23–25 and 3:1–2, such as references to Jesus's signs and references to people who witnessed Jesus's signs in Jerusalem to whom Jesus would not entrust himself and Nicodemus as a "man of the Pharisees."

Therefore, rather than understanding Jesus's encounter with Nicodemus as merely a face-off between two prominent rabbis, we see that in John's theology Nicodemus is presented as a prototype of a person who witnessed Jesus's teaching and signs but who did not truly understand Jesus's identity as Messiah and Son of God. Thus an understanding of the features of biblical discourse, and in the present case a proper identification of discourse boundaries, is absolutely essential to a proper and full-fledged interpretation of a given textual unit.

Other Definitions

To aid in the understanding of the discussion below and to clarify the terminology used, it will be beneficial to define several other important syntactical terms as well. The first such term is that of "phrase," which may be defined as any meaningful word cluster that lacks a verb form, such as a prepositional phrase plus an article plus a noun (e.g., "into the house"). Typically, prepositional phrases modify (i.e., explain or give additional information regarding) the main verb in a given clause or sentence. In the above example, "into the house" may modify "he went," indicating *where* a given person went. Phrases are thus part of what makes up a larger discourse.

Two more definitions will be helpful, those for "clause" and "sentence." A "clause" is any meaningful cluster of words that includes a verb, while a "sentence" is any complete thought expressed in form of one or several independent clauses. An example of a clause would be, "because he loved us." An example of a sentence would be, "Jesus died because he loved us." Notice the difference here. The former example is a coherent thought but not a complete one; the latter is both. Hence the notion of "sentence" comprises and includes that of "clause." Clauses may be dependent or independent clauses, the latter of which are sentences, while the former will be part of a sentence but not constitute a sentence.

At the very outset, it is also important to note that any *literary genre* itself, be it narrative, poetry, or parable, provides an important parameter for the discourse type of a given portion of text. We devoted the entire previous section of the present volume to a discussion of the interpretation of specific biblical genres.

LARGER SYNTACTICAL FEATURES AND SENTENCE STRUCTURE

Larger Syntactical Features

Larger syntactical issues in the Greek New Testament are raised by the presence of a variety of devices indicating incompletion or fullness of expression. *Ellipsis* represents a feature by which an incomplete idea requires the reader to supply a missing element which is self-evident (e.g., 2 Cor. 5:13: "If we are out of our mind, [it is] for the sake of God").

Zeugma is a special type of ellipsis in which a different verb is to be supplied, that is, one verb occurs with two subjects or objects while suiting only one. An obvious example is 1 Timothy 4:3: "They [i.e., the false teachers] forbid people to marry [and order them] to abstain from certain foods." Another New Testament instance of this phenomenon is 1 Corinthians 3:2: "I gave you milk to drink, not solid food [to eat]."

Aposiopesis is the breaking off of a speech or statement owing to strong emotion, modesty, or other reasons. New Testament examples include passages such as John 1:22 ("Who are you? [Give us an answer] to take back to those who sent us") and Luke 13:9 ("If it bears fruit next year [it should be allowed to grow]. If not, then cut it down").

Brachylogy is the omission of an element that can reasonably be supplied by the reader for the sake of brevity. A typical example involves the putting of a purpose clause at the beginning of a sentence prior to the main clause in order to preface it with the abbreviated form of a train of thought (e.g., Matt. 9:6; John 1:22; 9:36; 2 Cor. 10:9).

Hendiadys represents an arrangement of two or more expressions that essentially convey the same idea. Hence, an element of redundancy is present. New Testament examples include the reference to "kingdom and glory" in 1 Thessalonians 2:12 or to the "blessed hope and glorious appearing" in Titus 2:13. At other times, however, two ideas may be distinct and thus may not be found to truly represent this form of expression.

Pleonasm, finally, is a form of redundancy by which a previously expressed idea is repeated as a way of speaking (not for emphasis; the interpreter is cautioned not to jump to false conclusions here). This feature frequently involves the use of the word "again" (e.g., John 4:54; Acts 10:15; Gal. 1:17). Another frequent example is the phrase "he answered and said" or the phrase "the household master of the house" (Luke 22:11). Many modern translations eliminate this kind of redundancy in English (e.g., NIV: "the owner of the house").

Sentence Structure

As you may know, the original Greek manuscripts of the New Testament do not include punctuation such as periods, commas, colons, or semicolons. These were added by later critical editions of the New Testament, as were spaces between words (in the original manuscripts, Greek words run together). Nevertheless, divisions between units are discernible in places such as Luke's elegantly-crafted prologue (Luke 1:1–4; see also Acts 15:24–26; John 13:1–5; Heb. 1:1–3).

Asyndeton

An example of *asyndeton* (the absence of connectives) involving adjectives is 2 Timothy 4:2: "in season [and] out of season." Asyndeton also occurs in lengthy enumerations such as John 5:3: "a great number of disabled people—the blind, the lame, the paralyzed" (see also 1 Cor. 3:12; 1 Tim. 1:10; 2 Tim. 3:2; 1 Pet. 4:3). Asyndeton is also found when two or more verbs are juxtaposed rather one being subordinated to the other. An example of this construction is Matthew 5:24: "Go, first be reconciled" (see also Matt. 9:30; 24:6; Matt. 26:46 = Mark 14:12; Mark 2:11; 4:39).

On a larger discourse level, asyndeton between clauses and sentences is a common feature in the Gospels (e.g., Matt. 5:3–17; John 1:23, 28, 37–39, 41–42; 3:6–8). There are also many examples of rhetorical asyndeton in Paul's writings (e.g., 1 Cor. 7:18, 21, 27; 2 Cor. 11:23–28). Finally, asyndeton is also found between paragraphs and larger discourse units, especially in James, 1 John, and some of Paul's writings (e.g., Rom. 9:1), but not in Hebrews.

Parenthesis

Regular sentence structure may be interrupted by either *parenthesis* (the interjection of an independent additional thought) or *anacoluthon* (an incomplete thought). The need for either device arises when a writer finds it necessary to accommodate an afterthought or chooses to interject an additional piece of information that temporarily interrupts the flow of thought in a given passage. For example, John's Gospel features numerous asides or parentheses, informing the reader of translations, geographical or topographical locations, or other helpful pieces of information (e.g., John 1:38, 41; 9:7). In the book of Acts, an example of parenthesis is Acts 5:14, which interrupts the flow of Acts 5:13 and the narration of the result in Acts 5:15.

Anacoluthon

Anacoluthon refers to a sentence structure that includes an incomplete thought (e.g., Acts 7:40; 2 Cor. 12:17). It also includes pendent nominatives (e.g., Matt. 10:11) and expressions following an introductory participle (e.g., John 7:38: "Whoever believes in me, as the Scripture has said, *streams of living water will flow from within him*").

More complicated are instances where anacoluthon occurs after an intervening clause of a sentence. In those cases, after interjecting a thought, rather than resume the sentence structure of the original sentence, the author starts a new sentence with its own syntactical construction and does not complete the initial thought and thus does not follow smoothly from it. An example of this is Galatians 2:6: "As for those who seemed to be important—whatever they were makes no difference to me; God does not judge by external appearance—those men added nothing to my message" (see also Tertullus's speech in Acts 24:5–6). Other instances of anacoluthon involve the use of a participle in place of a finite verb (e.g., 1 Pet. 3:7, 9).

DISCOURSE ANALYSIS: OVERVIEW OF METHOD

Are you ready to go deeper in your study of Scripture? If so, you may want to get acquainted with a relatively new method that holds considerable promise for biblical interpretation—discourse analysis. The purpose of discourse analysis is the accurate discernment of the authorial intention expressed in a given text. The following overview of this method is based on the recognition that biblical interpretation should be conducted on the level of discourse rather than on the sentence or paragraph level.

As anyone perusing the literature on the subject will soon discover, there is considerable diversity in the specific method of discourse analysis adopted by different authors or groups (such as individuals associated with the Summer Institute of Linguistics). There is also a certain amount of variance with regard to specific terminology (e.g., some call discourse analysis "semantic structure analysis"; others subsume it under narrative criticism).

The purpose of the following overview is not to privilege any one of these methods but rather to pinpoint the underlying textual features that form the basis for biblical interpretation and that must be properly discerned and understood by the interpreter. We hope that you will be persuaded of the relevance, even necessity, of analyzing biblical discourse and incorporate the insights presented below in your method for personal Bible study.

Properly understood and implemented, discourse analysis has the potential to revolutionize the study of Scripture in that it shifts the emphasis from the work of the interpreter in breaking up units from his or her own vantage point to a careful analysis of the features of the biblical text itself. By providing the interpretive tools associated with discourse analysis (used in the present chapter in a nontechnical sense, that is, as the analysis of discourse apart from one specific method), we seek to equip the Bible student, teacher, and preacher to develop confidence and skill in tracing the concrete makeup and contours of the biblical text and to teach and preach it accordingly.

Major Steps in Discourse Analysis

In the following discussion, we will treat the following five aspects of discourse analysis: (1) boundary features; (2) cohesion; (3) relations; (4) prominence; and (5) situation. There is a certain logical flow to this sequence. At the outset, *boundary features* deal with isolating the beginning and end point of a given textual unit. *Cohesion* is concerned with features that weave together the fabric of a textual unit and constitute it as a coherent whole. *Relations* deal with the logic of the thought flow of a given passage, be it by indicating cause, purpose, result, or another coordinating or subordinating relation. *Prominence* seeks to discern emphasis, whether on the micro-level of an individual sentence or phrase or on the macro-level of the larger discourse or narrative (peak). *Situation*, finally, focuses on the way in which linguistic expression is part of the larger phenomenon of a speaker's or writer's embeddedness in a given culture, which has important historical, social, and cultural implications.

Boundary Features

A necessary first step is to screen the text for particular *boundary features* that set it off from the preceding and successive textual units. Some distinguish here between episodes, units, paragraphs, propositional clusters, and propositions. The identification of boundary features is critical for the proper delineation of a text for preaching or teaching and is thus of immense practical importance. Major boundary features include:

1. Initial markers, such as orienters ("I do not want you to be ignorant," 1 Cor. 10:1; "I praise you," 1 Cor. 11:2; "I want to remind you," 1 Cor. 15:1; "Finally," Phil. 3:1; 4:8), conjunctions, vocatives ("Dear children": 1 John 2:1, 12; "Dear friends," Jude 3, 17, 20), deictic indicators (such as adverbs of time or space; "After this he went down to Capernaum," John 2:12), topic statements ("Now about," 1 Cor. 7:1, 25; 8:1; 12:1), rhetorical questions introducing a new topic (Rom. 6:1–3, 15; 7:1, 7, 13), and changes in characters or setting (John 4:1–4).

2. Final markers, such as summary statements (Matt. 4:23–25; Acts 2:41; 9:31; Heb. 11:39–40), doxologies (Rom. 11:33–36; Eph. 3:20–21), colophons ("Amen" or "Goodbye"), or tail-head links (mention of a topic at the end of a section to be developed in the following unit; e.g. the mention of "salvation" in Heb. 1:14, which becomes the basis for subsequent exhortation, see Heb. 2:3).

3. Literary devices such as *inclusio* (John 2:11 and 4:54), chiasm (John 1:1–18), or other textual features such as changes in subject, object, or topic (e.g. the transition from icebreaker in Phlm. 4–7 to the business at hand in Phlm. 8–22); changes in time, setting, and participants (e.g., Matt. 5:1; 8:1, 5, 14, 16; 17:1); conjunctions or changes in verbal tense, mood, or aspect (shift from indicatives to imperatives from Phlm. 8–16 to Phlm. 17–22 or from Jude 3–16 to 17–23).

4. Repeated units (whether terms, phrases, clauses, sentences, or syntactical structures; e.g., Matt. 7:28; 11:1; 13:53; 19:1; 26:1. Of significant structural import is the phrase, "I was in the Spirit" or a similar expression, occurring in Rev. 1:10; 4:2; 17:3; and 21:10, by which the book of Revelation divides into four major visions).

Cohesion

A second important discourse feature is that of *cohesion*. Cohesion is provided by various lexical, thematic, or syntactical devices that make up the glue that holds a discourse together. Cohesion is the glue that provides a text with its unity. A text may be given cohesion by certain formal features (such as the alliterated five words starting with the Greek letter "p" in Heb. 1:1); semantic features (i.e., related word meanings in a given textual unit; e.g., 1 Tim. 5:3–16 on widows, or the "wealth and poverty" theme in Luke-Acts); or a text's pragmatic effect on its readers or hearers. Richard Young distinguishes four kinds of cohesion:

1. Grammatical cohesion (e.g., subject-verb agreement);

2. Lexical cohesion (the use of the same or similar words, e.g. Jas. 1:2–5);

3. Relational cohesion (conjunctions, relative pronouns and clauses, participles);

4. Referential cohesion (links between a given text and other textual units in a piece of writing), particularly anaphora (e.g., "thus," referring back to a previous clause or unit).

Relations

A third major feature of discourses is that of *relations*, that is, various ways in which statements or propositions are conjoined in a given text. We can discern the following major types of relations in biblical discourse:

1. Addition relations or coordination characterized by *equal* prominence (e.g., "So he went to her, took her hand and helped her up," Mark 1:31): these may be successive or sequential (i.e., chronological), simultaneous, or nontemporal.

2. Support relations characterized by *unequal* prominence: this may take the form of *orientation* (e.g., "After John was put in prison, Jesus went into Galilee," Mark 1:14); *logic* (be it reason-result, means-result, means-purpose, grounds-conclusion, condition-consequence, or concession-contra-expectation); or *clarification* (whether by way of restatement or expansion).

Prominence

A fourth discourse feature is that of *prominence* or emphasis. This refers to the observable phenomenon that certain aspects of a given discourse will stand out more than others, marking a point, theme, or plot. While readers are often oblivious to this dimension, it is nonetheless critical. In fact, if all features of a discourse were equally prominent, it would be virtually unintelligible, similar to a white bird in a blizzard or a black cat in a tunnel.

There are two kinds of prominence. *Natural* prominence relates to elements pertaining to the plot structure of a given pericope (its backbone). An example of this would be the reference to Jesus's performance of his "first sign" in John 2:11. *Marked* prominence is conveyed by a variety of elements, such as word order, morphemes (e.g., intensifying word forms), various grammatical features, figures of speech, repetition, orienters, rhetorical questions, anaphora, discourse proportion (i.e., relative length), asyndeton (lack of a conjunction at the beginning of a sentence), and personal names.

On a larger scale, coherent units in a certain discourse share a given topic, gradually progressing to a climax or *peak*, particularly in narrative discourse. For example, the Johannine farewell discourse, which extends from John 13:31 to 16:33, peaks at 15:1–8, Jesus's symbolic discourse on the vine and the branches. A change of participants, location, or pace (such as rapid closure) may ensue after the peak has been reached. An example of the latter is Jesus's raising of Lazarus in John 11:43–44, after which the narrative ends almost immediately. A typical discourse structure may include a title, stage, pre-peak episodes, the peak, post-peak episodes, and closure.

Situation

One final element is called *situation*, the real-life setting which is studied by a variety of disciplines. This field of study analyzes the nonlinguistic features of discourse such as social environment or shared knowledge, which is relevant particularly for biblical instances of interpersonal communication or dialogue. One relevant example here is that of *implicature*, that is, implicit yet necessary information for understanding a given discourse. In fact, much remains unsaid or unexplained because of a "presupposition pool" that is shared between the author and his readers (or, in the case of oral communication, between a speaker and his listeners).

The value of including this dimension in our analysis of discourse stems from the recognition that texts and their linguistic and literary aspects are part of a larger relational framework, which, in turn, is firmly embedded in a historical, social, political, economic, and general cultural framework. For this reason it would be both artificial and highly reductionistic to limit our study of the biblical text in a narrow manner to textual phenomena without recognizing that there are connotations to be discerned, underlying presuppositions to be made explicit, and the socio-linguistic and relational dimensions of language to be recognized.

To be sure, we must be careful not to confuse reading the text with reading between the lines of the text. The text must remain the final point of reference for biblical interpretation. Nevertheless, it is in the nature of human communication, both written and oral, that assumptions sometimes remain unstated and need to be supplied by the reader or interpreter. When Paul writes, "Don't you remember that when I was with you I used to tell you these things?" (2 Thess. 2:5), one only wishes that one had been privy to the previous teaching received by the Thessalonians. In 1 Corinthians, Paul most likely cites sayings common in the Corinthian church in order to address them (e.g., 1 Cor. 7:1: "It is good for a man not to marry").

For this reason it is part of the interpreter's role to unearth the implicit assumptions underlying a given text as part of the interpretive task. It also will be helpful to recognize that in many cultures, including first-century Palestinian Judaism, communication was frequently indirect, so that one must not cling to the surface meaning of a given phrase but seek to discern the underlying actual purpose or intended message of a given statement. An example of this is Nicodemus's opening gambit when visiting Jesus by night. Rather than taking his polite pleasantries at face value, it may be better to understand Nicodemus's words as a tacit inquiry as to the nature of Jesus's teaching (John 3:1–2; cf. 1:19, 22).

Sample Discourse Analysis: John 2:1–11

As mentioned, discourse analysis does not only pay attention to what might be called micro-elements of discourse such as the words denoting coordination, argumentation, orientation, or clarification, it also seeks to discern larger features or the *macrostructure* of discourses. These are discourse boundaries, whether initiatory markers, transitional devices, or concluding sequences, and various features of the internal structure of discourse, such as setting or staging, peaking, and closure.

John 2:1–11 may serve as an example. The *discourse boundaries* are set by the introductory phrase "On the third day" in verse 1 on the one hand and by the concluding statement of the pericope in verse 11 ("This, the first of his signs, Jesus performed at Cana in Galilee. He thus revealed his glory, and his disciples put their faith in him"). We should also note that verse 12 serves as a transitional statement between the pericopes narrated in verses 1–11 and verses 13–22, respectively. The *initiatory marker*, as mentioned, is the phrase "On the third day." This phrase, in turn, follows on the heels of repeated previous references to "the next day" (John 1:29, 35, 43).

The *concluding sequence*, as mentioned, is found in verse 11, where John makes reference to this being "the first of [the] signs" Jesus performed in Cana of Galilee (see the corresponding reference to "the second sign" in Cana in John 4:54, a literary *inclusio*). The features of the *internal structure* of the discourse in John 2:1–11 include a large variety of elements. The *setting* is provided in verses 1 and 2. The *peak* gradually builds from verse 3 until it is finally reached in verse 10, with suspense created in verses 7–9.

In keeping with the presentation of the different types of syntactical elements presented above, John 2:1–11 includes a large number of references ensuring the reader's orientation. The various persons are identified: Jesus's mother (v. 1), Jesus and his disciples (v. 2), the servants (v. 5), the master of the banquet (v. 8), and the bridegroom (v. 9). A variety of social or status implications are found in the text as well, such as the probable shame associated with people running out of wine at a wedding (v. 3).

Time markers place the event "on the third day" (v. 1), presumably from the last reference to "the next day" in John 1:43. Hence the present event concludes the narration of the first week of Jesus's public ministry, an important discourse structuring device hinging on time (1:35–2:11). On the other end of the discourse, the boundary is marked by the expression "after this" and the reference to Jesus staying in Capernaum "for a few days" (2:12).

The location is described, first, as Cana in Galilee (v. 1). Later, the action unfolds "nearby" where six stone water jars were placed (v. 6). Still later, the master of the banquet is shown to call the bridegroom aside (v. 9), indicating the private nature of the interchange. The private nature of previous interchanges is also implied with regard to Jesus and his mother (vv. 3–4), Jesus's mother and the servants (v. 5), and Jesus and the servants (vv. 7–8), respectively.

The above discussion on studying a given textual unit on the larger discourse level has demonstrated that meaning resides not on the individual word level, or even on the sentence level, but on the level of larger discourse units. The syntactical relationships sustained between a given unit and the previous and subsequent units (initiatory markers and closure) and the various internal discourse features (such as peak) are vital to a full and accurate understanding of the authorial intention expressed in the biblical text. It remains to illustrate the validity of these insights on a fuller and more detailed scale.

DISCOURSE ANALYSIS: SPECIFIC EXAMPLES

The various books of Scripture all can be looked at in terms of their macrostructure and their microstructure. *Macrostructure* refers to the breakdown of literary units on a larger scale. *Microstructure* means the arrangement of a smaller section of Scripture. In the next chapter, we will elaborate on the importance of interpreting the parts in light of the whole in greater detail. In the present unit we will gain some practice and experience in discerning the patterns underlying a book's macrostructure and microstructure to do just that.

Discerning the Macrostructure: Level #1

The first step in interpreting and learning to communicate the contents of a given book of the Bible is to discern the "big picture," that is, the macrostructure of the book. Take John's Gospel, for example. On a basic level, it is clear that the macrostructure presents itself as follows:

12.1. MACROSTRUCTURE OF JOHN			
1:1–18	1:19–12:50	13:1–20:31	21:1–15
Introduction	Book of Signs	Book of Exaltation	Epilogue

How do we know this is the book's macrostructure? In large part, we do so from internal clues left by the author. This includes various structuring devices, such as transitions, openings, conclusions, and the like. It also includes literary devices such as chiasm (an ABB'A' pattern), *inclusios*, and so on. Identifying the structure of a given biblical passage is often significant for interpretation since the literary layout is one of the authorially intended vehicles for communicating meaning and a particular theological message. The *medium* (structure, words) and the *message* thus work hand in hand in the way language and literature work, and we must be concerned with *both* (not just the latter) if we want to arrive at an accurate and full-orbed understanding of the text.

In John's Gospel, for example, the transitional phrase "now this" makes clear that 1:19 marks the beginning of the actual Gospel narrative. The first half of the book then presents Jesus's performance of several startling "signs" as proofs of his messiahship to the Jewish people. The conclusion of part one is found in 12:37–50, which provides a closing indictment of Jewish unbelief and sets the stage for Jesus's preparation of his new messianic community in part two.

The opening of John 13 represents a carefully crafted literary introduction, not just to the ensuing footwashing scene, but to the remainder of the Gospel as a whole, focusing on Jesus's perfect love for his followers (see esp. v. 1). This marks the cross as the climactic demonstration of Jesus's love for humanity, in keeping with the programmatic statement in John 3:16 that God so loved the world that he sent his one and only Son. Part two concludes with a purpose statement in 20:30–31.

The epilogue in chapter 21 is set off by the transitional phrases "afterward" and "again." Its major purpose is to draw together some of the themes—most notably, the relationship between Peter and the "disciple Jesus loved"—from the body of the Gospel. The Gospel concludes with an authenticating statement by its author and the customary affirmation that there were many more things that could have been included in the particular book (21:24–25).

This, then, is the macrostructure of John's Gospel. It cannot be stressed enough at this point that what the perceptive interpreter is after in discerning a given book's macrostructure (remember the "hermeneutic of perception") is not his own clever (or not so clever) alliterative devices in outlining a book but rather the structure *intended by the biblical author* as it can be reconstructed from the various literary clues described above that were left by the author in the text.

Discerning the Macrostructure: Level #2

On the next level of depth and thoroughness, and still on the level of macrostructure, the two major parts of the Gospel can be broken down further still into smaller pericope or narrative units. Along these lines, John 1:19–2:11 marks the first week of Jesus's ministry, punctuated by several references to "the next day" (1:29, 35, 43; 2:1: "On the third day"). At the same time, chapters 2 through 4 constitute the "Cana cycle," set off by the *inclusio* in 2:11 and 4:54 ("first sign," "second sign" in Cana).

The "Festival Cycle," which features Jesus appearing at various Jewish festivals and presents him as the fulfillment of the underlying symbolism of these feasts, comprises chapters 5 through 10. At the end of chapter 10, we find a literary *inclusio* referring to John the Baptist (who, on a historical level, is long dead; 10:40–42), which sets this off from the following unit. Chapters 11 and 12 constitute a bridge section narrating the conclusion of Jesus's public ministry and his performance of the climactic sign, the raising of Lazarus.

Part two of John's Gospel is built around two major units; Jesus's farewell discourse (chaps. 13–17) and his death, burial, and resurrection (chaps. 18–20). Within these sections, we can discern the following structure. John 13:1–30, narrating the footwashing and Judas's betrayal, constitutes the preamble to the farewell discourse proper, which occupies 13:31–16:33 and is followed by Jesus's final prayer (chap. 17). The passion narrative in chapters 18–20 follows the familiar contours.

The second half of John's Gospel is connected to the epilogue through two of Jesus's resurrection appearances in chapter 20 (vv. 19–23 and vv. 24–29, respectively) and a third such appearance in chapter 21 (vv. 1–14; see esp. v. 14). The final special commissioning of Peter corresponds to his earlier denials and complements the commissioning of the Eleven in 20:21–23. The juxtaposed presentation of Peter and the "disciple Jesus loved" continues the pattern of parallel characterization of these two figures in John.

The extended macrostructure of John's Gospel, including second-level headings, presents itself therefore as follows:

12.2. EXTENDED MACROSTRUCTURE OF JOHN

John	Level #1	Level #2	
1:1–18	Introduction		
1:19–12:50	The Book of Signs		
	1:19–51	John the Baptist and Jesus	
	2–4	The Cana Cycle	
	5–10	The Festival Cycle	
	11–12	Bridge: Climactic Sign, Concluding Indictment	
13:1–20:31	The Book of Exaltation		
	13–17	The Farewell Discourse	
		13:1–30	Preamble
		13:31–16:33	Discourse Proper
		17	Final Prayer

	18–20	The Passion Narrative	
		18:1–19:37	Arrest, Trial, and Crucifixion of Jesus
		19:38–42	Burial of Jesus
		20 [including vv. 30–31]	Empty Tomb, Appearances, Commissioning
21:1–25	Epilogue		

Discerning the Microstructure: Level #3

Now that we have discerned the two levels of macrostructure in John's Gospel, we are ready to look at the two levels of microstructure of a particular narrative unit. John 9 may serve as an example. It will be helpful initially to break the passage down into subunits and then to break each of these units down into even smaller sections. A look at the transitions reveals that chapter 9 is only loosely connected to chapter 8, which ends with a reference to Jesus slipping away from the temple grounds. On the other end, one notes the lack of overt transition between chapters 9 and 10 (though note the phrase "I tell you the truth" in 10:1), which suggests that 9:1–10:21 is to be treated as a narrative unit. This is convincingly underscored by the *inclusio* referring to the opening of the eyes of the blind in 10:21.

The unit is thus best understood as reflecting the following microstructure:

12.3. EXTENDED MICROSTRUCTURE OF JOHN: LEVEL #3	
9:1–12	The Healing of the Man Born Blind
9:13–17	The First Interrogation of the Formerly Blind Man
9:18–23	The Interrogation of the Man's Parents
9:24–34	The Second Interrogation of the Formerly Blind Man
9:35–41	The Pharisees' Spiritual Blindness
10:1–21	The Good Shepherd and His Flock

Discerning the Microstructure: Level #4

One final level of microstructure remains. Our example, again, is from John's Gospel, specifically, the unit narrating the healing in 9:1–12.

Clearly, the narration unfolds from the actual setting (v. 1), to the disciples' question which raises a theological dilemma (v. 2), to Jesus's response highlighting his messianic ministry (vv. 3–5), to the healing (vv. 6–7), to the mixed response of the man's neighbors to the healing (vv. 8–12). An important contextual link is the reference to Jesus as "the light of the world" in 9:5 which harks back to 8:12. Also, the evangelist translates Siloam as "Sent" (9:7), presumably to designate Jesus as the Sent One.

12.4. EXTENDED MICROSTRUCTURE OF JOHN: LEVEL #4	
9:1	Setting ("As he went along")
9:2	The Disciples' Question ("Rabbi, who sinned . . .?")
9:3–5	Jesus's Response ("Neither this man nor his parents sinned, . . .")
9:6–7	The Healing ("Having said this")
9:8–12	The Neighbors' Response ("His neighbors and those who had formerly seen him begging . . .")

The expressions cited in the parentheses above make clear that John uses various means of indicating discourse boundaries, such as initial markers or orienters (v. 1, "As he went along"), questions (v. 2, "Rabbi, who sinned?") and answers (v. 3), or orienters halfway through the unit (v. 6, "Having said this"). The additional relations detailed in verses 6–7 ("he spit on the ground, made some mud with the saliva, and put it on the man's eyes") build toward the preliminary climax or peak at the end of verse 7: "So the man went and washed, and came home seeing."

Interestingly, up to this point the main point of objection—the fact that the healing had taken place on a Sabbath (cf. 5:1–15, esp. v. 9)—is suppressed by the evangelist until the next narrative unit (cf. v. 14), which introduces Jesus's major antagonists, the Pharisees (v. 13). Thus 9:1–12 is focused on the remarkable nature of the actual healing, while the following unit, 9:13–34, focuses on the Pharisees' bone of contention: Jesus's alleged breaking of the Sabbath in performing the miracle. John 9:13–34, fittingly, climaxes in the final verse of the unit, verse 34, with the reference to the formerly blind man's expulsion from the synagogue.

By way of verbal repetition, the mention of the casting out of the blind man in the last verse of the previous unit (v. 34) and the first verse of the following unit (v. 35), the evangelist both sets boundaries and provides cohesion for his narrative. This is further underscored by the fact that Jesus, who had been silent in the narrative since the healing in verse 11, now resurfaces as a character in verses 35–41 (see the comments on the reintroduction of a character below).

Finally, 10:1 picks up seamlessly where 9:41 leaves off, introduced by Jesus's authoritative pronouncement, "Truly, truly, I say to you. . . ." The unit 10:1–21 comes to a close with an *inclusio* referencing the healing of the blind man in 10:21. The content of 10:1–18, of course, is Jesus's "Good Shepherd" discourse, in which he contrasts himself with the Pharisees, the major forces pursuing the formerly blind man's expulsion from the synagogue in the previous chapter. By contrast, while the Pharisees are blind guides (9:39–41), Jesus is the "good shepherd" of the sheep.

After discerning the microstructure of 9:1–10:21 and delineating this as the proper narrative unit, it will be helpful to locate its place in the macrostructure of the book. Per the above discussion, the unit is part of the Festival cycle that makes up chapters 5–10 and narrates Jesus's messianic signs. In fact, the healing of the man born blind is the sixth such sign, and the last sign included in the Festival cycle. Only the raising of Lazarus is still to follow.

The healing of the man born blind thus serves as the foil for the Pharisees' spiritual blindness to be revealed, similar to the anointing revealing the antagonism of Judas later on (see the comments on the account of Jesus's anointing by Mary in 12:1–8 above). The Pharisees' wrongheaded spiritual leadership and their expulsion of the healed man from the synagogue are contrasted with Jesus, the "good shepherd," who does not cast out anyone who comes to him (cf. 6:37). The healed man, finally, is the paradigmatic disciple who progresses all the way from blindness and spiritual ignorance to worship (9:38).

Conclusion

As we have seen, breaking down a given unit in Scripture both in terms of macrostructure and microstructure is absolutely essential for interpretation and yields rich insights that could not have been gained apart from locating the part within the larger discourse context.

Anyone teaching on or preaching from John 9 will be able to follow the above-outlined procedure and develop confidence in his or her ability to understand the literary plan and theological message of a portion of Scripture and communicate it with the authority vested in God's Word itself.

The above example shows how a proper apprehension of the structure, logic, and flow of a given passage will lead to a fruitful exploration of the biblical message in context. It is important to remember that this flow is part of the author's intended meaning just as much as is the meaning of individual words. While we believe in the verbal inspiration of Scripture, this does not mean that meaning resides in a string of isolated words. Rather, syntax connects these words within the larger context of discourse.

GUIDELINES FOR OUTLINING A BIBLICAL BOOK OR INTERPRETIVE UNIT

1. Discern the macrostructure: break down a book into its largest constituent units.

2. Discern the second level of macrostructure, discerning the subunits of the broadest outline of the book.

3. Determine the microstructure of a chosen narrative unit.

4. Determine the microstructure of one or several portions of the narrative unit.

5. Interpret this narrative unit in the context of the book as a whole.

KEY WORDS

Anacoluthon, Aposiopesis, Asyndeton, Brachylogy, Chiasm, Clause, Closure, Cohesion, Discourse, Discourse analysis, Discourse boundary, Ellipsis, Grammar, Hendiadys, Implicature, Inclusio, Orienter, Peaking, Pericope, Phrase, Pleonasm, Prominence, Relations, Semantics, Sentence, Situation, Staging, Syntax, Tail-head link, Thought flow, Zeugma.

ASSIGNMENTS

1. Perform a basic discourse analysis of the book of Philippians. Identify the boundary features and give attention to factors such as cohesion, relations, prominence, and situation. Conclude your analysis with a detailed outline of Philippians.

2. Perform a discourse analysis of the Old Testament book of Esther. Again, identify the major boundary markers and pay close attention to other relevant features of the text. Identify the peak of the narrative and sketch both the macrostructure and microstructure of the book.

KEY RESOURCES

Cotterell, Peter and Max Turner. *Linguistics & Biblical Interpretation.* Downers Grove: InterVarsity, 1989.

Erickson, Richard J. *A Beginner's Guide to New Testament Exegesis.* Downers Grove: InterVarsity, 2005.

CHAPTER 13 OBJECTIVES

1. To introduce the student to the science of determining word meanings.

2. To impress upon the student the importance of context and larger discourse units in biblical interpretation.

3. To present the student with a representative list of exegetical fallacies in order to guard him or her against the dangers of improper interpretation.

4. To equip the student with a sound method of studying individual words of Scripture as part of the larger goal of developing a proper method of interpretation.

CHAPTER 13 OUTLINE

A. Study of Languages (Linguistics)

B. Determining Word Meanings (Semantics)

C. Interpreting the Parts in Light of the Whole

D. From Word Study to Semantic Field Study

E. Word Study Fallacies

F. Conclusion

G. Guidelines for Determining Word Meanings in Scripture

H. Key Words

I. Assignments

J. Key Resources

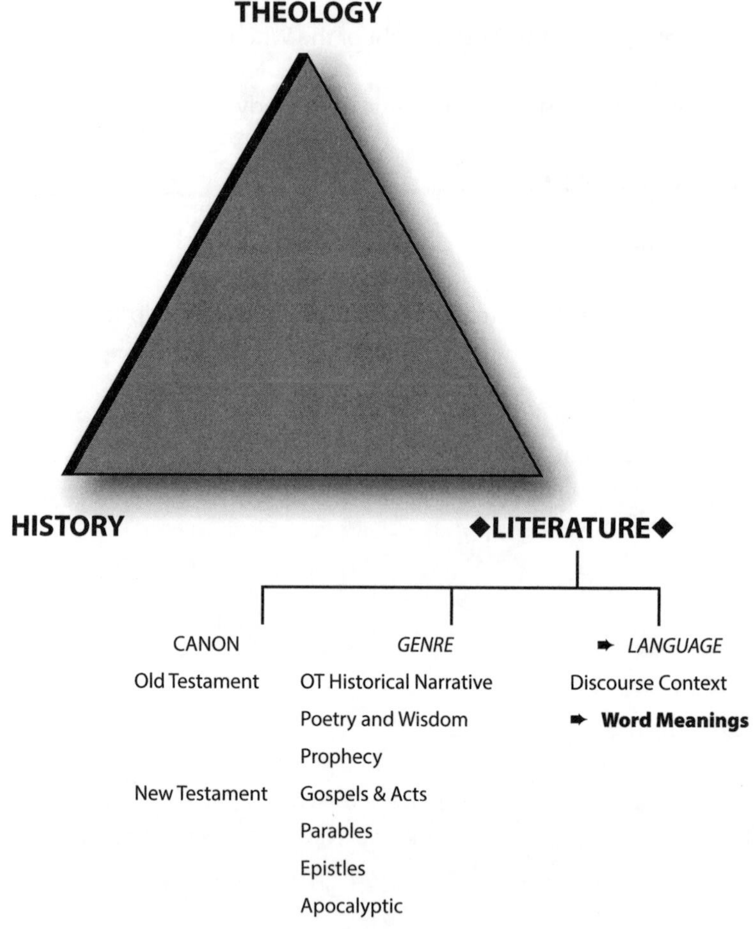
THEOLOGY
HISTORY
◆LITERATURE◆
CANON
Old Testament
New Testament
GENRE
OT Historical Narrative
Poetry and Wisdom
Prophecy
Gospels & Acts
Parables
Epistles
Apocalyptic
➡ LANGUAGE
Discourse Context
➡ Word Meanings

Chapter 13

A MATTER OF SEMANTICS: DISCERNING WORD MEANINGS

STUDY OF LANGUAGES (LINGUISTICS)

SOME INTERPRET SCRIPTURE AS IF word meaning were found on the level of individual words whose meaning can simply be looked up in a dictionary or be gleaned from a study of parallel passages in Scripture. While this may at times prove adequate, we have seen in the previous chapter that, understood more properly, word meaning is in fact determined by the use of a word in context, that is, on the larger discourse level. It remains now for us to apply this crucial insight to our specific word study methodology.

At the very outset, it is worth remembering that language, and the various literary forms and genres in which it finds expression in Scripture, is part of history and culture. That is, the linguistic forms in which Scripture has come down to us—in the original Greek, Hebrew, and Aramaic—are a reflection of the historical-cultural world in which God chose to reveal himself to his people in both Testaments.

In fact, the failure to appreciate that we are dealing here with *language*, which by its very nature is subjective and varied in style and often eludes being reduced to a simple formula or rigid dictionary definitions, hinders much of common biblical interpretation. What is language? In short, language is *convention*. It is the arbitrary assigning of a certain sequence of letters or symbols to a particular object or action. There is no reason why the object we know as "apple" should be designated by the successive letters "a," "p," "p," "l," and "e," other than that at one point in the past a language user or a group of language users determined to call this particular fruit by that particular name.

To be sure, once this usage had attained common acceptance, it became the standard, and new language users (such as children or non-native speakers) were taught that means "apple." The important lesson for us at this point is that there is nothing sacred, or absolute, about being an "apple." Language is a human convention, and as such is subject to change or modification. Words have a history and can take on new meanings over time or acquire additional connotations.

All that has been said thus far (and more will be said below) already makes clear that language is not a hard science like mathematics or quantum physics but rather a "soft," rather subjective and malleable affair. Perhaps this is why theologians and others who deal with religious absolutes and theological certainties have frequently had such a difficult time adjusting to the challenges presented with interpreting biblical texts. Unless we become students of language and literature *as well as* theology we will always be limited in our ability to "accurately handle the word of truth."

DETERMINING WORD MEANINGS (SEMANTICS)

As we have seen, *linguistics* is the field of research devoted to a study of the nature of language. A related field of study is the area of *semantics*, the science of determining word meanings. Over the past century, it has been increasingly understood that language is an intricately interwoven fabric. As John Lyons (1981: 75) observes,

> People often think of the meaning of words as if each of them had an independent and separate existence. But . . . no word can be fully understood independently of other words that are related to it and delimit its sense. Looked at from a semantic point of view, the lexical structure of a language—the structure of its vocabulary—is best regarded as a large and intricate network of sense-relations; it is like a huge, multidimensional, spider's web, in which each strand is one such relation and each knot in the web is a different lexeme.

Correspondingly, the Swiss linguist Ferdinand de Saussure distinguished between two linguistic phenomena: *langue* and *parole*, whereby the former constitutes the language system in its entirety and the latter specific words chosen by the language user for the sake of written or oral communication. In construing particular utterances or discourses, a speaker or writer draws on his general knowledge of a certain language system (e.g., English), made up of its stock of vocabulary and syntactical options. The Austrian philosopher Ludwig Wittgenstein posited the notion of "language games," showing that language users have a variety of options in accordance with the parameters of a given linguistic system at large.

The important implications of this kind of theory for the study of biblical words may not be immediately obvious, but they are significant nonetheless. Rather than study merely the specific word a biblical writer, such as Paul, was using in a particular instance, biblical interpreters will do well to study also other words Paul may have used in a given passage but chose not to use. This will be justified especially where Paul does use alternative or similar expressions elsewhere in his writings. This will result in a more realistic, more relevant, and richer picture of the message and meaning of a given text of Scripture. Since our underlying hermeneutical purpose is the determination of authorially intended meaning, and authors have a number of linguistic options to convey a particular proportion or meaning, the larger linguistic system must be taken into account.

INTERPRETING THE PARTS IN LIGHT OF THE WHOLE

What is the proper relationship between words and context in the study of biblical concepts? Many older treatments tend to detect meanings in biblical words that are actually supplied by the context in which those words are used. However, it is important to distinguish between information supplied by the context in which a word occurs and the component of meaning contributed by the word itself.

Among these two factors, context must have priority. The noted linguists J. P. Louw and Eugene Nida (1988: xvi) adduce the basic principle of semantic analysis "that differences in meaning are marked by context, either textual or extratextual. . . . Since any differences of meaning are marked by context, it follows that the correct meaning of any term is that which fits the context best."

Nevertheless, the fact that context must be given priority does not warrant the neglect of the other factor relevant for determining a term's meaning, namely, semantic field. The semantic field provides the word options available to the writer, the assumption being that a writer chose the word employed to communicate a meaning or nuance not provided by a different word. The following guidelines will be helpful here: (1) semantic field (i.e., terminology) and context are both important for the study of a biblical concept; (2) context has priority over semantic field; (3) if the second point is kept in mind, semantic field is an appropriate starting point to guide one to at least some of the most relevant contexts which need to be considered in one's study of a concept. Thus terminology (in the present case, biblical terminology) will serve as a guide to most of the relevant contexts where a given word or group of words is found. As mentioned above, therefore, rather than narrowly focusing on words in isolation, resulting in reductionism, part of the solution is an expansion of one's focus beyond *words* to *concepts.*

These insights with regard to semantic fields and biblical concepts, in turn, should be viewed within the larger framework of biblical discourses. In their important work *Linguistics and Biblical Interpretation*, Peter Cotterell and Max Turner draw the vital distinction between *lexical* and *discourse concepts.* The example provided by Cotterell and Turner is that of "Uncle George's old red bike," which later in a given discourse may be simply called "the bike." However, in the context of the discourse at large, "the bike" is not just any bike, but rather "Uncle George's old red bike." Or to use a biblical example, when reference is made in Revelation 13:1 to "the dragon" who stood on the shore of the sea, reference to the larger discourse unit of which the verse is a part leads the interpreter to the fuller reference to "the great dragon, . . . that ancient serpent called the devil, or Satan, who leads the whole world astray" (Rev. 12:9). The lesson is clear: biblical concepts must be understood and interpreted within the context of the larger discourse of which they are a part.

FROM WORD STUDY TO SEMANTIC FIELD STUDY

The old-fashioned notion of word studies has in recent years been increasingly replaced by the more refined approach of a semantic field study. By "semantic field" we mean a particular set of words that are linguistically related, be it by synonymy, antonymy, or some other association of meaning. Groundbreaking in this regard was the *Greek-English Dictionary Based on*

Semantic Domains compiled by Johannes P. Louw and Eugene A. Nida under the auspices of the United Bible Societies. Initially prepared as a resource for Bible translators, the innovative approach used by this dictionary has pointed the way forward to a more accurate and faithful appraisal of word meanings in both Testaments, particularly the New Testament.

In this dictionary, the vocabulary of the New Testament is grouped into a total of 93 semantic domains, which in turn are divided into two or more sub-domains each. For example, you might want to conduct a study of possessions in the New Testament. If so, you would want to include an analysis of several words related to wealth and poverty, be it nouns, verbs, adjectives, or adverbs, such as "rich," "poor," "wealth," "poverty," and so on, of course in the original Greek. Most of these terms are found together in Louw and Nida's domain 57, "Possess, Transfer, Exchange," which is divided into as many as 21 sub-domains.

Assume that your focus is on a study of wealth and poverty in the Gospel of Luke, a New Testament book where this theme is particularly prominent. Perhaps the ace for you to turn in order to locate specific instances of "wealth and poverty" vocabulary in the Gospel of Luke is *The Book Study Concordance*, which organizes the vocabulary of the New Testament book by book. This enables you to survey the vocabulary of any one New Testament book much more quickly than by the use of a conventional concordance. By way of scanning the English glosses even those interpreters who do not know New Testament Greek are able to delineate the contours of the Lucan theology of wealth and poverty.

The (partial) results present themselves as follows (references are to the Gospel of Luke):

13.1. SEMANTIC FIELD STUDY OF WEALTH AND POVERTY IN THE GOSPEL OF LUKE	
ptōchos, **"poor"**	
4:18	anointed me to proclaim good news to the poor
6:20	Blessed are you who are poor
7:22	the poor have good news preached to them, etc.
plousios, **"rich"**	
6:24	But woe to you who are rich
12:16	The land of a rich man produced plentifully
14:12	When you give a dinner or a banquet, do not invite your . . . rich neighbors, etc.

plouteō, **"be rich"**	
1:53	he has filled the hungry . . . , and the rich he has sent empty away
12:21	So is the one who lays up treasure for himself and is not rich toward God
ploutos, **"wealth, riches"**	
8:14	choked by the cares and riches and pleasures of life

A quick glance at passages show that wealth and poverty is indeed an important theme in Luke's Gospel. A semantic field study, rather than a series of isolated word studies, is better able to provide the interpreter with a full-orbed understanding of Luke's theology of wealth and poverty. It is not our purpose here to develop this theology further. The above listing of passages merely provides us with the relevant data from which this important Lucan theme can be profitably studied.

WORD STUDY FALLACIES

Now that we have laid out a responsible procedure for conducting semantic field studies, it will be helpful to take a look at several common fallacies that relate to determining word meanings. This is an important subject, because, as mentioned in the introduction to this volume, the biblical interpreter is ultimately accountable to God and charged with handling the word of truth accurately. This, in turn, involves discerning the meaning of individual words in context.

At this point it is worth remembering that our hermeneutic is founded on the two bedrock principles of (1) the integrity of Scripture (including its verbal inspiration); and (2) the importance of determining the meaning intended by the original author (rather than supplying a meaning of our own). Giving utmost care to the study of each individual word of Scripture flows directly from these two bedrock principles.

It has been said that a little knowledge is dangerous. This is nowhere truer than when it comes to the knowledge of biblical languages. Many a preacher has been known to parade his command of the Greek or Hebrew language before his congregation and to make confident assertions that would have made competent linguists or informed biblical scholars cringe. We therefore turn our attention now to the matter of word study fallacies.

Fallacy #1: The Etymological or Root Fallacy

We all have heard people say, "You know, the word X originally meant such-and-such," with the implication that knowing this original meaning of a given expression is significant for interpreting the meaning of the word in a later instance. But while this may at times be the case, it is not invariably so, and in many cases will be downright fallacious. To use an example from the English, the word "nice" comes from Latin *nescius*, which means "ignorant." How does knowing that the term underlying the word "nice" originally meant "ignorant" help the contemporary reader understand the use of the word in a particular written text (or oral communication)? The answer is that it does not help, and drawing on the root meaning of the word can be rather confusing and lead to wrong and unfounded conclusions, in some cases even bizarre or humorous ones. For example, "butterfly" does not mean "butter" + "fly," nor does "pineapple" mean "pine" plus "apple"!

This caution pertains also to conclusions drawn from the meaning of two or more component parts of a given expression. Among the common examples in this area is the Greek word *hypēretēs* which is properly translated "servants" in many English translations of 1 Corinthians 4:1. However, some have pointed to the fact that, taken by itself, the preposition *hypo* means "under," and the word *eretēs* means "rower"; hence, *hypēretēs* means "under-rower," as in "one who is part of a crew rowing a boat." The all-important question, however, is: Was Paul consciously drawing on rowing imagery when writing to the Corinthians? Or had the original metaphor been lost as a connotation that would have resonated in the writer's and readers' minds? If the latter (and in the present instance, there is good evidence that it had), it is fallacious to claim that Paul invoked an illustration from the realm of rowing in 1 Corinthians 4:1. It may be tempting for the preacher to suggest this, and hard to pass up an opportunity to impress the audience with one's knowledge of the original Greek, but such temptations must nonetheless be firmly resisted, for our quest for truth must override points made on flimsy linguistic foundations. Contextually, it appears that *hyperetēs* used in 1 Corinthians 4:1 is a virtual synonym of *diakonos*, "servant."

A further pitfall in this regard can be illustrated as follows. In several instances, Jesus is called *monogenēs* in John's Gospel (John 1:14, 18; 3:14, 18). Many have claimed that the best understanding of this word is that Jesus is the "only-begotten" Son of God. Even on the premise that the sum of a word's parts makes up the meaning of the word as a whole, however (which we have shown to be fallacious), the problem in the present instance is that *monogenēs* is derived not from *mono (monos,* "only") + *gennaō,* "beget" or "give birth"), which would add up to "only-begotten," but from *monos,* "only" + *genos,* "kind." Thus *monogenēs,* based on the meaning of its component parts, more properly means "the only one of a kind" (i.e., unique), not "only begotten." This is confirmed by the usage of the word in the Greek Septuagint (e.g., Judg. 11:34) and other New Testament passages (e.g., Luke 7:12; 8:42; 9:38), where the term is applied to only children who by virtue of being such were considered unique and particularly precious to their parents.

In short, then, we must avoid the etymological or root fallacy and study the contextual meaning of a given word in a biblical passage. Rather than focusing on *diachronic* study (the use of a given word "over time"), the emphasis should lie on *synchronic* study (the use of a word "at the same time" as the word under consideration). This way we will compare apples to apples rather than to oranges, will build our linguistic work on more proper foundations, and will more likely arrive at accurate conclusions with regard to the meaning of a particular biblical word in its proper context.

Fallacy #2: Misuse of Subsequent or Previous Meaning (Semantic Anachronism or Obsolescence)

As mentioned, language is a matter of convention, and words have a history. The relevance of these observations has already been shown with regard to the "root fallacy" above. It is also an issue related to the present set of fallacies. *Semantic anachronism* may be defined as the reading of a later use of a word back into earlier literature.

It may seem compelling to many preachers and people in the congregation that God loves a "hilarious" giver (2 Cor. 9:7), because the Greek word underlying "hilarious" is *hilaron,* but this conclusion is also certainly wrong, because "hilarious" is a later connotation taken on by the word in subsequent English usage. At the time of the writing of New Testament, the Greek word meant "cheerful" (NIV), not "hilarious," and the preacher should be content to leave it at that. No playing of laughing tapes during offertory, please!

Likewise, while it is true that the Greek word underlying "miracle" in the New Testament is *dynamis,* this does not mean that Jesus's miracles were "dynamite"! "Dynamite" is a later linguistic development that should not be read back into earlier usage. This would be committing the fallacy of semantic anachronism. Or, is Paul telling Romans 12:1 to render "logical worship" because the word modifying "worship" is Grk. *logikēn*? This improperly assumes that *logikēn* = "logical," which may or may not actually be the case. "Spiritual" or "reasonable" (orig. [changed in 2010 version]) is therefore a better translation. Another example of such a fallacy is the use of the word "bishop" to translate Greek *episkopos*. "Overseer" (e.g. 1 Tim. 3:2 NIV) is better; "bishop" carries unwelcome connotations of the later development of a three-tiered monarchical episcopate.

And are we really God's "poem" merely because the Greek word underlying "workmanship" in Ephesians 2:10 is *poiēma*, the word from which we get "poem" in the English language? Hardly. More properly understood, *poiēma* is related to the Greek verb *poieō*, which means "do" or "make," so that *poiēma* denotes the work of one's hands more generally, as in "workmanship" or "product," not necessarily the work of a poet, as in "poetry." Finally, when Jude urges his readers to "contend for the faith" (Jude 3), does the fact that the Greek word *epagōnizomai* is used to denote the word "contend" in this passage mean that we should "agonize over" our faith? This is hardly the case. We could give more examples, but the point is clear enough.

A related fallacy is that of *semantic obsolescence*, in which case the interpreter assigns to a word in a given biblical passage a meaning that the word in question had at an earlier point in the development of the language but that is no longer within the live, semantic range of the word. In other words, this meaning is semantically obsolete. A possible example is the meaning "to kiss" for the word *phileō*, which is quite common early on but seems to be largely obsolete in the New Testament. A New Testament instance where obsolescence can be detected with regard to a type of grammatical form is the almost complete loss of the superlative sense in most superlative forms. The important interpretive implication is that most superlatives should be understood to carry "elative" force, that is, convey simple comparison or even mere emphasis.

Or, conversely, interpreters may assign a particular meaning to a word that it took on at a later point in its semantic development but that it did not yet possess at the time period from which the text stems. An example of this latter fallacy is the imposition of the notion of martyrdom onto the New Testament instances of the *martys* word group (with the possible exception of certain instances of this word group in the book of Revelation). Another example is the translation, "On this rock I will build my *church*," of Matthew 16:18, even though "church" may anachronistically suggest the New Testament doctrine of the church as the body of Christ that was developed only subsequently by Paul. More properly, Jesus spoke of establishing his new messianic "community" (the more likely meaning of the term *ekklēsia* in the present example).

Fallacy #3: Appeal to Unknown or Unlikely Meanings or Background Material

The appeal to unknown or unlikely meanings or background material is one of the most common fallacies in biblical interpretation and preaching. One of the most serious negative consequences of this practice is that the actual explicit message of the text is set aside in favor of an alleged construal of background or word meaning, which substitutes the message intended by the given interpreter for that intended by the biblical author and ultimately God himself as the author of Scripture. In light of the above comments made about the importance of context, we must be careful in our use of lexical or background information so that we give preference to the connotation that is most likely in keeping with the surrounding and later context rather than resort to dubious extratextual pieces of information.

Perhaps one of the most egregious examples of the present fallacy in biblical scholarship of which I am aware is the argument by Catherine and Richard Kroeger in *I Suffer Not A Woman* (1992) that the term *authenteō*, commonly translated "to have authority," in 1 Timothy 2:12 should be translated as "to proclaim oneself the author of man." The Kroegers posited this previously unknown meaning on the basis of an alleged teaching in Ephesus at the time of writing, according to which women claimed that God created the woman first, and then the man, rather than the other way round. If so, Paul's prohibition against women occupying authoritative offices over men in the church would be recast as a prohibition for women to claim, wrongly, that God made, first Eve, and then Adam. The problem with this interpretation is that it lacks complete textual support, which is why few, if any, scholars have adopted this rendering.

Fallacy #4: Improper Construals of Greek or Hebrew Grammar or Syntax

In any given language, there are certain rules of proper word order, grammar, and syntax that, while capable of being broken, nonetheless are required for proper expression in that particular language. To cite an example in English, "Car kills man" means something quite different than "Man kills car," though the words are exactly the same. Word order makes all the difference. Or someone may say, "I is Andrew." We may still understand that the person's name is Andrew, but clearly the person is using improper grammar (in the present case, the third rather than the first person singular of the verb "to be").

The same principle applies in the biblical languages, Greek, Hebrew, and Aramaic. Properly understood, these fairly hard and fast rules of Greek or Hebrew grammar and syntax (as well as a certain semantic range, which means that certain words will be outside this range) can be the interpreter's best friend, for these rules set proper boundaries for correct or incorrect interpretation. The problem comes only where someone is either ignorant of what constitutes proper grammar in a biblical language underlying a particular text or where such a person willfully sets aside these rules in order to advance his or her own preferred interpretation even though it violates common usage with regard to semantic range, grammar, or syntax.

Let's look at a few examples of this fallacy. The first comes from Genesis 1:2. Many have attempted to show that Genesis 1:2 forms a parenthetical observation to Genesis 1:1 (e.g., the translation in the Anchor Bible of Gen. 1:1–3). Others have suggested that there is a gap between Genesis 1:1 and 1:2, so that a long period of time existed after the original creation, allowing for the fall of Satan and his hosts. Genesis 1:2 then becomes a subsequent recreation because of what the earth had become: "formless and empty."

The former view illegitimately assumes an unlikely grammatical structure, because the Hebrew verbal phrase here contains a perfect rather than the normal imperfect tense in a special construction denoting verbal sequence. The latter view would also demand an imperfect verb tense and call for a different construction with "formless and empty" if the meaning "became" were to be distinctly clear. Appeal to Isaiah's remarks that the Lord did not create the earth "to be empty, but formed it to be inhabited" (Isa. 45:18) likewise fails to substantiate the case for the gap theory, for Isaiah simply emphasizes the Lord's purpose in creating the earth rather than the process of his activity in doing so.

It is best simply to view verse 1 as a sovereign God's original creation and verse 2 as the opening conditions from which God proceeded in his further creative and fashioning work with regard to planet earth. The Hebrew construction in verse 2 is thus best viewed as conveying anticipatory emphasis. Having spoken of the universe, the text now moves on to consider the earth: "Now as for the earth."

A New Testament example comes from John 2:20, a verse in which translations commonly render the Greek original as indicating that the temple had been under construction "for 46 years." This seems to make good sense in that Jesus then would be saying that he can tear down and rebuild the temple in three days rather than the 46 years that it had already taken to do so in his day. The problem with this, however, is that the expression "46 years" in the Greek is in the dative rather than accusative case. Yet it is the accusative that would need to be used (an "accusative of time") if the above-cited interpretation were valid. On the former reading, the dative suggests, not duration *of* time ("for 46 years") but location *in* time: "at [a point] 46 years [ago]." Therefore what is most likely in view is the beginning of reconstruction of the temple 46 years ago in the past (location), not the extended period of reconstruction (duration) of the temple.

Fallacy #5: Improper Appeal to Alleged Parallels

Another very common fallacy is the improper appeal to alleged parallels, whether semantic or conceptual. Regarding the latter, Samuel Sandmel (1962) has written a well-known essay opposing what he calls "parallelomania," that is, the urge felt by some scholars to adduce parallels of questionable value. Often it appears that interpreters feel they can simply *assume* that a given passage constitutes an actual parallel without demonstration. Yet it must be stated unequivocally that simply quoting a similar-sounding passage and asserting that this is a "parallel" does not amount to and must never take the place of an argument supported by evidence.

During the heyday of the history-of-religions school, for example, it was common practice to explain virtually every feature of Christianity by appeal to other religions, particular the so-called "mystery religions." Scholars explained baptism in connection with secret initiation rites in those cults, and likened the Lord's Supper to sacred ritual meals. Similarly, they interpreted Old Testament legal observance and worship in light of other ancient Near Eastern religions. Somehow, it was always other religions that had a claim to originality, except for Christianity, which was always assumed to borrow its ideas from other religions!

Caution is always called for when we adduce a given parallel, because we must never assume that even the predominant usage of a given word or image prevails in each and every case. It is highly precarious simply to take the most frequently attested lexical meaning of an expression from a dictionary and to assume it obtains in a particular instance. There is no substitute for contextual interpretation, and what we said about the determinative role of context for word meanings above applies here as well.

For example, 1 Timothy 2:15 is commonly rendered, "But women will be saved through childbearing." Saved by childbearing? This sounds very un-Pauline, for according to the apostle, salvation is by grace through faith, not works (e.g., Rom. 3:21–28; Eph. 2:8–9). Some have sought to alleviate this difficulty by arguing that future salvation *on the last day* is in view here, but it is hard to see how merely transferring the point in time of salvation from the present to the future takes care of the problem.

A better solution involves a close look at the meaning of the Greek word underlying "saved." While the expression connotes religious salvation in most instances in Paul's writings, in its nonbiblical usage the word refers more broadly to rescue or deliverance from any kind of danger. In the New Testament epistles, this "danger" from which people are said to be delivered is normally sin and eternal death. However, the sense "rescue from danger" is still found in the New Testament in the several uses of the word *diasōzō* in the book of Acts in conjunction with Paul's shipwreck (Acts 27:43-44; 28:1, 4; cf. 23:24, which speaks of Paul being "taken safely" to Governor Felix). The Gospels use *sōzō* differently as well. There, the word refers to a person getting well or whole as a result of being healed by Jesus (e.g., Mark 5:23, 28, 34; 6:56; note that these people do not always experience religious salvation as well). In light of these semantic data and in light of the difficulty of translating *sōzō* with its common Pauline meaning, the question arises if there is an alternative way of rendering the term in 1 Timothy 2:15.

In fact, there is. Later in the same epistle, Paul urges Timothy to pay close attention to how he lives and to the content of his teaching, so that he may "preserve" or "ensure salvation" (NASB) for both himself and his hearers (1 Tim. 4:16). Clearly in this instance Timothy will not literally "save" himself or those who listen to him. Rather, Paul's concern is for the *spiritual preservation* of those under Timothy's care, the danger lurking in the form of the false teachers who sought to lead believers astray. Likewise, in 1 Timothy 2:15 Paul's probable intended meaning is not that women will literally be *saved* by childbearing (or even by "the" Childbearing of Mary) but that they will be *preserved* by adhering to their God-ordained role of motherhood (a figure of speech called synecdoche). The lesson, therefore, as mentioned, is this: one must never assume that the predominant meaning of a given word (in the present case, "save" for *sōzō*) will certainly prevail in a particular passage. The actual meaning of the word will be indicated by the respective context.

The same principle obtains when it comes to the use of common metaphors, such as sheep or infants. Many things may be said about either of these metaphors, but not all characteristics may be the point of a biblical writer's illustration. Since "sheep" is also a good illustration of another fallacy called "illegitimate totality transfer," we will discuss this example below, but a brief look at the way in which infants are used to illustrate spiritual truths in the New Testament will make the issue clear. In places such as Hebrews 5:12–13, the readers are chastised by the author who says that these believers are like babies who "need milk, not solid food! Anyone who lives on milk, being still an infant, is not acquainted with the teaching about righteousness." Conversely, "solid food is for the mature, who by constant use have trained themselves to distinguish good from evil" (Heb. 5:14). Clearly, babies are used as a negative example here. Believers ought to grow up. But consider 1 Peter 2:1–3. In context (1 Pet. 1:23), Peter wrote that believers have been born again to new life. As those who have been reborn spiritually, Peter proceeds to exhort the recipients of his letter, "Like newborn babies, crave pure spiritual milk, so that by it you may grow in your salvation, now that you have tasted that the Lord is good." Strikingly, here babies are used in a diametrically opposite fashion, as good examples of something the biblical author wants his readers to emulate. This means that we must not assume that a given type of illustration is used in the same way in every instance. Again, context must decide.

On a verbal level, the same principle applies. In English, "gift" means a present given to or a special ability possessed by a person. In German, "Gift" means poison. Context must decide—in this case, which language is in play? Depending on the language in which you are operating, you are advised to accept a gift in English but *not* in German! In our study of the Bible, too, we must beware of assuming too quickly that an *apparent* parallel is a *genuine* parallel. Again, merely quoting a similar-sounding passage and assuming without further substantiation that it will be self-evident to others that the alleged "parallel" explains the use of a given word in a certain passage is inadequate. Beware of "parallelomania" and recognize the all-important role of context in interpretation.

Fallacy #6: Improper Linkage of Language and Mentality

Conventional wisdom has it that Hebrew thought was concrete while Greek thought was abstract. This leads to corresponding assertions in the interpretation of specific biblical passages. Truth, for example, is said to be conveyed in the sense of a person's faithfulness in the Old Testament (in keeping with Hebrew thought) while the term is said to convey the notion of correspondence to reality in the New Testament (corresponding to the Greek way of thinking). This would be a nice theory if it were true; the problem is that the evidence does not bear this out, whether on a general or on a specific level.

On a specific level, to continue with our example of the concept of, and words for, "truth," both the Old and the New Testament feature both types of usage—"truth" in the sense of faithfulness and in the sense of correspondence to reality. In both Testaments, statements are said to be true (i.e., they correspond to reality), and in both Testaments truth is conveyed in personal terms, by people—or God—keeping his word and proving to be faithful (as suggested by the English word "fidelity" or the expression of one remaining "true" to his word).

On a general level, too, it has been shown convincingly that generalizations with regard to language use and word meanings on the basis of the mentality of peoples cannot be sustained. Are all French people gourmets? Are all Germans perfectionists? The list could go on and on. Yet we must not confuse grammatical and biological gender or hold that there is a necessary correspondence between the two. Do Germans believe girls are neuter because of the gender of "das Mädchen"? Did Greeks think sin was a uniquely or distinctively female trait because "sin," *hē hamartia*, is feminine in grammatical gender? If so, they must have thought "truth" was a feminine trait as well, since the Greek word for truth, *hē alētheia*, is likewise feminine in gender. Examples such as these illustrate that linking language to mentality is fraught with problems and is best avoided altogether.

Fallacy #7: False Assumptions about Technical Meaning

We have already made reference to Matthew 16:18, which is commonly translated as, "On this rock I will build my *church*." In light of the fact that the Greek word underlying "church," *ekklēsia*, only occurs one other time in all the Gospels combined (Matt. 18:17), we suggested that the translation "church" may be misleading since it suggests, erroneously, that this term had already become a technical term in Jesus's day when in fact it did so only in the days of the apostle Paul who developed the notion of the church as the body of Christ. For this reason we proposed that "community" may better convey the sense of Jesus's statement in Matthew 16:18.

Another possible instance where a technical meaning may be wrongly surmised is the New Testament doctrine of sanctification. The student of systematic theology would tend to assume that "sanctification" refers to the process of Christian growth following a person's conversion. It is often assumed that justification (a person being declared righteous on the basis of Christ's substitutionary cross-death) occurs at the time of conversion, while sanctification is a process that takes place subsequent to this event. However, as a study of the instances of "sanctification" terminology (especially the *hagiazō*, "set apart," word group) makes clear, according to the New Testament people are not only justified but also "set apart" ("sanctified") at the point of conversion (e.g., 1 Cor. 1:2; 6:11). For this reason the neat distinction between justification and sanctification in our systematics textbooks collapses. Both justification *and* sanctification take place at conversion, and the New Testament terminology for what we call "sanctification" is that of Christian growth (e.g., 2 Pet. 3:18).

Fallacy #8: Improper Distinctions Made Regarding Synonyms

One very common fallacious assumption in biblical interpretation is the notion that every difference in wording is theologically motivated. This assumption is fallacious because it fails to consider alternative possibilities such as that two or more different words which are roughly synonymous may be used owing to stylistic variation or other factors. This fallacy, in turn, is linked to another improper hermeneutical practice, that is, the unwarranted linking of sense and reference (see further below). The classic example is the use of two different verbs for "love" in John 21:15–17, *agapaō* and *phileō*. The state of affairs can be laid out as follows:

13.2. TWO DIFFERENT VERBS FOR "LOVE" IN JOHN 21:15–17	
v. 15	Jesus to Peter: "Simon son of John, do you love (*agapaō*) me more than these?"
v. 15	Peter to Jesus: "Yes, Lord, you know that I love (*phileō*) you."
v. 16	Jesus to Peter: "Simon son of John, do you love (*agapaō*) me?"
v. 16	Peter to Jesus: "Yes, Lord, you know that I love (*phileō*) you."
v. 17	Jesus to Peter: "Simon son of John do you love (*phileō*) me?"
v. 17	Peter to Jesus: "Lord, you know everything. You know that I love (*phileō*) you."

The standard explanation of the use of verbs for "love" in this passage is that the first two times Jesus uses *agapaō* to denote a divine form of love, while Peter only pledges a human form of love. The third time around, we are told, Jesus lowered himself to Peter's standard and used the "human" word for love, *phileō*, rather than the "divine" one, *agapaō*. This seems to be a very satisfying explanation of the data that only has one problem: it does not comport with the linguistic evidence from John's Gospel. In fact, both *agapaō* and *phileō* are used in John with reference to both divine and human love and function interchangeably in the Gospel! This means that the underlying semantic distinction between the two words for "love" in John 21:15–17 is illegitimate. Another explanation must be found. Most likely the two words are synonyms that are used alternatively for the sake of stylistic variation. This is strongly suggested by the presence of two other sets of synonyms for common words in the same passage: *ginōskō* and *oida* for "to know," and expressions such as "feed my lambs" or "tend my sheep."

Or take the use of the Greek word for "receive," *dechomai*, in 1 Thessalonians 1:6. In a recent sermon, the preacher made the point that the use of this particular word for "receiving" in the present passage, rather than the other Greek word for "receiving," *lambanō*, is significant, because it means that the Thessalonians did not merely "take" the word (as would be indicated by *lambanō*, they truly "received" it. However, once again, there is little support for making such a distinction between these two Greek words. More likely, they are virtual synonyms that are used with no discernible distinction in meaning. For this reason students and teachers of the Word should take care lest they find distinctions in their interpretation of biblical words even where the original authors did not intend to make such a distinction.

Fallacy #9: Selective or Prejudicial Use of Evidence

Virtually every one of us at one time or other has been guilty of selective or prejudicial use of evidence. By this we mean the practice of citing only the evidence that can be adduced in favor of a person's viewpoint while countervailing evidence is omitted or suppressed. Not only is this practice fallacious from a standpoint of thoroughness of research and presentation, it is also ethically suspect if not dishonest. Awhile back one researcher asked the other, "How is your research going?" To which the other person replied: "Great! I'm finding a lot of people who agree with my conclusions."

If this is your definition of research, it has to change, for whatever the above-stated procedure is, it is certainly *not* research. Research means the unearthing of *all* of the evidence, whether it agrees with one's own findings or not. Everything else is merely a matter of prooftexting or deduction, and while some may dress up their findings as research, unless they present the evidence in an even-handed, thoroughgoing manner, their arguments will likely fail to convince, because it will quickly become transparent that theirs is an exercise in dogmatism likely to convince only those already converted.

As mentioned, biblical interpretation, properly understood, requires a commitment to listening and perception of what is there. Proper procedure demands that the various alternatives be set forth and pros and cons be weighed before the interpreter settles on the interpretation that accounts best for all the data under consideration. This will flow from an honest search for truth that is willing to hold one's own predetermined notions in abeyance and to be seriously engaged by the data of the biblical text. In the end, this will also most likely convince others of a given view.

Fallacy #10: Unwarranted Semantic Disjunctions or Restrictions (Including Illegitimate Totality Transfer)

As in many other areas of life, so also in the realm of biblical interpretation, simplistic "either-or" alternatives are often suspect. An example of this "disjunctive fallacy" is the insistence by some that the Greek word *kephalē*, translated "head," in Ephesians 5:23 means "source" rather than conveying the notion of authority, when contextual study shows that *both* senses are present: the husband is to be a source of nourishment and encouragement to his wife, *and* he is put in charge of his wife as Christ is over the church as the head is over the body (Eph. 5:23–30).

Also in this category falls the unwarranted restriction of a semantic field, that is, the insistence that a word can only mean one thing when there is in fact a semantic range (i.e., a multiplicity of potential meanings). This problem may arise with a too narrowly conceived notion of formal equivalence, leading to the insistence that every instance of a given Greek or Hebrew word be translated with the same English word. However, this insufficiently accounts for the possibility—and often reality—that a word's semantic range in Greek or Hebrew on the one hand and in English on the other may differ. If so, it is not only legitimate but even imperative to render the same Greek or Hebrew word with a variety of English words. While this may make it harder to see from the English translation where the same word was used in the original, the practice of finding context-appropriate renderings will prove to be more accurate and faithful to the meaning intended by the original authors.

The opposite of the unwarranted restriction of the semantic field is the unwarranted adoption of an expanded semantic field, a fallacy that has also been called "illegitimate totality transfer." In this fallacy a word's entire semantic range is improperly considered to be part of the term's meaning in a specific context when, in fact, only one of the several possible meanings obtain in that particular instance. This is the fallacy at least suggested, if not committed, by the "Amplified Version."

A case in point is the biblical use of the shepherd metaphor. Many a preacher, when expounding on the meaning of a particular passage involving a reference to sheep, has imported all the characteristics of sheep, even though not all of these may be in play in that particular case. To be sure, Isaiah 53:6 says, "We all, like sheep, have gone astray," but is this the point of Jesus's statement, "My sheep listen to my voice; I know them, and they follow me" (John 10:27)? This is hardly so. In the former case, it is sheep's waywardness that is the point of the biblical illustration; in the latter instance, it is sheep's need for a shepherd and their following of his voice. Both are characteristics of sheep, but one is invoked in the former passage and the other in the latter. The fallacy of illegitimate totality transfer unduly lumps all the characteristics of sheep together and wrongly claims that all of these are relevant every time an illustration involving sheep is used.

Or take Jesus's reference to salt in his statement, "You are the salt of the earth" (Matt. 5:13). We've all heard sermons where the various characteristics of salt are mentioned at this point: salt is a preservative, salt provides seasoning, and so on. Did Jesus intend to invoke all of these attributes in the present passage? Maybe so, but this must be established on contextual grounds rather than be assumed merely on the basis that salt is mentioned.

Fallacy #11: Unwarranted Neglect of Distinctive Characteristics or Personal Style

As mentioned, language is convention, and as such inevitably involves a subjective element. This includes matters such as personal style, preference, and distinctive vocabulary, and even theology. Hence we must beware of the notion that "righteousness" must mean exactly the same in Matthew or Paul, or that the relationship between faith and works is construed in exactly the same way in Paul and James (compare and contrast the use of Gen. 15:6 in Gal. 3:6 and Jas. 2:23).

In terms of the interpretation of specific biblical passages, one example where this comes into play is John 1:17, where the evangelist writes that "the law was given through Moses; grace and truth came through Jesus Christ." In light of the fact that in Paul's writings a distinction is regularly made between observance of the law (which is unable to lead to salvation) and faith in Christ, some have construed John's message here in similar terms. In fact, some even inserted the adversative conjunction "but" between the two phrases (e.g., NLT: "For the law was given through Moses, *but* God's unfailing love and faithfulness came through Jesus Christ"), even though the word is absent from the Greek. However, as a contextual study of John 1:17 shows, both with regard to the immediate context and the context of the theology of the entire Gospel, the Pauline law-gospel distinction is not present in John. Instead, John 1:17 presents Jesus as the climactic fulfillment of earlier manifestations of God's grace, *including* the law. For this reason, John 1:17, rather than constituting a negative reference to the law (conveying its inability to provide salvation, cf. Rom. 3:21; Gal. 2:17–21; 3:23–25), presents the law in positive terms: it, too, was God's gracious provision, albeit one that was preliminary to his ultimate provision of grace and truth in Jesus Christ.

Or take instances of the Greek word *sarx*, "flesh," for example. In Paul, the term frequently serves as a synonym for "sinful nature," that is, it carries a negative connotation. In other passages, however, "flesh" is used neutrally to refer to humanity, without intended reference to human sinfulness (e.g., 1 Pet. 1:24–25 citing Isa. 40:6–8). In light of the personal style characteristics and distinctive vocabulary and usage of individual biblical writers, the interpreter must take care to allow for the context of Scripture to guide his or her study and to avoid a "one-size-fits-all" approach when it comes to word meanings or biblical concepts.

Fallacy #12: Unwarranted Linking of Sense and Reference

While the fallacy of an illegitimate linking of sense and reference is more subtle than some of the others and requires a bit of explanation, it is a fallacy nonetheless. For this reason it is worthwhile to understand the dynamics underlying this misuse. If *sense* is the actual meaning of a word in a specific context and *reference* is the object to which the word is referring, it is important to realize that part of a word's meaning in a given passage is supplied not by the word itself but by other words in its immediate context. The important implication of this realization is that it is improper to construe a word's lexical meaning on the basis of its contextual meaning as if the two were identical. They are not.

Take Paul's repeated reference to Timothy as his "coworker" (*synergos*; Rom. 16:21; 1 Thess. 3:2; also Titus: 2 Cor. 8:3; Epaphroditus: Phil. 2:25) as an example. Apart from being Paul's coworker, Timothy also was an apostolic delegate and what some might call a "senior pastor." Does the fact that Timothy, as Paul's "coworker," was also a senior pastor imply that the meaning for "coworker" includes "senior pastor"? This does not necessarily follow. Timothy was both, and so is a shared referent of both terms, but this still allows for the possibility that there may be others who were Paul's coworkers but not senior pastors. Ignoring this important fact would be to confuse sense (i.e., the contextual meaning) and referent (the object to which a given term is referring). For this reason it is fallacious to argue, as some have done, from the fact that Euodia and Syntyche in Philippians 4:2 are referred to as Paul's "coworkers" that this implies that they also served as pastors since this was true of Timothy. As we've seen, this follows neither logically nor is this conclusion linguistically sound. Whether or not these two women were pastors must be established on other grounds—such as Paul's teaching on women serving as pastors—not on the basis of the meaning of the word "coworker" alone.

As James Barr has shown in *The Semantics of Biblical Language* (1961), the failure to distinguish between sense and referent is endemic to the work of many theologians, including even respected reference works such as the ten-volume *Theological Dictionary of the New Testament.* As Barr has demonstrated, much of what is listed under the rubric of specific Greek *words* flows in fact from the study of biblical *concepts* conveyed through various contexts. The reason why this is fallacious is because by listing a given entry under a particular word the editors misleadingly suggest that aspects of the contextual meaning of a given word reside in the lexical meaning of the word itself rather than being contributed by the context.

CONCLUSION

In the present chapter, we considered an important dimension of the second, literature-related, aspect of the hermeneutical triad, language. Drawing on the findings of recent linguistic research, we attempted to establish sound procedures in determining word meanings, involving the more sophisticated use of a semantic field study approach.

To round out our discussion, we concluded the chapter with a discussion of several commonly committed word study fallacies, warning signs, as it were, that must be heeded by the skilled interpreter, lest he or she fall prey to a variety of questionable methods in the lexical study of words in Scripture.

GUIDELINES FOR DETERMINING WORD MEANINGS IN SCRIPTURE

1. Select the word or words to be studied. This should be a word that is significant for the interpretation of a given biblical passage.

2. Make sure you study a given Greek or Hebrew term or set of terms, not the English one. This is important since, depending on the particular translation, a given Greek or Hebrew word will be rendered by several different English words and vice versa. What we want to study is what a given word means in the original rather than in English. This is possible even for those who have not studied Greek or Hebrew through the use of New Testament tools such as Louw and Nida's *Greek-English Lexicon* and Köstenberger and Bouchoc's *The Book Study Concordance*.

3. If studying, for example, the different words for "love" in the Gospel of John, both nouns and verbs, and perhaps also adjectives and adverbs, identify the specific words by looking up the word "love" in the index volume (vol. 2) of Louw-Nida. Then locate the specific semantic domain (#25) in vol. 1 of Louw-Nida and determine which Greek words fall under this rubric.

4. Armed with this information, go to *The Book Study Concordance* and look up each of these Greek words under the respective heading. This will supply you with all (or at least most of) the relevant data for your study.

5. Conduct a contextual study of all the relevant passages. Lexicons and concordances can provide a quick overview of the semantic ranges for related words or can provide material for a more exhaustive study.

6. Categorize the passages according to types of usage (i.e., word meanings). This will yield the semantic range of the word or words.

7. In light of this semantic range, return to your base passage and see how it fits within the overall semantic profile of your word and what it contributes to the overall theology or concept or theme in question.

KEY WORDS

Connotation, Diachronic, Etymology, Illegitimate totality transfer, Lexis or lexical meaning, Linguistics, Parallelomania, Reference, Referent, Semantic anachronism, Semantic field, Semantic field study, Semantic obsolescence, Semantic range, Semantics, Sense, Synchronic.

ASSIGNMENTS

1. Engage in a close study of the "warning passage" in Hebrews 6:1–8. Identify at least three words requiring careful study. Use the findings of these individual word studies to shed light on the interpretation of this difficult passage.

2. After having read the section on exegetical fallacies, reflect on sermons you have heard or other biblical teaching you have received that fell prone to a given exegetical fallacy. List each of these and demonstrate their fallacious nature in light of the discussion in the course text.

KEY RESOURCES

Carson, D. A. *Exegetical Fallacies*. 2nd ed. Grand Rapids: Baker, 1996.

Cotterell, Peter and Max Turner. *Linguistics and Biblical Interpretation*. Downers Grove: InterVarsity, 1989.

PART 3
THEOLOGY

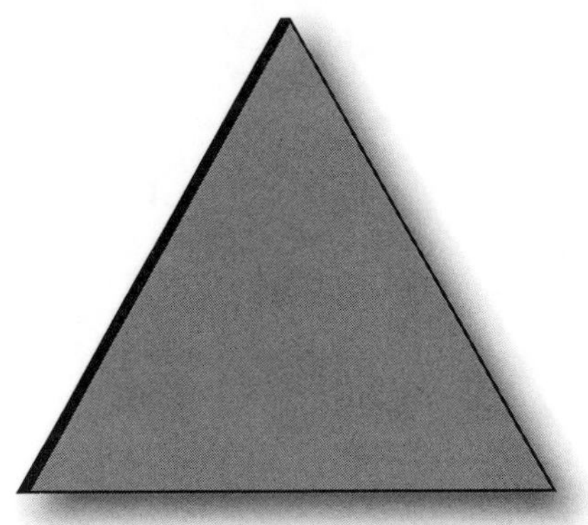

CHAPTER 14 OBJECTIVES

1. To acquaint the interpreter with the nature of biblical theology.
2. To acquaint the reader with some of the major issues in biblical theology.
3. To introduce the interpreter to important questions related to the method of biblical theology.
4. To familiarize the reader with important issues related to the use of the Old Testament in the New.

CHAPTER 14 OUTLINE

A. Nature of Biblical Theology

B. Issues in Biblical Theology

C. Method of Biblical Theology

D. Use of the Old Testament in the New

E. Guidelines for the Study of Biblical Theology

F. Guidelines for Studying the Use of the Old Testament in the New

G. Key Words

H. Assignments

I. Key Resources

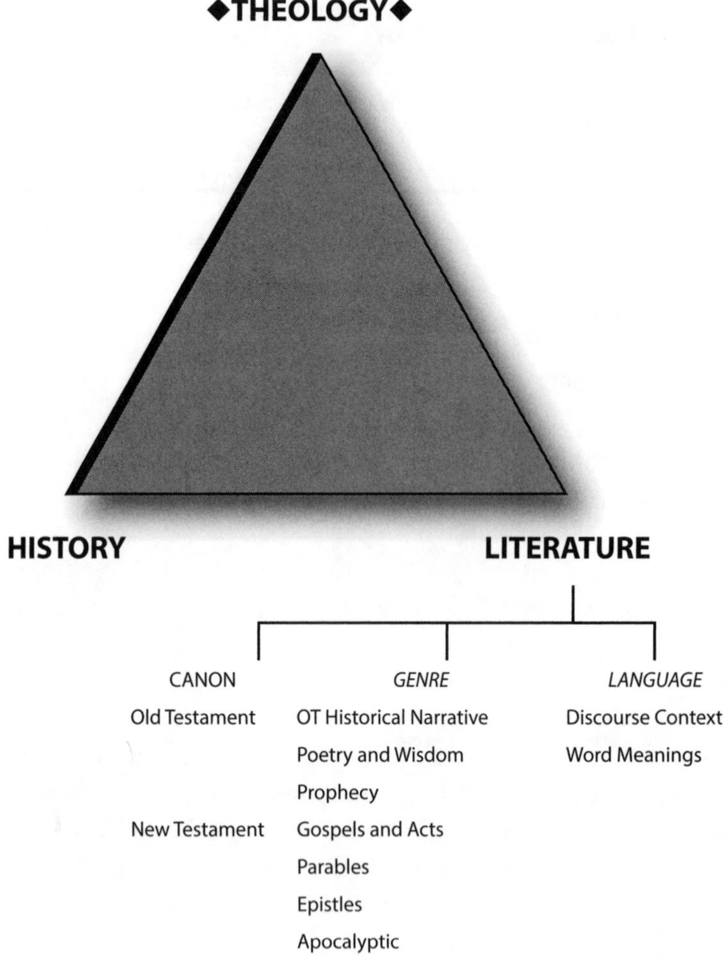
◆THEOLOGY◆
HISTORY
LITERATURE
CANON
Old Testament
New Testament
GENRE
OT Historical Narrative
Poetry and Wisdom
Prophecy
Gospels and Acts
Parables
Epistles
Apocalyptic
LANGUAGE
Discourse Context
Word Meanings

Chapter 14

MAKING THE CONNECTION: GETTING OUR THEOLOGY FROM THE BIBLE

NATURE OF BIBLICAL THEOLOGY

AT LONG LAST, WE HAVE arrived at the mountain top in our interpretive journey and reached the goal of our quest to interpret Scripture accurately. Having grounded our interpretation of Scripture in the first dimension of the hermeneutical triad, history, and having focused on interpreting the various literary facets of Scripture in descending order from the macro- to the micro-level—(from canon to genre to language), we have come to our final destination: the third and crowning aspect of the hermeneutical triad, theology. If we are not only grounded in the historical setting and well versed in the various literary dimensions of Scripture but develop a firm grasp of its theological message, we will indeed be workers who need not be ashamed but who correctly handle God's Word.

In our day, theology, or doctrine, is often given a negative connotation, as people look for an authentic expression of biblical Christianity. Doctrine is often viewed as a lifeless listing of a creed or confessional statement and contrasted with a vital spiritual firsthand experience of God. "Just give me Jesus," some say, but spare me doctrine and theology. Rather than viewing theology as nurturing and stabilizing elements in their journey of faith, many today view it as the enemy, or are skeptical at best if not indifferent or outright antagonistic. For reasons such as these, it is vital that we make sure that we derive our theology from the Bible rather than imposing our own preferred viewpoints onto Scripture. The quest for a sound, *biblical*, theology has in recent years come to be dealt with under the rubric "biblical theology."

What is "biblical theology"? The shortest possible answer is this: "Biblical theology is the theology of the Bible." That is, biblical theology is theology that is biblical—derived from the Bible rather than imposed onto the Bible by a given interpreter of Scripture. If so, then it follows that Old Testament theology and New Testament theology derives from the Old Testament and New Testament respectively.

For purposes of this chapter, we will focus our quest for theology on *biblical* theology. This will be important so as to ensure that our theological thinking is properly grounded in Scripture and its revelation of God, his Messiah, and things of the Spirit. While biblical theology should therefore come first, there is also a second step, commonly referred to as systematic theology.

When comparing biblical and systematic theology, the following differences may be noted. Biblical theology, as we will discuss shortly in more detail, is grounded in the historical setting and the narrative context and is inductive in nature. Systematic theology is more deductive in nature and seeks to organize various themes in Scripture in topical and abstract fashion. Ideally, systematic theology is systematized biblical theology.

Systematic theology, in turn, is informed by historical theology, the study of how interpreters and church leaders have conceived of the major doctrines of Christianity over the centuries. Other applied theological disciplines include ethics (which concerns itself with morality), philosophy (to the extent that it is concerned with religion), as well as homiletics (preaching), contextualization, missions, and evangelism.

That said, let us now delve more deeply into the topic of issues in biblical theology. One pertinent issue to be discussed under this rubric is the New Testament use of the Old Testament. As is our custom, we will close with relevant guidelines for the study of biblical theology and for the study of the use of the Old Testament in the New.

ISSUES IN BIBLICAL THEOLOGY

Defining biblical theology as the theology of the Bible, and our task as discerning that theology from the point of view of the biblical writers themselves, may seem clear enough. However, in practice there are several potential problems in this regard. First, it is commonly acknowledged today that no interpreter approaches Scripture without *presuppositions*. How, then, is it possible to turn away from ourselves and our preconceived notions of what a given passage of Scripture means?

First, it is important to keep in mind that not all presuppositions are necessarily problematic. For example, the presupposition that Scripture is trustworthy is in keeping with its own self-attestation and with its nature as the inspired Word of God (e.g., Psalms 19; 119; 2 Tim. 3:16–17; 2 Pet. 1:21–22). Likewise, Scripture itself assumes the existence of God when it says in its opening words that, "In the beginning, God created the heavens and the earth" (Gen. 1:1). The existence of angels (including Satan) is assumed as well; the Bible does not narrate the creation of angels.

Other presuppositions, however, may derive from tradition, personal experience, or prejudice, or other possibly questionable sources that must be checked so that they do not become hindrances to a proper apprehension of the biblical message. For example, I have often found that my students tend to assume that the interpretation of a given passage of Scripture by their favorite preacher is correct. This may well be, but it is still important to be open to all the evidence relevant for biblical interpretation, whether or not this supports the interpretation of our favorite Bible expositor.

In today's postmodern environment, the impression is often given that our subjectivity is so inescapable that the apprehension of absolute truth and interpretive objectivity are complete impossibilities—except, of course, in apprehending the postmodern contention that objectivity is impossible, which is held as absolutely true! In this regard, it will be helpful for us to distinguish between the intended meaning of a passage itself and the degree of confidence to which we can reasonably expect to attain in having arrived at this meaning.

In other words, the meaning itself may be clear; the problem is our lack of equipment in ascertaining it. If so, however, repeated reading, diligent study, and biblical education can be expected to close the gap. What is more, while 100-percent confidence will often be elusive, this does not mean that we cannot be reasonably confident that a given interpretation accurately approximates the originally intended meaning. To use an analogy from life in general, we are regularly called to make decisions on less than 100-percent certainty or complete information. But this does not mean that we cannot make good decisions, such as buying a reliable vehicle or entering responsibly into marriage.

Second, how does one determine the theology of the Bible? This raises the issue of *hermeneutical method* and procedure. As a survey of the history of doctrine and of biblical theology reveals, different interpreters have interpreted Scripture differently with regard to its major or central themes, resulting in at times conflicting theological systems. Issues such as the relationship between Israel and the church, the fulfillment of Old Testament prophecy, and the end times have been adjudicated differently.

This is not the place to deal with any of these issues in detail. In essence, this entire book is designed to set forth a responsible hermeneutical method that will enable the interpreter to derive the Bible's own theology through patient, repeated study. As we explore the three major aspects of the hermeneutical triad—history, literature, and theology; as we interpret a given passage in its larger canonical context; and as we familiarize ourselves with the characteristics of the various biblical genres, we will be equipped not merely to analyze individual biblical passages but also to develop a synthesis of the biblical teaching on the major topics it addresses.

Third, our apprehension of the theology of the Bible hinges on various other important foundations, such as the extent and composition of the biblical canon; the way in which the New Testament writers use the Old Testament; the relationship of the Testaments more broadly conceived; the issue of the unity and diversity of Scripture; and the question of whether or not the Old Testament, the New Testament (and certain New Testament writers such as Paul), and the Bible have a center and, if so, what it is. All of these are important issues which are dealt with in the relevant literature.

METHOD OF BIBLICAL THEOLOGY

How should we go about doing biblical theology? While we may be agreed in principle as to the purpose and goals of the discipline, the question remains as to the means and method of arriving at an accurate representation of the theology of the Bible on its own terms. As we seek to determine the best way to move forward methodologically, two important considerations must be stated at the very outset.

First, the method of biblical theology must be *historical*. That is, unlike systematic theology, which tends to be abstract and topical in nature, biblical theology aims to understand a given passage of Scripture in its original historical setting. For example, when interpreting the well-known passage, "'For I know the plans I have for you,' declares the LORD, 'plans to prosper you and not to harm you, plans to give you hope and a future'" (Jer. 29:11), we must ask who were the original recipients of this promise, and at what stage of Israel's history was this prophecy uttered.

Or consider another familiar passage on the issue of tithing:

> "Will a man rob God? Yet you rob me. But you ask, 'How do we rob you?' In tithes and offerings. You are under a curse—the whole nation of you—because you are robbing me. Bring the whole tithe into the storehouse, that there may be food in my house. Test me in this,' says the LORD Almighty, 'and see if I will not throw open the floodgates of heaven and pour out so much blessing that you will not have room enough for it'" (Mal. 3:8–10).

Biblical theology will seek to understand this passage in its original historical context before asking questions regarding its applicability for today.

Second, biblical theology will seek to study Scripture *on its own terms*, that is, pay special attention, not merely to the concepts addressed in Scripture, but to the very words, vocabulary, and terminology used by the biblical writers themselves. Rather than investigating "sanctification" as a broader topic, the biblical theologian will study the individual words that are used in the Bible to express what may be called the subject of Christian growth, words such as "set apart" or "grow." This is part of the express purpose of biblical theology: to initially seek to understand the theology of the Bible before systematizing its teaching on certain subjects and making application.

USE OF THE OLD TESTAMENT IN THE NEW

One important question in interpreting a given New Testament passage is, "Does the New Testament writer quote or allude to an Old Testament text?" In fact, the Old Testament is the major source of theology for the New Testament. Jesus frequently quoted the Old Testament, as did

Paul, Peter, the author of Hebrews, and others. In fact, we have already discussed Paul's use of the Old Testament in chapter 10 above. As a result, it is hard (if not impossible) to understand the New Testament apart from the Old. In what follows, we provide some important observations for interpreting passages involving the use of the Old Testament in the New.

(1) There are times when the New Testament's use of the Old is *structurally, thematically, and theologically significant*. In these cases, the New Testament writer establishes important structural connections between a given Old Testament theme and its New Testament counterpart or fulfillment. An example of this is Matthew 1–4, where the evangelist uses several "fulfillment quotations" to show that Jesus in the early stages of his ministry acted as the paradigmatic new Israel. In the temptation narrative, for example, Jesus repeats, yet supersedes, Israel's wilderness experience (Matt. 4:4, 6, 7, 10 citing Deut. 8:3; Ps. 91:11–12; and Deut. 6:16; 6:13, respectively). In these cases, we must not miss the Old Testament connection lest we miss the entire message of the New Testament passage in question. In other cases, a New Testament writer may use the Old Testament merely to establish a more limited exegetical point.

(2) While references to the Old Testament in the New are *frequent*, they are *not evenly spread*. For example, half of Paul's Old Testament citations are found in the book of Romans, and of these, half are found in chapters 9–11. This means that a given New Testament writer, such as Paul, did not quote the Old Testament in every case but only when he believed this was warranted in the context of his theological argument and his original readership. For example, in Galatians Paul dealt with Judaizers who claimed that Gentile converts to Christianity must be circumcised. Since his opponents were Jews, Paul used the Old Testament to show on scriptural grounds that the Judaizers' theology was mistaken, even on the basis of the Scriptures they cited in support of their view (see esp. Gal. 3:6–16 citing Gen. 15:6; Hab. 2:4; Deut. 21:23; etc.). In other cases, especially when dealing with a Gentile audience, Paul referred to the Old Testament less frequently, if at all (e.g., Colossians, Philippians).

(3) An important question to ask in the case of the New Testament's use of the Old is that of *warrant*: Why does a given New Testament writer

use the Old Testament at all rather than making a certain pronouncement on his own (apostolic) authority or stating a rationale that does not involve using Old Testament Scripture? In many cases, the reason is that his audience already accepted the authority of the Hebrew Scriptures. If he could show that his teaching was in accord with Old Testament teaching, his audience would be convinced and satisfied (cf., e.g., Paul's repeated references to Gen. 15:6 in support of his gospel of salvation by faith apart from works; see, e.g., Gal. 3:6; Rom. 4:3).

(4) Beginning students of Scripture sometimes assume that there is only one way in which the New Testament writers use the Old Testament. (Most commonly, the assumption is that this one way is prediction-fulfillment, that is, a New Testament writer citing an Old Testament passage to show that a given passage has been fulfilled in Christ.) Nothing could be further from the truth. While it is true that the *prediction-fulfillment* pattern accounts for a significant number of New Testament references to the Old (such as Matt. 2:6 citing Mic. 5:2), it is by no means the only type of usage.

Another important use involves *typology*, that is, the argument that an original pattern in Scripture—a "type," be it a historical person, event, or institution—has found a corresponding "anti-type" in the messianic or church age. An example of this is Jesus's reference to the serpent lifted up in the wilderness in John 3:14. Just as Moses lifted up the serpent in the wilderness and those survived who looked at the raised-up serpent in faith, so Jesus would be lifted up on the cross and everyone who looked at him in faith would live.

The discerning reader will detect in this pattern an analogy (Moses-Jesus; looking/believing/life–looking-believing-eternal life). Indeed, analogy is present, but in the case of typology there is also the additional historical grounding which relates an earlier incident in the history of God's dealings with his people to an end-time corresponding event which is likewise historical. This typological usage proved exceedingly convincing in a Jewish context where people believed that God acted consistently throughout the course of history. If it could therefore be shown that God had acted in a certain way in ages past, there was a high likelihood that he had acted similarly in more recent history or would act again in a similar way in the future.

An example of the latter case is from the book of Jude, where the author shows that God consistently punished rebellion and immorality in Old Testament times and that it was therefore certain that he would similarly punish the false teachers in his day, even though he had not yet done so, on the basis of typological correspondence (a Jewish technique called *midrash*, or commentary).

Yet other ways in which New Testament writers use the Old include *allegory* (e.g., Gal. 4:21–31), *analogy*, or *illustration* (Eph. 5:32). What all these uses of the Old Testament in the New have in common is that they add persuasiveness to the argument of a given New Testament author by seeking to demonstrate on the basis of the commonly accepted authority of the Hebrew Scriptures the truthfulness of their teaching regarding Christ or the church.

(5) *Direct citations* of the Old Testament in the New are only one form of the New Testament's use of the Old. Other forms of usage involve the employment of *allusions* or *echoes*. In the case of allusions, the question of criteria arises. In the absence of an extended literal quote, how can we be sure that a given New Testament writer intended to cite an Old Testament text? In response, the following constraints should be noted.

(a) *Authorial intent.* In order for a given use to qualify as an allusion, it must be authorially intended. Otherwise, we are no longer operating on the basis of an authorial intent hermeneutic but are moving into the realm of reader response. A New Testament passage may evoke the reminiscence of a certain Old Testament passage in the mind of the contemporary reader, but if it cannot be plausibly demonstrated that the New Testament writer intended to evoke this association, we should refrain from speaking of an "Old Testament allusion" in the particular New Testament passage in question.

(b) *Verbal similarity.* In order for a passage to qualify as allusion, there must be sufficient verbal similarity between the New Testament passage and the possible Old Testament source reference. In some cases, this may be only one or two words, perhaps even in different grammatical forms, possibly even involving the use of synonyms. But nevertheless, unless specific New Testament words can be matched with particular Old Testament words, any alleged allusions must normally remain in the realm of speculation, and caution should be exercised in those cases. Depending on the strength of these verbal similarities, it may be appropriate to distinguish in this category between *allusions* on the one hand (stronger similarity) and *echoes* (weaker, fainter similarity).

(6) A helpful indicator signaling the presence of an Old Testament quotation is the use of one of several *introductory formulas.* Examples of this are the following: "it is written"; "this took place in order that the words spoken by Isaiah the prophet might be fulfilled"; or a variety of other formulas. If such an introductory formula can be identified, the presence of an Old Testament citation is virtually certain, though in a few isolated cases it may be difficult to pinpoint the exact Old Testament passage quoted.

(7) In some cases, the study of the use of the Old Testament in the New involves *more technical biblical studies skills* where a particular question hinges on which version of the Old Testament a given New Testament writer used—the Greek Septuagint (LXX) or the Hebrew Masoretic text (MT)—and in some cases which particular textual variant, or even an unattested text form. In these cases, it is best to consult more technical commentaries or reference works in order to make sure one adequately understands the issues involved. An example of this is the use of Habakkuk 2:4 in Romans 1:17 where the Septuagint and the Masoretic text differ in their rendering, which is important for the way in which Paul quotes this passage in Romans.

(8) In other cases, the difficulty may not be so much on the level of source text and biblical languages but on the level of *theology.* It may be unclear how a given New Testament writer derives a particular point from the Old Testament passage he cites. How does Matthew find support for Jesus's parent's flight to Egypt in the statement in Hosea 11 that God would call his son out of Egypt? (The answer probably involves the use of typology; see above.) Or how can James at the Jerusalem Council in Acts 15:16–18 cite Amos 9:11–12 in support of the conversion of the *Gentiles* when the original text speaks of restoring the house of *David*? (Part of the answer is the reference to "all the nations" in Amos 9:12.) And who among us would have detected a possible reference to God giving gifts to the church in Psalm 68:18 as Paul argues in Ephesians 4:9? We could multiply examples. In those cases posing an exegetical difficulty, it will be wise not to jump to conclusions or to give up but to educate oneself by

consulting a technical commentary or good reference work and weighing the different options before coming to a more settled conclusion.

(9) A helpful distinction in the study of the use of the Old Testament in the New is that between a *hermeneutical axiom* and an *appropriation technique*. The former constitutes an underlying assumption which leads a given New Testament writer to use a particular Old Testament passage in a certain way. Most notably, such an axiom may be the conviction that Jesus is the Messiah predicted in the Old Testament. Paul, for example, became convinced of this when he met the risen Christ on the road to Damascus (Acts 9) and as a result reread the Old Testament in light of this newly-found hermeneutical axiom.

This made all the difference in the way Paul read the Hebrew Scriptures. Rather than believe that Jesus was crucified because he was cursed—in keeping with the statement in Deuteronomy 21:23 that "cursed is everyone who hangs on a tree"—Paul concluded that, on the premise that Jesus was the Messiah, Jesus's death was not for himself but for others—sinners in need of redemption—so that Jesus was not cursed but rather became a "curse *for us*"—for our salvation (Gal. 3:13). What a difference a new hermeneutical axiom makes!

Appropriation techniques, on the other hand, are specific ways in which the Old Testament is appropriated by a New Testament writer as part of his theological argument: prediction-fulfillment, typology, analogy, illustration, and so on. We have already discussed this matter under point (4) above.

(10) One final question relates to whether or not we should expect to be able to duplicate the use of the Old Testament by the New Testament writers. This is a difficult question to answer. On the one hand, we would expect the New Testament use of the Old to conform to historical-grammatical principles of exegesis that are reproducible by contemporary interpreters. At the same time, the New Testament writers operated under divine inspiration. Not that this inspiration necessarily overrode normal human thought processes, but it provides the New Testament interpretation of specific Old Testament passages with a type of authority that cannot legitimately be claimed by anyone today. For this reason, we will do well to exercise caution and to claim authority only for interpretations of the Old Testament that are made explicit in the New Testament.

GUIDELINES FOR THE STUDY OF BIBLICAL THEOLOGY

1. Determine the focus of your study: Is it the study of a particular theme in one or several biblical books? The study of a theme in one Testament or the entire Bible? Is it a study of two or several related themes?

2. Determine the relevant passages that need to be studied by means of lexical study, concordance work, study Bibles, and other reference works.

3. Engage in careful contextual study of each of the relevant passages in light of their historical context and the salvation-historical stage in the life of God's people Israel or the church.

4. Determine the original message to the intended recipients at the respective stage of salvation history.

5. Trace the Bible's teaching on your chosen theme throughout the respective books of the Bible or Testament or Scripture as a whole, carefully observing the terminology used by the respective biblical authors.

6. If desired, systematize the biblical teaching in the form of a systematized biblical theology and make proper application.

GUIDELINES FOR STUDYING THE USE OF THE OLD TESTAMENT IN THE NEW

1. Discern the hermeneutical axiom underlying a given use of the Old Testament in the New.

2. Determine the appropriation technique, whether prediction-fulfillment, typology, allegory, analogy, illustration, or other.

3. Ask the question of warrant: Why did the New Testament writer use the Old Testament in his argument?

4. Seek to determine the place the Old Testament quote or allusion has in the argument of the New Testament writer in the New Testament context.

5. Study the Old Testament context of the source quote and determine what role (if any) the original context has in its New Testament appropriation.

6. Engage in comparative study of the Hebrew text, the Septuagint version, and the New Testament citation. Note any important differences and attempt to explain their significance, in consultation with relevant commentaries and reference works.

7. Try to resolve any theological difficulties posed by a given New Testament use of the Old, in consultation with relevant commentaries and reference works.

KEY WORDS

Allusion, Anti-type, Appropriation technique, Biblical theology, Direct quotation, Echo, Hermeneutical axiom, Introductory formula, *Midrash*, Prediction-fulfillment, Systematic theology, Type, Typology.

ASSIGNMENTS

1. Study the theme of stewardship in Scripture. Decide on key terms to study, locate major passages, and sketch a biblical theology of stewardship.

2. Imagine that you were asked to write a biblical theology by a major evangelical publisher. Weighing the different possibilities for presenting such a biblical theology, provide an annotated table of contents in order to sketch the flow of your presentation.

KEY RESOURCES

Alexander, T. Desmond and Brian S. Rosner, eds. *New Dictionary of Biblical Theology.* Downers Grove: InterVarsity, 2000.

Beale, G. K. and D. A. Carson, eds. *Commentary on the New Testament Use of the Old Testament*. Grand Rapids: Baker, 2007.

CHAPTER 15 OBJECTIVES

1. To equip readers with the most helpful resources for serious Bible study and sermon/lesson preparation.

2. To discuss ways in which biblical interpreters can apply Scripture to their own lives and help others to do the same.

CHAPTER 15 OUTLINE

A. Introduction

B. Resources for Study
   1. English Bibles
   2. Bible Study Resources
      a. Concordances
      b. Theological/Exegetical Dictionaries
      c. Bible Encyclopedias/Dictionaries
      d. Bible Atlases
      e. Old and New Testament Introductions
      f. Charts
      g. Commentaries
      h. Systematic and Biblical Theologies
      i. Communicator's Tools
   3. Electronic Resources

C. Application
   1. Foundation
   2. Complexities

D. Guidelines for Application

E. Conclusion

F. Key Words

G. Assignments

H. Key Resources

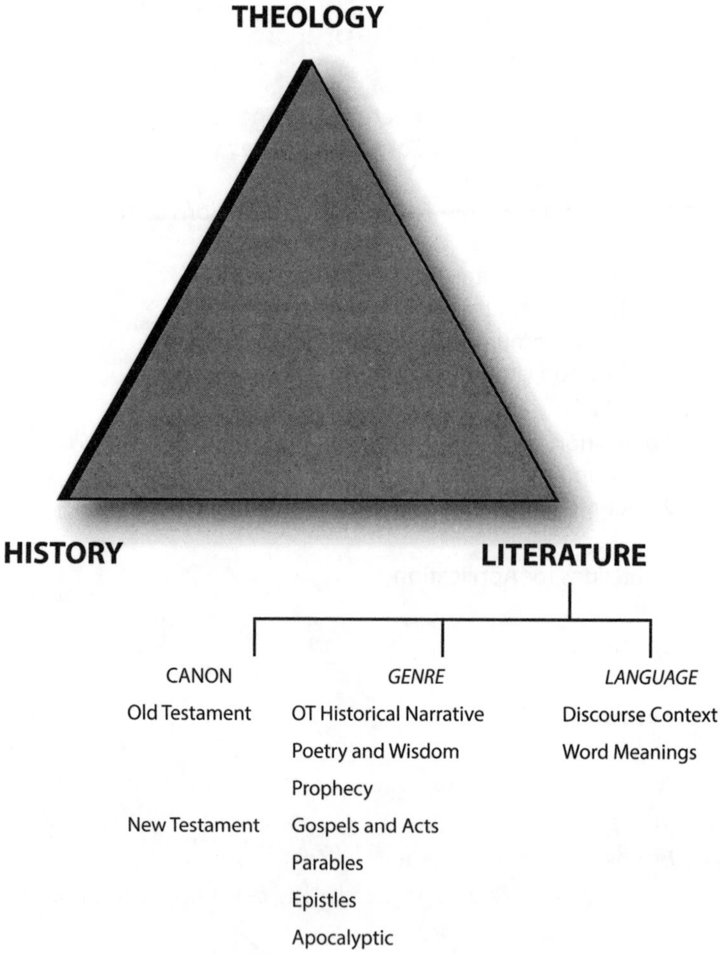

THEOLOGY

HISTORY

LITERATURE

CANON	*GENRE*	*LANGUAGE*
Old Testament	OT Historical Narrative	Discourse Context
	Poetry and Wisdom	Word Meanings
	Prophecy	
New Testament	Gospels and Acts	
	Parables	
	Epistles	
	Apocalyptic	

Chapter 15

GETTING DOWN TO EARTH: USING THE TOOLS, APPLYING THE WORD

INTRODUCTION

At the end of a book such as this, the critical question that must be asked is this. Now that we've learned about the hermeneutical triad of history, literature, and theology, and have discussed at some length principles for interpreting different genres of Scripture, not to mention principles for word study and discerning the structure of a given passage, what will you take away from reading and processing this book? Will you check off reading this book on some list and continue to interpret the Bible exactly the way you did before? Or will you apply what you've learned and let these principles transform your study of Scripture so that Scripture, in turn, will change your life and the lives of those with whom you will share what you've learned? This final chapter aims to help you put what you've learned from reading this book into practice.

RESOURCES FOR STUDY

While our primary focus must always remain the Bible itself, we would make our task more difficult than it needs to be if we were to neglect the many helpful resources that are available for studying Scripture. In fact, every serious student of the Bible should have a few reference works at his or her disposal to help him or her interpret Scripture. Just like a worker needs various tools to do his job well, so we will benefit from the use of helpful tools for studying the Bible. In what follows we will discuss several essential types of reference works and suggest standards in the field.

English Bibles

At last count, there were ninety English Bibles produced in the twentieth century and nine in the twenty-first. That's close to a hundred versions! What is more, with many translations available on the internet, you have a wide variety at your fingertips. All you need is an internet connection.

Regarding English translations, there are a wide variety of approaches. A good interpreter of Scripture will have several English translations on hand, from more literal ones to more idiomatic ones. Of course, the ideal is knowing the biblical languages so you can check the translations.

Bible Study Resources

Concordances

A concordance is invaluable in determining where a Greek or Hebrew word is used in the respective Testament because few English translations will be consistent in translating a given word (nor should they always be!). If you have a working knowledge of the biblical languages, there are several Greek and Hebrew concordances at your disposal. Otherwise, you can use one of the English concordances depending on your specific translation.

Theological/Exegetical Dictionaries

A theological dictionary is a collection of in-depth word studies that are designed to show the theological content of a given concept. Although such a compilation can be quite valuable, each entry should be critically evaluated. Regarding the New Testament, the revised *New International Dictionary of New Testament Theology* (*NIDNTT*) is well respected. Regarding the Old Testament, the work by Harris, Archer, and Waltke, *Theological Wordbook of the Old Testament*, is a time-honored resource. The new standard is the five-volume *Dictionary of Old Testament Theology and Exegesis* edited by Willem VanGemeren.

Bible Encyclopedias/Dictionaries

A solid essay-length treatment of various matters pertaining to the Old and New Testaments is very helpful. The standard in the field is the 6-volume *Anchor Bible Dictionary*. We would also recommend the *Zondervan Encyclopedia of the Bible*. Other helpful resources are *The Holman Illustrated Bible Dictionary* and *The New Bible Dictionary*.

Bible Atlases

Knowing biblical geography is often quite helpful in exegesis. Particularly helpful is the *ESV Bible Atlas*, which is exceptionally well-produced and comes highly recommended. Other helpful Bible atlases are the revised *Zondervan Atlas of the Bible*, the *Holman Bible Atlas*, and the *Kregel Bible Atlas*.

Old and New Testament Introductions

Solid, conservative introductions to the Testaments are invaluable tools for the exegete. With regard to the New Testament, we recommend *The Cradle, the Cross, and the Crown* by Köstenberger, Kellum and Quarles or *An Introduction to the New Testament* by Carson and Moo. In the Old Testament, Longman and Dillard's *Introduction to the Old Testament* is a standard, as are *A Survey of the Old Testament* by Andrew Hill and John Walton and *The World and the Word* by Eugene Merill, Mark Rooker, and Michael Grisanti.

Charts

Both Kregel and Zondervan have a series of books of charts that summarize chronological, archaeological, thematic, and other very good information in an easy-to-access format. Often these are both thought-provoking and informative.

Commentaries

To paraphrase the ancient teacher, "Of the making of commentaries, there is no end." Today, we have both academic and lay commentaries, preaching commentaries, application commentaries, background commentaries, and ever further subsets. With regard to buying commentaries, we suggest caution. First, avoid devotional commentaries in preparing an exegetically-based message (their place is in application, not interpretation). Academic exegetical commentaries (i.e., commentaries that deal with the original languages verse-by-verse) are the best for exegesis. They will cover the issues and debates that impact exegesis.

However, here the buyer must beware. The value of a commentary is often in the eye of the beholder. Few are written from a solidly evangelical perspective, and some series are mixed in this regard (e.g., the Word Biblical Commentary). What is more, a commentary series will also inevitably be uneven with regard to how well the individual volumes handle the text. It will benefit you to do some research on these matters before buying a commentary.

Overall, the rule is: don't buy an entire series, but pick the best commentaries on any given book of the Bible based on the credentials of the author of the commentary and on the available reviews of a particular volume. That said, series that are generally helpful are the Baker Exegetical Commentary on the New Testament (BECNT), the Zondervan Exegetical Commentary on the New Testament (ZECNT), and various other series depending on the particular volume and contributor.

Systematic and Biblical Theologies

A systematic theology with a Scripture index is often a very helpful resource to discern what matters of theology are germane to your text. This is not a foolproof method, but one that will get you thinking about the theological implications of your passage. Sometimes you will discover aspects of your passage that you would not have considered otherwise. A standard in the field is Wayne Grudem's *Systematic Theology* that comes in both an unabridged and abridged versions. Also highly competent is Millard Erickson's *Christian Theology.*

Biblical theology is a growing field with many useful recent publications. The most helpful series are the New Studies in Biblical Theology (NSBT), the Biblical Theology of the New Testament (BTNT), and the Biblical Theology for Christian Proclamation (BTCP) series. The NSBT series features biblical-theological studies on a great variety of topics; the BTNT series is covers in eight volumes the theologies of the entire New Testament, including Matthean, Markan, Lukan, Johannine, and Pauline theology as well as the theology of James, Peter, Jude, Hebrews, and Revelation. The BTCP series is a comprehensive series that is projected to cover both Testaments in a total of forty volumes.

Communicator's Tools

The ultimate job of the exegete is to communicate what he or she has learned to his or her hearers. To do this, there are a few items that ought to be in your library. The first group is a series of works on English grammar. You should have a good English dictionary to help you use words correctly. You should also have a good thesaurus to choose the correct word.

Beyond these basic grammar tools, the good wordsmith will also have a series of books, databases, or services that will prove helpful in finding quotes and illustrations. People will often remember your illustrations longer than your other content. That said, verify the content of a given illustration as best you can.

Electronic Resources

There are a great many electronic resources available to you either on the internet (both free and for pay) or through applications for your computer. Although information from the internet can be obtained quickly, be careful about internet sources.

First, avoid blogs. Only a blog from a recognized scholar or a person whose materials have been proven valuable over time should be seriously considered—and then verified.

Second, avoid websites by individuals who do not provide detailed documentation for their information. Sites such as Wikipedia (www.wikipedia.com) may be a good place to begin searching for information but are insufficient to use by themselves. You must verify every piece of information found on these sites by other reliable means.

Sites from trusted sources are the most valuable information. Some are trusted because of their institutional connection. Others are relied upon for having been useful over a long period of time or having come from a trusted scholar.

Another exceedingly valuable source of information is google books. At this website, you may search the contents of a very large (and growing) number of books. Books in public domain are available for free download. Many standard works in the field of biblical studies are available in this way. The problem with works in public domain is that they are rather old. As such, they don't reference the latest linguistic and archaeological discoveries or deal with current debates. They may also operate on the basis of outdated paradigms. This calls for discernment on the part of the user.

Newer books are often accessible as a "limited preview." Here a portion of the book is available to view online. Others are given in a "snippet view." Great is the rejoicing of the Bible student who finds his or her passage in a limited preview!

Amazon.com has pioneered the downloading of books through their Kindle platform. There will likely be more and more e-readers that enter the market. When we need a book, we now have the option of purchasing it at a discount and for immediate use.

When spending money on your Bible study library, consider purchasing a Bible software program. While the investment may seem high, you will be able to replace several resources such as concordances, atlases, lexicons, and other reference works. Low-end, low-cost software will often be insufficient. In general, pay as much as you can afford on your choice of Bible software.

Logos and BibleWorks are the major players in the premier Bible software category. Both can do all the grammatical and lexical searches the serious exegete will ever need. Each has a concordance function that goes beyond anything a printed concordance can do, and in a fraction of the time. You can also diagram sentences; compare translations; use lexicons; use and/or create cross references and notes; connect to external links; examine major biblical manuscripts; and browse exegetical resources.

Whatever version you choose, first, avoid thinking that the programs are perfect. All are dependent on human data entry at some point and involve subjective judgment. Second, the language tools are useless to you unless you know at least the basics of grammar and language (or look them up). Third, you must be familiar with the terminology employed by the program. Fourth, your search is only as good as the parameters you set. Be careful when setting your search parameters!

APPLICATION

With this, we've arrived at the final stop on our journey: application. This textbook has been occupied with the (often multi-faceted) task of interpreting Scripture. Yet, if we become experts at interpreting Scripture *alone*, we fall short of our ultimate calling: to glorify Christ with our lives. We do so only when we live out what we know. What is more, if we interpret a passage with 100% percent accuracy and even wow our audience with our eloquence and skill in communicating a given portion of Scripture but fail to tell our audience how to apply the truths we have taught, we have fallen short.

The famous preacher, Charles Spurgeon, made the following statement in his *Lectures to my Students* (1875: 27–28): "We have all heard the story of the man who preached so well and lived so badly, that when he was in the pulpit everybody said he ought never to come out again, and when he was out of it they all declared he never ought to enter it again. From the imitation of such a Janus may the Lord deliver us." Fundamentally, this is not so much a failure of *interpretation* as it is a failure of *application*.

Application, then, is the believer's obedience to the correct interpretation of God's Word. The two together enable the believer to glorify Christ. While obedience requires a certain amount of knowledge, knowledge without application is futile. In the preceding pages, we've repeatedly addressed the question of how to apply various portions of Scripture, such as the Law or the Epistles, in light of the complex hermeneutical issues involved. As we conclude, we'll give some general instruction regarding the application of the Bible to our lives.

Foundation

The foundation for mature obedience to Scripture begins with the *conviction that it is the word of God*. For most of you, this conviction is one of the reasons why you're reading this book. That Scripture is the word of God strongly implies that we should obey it. Notice that Paul connects inspiration and obedience in 2 Timothy 3:16–17: "All Scripture is given by inspiration of God, and is profitable for doctrine, for reproof, for correction, for instruction in righteousness, that the man of God may be complete, thoroughly equipped for every good work."

The second motivation is that *Scripture presents truths to be obeyed* by those who desire to follow God. Jesus summed up his teaching in Matthew 7:24: "Therefore everyone who hears these words of mine and puts them into practice is like a wise man who built his house on the rock." He habitually closed his parables with the words, "He who has ears to hear, let him hear" (e.g., Mark 4:9). Similarly, James wrote, "Do not merely listen to the word, and so deceive yourselves. Do what it says" (Jas. 1:22).

The third conviction is that *Scripture is as relevant to us as it was to its first readers*. The Bible everywhere assumes this. In fact, the very existence and preservation of the Bible attest to the conviction that people of all times and places need the word of God. Paul made this point repeatedly with regard to the Old Testament. In Romans 15:4, he wrote, "For everything that was written in the past was written to teach us, so that through endurance and the encouragement of the Scriptures we might have hope." In 1 Corinthians 10:6, he maintained, "Now these things occurred as examples to keep us from setting our hearts on evil things as they did."

We might say more, but we will close our foundational discussion with one last principle: *obedience is the way to please God and glorify him in this life*. The last book of the Bible opens and closes with this point: "Blessed is the one who reads the words of this prophecy, and blessed are those who hear it and take to heart what is written in it, because the time is near" (Rev. 1:3); "Behold, I am coming soon! Blessed is he who keeps the words of the prophecy in this book" (Rev. 22:7).

Complexities

That said, there are some complexities to navigate when applying the Scriptures. First, not every command found in the Bible is directly relevant for us today. For example, certain Old Testament laws such as the dietary laws no apply to us today because they are directly abrogated by Jesus: "in saying this, Jesus declared all foods clean" (Mark 7:19). Or consider the matter of eating meat that had previously been sacrificed to idols. To be sure, this was a pressing issue for first-century Christians living in a pagan environment. But how is this matter still relevant for believers in the Western world in the twenty-first century?

To complicate matters yet further, the Bible doesn't directly address many of the ethical issues facing modern civilization. Euthanasia, genetic manipulation, and cloning are just a few of the issues we face that the ancients did not. How are we to address these issues? Is it pointless to look to the Bible when grappling with these questions?

Human beings have lived and continue to live in a variety of circumstances and cultures. Even in our lifetime, we've experienced varying levels of technological sophistication. Because life is not stagnant, no piece of writing can reasonably be expected to address every conceivable situation. Not only would such a work be highly unwieldy, it would also be unbearably boring, resembling a detailed, unending list of do's and don'ts rather than a set of principles to live by.

The book God gave us embodies, in a variety of genres, the story of creation, fall, redemption, and consummation. Along the way, the inspired writers of Scripture enunciate numerous principles for applying the word of God to our lives. God is our Creator; we fell in disobedience; Christ paid the price for our sins; repentance and faith in him secure our salvation. In cases where the situation described in Scripture matches our own, the biblical instructions are directly applicable to us. In cases where a given scenario in Scripture differs from the one we are facing today, we should look for the underlying *principle* beneath a given command.

That said, many (if not most) of the situations and commands contained in Scripture are very germane by virtue of our common humanity (and sinfulness!). Take the repeated biblical injunctions to forgive as an example. Because we are still sinners, we still sin, and still need to extend, and ask for, forgiveness. Many, many commands in Scripture operate in this way.

Nevertheless, it's true there are some passages in Scripture that are less directly applicable. A case in point, as mentioned, are Old Testament dietary laws. Should we ignore these kinds of Old Testament passages completely because the teachings they contain have been superseded? Or is there some remaining health value in the dietary restrictions and strive to abide by these? Neither option seems entirely satisfying. A solution emerges once we consider the purpose of these laws, that is, the principle that is given as the grounds for these commands: "But you are a people holy to the LORD your God" (Deut. 14:21; cf. Deut. 14:1–2). Thus, the food laws were a sign of Israel's separation from the pagan world around them and her consecration for God. The Jewish people were not to be like the other surrounding nations. With the arrival of the new covenant, the inclusion of the Gentiles renders this particular badge of separation outmoded. God makes both Jew and Gentile one new entity in Christ. But *the principle* is not abrogated. The people of God are *not* to be like everyone else, but are to remain separate from the world and holy for God. Like Israel of old, they are to be his treasured possession. The obvious application, then, is that it is not the surrounding culture that should dictate our behavior; it is the will of God.

At times, the procedure we have suggested here is called "principlization," though we prefer the term "contextualization." We suggest you use the following steps to guard against drawing questionable applications from the text.

GUIDELINES FOR APPLICATION

Steps of Application

Step 1: Apply the correct historical-grammatical exegesis of the text to find the intended purpose of the author. Application is always built on interpretation. If the interpretation is wrong, the application will be wrong as well. Use the tools you have been given in this book to determine the original meaning of the text. Enter its world, drink deeply from the well of Scripture. What is the main idea of the text? How does the author communicate it to us? What was his purpose and intent? It is imperative that you understand your passage for its own sake before you move on to application.

Step 2: Evaluate the level of specificity of the original application(s). The major question here is whether the passage is dealing with an issue that is so conditioned by cultural or covenantal issues that it is impossible to apply the text directly. Generally, it is not terribly difficult to discern these culture-bound matters. But be careful. Make sure that you don't make culture rule over you rather than allowing God to rule over culture. Try using the following criteria to help you determine whether or not a command in Scripture is specific to one particular culture.

a. *Criterion of purpose.* The issue here is that the purpose of the rule generates the rule. So, then, it supersedes the rule itself. The good news is that the biblical authors (including the Holy Spirit) had a purpose in mind when they wrote the text. Discover that purpose. It will guide you to the application for today's hearers. So, for example, Peter's injunction to "Greet one another with a kiss of love" (1 Pet. 5:14) is generated by the desire for people in the body of Christ to show warm affection for one another, not just press lips.

b. *Criterion of cultural correspondence.* In determining whether or not a given biblical injunction is culturally conditioned (most are to one degree or another), we must ask, what is the correspondence to our culture? Are these cultural practices present in our culture? If the answer is yes, then we can apply the principle more directly. If no, then we look to the underlying principle. For example, we can put Peter's directive, "Submit yourselves for the Lord's sake to every authority instituted among men"

(1 Pet. 2:13–14) into practice fairly directly, while the application of Paul's injunction in 1 Corinthians 8 not to eat meat sacrificed to idols is more indirect, along the lines of not violating the conscience of other, less spiritually mature believers, who, rightly or wrongly so, may be offended by what they see us do.

c. *Criterion of canonical consistency.* Is a given type of conduct viewed consistently throughout Scripture? If so, the same stance obtains today as well. For example, Scripture proscribes homosexuality in both Testaments (Gen. 19:1–11; Lev. 18:22; 20:13; Rom. 1:18–32; 1 Cor. 6:9–11; 1 Tim. 1:8–10; Jude 7); thus it should still be viewed as contrary to God's design today.

d. *Criterion of creation order.* An injunction should be viewed as transcultural if the biblical author invokes the original creation. See, e.g., 1 Timothy 2:12–14: "I do not permit a woman to teach or to have authority over a man; she must be silent. *For Adam was formed first, then Eve.*" The appeal to Adam and Eve suggests that the prohibition is not limited to the situation in Ephesus. If the grounds of appeal is universal, then so is the command.

Step 3. Identify cross-cultural principles. This step is unnecessary if a passage treats a situation that is part of our experience. Prohibitions against sin, invitations to enjoy the salvation afforded in Christ, treatments of loneliness, betrayal, fortitude in the face of trials, suffering for the cause of Christ, are all universally possible experiences for the believer. The main idea of the text applies directly in such situations.

However, if a particular command, example, promise, or warning cannot be applied universally without alteration, what do we do? First, we identify the principle underlying the command, example, promise, or warning. Here, we must be careful not to identify a principle that is too broad or only part of the main idea of the text. Scott Duvall and Danny Hays (2005: 24) give sound advice when identifying such a principle:

a. *The principle should be reflected in the text.* That is, the text is pointing to this principle. It is often stated in the text itself. See, for example, the grounds given for the dietary laws in Deuteronomy 14 mentioned above. The principle underlies the text; it is not just tangential to the passage.

b. *The principle should be timeless and not tied to a specific situation.* This is moving into the area of application before you are ready. Avoid being specific regarding the distinction between modern and ancient. It should apply readily to both.

c. *The principle should not be culturally bound.* It is extremely easy to remove an item from a foreign culture. It is far more difficult to remove ourselves from ours. We believe the key here is to work at envisioning the principle from the ancient context.

d. *The principle should correspond to the teaching of the rest of Scripture.* Use the whole canon to test your principle. If your principle is in violation of clear teaching elsewhere, your principle is flawed.

e. *The principle should be relevant to both the biblical and the contemporary audience.* If an ancient reader were to be able to read your principle, it should make absolute sense to him or her just as it does to you.

Discerning principles in culturally loaded contexts is not something to take lightly, nor do we elevate them above the text itself. If we have exegeted well, having accurately determined the meaning of the text, then the underlying principle should be easy to recognize.

Step 4: Find appropriate applications that embody broader principles. The communicator has clearly explained the meaning and purpose of the biblical text and now has discerned the underlying principle (often given directly in the text). It is time to suggest applications first for ourselves and then for our hearers. It is not as if there are generally two applications but the first one to apply the application and to respond to the invitation is the preacher or teacher.

Now a caution: we do not discern principles, cut them free from their text, and arbitrarily apply them to all kinds of situations. We apply them to legitimately similar situations today. The principle that generated the command or action in the text should be applied appropriately in similar situations today. As Klein, Hubbard, and Blomberg (2004: 501) observe, "[T]hus, we may give a hearty handshake instead of a holy kiss; we may set up inexpensive food banks instead of leaving our fields to be gleaned; and we should be concerned about the effect of consuming alcohol in the presence of a recovering alcoholic, even if we are never faced with the dilemma of whether or not to eat meat sacrificed to idols."

In application, we no longer deal with theory, but with practice. We no longer describe the abstract, but the concrete. You should give practical suggestions of how the text applies to your audience today and suggest specific points of application. You should be persuading your listeners to conform their lives to the truths of the passage of Scripture you have just presented.

CONCLUSION

Having applied the truth of God's Word to our lives and communicated it to others, our interpretive journey has come to an end, at least as far as this book is concerned. The challenge of interpreting and applying Scripture, of course, is the task of a lifetime. In the preceding pages, we have sought to lay the foundation for the interpretation of Scripture within a proper biblical framework. On the basis of the recognition that the Bible was given to us by revelation from God under the inspiration of the Holy Spirit, we have used the hermeneutical triad of history, literature, and theology as the basic grid for biblical interpretation. We noted that before we turn to the task of interpretation, it is vital that we engage in proper preparation, which includes an awareness of our presuppositions and personal background, a prayerful disposition and a high view of Scripture, and a suitable method.

At the beginning of our interpretive journey, we focused on the first dimension of the hermeneutical triad: history. Chapter 2 explored the study of the historical setting and cultural background of a given passage of Scripture. The next section took up the bulk of our travels through the biblical landscape, dealing with the second dimension of the hermeneutical triad, literature. We began this section with a big-picture survey of both Testaments (chapters 3–4). After this, we focused on the study of the different genres of Scripture: in the Old Testament, narrative, poetry and wisdom, and prophecy (chapters 5–7); in the New Testament, narrative (Gospels/Acts), parables, epistles, and apocalyptic (chapters 8–11). In chapters 12 and 13, we focused on the language of

Scripture, specifically breaking down the discourse and determining word meanings. In chapter 14, we reached the goal of our interpretive journey: theology, the third dimension of the hermeneutical triad. With this, we were ready to "get down to earth": using the tools and applying God's Word to our lives.

Our prayers are with you as you hone your interpretive competencies for the glory of God, seeking to grow in (1) historical-cultural awareness; (2) canonical consciousness; (3) sensitivity to genre; (4) literary and linguistic competence; (5) a firm and growing grasp of biblical theology; and (6) an ability to apply and proclaim passages from every biblical genre to your own life and to the life of your congregation. In the spirit of 2 Peter 1:3–11, we would also encourage you to cultivate the following interpretive virtues:

- Be submissive: Take on a submissive stance toward Scripture. Do not domesticate Scripture, or use biblical interpretation to serve your own ends. Approach Scripture with reverence as the Word of God.

- Be humble: Don't be dogmatic or arrogant. Focus on issues, not people.

- Be spiritual: Read 1 Cor 2:10b–16. Ask God to illumine your study of Scripture.

- Be sensible: Be mindful of the importance of balance. In your interpretation of Scripture, do not go out on a limb. Distinguish between possible, plausible, and probable interpretations. Beware of exegetical fallacies.

- Be seasoned: Be knowledgeable, develop experience. Be aware of the relevant issues and any potential pitfalls.

- Be committed to proper interpretive procedure: Make the hermeneutical triad your own and use it regularly. Look at every passage you study from the vantage point of history, literature, and theology.

- Be intentional and deliberate. Don't be haphazard in your interpretation of Scripture. Good hermeneutics does not happen by chance. It takes careful thought, planning, and effort, and requires the use of a sound interpretive method.

- Be consistent: Make sure your interpretive outcome and application are coordinated, not arbitrary.

- Be perceptive: Be quick to listen and slow to speak. Listen to God's Word carefully and aim to perceive what is there. Cultivate the ability of seeing and perceiving.

- Be conservative: Exercise interpretive restraint. Do not unduly exaggerate, illegitimately extrapolate, or otherwise exceed the evidence.

- Be courageous: If necessary, be prepared to swim against the stream of tradition. Scripture must have priority and be in a place of ultimate authority.

- Be exegetical: Don't cover up bad exegesis by generalizations, grand theories, or other improper interpretive moves.

We close this volume the way we started—with a call to all of us to heed Paul's exhortation to Timothy: "Do your best to present yourself to God as one approved, a workman who does not need to be ashamed and who correctly handles the word of truth" (2 Tim. 2:15). In a day when man-made solutions to the world's problems abound, those who are called by God to shepherd his flock must be faithful to his charge: "Preach the Word; be prepared in season and out of season; correct, rebuke and encourage—with great patience and careful instruction. For the time will come when men will not put up with sound doctrine" (2 Tim. 4:2–3).

These are indeed times when the truth of God's Word is regularly rejected, ridiculed, and set aside as irrelevant. But God's Word is not bound—it is "living and active," and "sharper than any double-edged sword, it . . . judges the thoughts and attitudes of the heart. Nothing in God's creation is hidden from his sight. Everything is uncovered and laid bare before the eyes of him to whom we must give account" (Heb. 4:12). God's Word has real authority and power, but only to the extent that it is faithfully and properly interpreted and proclaimed. To this end, may this book make a small contribution, for the good of God's people and for God's greater glory.

KEY WORD

Contextualization.

ASSIGNMENTS

1. Look up Romans 1:16–17 in five different Bible translations, including the NIV, the NASB, and the CEV. Note any significant differences and then consult at least two commentaries to see what accounts for the differences. Then, indicate your preference for a given rendering and explain why you prefer it over the alternative renderings.

2. Plan a series of lessons or messages on the book of Ruth. Read through the entire book at least twice. Then, prepare a series of lessons or messages. Make sure to break down the book into an appropriate number of units and to include a series of points of application.

KEY RESOURCES

Doriani, Daniel M. *Getting the Message: A Plan for Interpreting and Applying the Bible.* Phillipsburg, NJ: Presbyterian & Reformed, 1996.

Duvall, J. Scott and J. Daniel Hays. Chapter 13. "Application" in *Grasping God's Word: A Hands-On Approach to Reading, Interpreting, and Applying the Bible.* 2d ed. Grand Rapids: Zondervan, 2005.

REFERENCE LIST

Chapter 2

Duvall, J. Scott and J. Daniel Hays. 2005. *Grasping God's Word,* 2d ed. Grand Rapids: Zondervan.

Osborne, Grant. 2006. *The Hermeneutical Spiral.* Rev. ed. Downers Grove: IVP Academic.

Chapter 7

Collins, John J. 1984. *The Apocalyptic Imagination.* New York: Crossroads.

Duvall, J. Scott and J. Daniel Hays. 2005. *Grasping God's Word,* 2d ed. Grand Rapids: Zondervan.

Chapter 8

Klein, W. Williams, Craig L. Blomberg, and Robert L. Hubbard Jr. 2004. *Introduction to Biblical Interpretation.* Rev. ed. Nashville: Thomas Nelson.

Osborne, Grant. 2006. *The Hermeneutical Spiral.* Rev. ed. Downers Grove: IVP Academic.

Chapter 9

Osborne, Grant. 2006. *The Hermeneutical Spiral.* Rev. ed. Downers Grove: IVP Academic.

Stein, Robert 1978. *Method and Message of Jesus' Teachings.* Philadelphia: Westminster.

Chapter 11

Collins, Adela Yarbro, David Hellholm, and David E. Aune. 1986. *The Power of the Apocalypse*. Philadelphia: Westminster.

Collins, John J. 1979. "Introduction: Towards the Morphology of a Genre." *Semeia* 14: 1–20.

Chapter 13

Lyons, John. 1981. *Language, Meaning and Context*. London: Fontana.

Louw, J. P. and Eugene Nida. 1988. *A Greek-English Lexicon of the New Testament Based on Semantic Domains*. 2 vols. New York: United Bible Societies.

GLOSSARY

***A fortiori* argument**: argument from the lesser to the greater

Account: presentation of history that includes theological interpretation

Allegory: series of related metaphors

Alliteration: subsequent words starting with the same letter

Allonymity or allepigraphy: the theory that a later author edited what the original author wrote while attributing the writing to the original author or writing in another person's name without intent to deceive

Allusion: an authorially-intended reference to a preceding text of Scripture involving verbal or, at a minimum, conceptual similarity

Amanuensis: scribe or secretary who wrote down the message of the author of an epistle, whether by way of word-by-word dictation or by filling out the sense of a missive

Anacoluthon: a sudden shift in grammatical construction

Announcement of judgment: a prophetic oracle involving the stating of an accusation and the pronouncement of the ensuing judgment

Antagonist: the person opposing the protagonist

Anthropomorphism: ascription of human characteristics or qualities to God

Antithetic parallelism: two poetic lines expressing sharp contrast

Antitype: a later pattern of God's dealings with his people that corresponds to an earlier instance (see Type below)

Apocalypse: a genre of literature with a narrative framework in which a revelation is mediated by an otherworldly being to a human recipient, disclosing a transcendent reality that is both temporal and spatial

Apocalyptic: a world view anticipating God's climactic and cataclysmic intervention in human history at the end of time

Apocalypticism: denotes a worldview, ideology, or theology merging the eschatological aims of particular groups into a cosmic and political arena

Apophthegm: short, witty, and instructive saying

Apocryphal: extrabiblical, not belonging to the canon of Scripture

Aposiopesis: the breaking off of a speech or statement owing to strong emotion, modesty, or other reasons

Appropriation technique: specific ways in which the Old Testament is appropriated by a New Testament writer as part of his theological argument

Archetypal plot motifs: narrative elements found across the spectrum of literature

Aretalogy: string of "I am" statements

Assonance: succession of words containing the same sounds, especially vowels

Asyndeton: lack of a conjunction at the beginning of a sentence

Biblical theology: a discipline of biblical study that seeks to investigate Scripture as originally given in its historical context and on its own terms (in distinction from systematic theology; see below)

Bicolon: parallel thought over two successive lines of poetry

Bookending: the technique of returning at the end of a unit to a theme, subject, or word(s) mentioned at the beginning of that section

Brachylogy: the omission, for the sake of brevity, of an element that is not necessary for the grammatical structure but for the thought

Characterization: the depiction of major and minor figures in the narrative

Chiasm: a literary device in which the second half of a composition takes up the same words, themes, or motifs as in the first half, but in reverse order (A B B′ A′ pattern)

Chreia: pronouncement story

Clause: any meaningful cluster of words that includes a verb

Closure: the concluding statement in a given discourse unit

Cohesion: the glue that holds a discourse together

Concreteness: a feature of Hebrew poetry that involves a graphic description appealing to the reader's senses

Connotation: the meaning added to the lexical meaning or denotation by the context

Contextualization: the application of a given truth or principle in a particular cultural context

Covenant: a sacred contract or agreement

Covenant lawsuit: a type of prophetic judgment speech in which God summons his people to appear before him for covenant violations

Denotation: the "dictionary" definition of a word apart from a particular context

Denouement: the final clarification or resolution of a narrative or dramatic plot

Diachronic: the study of language "over time"

Diatessaron: Grk. "through four"; first parallel presentation ("harmony") of the four canonical Gospels Matthew, Mark, Luke, and John by the second-century church father Tatian

Diatribe: a technique for anticipating objections to an argument, raising them in the form of questions and then answering them (e.g., Romans 6–7)

Direct quotation: an explicit, verbatim citation of an Old Testament passage, usually fronted by an introductory formula (in distinction to Allusions or Echoes; see definition of these)

Disclosure formula: indication that author wants to inform his readers about a given subject (e.g., "I do not want you to be ignorant")

Discourse: any coherent sequence of phrases or sentences, whether a narrative, logical argument, or poetic portion of text

Discourse analysis: a study of a textual unit for the purpose of discerning various features of the text such as boundary markers, cohesion, prominence, relations, and situatedness

Discourse boundary: the opening and closing phrases or devices marking the beginning and end of a given discourse unit

Disputation: a literary device that deals with a given topic by way of presenting different sides of an argument, often involving declaration, discussion, and refutation

Domestic code: norms having to do with reciprocal responsibilities between the members of a household

Dual authorship: the Bible's authorship by God as well as human authors

Echo: an authorially intended reference to a preceding text of Scripture that exhibits a proportionately lesser degree of verbal similarity than an allusion

Eclectic approach: an approach (in the present context, to the book of Revelation) that draws on several or all of the other approaches (preterist, historicist, idealist and futurist)

Ellipsis: a feature by which an incomplete idea requires the reader to supply a missing element that is self-evident

Emblematic parallelism: two poetic lines showing progression of thought involving simile

Emperor cult: the mandated, enforced worship of the Roman emperor as deity

Eschatological: end-time

Eschaton: the end of history

Eternal State: heaven

Etymology: the root (i.e. original) meaning of a word

Exhortation speech: an instructional message in which the recipients are urged to follow the Lord and his standards

Exodus: God's deliverance of the Hebrews out of Egypt, his guidance of them through the wilderness, and eventual bringing them into the Promised Land

External elements of narratives: features outside the narrative, such as author, narrator, and reader

Futurist approach: interpretation of Revelation as primarily depicting future events

Gallio inscription: ancient artifact mentioning the name of the governor of Achaia by that name

Gezera shawah: rule of equivalence, that is, the principle of Scripture interpreting Scripture

Grammar: specific features of syntax, such as a certain kind of genitive or participle (form)

Hellenism: the Greek way of life including various aspects of Greek culture, the Greek pantheon (gods and goddesses), and Greek philosophy, which spread throughout much of the Greco-Roman world in NT times

Hendiadys: an arrangement of two or more expressions that essentially convey the same idea

Hermeneutical: pertaining to interpretation, in the present context the interpretation of biblical texts

Hermeneutical axiom: an underlying assumption that leads a New Testament writer to use an Old Testament passage in a certain way (e.g., Jesus is the Messiah)

Hermeneutics: the theory and practice of interpretation, in the present context biblical interpretation

Herodians: a political party mentioned alongside the Pharisees in the New Testament that may have been friendly to the Herodian dynasty

Highlighting: the literary technique of drawing attention to a particular detail in the story

Historicist approach: interpretation of Revelation as forecasting the course of history in Western Europe

Horizontal reading: comparison of the presentations of a given event by the different Gospels

Hyperbole: a form of overstatement in which literal fulfillment or portrayal is impossible

Hypocatastasis: figure of speech in which the comparison is implied by direct naming

Idealist approach: interpretation of Revelation focusing on the symbolic portrayal of spiritual and timeless truths regarding the end times

Illegitimate totality transfer: the improper assumption that a word in a given context means everything the word can mean in a variety of different contexts

Implicature: implicit yet necessary information for understanding a given discourse

Implied author: persona created in text by real author

Implied reader: the reader to whom a given piece of writing is ostensibly addressed

Inaugurated eschatology: aspects of the end times that have already begun to be a present reality in the lives of believers

Inclusio: the occurrence of a given word or phrase at the beginning and at the end of a discourse unit for the purpose of marking this portion of material as a textual unit

Inerrancy: the attribute of Scripture as being free from error in the original autographs

Infallible: the attribute of Scripture as being trustworthy and unfailing

Inspiration: the process by which God caused human authors to produce inerrant Scripture

Instructional account: various forms of prophetic material, including disputation and exhortation speeches, satire, or wisdom sayings

Interlude: a literary feature interspersing additional material into a given unit

Internal elements of narrative: features of the narrative itself, including setting, plot, and characterization

Intertextuality: relationship between texts

Introductory formula: a phrase preceding a direct Old Testament quotation in the New Testament, such as "it is written"

Irony: device in which the writer states the opposite of what is intended

Ladder parallelism: two or more poetic lines displaying progression in form of numerical sequence

Lament: a special type of a prophetic announcement of judgment similar to the woe oracle in which the prophet deplores the state of affairs among God's people

Law: in the Bible an expression of God's will and moral standards for human conduct delivered as instructional material

Lexis or lexical meaning: a word's meaning as listed in a dictionary

Life setting: the circumstances surrounding the original composition of a biblical document

Linguistics: the study of the nature of language

Maccabees/Hasmoneans: a political dynasty that arose in reaction to Greek rule during the Second Temple period and that led to a century of Jewish self-rule

Markan priority: theory that Mark was the first to write his Gospel

Matthean priority: theory that Matthew was the first to write his Gospel

Messiah: God's promised, anointed, and divine representative who would deliver his people and rule as king in earth's final state

***Midrash*:** Jewish commentary-style interpretation or exposition of a religious text

Millennium: the one-thousand-year reign of Christ at the end of time depicted in Revelation 20

Mirror-reading: the (often doubtful) interpretive practice of inferring the circumstances surrounding the writing of a given text from explicit statements made in the text

Monocolon: an individual poetic line that does not combine closely with another line

Narrative: a literary genre that builds its sentences and paragraphs around discourses, episodes, or scenes

Narrative time: the way in which time is portrayed in a given narrative, as opposed to chronological time

Narrator: person telling the story

Nero *redivivus* myth: the belief that the Roman emperor Nero (A.D. 54–68) did not truly die but was still alive and would return

New covenant: in Old Testament prophesies, God's future bestowal of blessings upon his redeemed people in the Promised Land

Old Testament Canon: that body of writings accepted as reflecting divine inspiration and authority

Orienter: an initial marker indicating a boundary feature in a given discourse

Ossuary: ancient bone box containing the remains of a deceased

Parable: true-to-life or realistic story told in form of an extended simile, short story, or allegory to teach a spiritual lesson

Parallelism: the practice of using similar language to express corresponding thoughts in succeeding lines of poetry

Parallelomania: the adducing of parallels of questionable value

Parataxis: unconnected juxtaposition of sentence units or clauses

Parousia: second coming of the Lord Jesus Christ

Peaking: the height of action reached in a particular discourse unit

Pericope: narrative unit

Pesher: Jewish verse-by-verse commentary

Pharisees: a prominent Jewish sect that was known for its scrupulous attention to minutiae of the law and served as major antagonists of Jesus in the Gospels

Phrase: any meaningful word cluster that lacks a verb form

Pleonasm: a form of redundancy by which a previously expressed idea is repeated as a way of speaking

Plot: the arrangement of events in the story

Prediction-fulfillment: a phenomenon by which an Old Testament prediction is fulfilled in the New Testament

Preterist approach: interpretation of Revelation that focuses on the book's message to its contemporary, first-century readers

Progressive dispensationalism: belief that the various eras of salvation history (dispensations) progressively overlap in keeping with the "already/not yet" tension of inaugurated eschatology

Progressive parallelism: a succeeding line (or lines) supplements and/or completes the first line

Prominence: elements in a discourse that stand out, be it by way of natural or marked emphasis

Prooftexting: the use of isolated portions of text (prooftexts) to support a given interpretation

Prophetic narrative: an account of the prophet's calling, life, and work

Prophetic-apocalyptic: the likely genre of the book of Revelation, combining prophetic and apocalyptic features

Protagonist: the main character of a story

Proverb: short memorable statement of the true state of things as perceived and learned by human observation over extended periods of experience

Pseudonymity: a writing in which a later follower attributes his own work to his revered teacher in order to perpetuate that person's teachings and influence

Pun: a play on words in which one word may have more than one meaning or two similar-sounding words intentionally used to suggest two or more different meanings

***Qal wahomer*:** argument from the lesser to the greater (lit. "light and heavy")

Rapture: meeting between believers alive at the time of Christ's return and their risen Lord per 1 Thessalonians 4:13–18

Real author: actual writer of a given document

Reference: the linguistic procedure by which a word points to an extra-textual object

Referent: the object to which a word points

Relations: various ways in which statements or propositions are conjoined in a given text

Report: a narrative providing historical information

Royal grant treaty: privileges or benefits granted by a king to a vassal or servant for faithful and loyal service

Sadducees: a major Jewish sect that together with the Pharisees made up the Jewish ruling council (Sanhedrin) and served as antagonists of Jesus in the Gospels

Salvation-historical: related to God's plan of salvation unfolding in Scripture

Salvation oracle: prophecy that deals with God's saving work, such as a promise of deliverance, a kingdom oracle, or apocalyptic

Sanhedrin: the supreme Jewish ruling council, traditionally made up of 70 men, that had religious and political authority over Jewish affairs

Satire: an attempt to demonstrate through ridicule or rebuke the vice or folly of that which appears to be improper or ill-conceived

Second Temple period: time between the rebuilding of the temple subsequent to the return from the exile and the destruction of the temple in A.D. 70

Semantic anachronism: the imposition of the later meaning of a word onto earlier uses

Semantic field: a group of words that are related in meaning

Semantic field study: the study of the meaning of a word and related words

Semantic obsolescence: rendering a word with a meaning it once possessed but that has since fallen into disuse

Semantic range: the variety of meanings of which a word is capable in different contexts

Semantics: concerned with the meaning of individual words based on the recognition that word meaning is to be discerned in context

Sense: the meaning of a word in context including the word's connotation

Sentence: any complete thought expressed in the form of one or several independent clauses

Septuagint: the Greek translation of the Hebrew Scriptures (Old Testament) that was widely used in the early church and is frequently cited in the NT

Setting: information as to the place, time, and circumstances of a given event

Similar parallelism: two poetic lines conveying closeness of thought and expression

Simile: simple comparison, usually linked by "like" or "as"

Similitude: extended simile

Situation: set of circumstances

Staging: the presentation of setting of a given action or event

Staircase parallelism: a thought stated in the first line is completed by a succeeding line beginning with similar phraseology

Stanza: a group of lines within a poem

Stitching: an author's practice of linking successive units or subunits of a poem by means of repeating a word, phrase, or idea

Strophe: portion of a poem containing several stanzas

Sufficiency of Scripture: notion that Scripture, while not exhaustive, is complete and fully adequate in matters of faith and practice

Suzerainty treaty: an agreement whereby the enacting party imposes covenant stipulations upon a vassal

Synchronic: the study of language "together with" (i.e. at the same) time

Synoptic Gospels: Grk. "seeing together"; common designation for Matthew, Mark, and Luke owing to the similarities between these Gospels

Syntax: refers more broadly to relationships between words in the larger scheme of discourses and sentence structures

Systematic theology: a form of presentation of biblical teaching which is essentially topical in nature (in distinction from biblical theology; see above)

Tail-head link: mention of a topic at the end of a section to be developed in the following unit

Terrace pattern parallelism: type of staircase parallelism in which the beginning of the second line repeats the end of the first line

Terseness: feature of Hebrew poetry that involves succinctness of stating a point

Theodicy: vindicating the righteousness of God and his ways when called into question

Thought flow: discourse structure as conveyed by various discourse features per discourse analysis

Transitivity: the ability of the audience to grasp and comprehend an allusion and its source text

Tricolon: three lines of poetry forming a distinct unit

Type: an instance of a historical person, event, or institution that exhibits a pattern of God's dealings with his people in salvation history

Typology: an escalating pattern in salvation history in which a later antitype is found to correspond to one or several original types

Vertical reading: initial study of a given incident in the Gospel in which it is narrated

Vision or dream report: instance in which a prophet receives God's message in a vision, which he in turn is to proclaim to his people

Woe oracle: a special type of a prophetic announcement of judgment that involves (1) invective (the pronouncement of woe); (2) threat (the details of coming judgment); and (3) criticism (the reason for the coming judgment)

Zealots: first-century Jewish group engaging in active and violent resistance toward the Roman occupation force in Palestine

Zeugma: a special type of ellipsis in which a different verb is to be supplied

Zoomorphism: ascription of animal qualities to God

SCRIPTURE INDEX

2 Corinthians

SUBJECT INDEX